THE
AUTOMOBILE
AND
American Culture

THE
AUTOMOBILE
AND
American Culture

David L. Lewis and Laurence Goldstein, Editors

Ann Arbor   **The University of Michigan Press**

1991   1990   1989   1988   7   6   5   4

Library of Congress Cataloging in Publication Data

Main entry under title:

The Automobile and American culture.

1. Automobiles—Social aspects—United States—
Addresses, essays, lectures. 2. Automobiles—United
States—Literary collections. I. Lewis, David Lanier,
1927–   . II. Goldstein, Laurence, 1943–   .
HE5623.A812   1983   306'.46   83-10293
ISBN 0-472-08044-X (pbk.)

Grateful acknowledgment is made to the following persons and organizations for permission to use copyrighted material:

Arc Music Corporation for "Maybellene" (W & M: Chuck Berry, Russ Fratto, and Alan Freed) © 1955 by Arc Music Corp., New York, N.Y., and "No Money Down" (W & M: Chuck Berry) © 1956 by Arc Music Corp., New York, N.Y. Used by permission.

Big Seven Music Corporation for "Speedoo" by the Cadillacs.

Fred Rose Music, Inc. for "Ramblin' Man" by Hank Williams.

Nikki Giovanni for "The Beep Beep Poem" from *Cotton Candy on a Rainy Day*. Copyright © 1978 Nikki Giovanni. Reprinted by permission of the author.

Globe Music Corporation for "V-8 Ford Blues" by Willie Love. Used by permission.

Harcourt Brace Jovanovich, Inc. for "Portrait of a Motorcar" from *Cornhuskers* by Carl Sandburg, copyright 1918 by Holt, Rinehart and Winston, Inc., renewed 1946 by Carl Sandburg. Reprinted by permission of Harcourt Brace Jovanovich, Inc.

Margaret Held for an illustration by John Held, Jr.

The Iowa Review for *☞* by Joyce Carol Oates. Reprinted by permission of the Iowa Review.

Isalee Music for "Aimlessly Drifting" by Chuck Berry.

Iwo Music for "Swing Low, Sweet Cadillac" by Dizzy Gillespie.

MCA Music for "How Long, How Long Blues," Words and Music by Leroy Carr. © Copyright 1929 by MCA Music, a division of MCA, Inc., New York, N.Y. Copyright renewed. Used by permission. All rights reserved.

Bruce Springsteen for "Cadillac Ranch" and "Born to Run" by Bruce Springsteen. Used by permission.

William Stafford for "Traveling Through the Dark" and "Written on the Stub of the First Paycheck" from *Stories that Could Be True*. Copyright © 1960 by William Stafford. Reprinted by permission of Harper & Row, Publishers, Inc.

The Washington Post for "Our Romance with the Auto Is Over" by Michael Barone. Copyright The Washington Post, August 24, 1982.

Whitney Museum of American Art for Robert Bechtle's *'61 Pontiac*. 1968–69. Oil on canvas. 60 × 84 inches. Collection of Whitney Museum of American Art. Richard and Dorothy Rogers Fund.

PREFACE

During America's bicentennial, the Associated Press asked leading journalists to name the most important developments in U.S. history; 272 responded. They gave first ranking to the Revolution, followed by the drafting of the Constitution, the Civil War, and World War II. "Henry Ford, his Model T, and the rise of the automobile" was rated tenth, comfortably ahead of the Vietnam War, the New Deal, the Louisiana Purchase, the 1954 Supreme Court decision outlawing school segregation, and such technological advances as the development of television, aviation, and the electrification of the nation.

The journalists' opinions merely corroborated what Americans already knew—that the automobile has had an extraordinarily potent influence on this country. Nobody needs to be told that the auto industry has been the nation's, indeed the world's, leading business activity since the early 1920s. But the cultural impact of this single invention has attracted much less attention until recently, perhaps because the car has been around only one long human lifetime. It is still a new fact in the American consciousness, for all its shopworn familiarity.

The auto has generated love-hate feelings since its inception. Many turn-of-the-century citizens compared it unfavorably with the horse, and many more complained that it raised too much dust, ran over too many chickens, made deafening noises, produced foul odors, and further separated the classes from the masses. But naysayers were swept aside, or joined the automotive parade, and cars chugged, then raced ahead, changing the face of America and profoundly affecting manners and morals forever. We still complain that vehicles disturb tranquility, pollute the environment, kill us off in large numbers, and strain our pocketbooks. But only a handful of us have traded motor vehicles for mopeds, much less bicycles.

Today American motorists and the auto industry face more uncertainty than they have ever known. The vast majority of Americans will continue to move about in cars, and the industry will survive, almost everyone agrees. But it is also widely believed that motoring and the industry are in a state of transition, and that the halcyon days for both lie behind, not ahead.

Aware that the past casts a giant shadow and that America retains a high level of auto consciousness, in 1979 the University of Michigan's *Michigan Quarterly Review* (*MQR*) deemed it timely and worthwhile to analyze the car's influence on American culture, and to peer a few kilometers down the road as well. The magazine's call for contributions produced more that 450 poems, 86 short stories, 41 essay-length works of nonfiction, a dozen memoirs, and scores of graphics. Gratified by the number and quality of the submissions, *MQR* decided to combine the Fall 1980 and Winter 1981 issues, so that the awesome range of voices and themes would have ample space for expression.

"Scholarly" and "popular," happy and disgruntled, the selections included the reminiscences of those whose lives were touched by the auto and its makers; appraised the manner in which artists made use of cars; and examined how the auto altered the topography and folkways of America, then blended into the environment it created. The polemical writings, fictive and poetic as well as essayistic, left no doubt that the automobile remains the central symbol of the American genius, for good or ill. The final document was the most comprehensive ever devoted to the auto and American culture. It was expected not only to entertain for a season, but to serve as a significant reference work for any future analysis of the car culture in America.

That expectation was realized. The issue's first printing quickly sold out; so did the second. Meanwhile, the volume was critically acclaimed by scholars and favorably reviewed by dozens of publications as diverse as the *Wall Street Journal* and *Sioux City Argus Leader; Chronicle of Higher Education* and *Technology and Culture; Michigan History* and *Environmental Action; Motor Trend* and *Horseless Carriage Gazette.* The reviews confirmed our belief that the reading public would be served best by a collection that mingled objective and subjective accounts of the automobile's history and identity. New perspectives and new interdisciplinary connections emerged from the collage of writings that surprised even the experts on this subject, and offered them the opportunity to test new hypotheses. Indeed, the breadth of the anthology made it useful as a reference work for college and university courses in a variety of fields.

When the third printing sold out, it became apparent that the issue, augmented by six new essays, should be published by the University of Michigan Press. We hesitate to say that bigger is better, but it is inevitable that the new model looks more attractive to its producers than the old. We hope that this version of a modern classic will bring an equal amount of satisfaction to the reader.

CONTENTS

I. THE FIRST DECADES

JOHN B. RAE

WHY MICHIGAN?

It is almost always easier to ask questions than to answer them; this is
certainly true of the question I will attempt to answer here: Why did
Michigan become the capital of the automotive world? Speculation on
this subject has ranged from superficial theorizing to scholarly analysis. It is not my intention here to review the literature or to itemize in
detail the points of view that have been expressed. Rather, I wish to
consider the various forces that were operating during the formative
years of the automobile industry and see if some reasonable assessment of their influence can be made.

It would be a great help if the motor vehicle had only been invented in Detroit: if, for instance, the conversation overheard in a
Pullman smoking room by Frederick L. Smith, for many years president of the Olds Motor Works, were an authentic account of what
happened:

"Who invented the automobile anyway?"

"Henry Ford. Started as a racer by beating Barney Oldfield on the
ice at Detroit. Right after that he built a plant to turn out the same
kind of car in fifty thousand lots."

"Doesn't he own the Lincoln now?"

"Yeah, owns the Lincoln and the Packard, Cadillac, Buick—all the
big ones and a lot of the little ones besides."

So much for remembered history—although I must record my admiration for the feat of packing so much inaccuracy into a single short paragraph.

Actually, the horseless carriage was born in Germany and brought up in France, where the true automobile, as distinguished from a buggy with a motor attached, first appeared, and where industrial production in significant quantities was first achieved. The first American gasoline car was built in Springfield, Massachusetts, not in Michigan. Credit for being the birthplace of the American automobile industry can be allocated to Springfield; or to Hartford, Connecticut, where Albert A. Pope and Hiram Percy Maxim began quantity production of electric automobiles in 1897, with a few gasoline cars on the side; or to Cleveland, Ohio, where Alexander Winton began the regular commercial manufacture of gasoline automobiles, also in 1897. At this time to be sure, Henry Ford and Ransom E. Olds had built their first experimental cars, but neither would be an important producer until after the turn of the century. Then, however, events moved with astonishing rapidity. Detroit was barely visible on the automotive scene in 1900. For the next several years it was only one of several promising centers of automobile production, competing with Hartford, Cleveland, Buffalo, Toledo, Indianapolis, and St. Louis, to say nothing of Kenosha, Wisconsin; Moline, Illinois; Kokomo and Elkhart, Indiana; Hagerstown, Maryland; Elyria, Ohio; and York, Pennsylvania. By 1910, however, Detroit was clearly in the lead, and five years later it was unmistakably and unchallengeably Motoropolis. Again, why?

We might begin with environmental factors—what Merrill Denison in *The Power to Go* refers to as the industrial ecology of the region. It is an undeniable fact that Detroit enjoys an advantageous geographical position, with easy access by water to coal and ore and other materials. The same argument could be made for Chicago, Toledo, Cleveland, and Buffalo, with the additional consideration that at the beginning of the century the Lake Erie ports were closer to the principal market area. Michigan, it is argued, was in the hardwood forest area, so that the state became a major center of carriage and wagon manufacturing, and from this it was a short step to powered vehicles. It is a good argument as far as it goes—the carriage business in Michigan produced Billy Durant, J. Dallas Dort, and Charles W. Nash—but the hardwood stands extended well south into Indiana and Ohio, and the world's largest single manufacturer of horse-drawn vehicles in 1900 was the Studebaker Brothers Manufacturing Co. in South Bend, Indiana. Geographical location and resources therefore have their place, but they are not a sufficient explanation by themselves.

Next, we might look at the economic factors. We can accept the thesis that Detroit at the beginning of the century was well-equipped to offer the automobile industry a home. It was a city of diversified, largely small-scale industrial enterprises, offering an abundance of machine-shop facilities and skilled labor. These were assets; indeed they were an indispensable base for the initiation of automobile manufacturing. Very comparable conditions existed at this time in Birmingham and Coventry in England and help to account for the concentration of British automobile manufacturing in that area. But in the United States these assets were by no means confined to Detroit. They could also be found in the Connecticut valley, where the American gasoline automobile was born.

It also has been suggested that Detroit had the advantage of having no existing industrial commitment such as Pittsburgh had to iron and steel or Cleveland to oil refining—industries, that is, in so dominating a position that they were likely to attract the best business talent of the community. This argument may have some weight, but the record indicates that plenty of able entrepreneurs in those cities were willing to risk involvement with the horseless carriage. Pittsburgh was the original home of the Autocar, best known as a one-time popular truck, and Cleveland could claim such famous automotive names as Winton, Peerless, Stearns, Chandler, Jordan, and White. In any event, Detroit's position in this respect was matched by Toledo and Indianapolis, and in fact until about 1905 Indianapolis had more automobile plants than Detroit.

There is one legend that definitely should be demolished before we proceed further. This is the claim that the automobile industry located where it did because Middle Western bankers were more enterprising than their Eastern competitors and more willing to take chances in backing a new industry. I am not questioning the merits of Middle Western bankers; I am just saying that on the basis of the facts, this legend is just a legend. The Electric Vehicle Company of Hartford, Connecticut, the organization that made the unhappy attempt to exploit the Selden patent, was the first incursion of high finance into the automobile industry. The venture was backed by a syndicate that included William C. Whitney, P. A. B. Widener, Thomas Fortune Ryan, and Anthony M. Brady—surely an impressive enough representation of the Eastern money market to satisfy the most exacting requirements of historical scholarship. Nor was this entirely a speculative operation. The promoters really meant to manufacture electric automobiles; the nuisance value of the Selden patent was an afterthought.

On the other hand, when the Briscoe brothers of Detroit joined with Jonathan D. Maxwell to form Maxwell-Briscoe in 1903, they were unable to get local support because, as Benjamin Briscoe explained in later years, "there was a feeling on the part of local capitalists that the business was growing too fast, and that the automobile had then reached the limit of its possibilities." Detroit may have been foreordained to become the automotive capital of the world, but for some of its inhabitants in 1903 the finger of fate seems to have been wavering uncertainly.

Maxwell-Briscoe got assistance from an eastern banking source, namely the House of Morgan, which had dealt with the Briscoes as successful manufacturers of sheet metal products. Ransom E. Olds got his first financing from a lumber and copper magnate, Samuel L. Smith; the Ford Motor Company was launched with $28,000 put up by Alexander Malcomson, who was a coal dealer; and Hudson got its name because J. L. Hudson, the Detroit department store owner, contributed $90,000 to get the enterprise started. The truth of the matter is that most of the pioneer automobile manufacturers, regardless of location, had little association with the conventional money markets. The standard procedure was to buy from suppliers on credit and sell to dealers for cash, so that insofar as banks provided capital for the automobile business in its early years, it came mainly from the dealers' local banks.

We have therefore an assortment of factors and forces that might account for the rise of Michigan to its position of preeminence in motor vehicle manufacturing. No one of them was a sufficient cause by itself to produce the eventual result. No one of them was an asset possessed exclusively by Michigan. Perhaps it was the combination of all of them that was decisive. A deterministic explanation might hold that Michigan happened to be the one location in the United States where conditions were such that all these elements could combine and react spontaneously on each other to set the necessary chain of events in motion.

I do not subscribe to this theory. I do not believe that there was any compelling reason for these impersonal forces to operate by themselves. There had to be a catalyst, and this catalyst was a remarkable concentration in time and place of a group of individuals who became attracted to the possibilities of the motor vehicle and who brought to it exceptional entrepreneurial and technical talent. The opportunity admittedly was there to be grasped, but someone had to grasp it.

Of the men who did the grasping, most were of Michigan origin: Henry Ford, Ransom E. Olds, Roy D. Chapin, Henry B. Joy, William C. Durant, Howard E. Coffin, John and Horace Dodge, Benjamin and Frank Briscoe, to give a partial list. Others like Vermont Yankee Henry M. Leland became Michigan residents by choice. The story used to be told that Leland came to Detroit by a very fortuitous chance. When he left Brown and Sharpe of Providence, Rhode Island, to go into the machine tool business for himself, he allegedly planned to settle in Chicago, but arrived during the Haymarket Riot and was so horrified that he took the first train out he could get, and it happened to be going to Detroit. It makes a good story, but the facts are that the Haymarket Riot occurred in 1886 and Leland arrived in Detroit to establish the machine tool firm of Leland, Norton, and Faulconer (later Leland and Faulconer) in 1890. A main-line passenger train in those days might have been late, but hardly that late.

These men and their associates are the people who in a short span of time—the fifteen years from 1900 to 1915 will cover it adequately—transformed the fledgling automobile industry and gave to the world a new technology of production. This feat was accomplished in Michigan. They were as complete a cross section of their contemporary society as could have been devised. Joy, who moved Packard from Warren, Ohio, to Detroit, was a millionaire and Durant grew up in the home of a wealthy grandfather who had been governor of Michigan. At the other end of the spectrum Charles W. Nash started out as a penniless orphan working as a migrant laborer. Chapin and Coffin, founders of the Hudson Motor Car Company, went to the University of Michigan, but few of the others finished high school, which was characteristic of the early years of the twentieth century. Many had technical training or experience. Coffin was exceptional in having an engineering degree. The others followed the more usual pattern for their time of coming up through apprenticeship and on-the-job training, like Leland Olds, Maxwell, the Dodge brothers, Chevrolet, and of course Henry Ford, the farm boy who liked machinery and disliked horses. Others, like the Briscoes and David Buick, were established businessmen who succumbed to the lure of the horseless carriage.

They and all the others who were similarly lured are described in

George F. May's book, *A Most Unique Machine. The Michigan Origins of the American Automobile Industry* (Grand Rapids, 1975). They were a diverse group, but they had one thing in common. They became utterly dedicated to the manufacture of motor vehicles, to the point where they seem to have preferred to go broke making automobiles than to get rich doing anything else. The attrition rate in the motor vehicle industry has been high. Since the Duryea car first appeared in Springfield, Massachusetts, in 1895, some 1900 companies producing over 3000 makes of cars have been identified in the United States. However, whereas in other areas the demise of an automobile company was usually final, in Michigan the men who got knocked out in the bruising competition of those early days kept getting up and charging back into the battle again.

Two prime examples of this phenomenon were Byron F. "Barney" Everitt and William F. Metzger, who bobbed in and out of the automobile industry for a quarter of a century, never quite reaching success but also never willing to give up. Everitt had been a carriage builder and supplier of bodies to Olds. In 1903 he joined other Detroit businessmen to organize the Wayne Automobile Company. Metzger sold bicycles and cash registers, then became Detroit's first automobile dealer, and in 1902 joined Charles B. King to establish the Northern Automobile Company. Neither company had any great success, and in a short time they were combined as EMF (Everitt-Metzger-Flanders), with Everitt and Metzger joined by Walter E. Flanders, former production manager of Ford and one of the earliest of a long and distinguished line of automobile men to part company with Henry Ford. EMF was then taken over by Studebaker, an event that put a Studebaker factory in Detroit until 1925. There were also short-lived attempts to produce Everitt and Metzger cars.

Three names stand out in the long list of Michigan entrepreneurs who were responsible for making Detroit into Motoropolis: Ransom E. Olds, Henry Ford, and William C. Durant. Olds almost anticipated Ford. The Oldsmobile buggy, the "Merry Oldsmobile," was the first popular, quantity produced gasoline car, although its light construction would have prevented it from taking the place later filled by the Model T. Olds' important contribution was that the Olds Motor Works became a seedbed for automobile men: Chapin, Coffin, Maxwell, Robert C. Hupp. The Dodge brothers built the transmissions for the early Oldsmobiles, the Briscoes the bodies, and Leland and Faulconer the engines, and all became motor vehicle manufacturers on their own. Henry Leland was called on to take over Henry Ford's second unsuccessful venture into automobile production in 1902. He transformed it into Cadillac, and impressed on the American automobile industry his own exacting standards of accuracy and precision. John and Horace Dodge were among the founders of the Ford Motor Company in 1903 and subsequently, as we know, went into business for themselves. Benjamin and Frank Briscoe tried unsuccessfully to help poor David D. Buick to get his car into production, and then joined forces with Jonathan D. Maxwell to organize the company (Maxwell-Briscoe) from which the Chrysler Corporation is directly descended.

Ford has of course been written about voluminously, and there is no need to go over well-trodden ground. In terms of concentrating the automobile industry in Michigan there are three salient items in the Ford story. First, Henry Ford clearly had the concept of a "car for the great multitude" almost as soon as he became interested in horseless carriages. He was not alone in having the idea; he was alone in sticking to it with grim persistence, through several false starts, until he brought it to fruition. Second, he avoided the error of competitors, which was to start off by trying to design a vehicle that could be built cheaply. Ford sensed that the first essential was to design an automobile that would meet the requirements of a "car for the great multitude"—durability, simplicity, and ease of operation and maintenance. When he found this design in the Model T, then he tackled the problem of producing it cheaply. Third, the responsibility for the key decisions—the concentration of a single standard design, the Model T of happy memory, and the adoption of the moving assembly line—was Ford's and Ford's alone. It makes no difference who thought of them first. Henry Ford was president of the company and its majority stockholder. If these decisions had proved wrong, his neck was out farther than anyone else's; with his previous record of failure, his career in the automobile industry would have been irretrievably finished. So it seems quite proper to give Ford the major share of the credit for his company's achievement; there is plenty left over for Couzens and Knudsen and Wills and the rest of the talent that moved in and out of the Ford Motor Company.

But while Henry Ford could introduce mass production, he was not the man to create a smoothly functioning industrial organization, capable of adapting readily to future changes either in automotive technology or consumer preferences. As it turned out, William C. Durant was not the man to do it either, but at least he had the right idea of how to tackle the problem, and he put the idea into operation in Michigan. Let me emphasize that it did not have to happen there. Billy Durant came into the automobile industry in 1904 by taking charge of a bankrupt firm—Buick—that had achieved a production record of 22 cars in three years. There were certainly more promising companies elsewhere that could equally well have provided the nucleus for General Motors. All they lacked was a Billy Durant.

In contrast to Henry Ford, Durant was a successful, prosperous businessman at the time he turned to manufacturing automobiles. The Durant-Dort Carriage Company of Flint was one of the country's leading producers of carriages and wagons. Like Ford, Durant had a vision of a great future for the motor vehicle; in fact, when he began to implement his dream, he alienated some of his prospective financial support by predicting that automobile production in the United States would in the foreseeable future reach 500,000 cars a year. Ford and Durant approached their goals by different routes. Ford set up an essentially monolithic structure, putting his whole effort into a single standardized model aimed to sell at the lowest possible price. Durant envisaged a vast corporate organization building a variety of models to appeal to a wide range of tastes and price levels, and including its own parts manufacturers. In pursuit of this aim he founded General Motors in 1908, the same year that saw the Model T put on the market.

Durant himself was too mercurial, too erratic, to make his dream work. Eventually it would take Alfred P. Sloan, Jr. to turn Durant's vision into reality, but let us give Billy the credit due him for having the vision in the first place. And the corporation he founded had its roots in Michigan: Detroit, Flint, Pontiac, Lansing. It was Durant also who, during his first temporary exile from General Motors, joined with Louis Chevrolet to give the automobile world the car that would eventually match the Ford in popularity.

The combined weight of Ford and General Motors, plus the companies that sprouted from the Olds Motor Works and the others who have been mentioned, created a concentration that grew on itself. For those who wanted opportunities in the automotive field, the vicinity of Detroit was manifestly the place to be. It was in a sense, the gravitational attraction of the mass, but the mass had to be created first.

It was never predetermined that this should be so. To be sure, Ford, Durant, Olds, Chapin, and the rest found favorable conditions for the creation of this new industrial enterprise, but favorable conditions do not produce results by themselves. In the last analysis the human factor is decisive. There were plenty of men in the same or similar environments who either did not see the opportunity at all or who tried to seize it and failed. The struggle for survival in the automobile industry has been drastically Darwinian. Those who succeeded had to possess a distinctive combination of qualities: technical skill, business acumen, faith that the automobile really had a future, and above all an unshakeable determination to build cars.

I do not know why during the critical early years of this century a greater concentration of individuals with these qualities appeared in Michigan than elsewhere. There certainly was no common pattern or single mold to explain them. The vital point is that they were there, in the right place, at the right time, and with the right talents.

CHARLES MADISON

MY SEVEN YEARS OF
AUTOMOTIVE SERVITUDE

*What follows is a memoir of working conditions in the early auto-
mobile industry. It is excerpted from a recently-completed book-
length manuscript.*

Having survived the October 1905 pogrom in Kiev, my father decided to emigrate to the United States, where his daughter from
a previous marriage had gone to Detroit with her husband's family
two years earlier, in order to escape further Russian persecution.
We reached Detroit in July 1906. A quasi-intellectual but a poor
provider, he was forced to accept work with a local tailor at a dollar
a day. In dire need of additional income, he acquiesced in the urging
of a neighbor that I, the oldest of five children, though only eleven
years old, sell matches to housewives as a means of supplementing
the family's income. Proud to be of help, I strove to maximize
my sales and was soon earning nearly as much as my father. In
September, when my younger brothers were enrolled in a public
school, my mother insisted that I continue peddling during the coming year. The following summer my father found work which paid
him eleven dollars a week, and he was happy to have me enter school
in September. Two months later, however, a neglected cold brought
on pneumonia, and father died in December. As the oldest of the
children, I persuaded the principal to let me attend school only
mornings in order that I might again peddle matches the rest of
the day.

With the approach of spring and my fourteenth birthday I considered myself mature enough for adult work. On perusing the want ads
in the Sunday newspaper I saw that the small Grabowsky Truck
Company was in need of an office boy. Early the next morning I
hurried over to the Grabowsky factory. My eagerness to get the job
impressed the man who interviewed me, and I was employed at five

dollars a week. I realized of course that I could earn more than that by peddling matches, but I was willing to make the sacrifice because I considered it more dignified to have a regular job and because of the chances for advancement. The work was not difficult. I ran errands for the small office staff, distributed the mail, and did various odds and ends asked of me. I had to work on Saturdays, but that caused me no mental anguish, as I was by then far along toward agnosticism without having ever heard of the term.

Sundays, as before, I joined my brothers in selling newspapers, but I would leave them around ten o'clock and go with my shoeshine kit to the back doors of saloons where I had most success in finding customers. The current price for shining shoes was five cents, but some of the drinkers would give me a dime. For two hours or more I would go from saloon to saloon and solicit the men standing at the bar. One Sunday a mulatto girl was at the bar with a man, and when I asked if she wanted her shoes shined she readily agreed. I was startled when she gave me a half dollar and told me to keep the change. The man with her protested, telling her indignantly that just because she had earned eighteen dollars that night she should not squander them. But she maintained laughingly that the "kid" no doubt needed the money more than she did. I thanked her and hurried out, as if ashamed. What was not clear to me then, although I assumed there was something illegitimate about it, was later explained to me by one of the older boys to whom I mentioned the windfall; she was a prostitute and had many men that night. In my innocence I was both repelled and ashamed, prostitution being to me a degrading and ugly activity.

THE AUTHOR AT AGE 19

Although prostitutes remained to me immoral beings to be avoided, I found myself more tolerant toward them during that summer. Grabowsky was located on Champlain Street (later changed to Lafayette Street), in 1909 a concentration of brothels. Now and then, one of the girls would call me as I passed by, ask me to do an errand for her, and pay me a dime for the service. These girls seemed to me no different from other young women, and I could not help wondering what had caused them to become prostitutes. On reflection I tended to feel sorry for them even as I condemned them for taking what must have seemed to them an easy way out. Yet I did not mind joining the factory men who crowded the windows on Friday afternoons to watch the girls on the back porches sitting scantily dressed and drying their hair.

Eager to earn more money and aware that I could do so by learning how to work a drill press, the simplest of machines in the factory, I asked one of the men to teach me how to operate it. He was most obliging, and took pains to show me how to put the piece to be drilled in the chuck, tighten it firmly, start the soda water flow on the drill, and press steadily but not too hard until the hole was drilled. He explained that pressing too hard would break the drill and that the drill must be kept sharp for the best results. He then let me drill several pieces under his guidance. Satisfied with my performance, he advised me to go to one of the larger factories on Piquette Street and apply for a job. "Tell the guy you're past sixteen and have worked here for several months," he said. "Ask for as much per hour as you think you can get." I felt very grateful to him and told him so.

At the end of the week I quit my job, and early the following morning I reached Piquette Street and entered the employment office of E. M. F. (Everitt, Metzger, and Flanders), the first factory I came to. I was asked to fill out a questionnaire, and on the line asking the expected rate per hour I dared not put down more than 12½ per hour—fearing that if I asked for more I might not be employed. I figured that working ten hours a day and six days a week I would earn seven and a half dollars a week. The clerk examined the sheet, looked at me quizzically, and told me to start work the next morning at 6:30.

I reached the factory a few minutes early and was taken to one of a row of drill presses. The straw boss showed me how to regulate the flow of soda water to keep the drill from overheating, pointed to the boxful of parts to be drilled, and told me to call him if I needed any help or if the drill got dull. I thanked him and proceeded to put a part in the chuck. I can see myself now, dazed and scared, fearing to look around me, praying to God in whom I did not believe to help me do everything right. I concentrated on the work and was not aware of the time, although I did begin to feel tired and hungry, when I heard the shrill noon whistle and the machinery came to a halt. I wiped my soda-wrinkled hands on a piece of cotton waste given to me by the straw boss, found a place to sit down, and ate the sandwich and apple I had brought with me. The lunch period lasted a half hour.

During the afternoon I began to gain confidence in my ability to operate the drill press, and glanced furtively to each side to see several youths older than I working at either side at the other drill presses. I could see they were Polish and feigned ignorance of their presence. The straw boss, who impressed me as a decent fellow, obviously of American stock, still in his early twenties, came over several times during the afternoon to check my work and to sharpen the drill. He spoke encouragingly to me, and I felt pleased when the five o'clock whistle blew. I put things in order and left for home, by then feeling too tired to think of anything but relaxing my fatigued body. Riding on a streetcar I became aware of my changed status, feeling myself an adult with obvious responsibilities and perquisites.

As I had feared, the half dozen Polish youths, experienced enough at their work not to have to concentrate on it, began to pass disparaging remarks at my expense. To them I was of a different breed, a Jew who snubbed their very existence. The more I ignored their insults, the more aggressive they became. I knew, however, that I was no match for any of them, being both younger and weaker than they. At lunch I avoided them by joining an older group of American workers; at five o'clock, or at seven when we had to work overtime, I hurried past them to get on the first streetcar going in my direction.

One of the Polish youths, who I noticed was mocked by the others, began to assert his hatred of Jews and to pass derogatory remarks in my direction. The others, annoyed by my aloofness, egged him on in their eagerness to start a fight between him and me. Seeing an opportunity to ingratiate himself with them, he called me "a dirty sheeny." My irritation getting the better of me, I called him "a dirty Polack." "Take that back," he shouted and hurried over to me. "Go to hell," I responded, trembling with fear and anger. He punched me in the face, and I hit him back as hard as I could. But I was no match for him, and he was getting the better of me. When my nose began to bleed, I shouted in pain. Just then the straw boss hurried over along with two nearby workers. We were immediately separated, and the straw boss scolded my antagonist for the disturbance. He took me to a sink where a cold compress soon stopped the flow of blood. In a few minutes I felt better and returned to my machine. I noticed that the youths around me looked subdued.

Shortly before five o'clock Jack Conrad, one of the older workers with whom I sometimes spoke during lunch, came over to me and whispered to go home with him, as he was sure I would be attacked by the Polish youths once I was out of the factory. On the streetcar he told me I needed to develop my puny muscles. He informed me he was a physical culturist and had a basement full of muscle builders. At his invitation I went with him to his basement and was amazed by its athletic gear. He gave me a list of exercises with a pair of Sandow spring dumbbells. With a smile he said he knew I was not yet sixteen despite my height and that if I was to work in a factory I needed to be able to defend myself from rowdies. I felt very grateful to him and insisted on buying the dumbbells. Before leaving he told me, "You do those exercises every morning and evening, and soon you'll not only develop your muscles but build up your entire body. You're a good kid, and I don't like to see you messed up by rowdy Polacks."

Conscientiously I rose every morning twenty minutes earlier day after day and performed the numerous exercises and repeated them before going to sleep. It became my aim to develop myself physically—to possess a strong body in a sane mind, as was preached by Bernarr McFadden in his magazine, *Physical Culture*.

In the factory the Polish youths ceased bothering me, and I made no effort to associate with them. I had an idea that the straw boss had warned them that he would dismiss anyone who annoyed me. I did my work conscientiously, and soon learned how to sharpen the drill and use it with care. When a fresh lot of new parts required a different size drill and chuck, the straw boss helped me with the change. All seemed to be going smoothly, and I kept Conrad informed of my progress with the exercises.

After working for nearly two months and feeling proficient at the job, I felt emboldened to think of asking for an increase in my hourly wage. About that time I was called to the office and informed that owing to a new law concerning employment of youths under eighteen I was to sign a pledge not to sue the company for damages in case of an accident. I refused, maintaining that as the chief provider of my family I could not agree to such a pledge. Annoyed by my recalcitrance, the clerk told me to get my belongings and return for the money I had earned up to then. I felt both terrified at losing my job and proud of my refusal to risk the family's income in case of an accident to me. Returning to the shop, I explained to Conrad and the straw boss the reason for my dismissal. I then returned to the office to wait for my final envelope.

As I wondered where I was to look for work, it occurred to me that only a block away, on Piquette and Beaubien, was the factory of the Ford Motor Company. I hurried over to Ford's employment office and applied for a job. On the application form I stated my age as eighteen, my experience as a drill press operator, and my request for fifteen cents an hour. The clerk asked me no questions after glancing over the sheet, gave me a brass check with a number, and told me to return the next morning at 6:30. I thanked him, hurried back for my pay envelope, and decided to celebrate by going to a cinema for ten cents.

In the spring of 1910 many of Ford's operations were being moved to a new mammoth plant in Highland Park facing Woodward Avenue. At the time of the move I applied to the foreman to let me operate a lathe, and he was good enough to let me do so. I was already familiar with its operation from close observance of those near me. My main reason for the request was that the lathe demanded greater skill to operate than other machines and therefore entitled the operator to a higher rate of pay. In my favor was my ability to read a micrometer, as the work often required accuracy to the thousandth of an inch when trimming the face of a gear. And, as I expected, my pay envelope soon indicated the payment of twenty cents an hour.

Although I was only fifteen, I began to consider myself a skilled machine operator, the highest paid worker below the class of toolmaker. If I were ambitious in that direction, I would have begun to study mathematics and other subjects needed by a toolmaker; but, without giving the matter deliberate thought, I knew I was not really interested in being a machinist. More and more I began to feel repelled by the dirt and grime and dullness which were inevitable in machine work. I also knew I could not aspire to office work in view of my limited education; nor did I then think I had any chance of going back to school.

One day it occurred to me that I might become a draftsman—an occupation that approached professional status and remuneration. I had previously learned to read blueprints of automobile parts, and knew they were prepared in the drafting room at one end of the building which had the appearance of an office.

After days of contemplation and soul searching I forced myself to approach the superintendent's office and told him of my ambition. He regarded me quizzically, and I wondered if he weren't amused by my stuttering. After asking me about my background and experience as a machine operator, and my assurance that I would attend night school to take the necessary courses, he nodded and gave me a note to the head of the drafting department.

The man to whom I applied—and I can still see his thinning hair and bulbous nose—seemed annoyed as he read the note. He told me he had no need of an apprentice, but since the superintendent requested it, he would take me in. I sensed that he did not like me, but I was too eager to get into the drafting room to let my pride get the better of me. So I thanked him, and said I would quit my job in the factory and come to him the following morning. I also discussed with him the courses I needed to take, and he suggested that I study algebra and drafting at the YMCA school. He then distressed me by informing me that an apprentice's pay was fifteen cents an hour. Tears came to my eyes as I pointed out that I had been getting twenty cents an hour and needed the money to help support my younger brothers. But he only said that I could return to the factory if I wished. I quickly figured that I must not give up the opportunity to better myself even though it meant a cut in my income, hopefully for a short time; also that with greater knowledge and experience I might in time be earning more than twenty cents an hour. Thus resolved, I meekly acquiesced. That evening I enrolled in the two suggested courses.

On my arrival the next morning, neatly dressed, I had to wait for some time before the man was free to see me. He took me into the blueprint room and began to show me how to place a drawing and blueprint paper together and place them in a revolving large glass tube lighted within and letting the two sheets emerge from the other side. The blueprint paper was then put in an acid vat, kept there for several minutes, and hung to dry. I saw at once that the lines and letters of the drawing appeared in white on the acid-wetted sheet. At first I was quite interested in seeing that the application of light and acid turned what seemed to me an ordinary blue sheet of paper into a usable blueprint. I also liked to see the strongly lighted large glass tube turning around and around, and I thought it was fun to place the blue sheet in the vat and then take it out with tongs and hang it on a laundry-like line. Soon I made numerous copies of each drawing, as requested, and began to recognize some of the blueprints I had used in the factory.

After a week of this work I quickly mastered the process, and my interest in it began to slacken. With my patience decreasing daily, after three weeks I asked to be transferred to the drafting room. My boss quickly informed me that I would have to remain six months in the blueprint room before I would be considered for the promotion. The news dismayed me. Bored with the work and feeling underpaid, I shuddered at the thought of having to wait more than five months before I could begin working on a drafting board. I felt that the course in mechanical drawing was fast equipping me to do professional drawing. Angered by the man's attitude and, as I realized, increasingly disillusioned by the mechanical nature of drafting, I told him I couldn't wait that long and was quitting. He made no effort to keep me.

I thought of returning to the lathe division to ask for my job back, but a sense of pride stopped me. That same day, reconciled to a return to machine work, I proceeded to the Dodge Brothers large new factory in Hamtramck, and obtained work at twenty-two cents an hour. What pleased me also was the more relaxed atmosphere in the machine shop. While at Ford, I, like other workers, was frequently timed by efficiency experts, a way of driving a worker to function at maximum speed, and a cause of constant tension. The Dodge foreman, on the other hand, expected men to work steadily and well, but snapped no whip of forced exertion.

Due to my YMCA courses and a speech clinic I attended the next year, my savings were very low, and the need of additional income gradually turned my attention to Ford's widely publicized policy of paying five dollars a day for eight hours of work. Publicity about Ford's largesse had brought thousands of men from all over the country to Highland Park. Reading about the brutal handling of these applicants and knowing of the slave-driving methods of the factory, I for a time fought back the temptation to seek work there. I liked the atmosphere at Dodge, even though it meant two more hours of work at almost half the pay. But the urge to earn more money was soon strong enough for me to yield to temptation.

One cold Monday morning I took the streetcar to Highland Park and hurried to the employment office. A long line of men was already waiting for the door to open. When it did, the crush to enter was fierce, but guards forced the men to keep in line and await their turn. Since many of them were without experience as machine or assembly operators, most of them were rejected in quick order. When my turn came, my experience as a lathe operator and my previous employment with the company impressed the interviewer and he hired me. Pleased with my success, I went to see the foreman at Dodge Brothers, and explained to him my need of additional income and told him of my gratitude for his friendly behavior toward me. He shook his head in regret, told me I'd be sorry, and generously stated that when I was ready to return he'd see what he could do for me.

I found the Ford plant greatly reorganized, and I was assigned to a lathe in a new section. The harried foreman told me that my operation had been timed by an efficiency expert to produce a certain number of finished parts per day. I timed myself to see what I could actually do, and realized that I might achieve the quota only if all went well and I worked without letup the entire eight hours. No allowance was made for lunch, toilet time, or tool sharpening. I refused to disallow necessary delays, although I managed to keep the machine going while munching my sandwich. When I failed to produce the assigned quota of finished parts, the foreman scolded me. The next day another efficiency timekeeper with a stopwatch was assigned to observe my work. After an hour of making notes as I worked he told the foreman I was too slow in placing the part in the machine and was making no effort to speed up. I defended myself as best I could, asserting that it was humanly impossible to keep up the expected pace. I was annoyed enough to accept dismissal without regret, but no action was taken against me. I continued to work at a fast pace, but made no real effort to produce the assigned quota.

I later concluded that the speedup policy was intended to get the maximum production out of the workers by requiring them to produce their operations at a high rate of speed without ever actually meeting the demanded quota. Much as I resented a policy I considered inhumane, I tried to resign myself to it in the hope of earning five dollars a day. I was therefore shocked and angered when my first pay envelope revealed that I was being paid twenty-five cents an hour or two dollars a day. When I questioned the foreman about this, he told me blandly that the arrangement was to begin paying five dollars a day only after a worker had been with the firm six months and had proved his ability to maintain his quota requirement. The unethical nature of this policy outraged me, and I told him

I was quitting at once. Much as I wanted to earn the higher wage I refused to yield to the company's duplicity. The decision to quit gave me a feeling of pleasant relief, as if I had freed myself of an unpleasant burden.

Feeling sheepish, but in good spirits, I returned to the Dodge factory, admitted to the foreman that I had been a fool for leaving him, that the Ford lure was a mean deception, and that I would be grateful to get my job back. Even now I don't know why he was so friendly to me—so unlike the cold and crusty Ford foreman. But he not only agreed to take me back, but to put me on a newly established piecework system which enabled a speedy worker to earn more than his previous hourly wage.

I was glad to be back at my machine, and soon found it possible to earn three dollars or more daily without unduly forcing myself. It pleased me even more that, while I had felt too fatigued after leaving the Ford factory to do any serious reading or attend a play or concert (my urge toward intellectual cultivation was becoming my main interest), I was now able to indulge in such intellectual amenities. For some time thereafter the painful Ford interlude was a rancorous memory—a form of hell on earth that turned human beings into driven robots. I resented the thought that Ford publicists had made the company seem beneficent and imaginative when in fact the firm exploited its employees more ruthlessly than any of the other automobile firms, dominating their lives in ways that deprived them of privacy and individuality.

About that time Dodge Brothers decided to rescind its contract with Ford in order to produce a car of its own. A notice on the bulletin board announced that employees on piecework schedules might produce to the limit of their capacities without fear of reduction in payment per piece and that they could work as much overtime as they wished. The aim of the firm was to complete the Ford contract for engines as quickly as possible in order to reorganize the plant for the production of the Dodge car.

The temptation to earn more money was too strong to resist. A number of workers and I began to speed up our work and to remain at our machines as late as we could, occasionally as late as eleven o'clock at night, willing to lose sleep in order to return to the factory by six-thirty the next morning.

Although I did not find the long hours of work as depressing as the fewer hours at Ford, knowing it was voluntary, I was keenly aware of having become for the duration a robot operating a lathe for twelve or more hours a day in order to earn the extra money. During these several months I actually managed to save over a hundred dollars. But I had time for nothing else.

Early in May the firm announced that it would close the plant a week hence for reconstruction and reorganization and that notice would be given to employees when work on the Dodge car would begin. I looked for another job, and found one a few days later in one of the Studebaker factories.

I began to have an impulse to write soon after I began to read books I admired. Despite the puerility of my early efforts, the urge to write persisted. After several attempts at writing fiction and a biography of my father, I conceived the idea of writing verse in rhyme—my conception of the way poetry was written. Without being conscious of it, I felt a desire to give expression to my repressed sensual yearnings for the ideal girl with whom I would one day want to share my life. I also felt a strong, if less potent desire to exalt my love of nature and human ideals—largely in emulation of the volumes of verse in the Harvard Classics which I had bought and read religiously since my seventeenth year. I soon found a textbook on the writings of verse. I became engrossed in the discussion of rhyme and meter, the difference of iambics from trochees, how an anapest differed from either, the number of feet used in various poems, the nature of blank verse, the sonnet, the triolet, and other line combinations. By the time I left the library at its closing my mind buzzed with technical terms, with measures and feet, with the beauty and imagery of great poems.

As my work on the lathe had long become routine enough to require little attention and less thought, my mind was free to grope for words and rhymes. Lines of poems evolved in my consciousness. Verses on human aspiration, on individual endeavor, an aspect of nature, or a sensual emotion came to me with little effort.

I kept a pad and pencil near me, and as a line formed itself in my mind I wrote it down during moments when the lathe was in motion. This literary activity in no way interfered with the speed and accuracy of my work, as the two functioned on different and unconflicting levels. It sometimes took me an hour or more before I completed a quatrain; and as I did not try to form a line unless the words came to me readily, I often wrote nothing for hours. I was careful not to let anyone see what I was doing, and neither the straw boss nor the workers near me were curious about my scribbling. In the evening, in the privacy of my room, I examined the written sheets, went over each line critically, altered words to conform to the meter and imagery, and copied the verses in my clearest script. Some evenings I ended with two satisfactory quatrains; at other times I would scrap what I had written as too prosaic. Sooner or later I would have a complete poem, usually in iambic meter, and the rhymes as nearly correct as I could make them. Even then I would later read and reread the lines, making corrections and changes and recopying the entire poem. I was not conceited enough to assume that this writing had poetic merit, but I was satisfied that it expressed as best I could the emotions and ideas that moved me to write them. It never even occurred to me that I should send a poem to a magazine; it was enough for me that I was able to express my individuality in the midst of so many identical machines.

My thoughts in 1915 were mostly concentrated on the resumption of my education. To this end I went to Central High School and talked to David McKenzie, the principal. I told him about my background, my years as a machinist, my study of the Harvard Classics, my courses at the YMCA, my written verses, and my eagerness to go to college. Aware of my age and intellectual maturity and impressed by my verses, he was good enough to plan a schedule of courses that would make it possible for me to graduate in one year assuming that I could take twice the usual number of courses. I did so successfully, and was able to enroll at the University of Michigan in the fall of 1917.

Early in September I quit the factory and went to Ann Arbor to register, arrange for living quarters, and look for a part-time job to pay for my board. Unable to find work for my board and aware that I could not afford to spend my savings the first year, I saw no alternative but to return to Detroit in search of work Friday nights. With nearly all the factories manufacturing war materials around the clock, I persuaded a foreman I knew to let me work the twelve-hour night shift Fridays from six to six at forty cents an hour. To do this I had to take a train from Ann Arbor immediately after my last Friday class, get to Detroit in time to have a hurried supper, and change clothes before reaching the lathe I was to operate. On leaving the factory Saturday morning I would go to my sister's apartment for several hours of sleep.

In June of 1918 I found an envelope from the draft board. I learned that I was to report for guard duty in the East, having been given 4F status because of my nearsighted right eye. I went to the board's office downtown, my mind agitated by fear and resentment.

The man on duty told me that the delay in my appearance had kept me from being sent East with other 4Fs—as if I had lost a fine opportunity. He then asked me what I expected to do during the summer, and I told him that I was an experienced lathe operator and planned to work in a factory. He thought for a moment, then said that if I could get work in the Studebaker factory, which was working on shells for the army, I could remain there until the end of the war. I agreed and mumbled my thanks, realizing with concern that if the fighting did not end by September I would have to stay out of the university until it did. Having no alternative, however, and glad not to have to do guard duty in some army camp, I went directly to the Studebaker factory—formerly the E.M.F. plant where I first worked on a drill press—and had no difficulty being employed as a lathe operator at fifty cents an hour. Later I learned that the firm had a cost plus ten percent arrangement with the government, and that the company found it advantageous to increase costs to a maximum.

The long hostility of automobile manufacturers to labor unions had successfully destroyed attempts at organization. The companies usually dismissed employees who joined the machinist union. Conditions changed for the better when the United States entered the war and began to contract with companies to produce war materiel. To keep workers from striking the government stipulated that manufacturers must not prevent their employees from joining unions of their choice. The War Labor Board, headed by liberal officials, was quite strict in enforcing this provision. Union leaders readily took advantage of the favorable situation and sent organizers to factories working on military supplies. Approached soon after I began to work, I willingly gave the five-dollar initiation fee and agreed to pay monthly dues. I had of course long resented the exploitation of American workers, and therefore hoped that the new tolerance toward labor would result in the establishment of unions in the mass industries.

With the summer nearly over and with talk of peace remaining little more than hopeful gossip, I realized that Allied victories notwithstanding, the continued fighting would keep me from returning to the university in September. My work on the lathe was routine drudgery, and my one consolation was that every workday added to my savings. Yet I did not stint on what I considered cultural enhancement. When I learned that Enrico Caruso and Geraldine Farrar were scheduled to give concerts in Detroit, I was determined to hear them—having greatly enjoyed both on records. Tickets for these performances were five dollars—to me an extraordinary extravagance—but the thrill of hearing them in person made the amount inconsequential.

Early on November 7 I was awakened by prolonged factory whistles, and the morning newspaper announced in big black headlines that the fighting had ended and an armistice had been arranged. Factories and stores closed, and tens of thousands of men and women began to hurry from every part of the city to Cadillac Square facing City Hall. Their holiday mood was heightened by the excitement of emotional release after prolonged worry and fear, so that many behaved with joyfully excessive frivolity. Men and women hugged each other and kissed freely; many shouted out of sheer animal exuberance, determined to join the crowd in the expression of strong emotional relief. This overflow of pent-up emotion grew from moment to moment and brought about an unrestrained feeling of human love and excited ecstasy.

I joined the gathering crowd fairly early, exhilarated that the killing had stopped. Yet part of me kept thinking of the millions of young men dead and wounded, of the tremendous devastation and waste, and wondering what it was all for. After mingling with the crowd for several hours I began to feel slightly feverish and returned to my room. I had contracted the flu, then raging throughout the country.

When I returned to the factory after a week's absence, and offered an explanation to the foreman, he looked sourly at me and said that the government contract had been terminated and that all union members were to be dismissed at the end of the week. Management's callousness outraged me, not so much for myself as for the men with families to support who might be blacklisted and have difficulty in finding work elsewhere. As for myself, I felt a sense of release.

I returned to Ann Arbor for the second semester and soon was immersed in my studies. Although I worked in automobile factories during the next three summers, simply to earn some money, I no longer regarded myself as part of the work force. Later, the memory of my years of servitude in machine shops was a confused dream from which one awakens with relief.

MARK S. FOSTER

THE AUTOMOBILE AND THE CITY

In 1980 Americans are, at long last, finally realizing the enormous social and economic costs of their intense love affair with the automobile. Certainly the past decade has marked profound changes in the image of the motor vehicle. Until recently, the automobile symbolized the youthful vitality of the economy, as well as freedom and independence for most Americans. Today, American automobile companies are in perilous economic straits, unable or unwilling to match European and Japanese competition. Many Americans believe the motor vehicle symbolizes the growing weakness and vulnerability of this country's position in world affairs, and that they are themselves the hostages of big oil firms and oil monopolists in the Middle East. Closer to home, urbanites and policy makers worry about the automobile's long-range impact on the cityscape and its future in metropolitan America. Critics have long charged that the motor vehicle encouraged thoughtless use of land and intensified air pollution. Today, their immediate concern is that its negative impact upon public transportation has created a situation in which even short term fuel shortages will seriously impair the mobility of urban dwellers, particularly suburbanites.

In the process of mapping out future energy alternatives, thoughtful transportation planners, energy consultants, and politicians ask how Americans got themselves into such a vulnerable position. Why, indeed, did the automobile surpass all other transportation systems, both in the popular imagination and in passenger miles? Their sophisticated analyses reflect many of the complexities of present-day problems, but the majority of studies reveals a limited historical sense of the process by which Americans became almost wholly dependent upon the automobile for personal mobility. This essay suggests that one means of understanding the rapid evolution of automobile popularity is an examination of American attitudes toward technology. Americans have traditionally manifested remarkable enthusiasm toward technological advances. On one level, Henry Ford and Alfred P. Sloan, Jr. demonstrated genius in the art of practical application of

24

new automotive technology. However, genius in this arena has too often been coupled with the unrealistic and even arrogant assumption that the influence and negative side effects of technological advances could always be controlled. The idea underlying these assumptions was that technology was inherently neutral, and that it automatically connected itself to clear-cut ends such as better transportation. An historical examination of the American response to the automobile in the twentieth-century city provides a fascinating case study of the results of such unambivalent enthusiasm.

One cannot overlook the fact that as the new century dawned, there were some hostile critics of the automobile. Since early motor vehicles usually cost several thousand dollars, a few social critics dismissed them as expensive toys, appalling manifestations of "conspicuous consumption" by the very rich. In both rural and urban areas, some Americans were frightened by the new sounds and smells of the gasoline-powered buggies. While horsemen initially snickered at motorists struggling with unreliable vehicles, their derision turned to envy soon enough. Eventually, of course, most succumbed to temptation and purchased automobiles.

A variety of factors, including lower motor vehicle prices and better roads, conditioned Americans to rapidly accept automotive technology early in the new century. Although some of their reasons for adopting the automobile were practical, there is strong evidence that many consumers were simply fascinated with the mechanical appeal of the motor vehicle. Playwright Cleveland Moffett envisioned as early as 1900 the irresistibility of the contraptions, particularly to middle-class males. Moffett predicted that many would give in to their desire to own one when they witnessed a friend "rolling down the avenue on some trim, swift-moving contrivance that buzzes and flashes past to the general admiration."[1] Three years later, automobile enthusiast James P. Holland observed that "a thing of life and beauty, moving smoothly and swiftly, of its own power, among the lumbering vehicles of a century ago," could not fail to fascinate Americans.[2] Apparently, many buyers appreciated the fact that while early cars were difficult to operate, persons of average mechanical aptitude could provide their own maintenance and repairs.

---

[1]Moffett, "Automobiles and the Average Man," *Review of Reviews* 21:6 (June, 1900), p. 704.

[2]Holland, "The Future of the Automobile," *Munsey's Magazine* 29:2 (May, 1903), p. 172.

While prescient observers almost immediately anticipated the motor vehicle's ability to enhance the mobility and reduce the isolation of small town and rural dwellers, it took them somewhat longer to perceive its potential impact upon the American city. While they were obviously aware of its capacity for increasing the mobility of urban residents, they were slower to understand how it might drastically alter the physical urban environment. Like earlier technological advances, including structural steel, electricity, elevators, and the telephone, the automobile would permit significant expansion of usable urban space. While structural steel and the elevator allowed vertical urban growth, the electric trolley and the automobile augmented horizontal growth.

At the end of the nineteenth century, decentralization of the city seemed to be an imperative social goal. American cities had been growing increasingly crowded for many years, and huge influxes of immigrants and native Americans into urban areas in the late nineteenth century made congestion even worse. Reformers such as Jacob Riis, Jane Addams, and Lawrence Veiller publicized the horrors of slum life. While some "genteel racists" believed that the poor were disadvantaged because of inherent defects, many urban progressives were persuaded that poverty and its accompanying social disorders were largely the results of the squalor and crowding of the typical industrial city. Thoughtful urban decision makers supported any changes which permitted urban dwellers to escape the slums. Although some city engineers and planners adopted the strategy of reviving existing slum areas through better tenement design, improved urban services, lower utility rates, and more park space, growing numbers of planners frankly encouraged flight to outlying areas.

In the last decade of the nineteenth century the electric trolley offered the best means of decentralizing the metropolis. Municipal engineers, planners, and reformers thus at first endorsed the principle of generous franchises for electric street railways. At least from the standpoint of promoting horizontal growth, such policies were extremely successful. Many scholars have documented the impact of the street railway in encouraging suburban growth between 1880 and World War I.[3] Significantly, trolley suburbs attracted not only the

[3]The literature is far too extensive to list here. An excellent starting point is Sam Bass Warner, Jr., *Streetcar Suburbs: The Process of Growth in Boston, 1870-1900* (Cambridge, Mass.: 1962).

wealthy, but large numbers of working-class residents as well.

Unfortunately, many turn-of-the-century street railway operators arrogantly abused their franchises, and reformers eventually turned against them. According to numerous urban critics, the trolley companies too often charged outrageous fares, bribed politicians, and paid unconscionable bonuses to corporate directors. In addition, they paid low wages and subjected their workers to dangerous working conditions. Careless motormen and rickety, poorly maintained equipment frequently teamed to create grisly accidents, but in the early twentieth century, most urbanites had little choice but to take the trolley or walk. Perhaps most maddening from the standpoint of the reform-minded, trolley operators too often assumed a "take-it-or-leave-it" attitude toward patrons.

The growing antagonism between public officials and mass transit companies created long-term problems, particularly for street railways. But World War I escalated urban expansion and inflation, two factors which damaged mass transit even more severely. As wartime prosperity encouraged physical expansion of manufacturing districts and suburban neighborhoods, city officials and patrons initially urged street railways to expand their service into new areas. Many transit operators refused these requests. Severe inflation doubled the cost of living between 1914 and 1920, and trolley operators' capital construction costs soared. Many companies were bound by long-term contracts to supply service for a fixed fare, usually a nickel. Essentially, they were being asked to provide longer rides for fares which halved in value in six years, and they were to finance the extensions themselves.

Street railway operators were understandably reluctant to undertake the expansions needed to make their service competitive with that which the automobile could provide. For their part, public officials, remembering the operators' past transgressions, were generally unsympathetic to the companies' requests for fare increases which might have permitted them to extend some lines. Although transit companies supplemented trolley service with bus lines, their responses to rapidly changing consumer demands were generally tardy, hesitant, and uncoordinated. By the 1920s, many urbanites no longer cared whether mass transit operators extended any type of service to newer areas; they had switched to motor vehicles.

In the years preceding World War I, the excesses of trolley operators had received considerable publicity, and reformers demanded stricter regulation with increased stridence. These demands were not merely the voices of a tiny lunatic fringe. Unfortunately for the long-range future of mass transit, the misdeeds of early trolley operators also cost them the support of knowledgeable, conscientious municipal engineers and planners at the same time they alienated many patrons. This is not to suggest that even with enthusiastic support from public officials, mass transit could have prevented large-scale use of automobiles on city streets. But if trolley operators had provided better service during their heyday, they might have prevented the general apathy over their later fate. Most important, mass transit companies might have created a climate more conducive to public funding for trolley lines and their subsidiary bus operations as losses mounted in the years of the automobile's ascendancy. One result might have been that present-day mass transit operators would enjoy greater financial health and public acceptance.

That the excesses of trolley operators led to regulation and even municipal ownership in the early twentieth century is not the key point. Other large utilities simultaneously experienced a loss of public support. City governments purchased and operated water, gas, and electric companies, and state agencies regulated those remaining in private hands. Superficially, it appeared that all public utilities were treated alike. The critical difference was that only mass transit faced a deadly, potentially destructive new competitor: the automobile. Popularization of the motor vehicle posed two ironies. First, it drastically weakened public support for street railways just when they most needed it for survival. Second, the decentralization accelerated in part by the automobile increased consumer demand for virtually every other public utility. The burgeoning of automobile suburbs, particularly after 1920, meant the laying out of many miles of new electric, water, and gas lines.[4] While other utilities thrived, mass transit patronage withered.

Eighty years ago, no urban observer, no matter how prescient, could have anticipated the stunning rapidity of the rise of the automobile and the simultaneous collapse of the street railway. Although muckraking reporter Ray Stannard Baker labeled motor vehicle production "a gigantic industry of two continents," in 1899, the truth was that most automobile "manufacturers" struggled to produce a

---

[4]For an excellent account of this trend, see John G. Clark and Mark H. Rose, "Light, Heat, and Power: Energy Choices in Kansas City, Wichita, and Denver, 1900-1930," *Journal of Urban History* 5:3 (May, 1979), pp. 340-364.

few cars a week in makeshift plants and repair shops.[5] It is difficult for modern-day readers to conceive of a time when dozens of automobile producers, with capitalization of only a few thousand dollars, confronted hundreds of mass transit operators, whose assets were reckoned in millions. Seventy or eighty years ago, however, the David and Goliath roles of mass transit and the automobile companies were reversed. Civic reformers, while not necessarily opposed to "bigness" per se, may well have cast friendly eyes upon the bicycle shop operators producing the earliest automobiles.

Whether or not most urban decision makers consciously desired to punish the more obnoxious street railway operators, they were clearly fascinated by the promise of the new automobile technology. As the century opened, they would have welcomed any device which appeared to offer relief of intolerable urban congestion. While the general public perceived the automobile as a mass transit vehicle only in the 1920s, some urban observers foretold its potential for moving large numbers of residents much earlier. A 1901 *Electrical World and Progress* editorial predicted its future as an important factor in urban transportation.[6]

The automobile eventually overwhelmed urban policy makers by sheer numbers. Between 1900 and 1920 motor vehicle registrations multiplied a thousand-fold, from 8,000 to 8,000,000. During the 1920s registrations tripled again. Despite a leveling of numbers during the Depression and World War II, postwar prosperity brought huge increases, and multi-vehicle families became commonplace. By 1980 there were almost 120 million automobiles, or one for every other American.

Surely it is unfortunate that all too many splendid street railway lines succumbed to the "flivver." But several points must be raised in defense of urban policy makers. First, no pre-twentieth-century technological advance had ever wielded so much potential for internally shaping the urban landscape as did the automobile. Obviously street railways initiated decentralization. One may logically argue that the telephone more profoundly altered concepts of space and time in interpersonal communications, and that structural steel wrought more

---

[5]Baker, "The Automobile in Common Use: What it Costs, How it is Operated, and What it Will Do," *McClure's Magazine* 13:3 (July, 1899), p. 195. Henry Ford did not open his famous assembly line production unit until the second decade of the twentieth century.

[6]Quoted in "Automobiles—Toys or Tools," *Literary Digest* 23:20 (November 16, 1901), p. 605.

drastic changes in the image of "urbanness." But no other device opened up so much space for human habitation and other use in such a brief period.

While many present-day critics lament that the automobile symbolizes technology run amuck, several factors should soften criticism of those who made the crucial urban transportation decisions of the past. Sixty or seventy years ago, while urbanites were aware that exhaust fumes emitted an unpleasant odor, few connected them to hazardous health conditions or ugly air pollution. In fact, many early municipal engineers were aware of George Waring's widely publicized studies of the health hazards created by tons of horse manure on city streets; hence the motor vehicle appeared to be a more attractive alternative.[7] If earlier decision makers had possessed the medical knowledge and the sophisticated information retrieval systems we take for granted today, they would have been far more aware of the indirect, long-range effects of some of their critical transportation policies, and they might have altered them accordingly.

In the early years of the automobile, the planners' faith in the ability of technological and engineering advances to solve problems appeared justified. For example, between 1900 and the 1940s the science and technology of safety and traffic control evolved rapidly. While the number of automobile accidents increased steadily, injuries and fatalities per passenger mile declined. In urban areas, planners and traffic engineers generally assumed that the latest advances would eventually enable them to overcome the inherent problems of automotive movement.

Today it appears obvious that the faith in traffic control innovations as a means of solving automobile congestion was naive. In defense of yesterday's planners, one should recall that turn-of-the-century traffic control was truly primitive and that there were vast opportunities for improvement. In most cities, police on foot and a few mounted patrolmen exerted only minimal control of massive horse and wagon team snarls in the preautomobile age. Turn-of-the-century concepts of traffic relief were equally unsophisticated. Although planners such as Daniel Burnham sketched large-scale parkways and regional highway networks for Chicago, most thought only in terms of widening existing streets. Traffic signals were almost unknown in 1900 and were manually operated until the 1920s. By the latter period, munic-

---

[7]Clay McShane, "Transforming the Use of Urban Space: A Look at the Revolution in Street Pavements, 1880-1924," *Journal of Urban History* 5:3 (May, 1979), p. 298.

ipal engineers were experimenting with electric signals and synchronized patterns of traffic movement. Other transportation planners weighed proposals for multi-level streets to accommodate growing numbers of automobiles. While some worried that motor vehicles on city streets were already out of control, John C. Long of the American Automobile Association (AAA) captured the optimism of the 1920s in assuring automobilists that "it is the American temperament to wait until a situation is intolerable and then go out and lick it in short order."[8]

Perhaps the major factor contributing to traffic planners' confidence was their belief that they could solve congestion problems by diverting traffic away from densely settled areas. While traffic planners did not consciously abandon central business districts, most of the traffic plans of the 1920s promoted gridiron patterns of vehicular movement over entire regions rather than radial connections from suburbs to downtown. Long before the Interstate Highway Act of 1956 encouraged the rise of huge shopping complexes adjacent to freeway interchanges, the limited access and "bypass" roads of the 1920s encouraged urbanites to patronize businesses on the outskirts of town.

Another confidence builder in the minds of many transportation planners was their belief that sophisticated advances in highway building design and traffic engineering would permit them to guide and control motor vehicle use. Following the unsophisticated techniques of merely widening existing streets and the generally impractical multi-level plans of the early twentieth century, highway builders adopted the first limited-access highways in the 1920s. By the late 1930s they were building the first modern freeways. In their view, improved lighting, more scientific banking of roads, and the most up-to-date surfaces would not only enhance safety but speed up traffic flow.

Although some transportation historians have overestimated its importance as a factor behind the decline of mass transit, another cause of the popularization of the automobile and emphasis on urban road building was federal government policy. In the sense that roadways formed vital links in the national communications network, federal aid for better highways followed a tradition dating at least from Henry Clay's American System in the early nineteenth century.

[8]Long, "What City Planning Means to the Motorist," *American Motorist* 17:7 (July, 1925), p. 10.

In contrast, with the exception of some interurban electric lines, the trolley operated within cities and received little, if any, federal assistance.

The federal government did not develop a specific urban policy until the 1930s, when it financed construction of public housing projects on a limited scale. Considering the government's record in urban renewal, perhaps transit operators were fortunate to be largely ignored before the 1970s. The important point, however, is that mass transit systems in most cities were in serious decline long before the federal government developed an urban policy. Before the energy crisis of the 1970s, it was obvious that neither federal officials nor taxpayers were willing to make the commitments necessary to revive mass transit. Indeed, it is by no means certain that the necessary determination exists even today.

Even had they accurately foreseen the hidden dangers of mass adoption of the motor vehicle, planners and traffic engineers probably could have done little to stem the mounting tide. The primary reason is that they possessed little political power. Until about World War II, most planners had little formal training. Most planning boards were rag-tag collections of landscape architects, lawyers, zoning experts, and municipal engineers; in most cities, planners served in an advisory capacity only, with little or no "line" authority. Except for enacting rudimentary traffic controls, government agencies demonstrated little effectiveness in regulating motor vehicle use.

The most serious charge against planners and early traffic engineers is that they were incredibly short-sighted. In fact, public officials hailed the automobile just as they had initially welcomed street railways. By the time they began to realize the dangers posed by excessive motor vehicle usage, it was too late for them to effect anything but the most superficial restrictions. Early twentieth-century public officials had experienced a real struggle taming the street railway industry, and by mid-century, the automobile companies and their allies were far more powerful politically than mass transit interests had ever been.

Today the factors contributing to the outstanding political success of motor vehicle interests seem obvious, but public officials of the past dealt with largely new forces. One might justifiably argue that railroad interests exercised as much or more political control until about 1910 as did the motor vehicle lobby in the mid-twentieth century. However, in contrast to the crude, overtly corrupt methods of persuasion used by nineteenth-century railroad moguls, efforts of the motor vehicle lobby appeared sophisticated and low key.

Contemporary observers were in awe of the speed with which automobile interests became leaders in effective political lobbying. Certainly they dramatically surpassed mass transit spokesmen in their efforts to win friendly legislation from all levels of government. The reasons are not difficult to divine. Unlike mass transit operators, automobile manufacturers enjoyed support from an army of ancillary businesses. By the 1920s the American landscape was liberally sprinkled with automotive services and related enterprises, and the economies of several important cities were dominated by motor vehicle and parts production. Among the many interests promoting greater use of motor vehicles were parts manufacturers and tire dealers, oil companies and service station operators, highway builders and civil engineers, and land developers.

In addition to boosting automobile use, these powerful business interests formed lobbies to promote better streets and highways. Many present-day social critics haven't forgiven them for purportedly despoiling much of the countryside and turning cities into asphalt jungles.[9] Yet we should remember that sixty years ago, America's roads and streets were in extremely poor condition, and the majority of citizens approved major efforts to improve them. As the twentieth century unfolded, such powerful pressure groups as the American Road Builders Association (ARBA) joined hands with important public officials' groups such as the American Association of State Highway Officials (AASHO) to encourage massive road building efforts. At the grassroots level, the AAA effectively boosted automobile use for touring, and other supporting institutions ranged from the Lincoln Highway Association to the National Association of Manufacturers (NAM). Perhaps most important, public officials were impressed by arguments that motorists were willing to "pay their own way," through gasoline taxes, which would be used for constructing and maintaining roads.[10]

The efforts of the motor vehicle and highway lobbies initially created a far more obvious impact upon rural life than urban society.

[9]See, for example, John Keats, *The Insolent Chariots* (Philadelphia: 1958); Ronald A. Buel, *Dead End: The Automobile in Mass Transportation* (Englewood Cliffs, N. J.: 1972); James Flink, *The Car Culture* (Cambridge, Mass.: 1975); and Lewis Mumford, *The City in History: Its Origins, Its Transformations, and Its Prospects* (New York: 1961), pp. 505-510.

[10]See John C. Burnham, "The Gasoline Tax and the Automobile Revolution,"*Mississippi Valley Historical Review* 68:3 (December, 1961), pp. 435-459.

The Good Roads Movement emphasized "dragging many farmers out of the mud" at least through the 1920s, a period during which the majority of urbanites still relied upon mass transit for most of their journeys. Almost unnoticed by many national observers was the extent to which urban decision makers had shifted from a policy of encouraging development of mass transit to one of promoting the automobile as a carrier of urbanites.

The automobile unquestionably came of age in the 1920s, in the city as well as the country, and the decade marked critical decisions for the future of urban transportation. The ascendancy of the motor vehicle over mass transit in urban America was by no means wholly accidental. Nor was it simply the result of a selfish conspiracy by automotive and highway interests. Significantly, in many important American cities, planners and traffic engineers considered and consciously rejected proposals for upgrading trolley systems or building modern subway and elevated lines. Some traffic engineers considered trolley cars too slow and unwieldy; as symbols of an "outmoded" form of transit technology, they cluttered urban streets, particularly in congested areas. Their reasoning against modernized rapid transit was based on arguments which have a familiar ring today. Critics charged that subways were both expensive and inflexible, and that by encouraging more skyscrapers, they would eventually add to the congestion they were designed to relieve. While elevated lines were cheaper to construct, opponents cited their ugliness and noisiness as primary objections. Policy makers in Los Angeles, Seattle, and Detroit all rejected combined subway and elevated systems in the 1920s; and between World War I and the 1960s, only Chicago initiated a major new subway system. Rightly or wrongly, planners concentrated on the more efficient movement of automobiles.

Even before the energy crisis, the American love affair with the automobile was showing some signs of stress. By the late 1950s, if not sooner, it was evident to some urbanologists that "autopia" was an empty dream. Not only were automobile suburbs experiencing mounting criticism from many quarters, but the failure of automotive technology and highway design alone to provide efficient urban transportation systems was increasingly obvious. Defenders of the automobile observed that late twentieth-century Americans took for granted the luxury of unprecedented physical mobility. Critics countered that motor vehicles had dehumanized the city by destroying viable neighborhoods, turning parks into parking lots, and befouling the atmosphere. They also charged that Detroit had robbed Americans of any element of choice. If anything, urban transportation had regressed in the age of the automobile. Colonial Americans had little choice but to walk to their jobs in the city. Their heirs had almost no alternative but to drive.

In retrospect, urban transportation planners in the first half of the century obviously made serious mistakes in concentrating their efforts on the automobile. Today, urbanologists representing an impressive cross section of disciplines lament that earlier planners did not make the commitments required to preserve or revive mass transit. In the energy-short world of the 1980s, even a return to the trolley seems a noble dream. Yet before we dismiss the urban transportation planners of the early twentieth century as unwitting stooges of the automobile industry, we should recall the political, economic, and social milieu they confronted. In fact, most of the pro-automobile decisions they made appeared eminently sensible at the time. In the midst of a major suburban boom in 1924, Los Angeles planner Gordon Whitnall observed that

> When we faced the matter of subdivisions in the County of Los Angeles . . . subdivisions which were coming like a sea wave rolling over us . . . we reached the conclusion that it would be absolutely necessary to go out and try to beat the subdividers to it by laying out adequate systems of primary and secondary highways at least, thus obtaining the necessary area for highways and boulevards.[11]

After World War II, as suburban sprawl assumed massive dimensions, regional planners echoed Whitnall's ideas. Realizing that transportation corridors represented one of the most permanent metropolitan features, urban planners felt they had little choice but to lay out new superhighways to provide access to the suburbs.

From the perspective of this writer, it seems that contemporary urban planners have learned from some of their past mistakes even while repeating others. In the energy-short world of 1980, few transportation planners talk of further urban decentralization. Instead, they talk in terms of space-saving, energy-efficient "cluster" developments along "high-density" traffic corridors. However, contemporary transportation planners may be articulating Americans' supreme faith in technology in overestimating the potential of mass transit to solve our energy crisis and urban problems in general. Thanks to

[11]*Proceedings of the Sixteenth National Conference of City Planners, April 7-10, 1924, Los Angeles, California* (Baltimore: 1924), p. 10.

more sophisticated preliminary studies, most urban decision makers are more aware of the indirect effects of their commitments than were their predecessors. Most now recognize that contemporary decisions about transportation will influence social, economic, and political affairs, not just movement of people. They must be constantly aware that the problems of solving mass transit needs are exceedingly complex, and that no standard combination of modes can work in all metropolitan areas. They must also remember that it took at least a century to spread out the modern metropolis, and that we will be well into the twenty-first century before cities can be significantly reshaped by even the most sophisticated, futuristic mass transit systems we build today. Even then, we will undoubtedly still face old problems and new challenges.

REYNOLD M. WIK

THE EARLY AUTOMOBILE AND THE AMERICAN FARMER

The arrival of the automobile during the first years of this century had a profound influence on rural Americans. Not only did it substantially alter modes of travel, it affected the economy, changed the structure of social life, and became part of the cultural fabric of rural civilization. The sociologist Newell L. Sims, writing in 1928, claimed that the automobile had become the most revolutionizing force yet experienced by rural society.

Since farmers and ranchers were among the most isolated people in the United States, the benefits flowing from an improved system of transportation were substantial. In 1900, approximately half of the nation's population lived in the country, scattered across two billion acres of terrain. This usually meant that farm families lived far away from neighbors. Many rural folks spent their whole lives in one location; some never traveled more than fifty miles from home.

In addition, those in agriculture had long needed an improved mode of travel. For centuries they had relied on animals to aid them in working the land, marketing their products, securing supplies, and getting to social functions. Their mobility had been restricted to travel by horseback, bicycle, and a team of horses hitched to the "surrey with the fringe on top." Railroads and steamboats had specific routes and fixed schedules, but these services were often inconvenient or impractical.

At the turn of the century, the first automobiles appeared in the cities, where people of wealth could afford the new luxury. These early cars were viewed as toys of the rich, items of conspicuous consumption and leisure. When city dudes began invading the countryside with their "Red Devils," their actions were resented as threats to the tranquility of the rural scene. The editor of *The Breeder's Gazette*, in 1904, stated that the auto craze smacked of aggression by city mobsters who were turning the country roads into avenues of terror, and that these criminals were no more fit to be at large than so many mad dogs. Farm journals often alluded to "The Murderous Automobile," "The Deadly Auto," and the "Auto Menace."

The danger came when motor cars frightened horses on the roads, causing runaways which could injure or kill the occupants of horse-drawn vehicles. As a result, some farmers refused to let their wives or children travel on busy thoroughfares. Many ruralists insisted that city drivers should buy land and build their own roads. Some malcontents suggested that urban drivers who raced their cars merely for pleasure should be denied use of the highways except on Sundays and holidays. In some parts of the country, extremists urged vigilantes to take matters into their own hands by digging ditches across the roads, or by using chains, ropes, logs, barbed wire, broken glass, and sharp blades of steel to discourage motor travel. A few carried shotguns for self-defense.

Other protesters were motivated by economic interests, for the 14,000,000 horses in the nation represented a major vested interest which now seemed threatened by the new auto industry. Likewise, a sentimental affection for horses added voices to the anticar crusade. For horse-lovers no automobile was as beautiful as a team of high-stepping steeds with thunder in their manes and fire in their nostrils. Besides, horses did not belch fire and smoke, explode, or die from mechanical malfunctions. In some localities farmers advocated a ban on all cars on country roads, while in others regulations were adopted to control auto traffic. One local ordinance required the motorist to light a Roman candle upon sighting a horse-drawn vehicle, while another stipulated that an automobile must be preceded by a person carrying a red flag. Another restriction held that car owners must telephone ahead to the next town to warn people that a motor car was in transit. More reasonable measures required motorists to stop their car if an approaching team of horses appeared frightened, and to remain stationary until the team had passed by.

The horse versus car controversy was symptomatic of a basic cultural conflict. The automobile was the first invention with the power to significantly transform an agricultural way of life. As man's relationship to the land underwent radical readjustment, some said that if God had intended people to drive automobiles he would have mentioned as much in the Bible. But more realistic farmers began wondering how things would change if the car began to take over the countryside.

In the meantime, the owners of automobiles began defending

themselves. They argued that if the auto scared horses, so did farm steam engines, railroad locomotives, flying newspapers, parasols, strange noises, and almost anything unusual. Moreover, horses were expensive to maintain because they usually ate as much grain and hay as could be produced on five acres of land. In addition, they could die from disease or accident. When excited they could be dangerous. Even the trusted old nags and hammerheads could turn mean on occasion and become killers. In 1909, for example, 3,850 lives were lost in the United States because of accidents involving horses.

However, it is a misconception to believe that all farmers opposed the introduction of the automobile. Most of them had worked with machinery for years and, thus, were familiar with technological innovations. Ever since 1807 they had operated agricultural steam engines for threshing grain, ginning cotton, sawing wood, and other belt work. In fact, before anyone had seen an automobile, approximately 75,000 farm engineers were operating their steam engines in the grain-growing regions of the nation. They were also beginning to use stationary gasoline engines in the 1890s before the advent of the motor car. In 1900, *Country Gentleman* and *Nebraska Farmer* carried ads for gasoline engines but none for automobiles. The skills acquired in operating these gas engines were later transferred to the driving of the early automobiles. *Motor Age*, in 1910, claimed farmers had more ability to repair automobiles than did 80 percent of city drivers.

The introduction of auto travel in rural areas was enhanced when farm families noticed that local doctors made practical uses of the motor car. In most rural communities the first cars ever seen were driven by doctors who benefited from a faster mode of travel. Henry Ford recalled that his first enthusiastic customers were country doctors. A physician in South Dakota, in 1902, said he had used a car in his practice for two years in a region where no other motor vehicle existed within a radius of fifty miles. One winter day, despite a severe blizzard in which the snowdrifts reached the hubcaps, he managed to make a ten-mile trip in twenty-two minutes. In 1898, another doctor drove his car 24,000 miles, usually making ten calls a day and covering 100 miles. There were times on torrid summer days when liverymen refused to lend their rigs to doctors for fear the horses would die from the heat. In November, 1905, *Horseless Age* published eighty-nine letters written by doctors who described their early experiences with automobiles. One doctor told of rushing to a farm home one night and finding his patient in need of an immediate operation.

When the kitchen kerosene lamp threw insufficient light, he detached the acetylene lamps from his car, extended the gas tubing, and placed the lamps in the room where the operation was performed. One doctor thought he might make $20,000 a year with an automobile because he could visit more patrons and would be the first on the spot in cases of injury. He added in sanguine fashion, "I would be the envy of all horse owners and the pet of all the charming young women in the country around." A contemporary insisted the motor car reduced fatigue. He confessed that on one occasion when driving horses he was so tired when he reached a farm where he found a boy with an abscess on his neck, that he paused at the bedside to rest a moment and fell sound asleep. He awoke the next morning and returned home, forgetting to open the abscess, and had to make a return trip to finish the job.

Furthermore, the automobile tended to reverse the manner in which health care was delivered to people in rural communities. When only doctors owned cars, they drove into the countryside to practice medicine; when the farmers later bought automobiles, the rural people were driven into town to see doctors in offices or in local hospitals. As a result the urban hospitals and clinics were enlarged to care for a larger number of patients. Whereas most all of the rural childbirths in 1900 occurred on the farm with the aid of midwives or doctors, by the 1920s most farm children were born in city hospitals.

After 1908, the American farmer went on an auto-buying spree, spurred by an improved agricultural economy, the improved dependability of motor cars, and a growing knowledge of their practicality in a rural environment. It was estimated that half the automobiles sold in Iowa in 1910 were purchased by farmers, while the editor of *American Agriculturist* claimed that farmers were the largest group of car-buyers in the nation.

As these sales increased, some businessmen feared the expenditures would drive farmers into debt and lead to foreclosure on home mortgages. Some bankers urged rural people to refrain from putting money into these machines when better investments could be made in land or livestock. In addition, automobiles were a luxury that encouraged young people to neglect their work and go gadding all over the countryside.

In response, the agrarian crowd insisted that better transportation was a necessity rather than an idle diversion. They would go on buying cars because they thought they knew more about farming than did city bankers who lived off the interest of other people's money.

Furthermore, cars would tend to keep young people on the old homestead, and this would act as a deterrent to the urban movement. If the whole family could go for a spin after a hard day's work, the outing would lift the spirit and provide more zest for life. Young people would stay on the job and work harder knowing that there would be some pleasure in the evening hours. Many farm journals featured pictures of farm families gliding over country roads, giving the impression that life in the country *could* be idyllic.

Though skeptics insisted that farmers were still subject to long hours of hard work, exposure in bad weather, the onerous task of milking cows, and meager economic returns for their labor, the increased mobility provided by automobiles did reduce the boredom prevalent in rural areas. In preauto days, the husband usually did most of the traveling when doing business in town. With the motor car, however, the whole family could go shopping, especially on Saturday nights when the small towns were crowded with folks who enjoyed meeting their friends. In the Model T days, farmers in overalls could be seen driving down the road, wives beside them and five or six children in the back seat, side curtains flying in the wind—a happy and joyous crowd. A *Collier's* editorial in 1909 hailed the auto as the strongest force for family and social solidarity in rural America, stronger than telephones, the phonograph, rural free delivery, or university extension work.

Farm women, likewise, were emancipated from drudgery. *Rural New Yorker*, in 1913, mentioned a farm wife who drove forty-one miles to visit her married daughter, then stopped in the city of Cleveland to shop in a large department store before returning to prepare supper for the family. Another farm woman in Kansas cultivated corn in the forenoon, washed clothes in the afternoon, then took a sixty-mile drive to town to hear a band concert. Such liberating opportunities extended to the whole family, which increasingly enjoyed holiday outings. These could be one-day affairs such as attending the Chautauqua, the state fair, the circus, or religious camp meetings. Others were longer sightseeing ventures such as camping out en route to a national park or other scenic spot. This wanderlust led over strange roads, along creeks, under shade trees, and past lakes in the quest to see nature at close range. Farmers could be seen on the highway with their cars piled high with camping gear, tents, suitcases lodged between the front fenders and the hood, and crates of supplies lashed to the running boards. One farm family, in 1915, camped near Lake Tahoe in California supplied with citronella oil to ward off mosquitoes, thermos bottles, sleeping bags, camp chairs, an iron stove with a length of stove pipe, a Coleman lantern, boxes of groceries, flashlights, and a Colt revolver. Officials in Yellowstone Park observed that rural visitors outnumbered urban visitors by two to one.

Meanwhile, some farmers were ingenious enough to design special apparatus for camping purposes. Hinges were placed on front seats so they could be folded back to form a bed. Wooden frames were made to fit on the tops of seats to hold a mattress, and it was not unusual to see a homemade camper body mounted on the chassis. These appeared on the road about ten years before the auto manufacturers began building them in 1933.

These peripatetic outings were encouraged by writers who claimed automobile rides were beneficial to health. The fresh air would bring color to the cheeks, a new burst of energy would ensue, and the car motion would soothe the nerves and provide therapeutic benefits. After all, babies were cradled to sleep, youngsters enjoyed rocking horses, and grandmothers spent hours in rocking chairs. Some auto enthusiasts even claimed auto travel cured specific diseases such as tuberculosis. An octogenarian in California said he had gone West to die from consumption, but his Model T had rapidly improved his health and added years to his life. In *Combustion on Wheels*, David L. Cohn repeats the famous limerick:

> There was a fat man from Fall River
> Who said as he drove his Ford Flivver,
> "This bumping and jolting
> To me is revolting,
> It's hell; but it's good for the liver."

In the meantime, the needs of early motorists ushered in a new era of highway construction. The old dirt roads and prairie trails would not do; in the spring they became quagmires, and summer rains made them virtually impassable. A farmer had to traverse roads with ruts axle deep and "take a run" for mudholes and waterlogged ravines and sloughs. If he were lucky he emerged triumphant, if not he bogged down in the mire. To extricate the car, rope could be wrapped around the tire and between the spokes of the wheel to form a homemade set of chains. Some bolted a pulley to a rear wheel, then drove a stake in the ground in front of the automobile and used the motor to activate this block-and-tackle system. At times fence posts were used as a lever to raise a wheel out of the muck, but if all tactics failed the last resort was to "Get a Horse."

Fortunately, help was on the way. In 1908, Wayne County officials in Michigan laid the first mile of concrete road in the nation, while other road supervisors began grading roads and providing more gravel and macadam surfaces. In 1916, the Federal Road Act set aside $500,000 for road improvements. This federal legislation was enacted, according to John B. Rae, only after the Congressmen had agreed that the law's official intent was the promotion of farm-to-market transportation.

Cognizant of these bad roads, Henry Ford, in October, 1908, sold his first Model T, an automobile especially designed to travel over difficult terrain. The twenty-horsepower motor was mounted on a steel frame affixed to a chassis equipped with wheels 30 inches in diameter, thus providing good clearance for deep ruts, rocks, and tree stumps. The motor and transmission weighed 400 pounds, giving the car good power and light weight. The Tin Lizzie was only 100 inches long, could turn in a twelve-foot circle, and had the fortitude to keep chugging along even when misfiring on one or two cylinders. It could go almost anywhere. One of the virtues of the Model T was its simplicity of construction. The average person could cope with its idiosyncrasies by resorting to twine, baling wire, clothespins, chewing gum, or barbed wire taken from roadside fences. In most cases the only tools needed were a screwdriver, monkey wrench, hammer, and pliers. The Model T contained 5,000 separate parts, half of which could be bought at local garages for less than fifty cents. A Ford roadster could be purchased for $260 in 1923. Louis Cook, writing in *Ward's Quarterly* in the summer of 1965, recalled that the Model T's planetary transmission was somewhat similar to that of modern automatic drive cars. "A weekly ritual was the tightening of low, reverse and foot-brake bands, reachable through the inspection plate on the top of the transmission," he noted. "If the bands were worn out in remote areas they could be replaced by old trunk straps, sections of boots, or threshing-machine belting."

Although the sale of fifteen million Model Ts put America on wheels and made Ford a billionaire, most farmers believed the car could be improved. Approximately 300 letters a day reached the Ford Motor Company in Dearborn, Michigan. The inventive spirit conjured up such notions as a whistle on the gas tank to warn the driver when he was low on fuel and speedometers designed to flash multicolored lights on the side of the car to indicate its current speed. One farmer said he did not need a speedometer because when he went ten miles an hour the fenders rattled, when he made twenty miles an hour the transmission growled, and when he reached thirty miles an hour his false teeth fell out.

A housewife, while preparing supper, might take pencil and tablet paper, and, as grease from the frying pan splattered the page, write to "Dear Mr. Ford," asking him to install heating units on the manifold so the baby's bottle could be warmed or eggs fried while on the move. Some women wanted the running boards mounted on hinges with a trip rope attached to the steering column; then, if a villain jumped on the running board, the driver could pull the rope to dump the miscreant on the ground. Others wanted to see the exhaust pipe placed near the steering wheel so the driver could warm her hands on cold winter days.

One farmer suggested that cars be built to a sharp point so there would be no head-on collisions, while another advocated attaching a log under the car which could be lowered to the ground to act as a brake. Other writers asked for spittoons on the dash, altimeters to show elevation above sea level, an electric plug to heat flatirons, inflated cushions, mechanical traps to catch auto thieves, bumpers on all sides to get more protection, tires filled with oats and water to swell the tubes to the correct pressure, and a myriad of carburetors or attachments which would enable the car to get forty or fifty miles on a gallon of gas.

Although most of these ideas were impractical, many were enlightened, innovative, and far ahead of the times. For example, there were correspondents in 1919 who urged Ford to install four-wheel brakes, yet several years elapsed before the concept was adopted by the company. From 1912 to 1941 thousands of letters begged Ford engineers to put directional lights on the rear of the car to indicate when a driver was about to make a turn. Again company officials ignored such pleas until after World War II—a lag of about thirty years. Other practical suggestions by customers included self-acting windshield wipers, screens to keep out flies, side vents in the body to admit cool air, seats that tilted back like a barber chair, and rubber fenders made out of tire casings which would flap back into shape after collisions. Some farmers claimed they had built automatic transmissions as early as 1920. There is proof that rural motorists possessed considerable mechanical acumen, and at times were far ahead of engineers in the leading automobile companies. Their identification and cooperation with the automobile manufacturers helped to extend the car culture even deeper into rural and wilderness America.

During this time, the automobile became the most versatile power unit on the farm. In the busy season if a mower, cultivator, or grain binder broke down, the operator could jump into his car and rush to town for repairs. On threshing rigs, stopping for repairs could idle as many as twenty-five hired men. If repairs could be made quickly the time saved might mean the difference between a profit or a loss for the thresherman.

Furthermore, rural people found many uses for their cars. Milk cans, pails of eggs, and chicken crates were placed in the back seat of touring autos and carried to market. At times, pigs, goats, and sheep were crated and tied to the running boards for travel to city stockyards. During bad weather newly-born calves were picked up by car and hauled to the barn. Ranchers were known to use cars instead of horses to mend fence, herd cattle, or even to rope and brand calves.

It was a common sight to see automobiles hitched to four-wheel trailers which carried wagon boxes capable of hauling fifty bushels of grain. These were convenient for hauling grain to local elevators, bringing coal to the farm, and carrying water to livestock. At times cars were used for operating hay stackers or in pulling rakes in the hay field. In fighting prairie fires in the plains states, these trailers were used to carry barrels of water and fire-fighting equipment. Several firms built attachments to convert Model T cars into tractors. Steel drive wheels equipped with lugs replaced the regular rear wheels of the car, reduction gears reduced the speed of the car to about three miles an hour, and improved cooling systems for the motor were installed. Advertising copy showed these conversion units, which cost from $150 to $250, pulling gang plows, grain binders, and discs, and hauling freight. Although these units proved of some help in lighter work, such as in gardens or orchards, they were unsuited for heavy field work because they were not designed to be driven under full load in the heat and dust of the fields.

A more satisfactory adaptation of motor power to agriculture was the use of automobiles for belt work. A pulley could be bolted to a rear wheel that was then jacked off the ground. As the motor spun the wheel, the pulley drove a belt to power feed mills, corn shellers, water pumps, churns, grindstones, washing machines, silage cutters, and portable grain elevators. When the belt was removed the car resumed its normal use.

Automobility also strongly influenced the character of rural education. Traditionally, the one-room schoolhouse served the elementary students in each township. They were usually within walking distance, and the teachers often lived with one of the farm families during the school year. However, the auto improved transportation so much that the rural schools began to consolidate; one larger school replaced several smaller ones. More rural schools were abandoned when school boards bought school buses to transport rural youngsters into city school systems. Michael L. Berger, in *The Devil Wagon in God's Country*, calls attention to the debate as to whether the consolidated schools were better than the old-fashioned one-room country school. He cites evidence that indicates that the larger schools did improve student attendance, the school libraries and teaching materials were better, and there was more visitation between school officials and parents. Since most school districts contained more city voters than rural voters, the trend toward consolidation became inevitable.

At the same time efforts were made to educate students in matters of health. In the 1920s various state board of health organizations established school clinics in which doctors, dentists, and nurses visited the schools to check the students' health and to encourage better health habits such as brushing the teeth, using separate drinking cups, and using handkerchiefs. A farmers' bulletin in 1926 pointed out that most city schools had mandatory medical inspection programs while only eleven states required such services in rural schools.

Moreover, auto travel encouraged more farm young people to attend high school. With a car they could stay home for the daily chores and then drive to school for classes. Thus the automobile became instrumental in increasing the total attendance in high schools, a factor of immense importance in the future careers of young farmers.

It would be difficult to overestimate the importance of the auto in matters of education. Travel itself was educational. With an automobile it was easier to attend special events such as the circus, rodeos, auto shows, and auction sales. Now it was possible to get to programs sponsored by the county agent or to see demonstrations by faculty members of the state agricultural colleges. One could attend more political rallies; it was said that William Jennings Bryan was always good for forty acres of parked Model Ts. From 1915 to 1920 regional tractor shows were held throughout the major grain-growing states. At these three-day exhibitions, farm tractors demonstrated their value by plowing fields and operating farm machinery. Crowds ranged from 70,000 to 100,000 people, most of them from farm families.

Similarly, the increased mobility provided by the internal combustion engine affected the religious life in rural regions. In the horse-and-buggy days, country churches tended to be small, and served only those who could travel relatively short distances. Frequently Sunday School classes met in the local schools for convenience. Attendance was often restricted by a shortage of rural pastors, the difficulty of travel in bad weather, and a reluctance of some to work their horses on Sunday when they needed a rest. The arrival of the auto tended to increase church attendance, for it was now easier to get out on Sunday morning, especially for the elderly and shut-ins. Some farmers traveled thirty or forty miles to church, while ministers could go long distances to attend the sick and the infirm. Funeral processions were speeded up, and no longer were families exposed to bitter cold during the slow movement of horse-drawn vehicles from church to cemetery.

The ease of travel also exposed farmers to a broader range of religious ideas, fostering a greater degree of tolerance. After attending county and state Sunday School conventions of interdenominational Bible camps, ruralists were less inclined to believe that they and they alone had a monopoly on truth. In this context the automobile may have helped to preserve and promote that "sweetness and light" which humanists of the previous century warned would be wiped out by modern technology.

Mired in the countryside for centuries, farmers were among the first and most enthusiastic joiners of the automotive parade. As they chugged and rattled their way over dirt roads past their neighbors' mailboxes and the crossroads, and finally hit the blacktop that led into town, they had traveled a distance far greater than the few miles from farm to feedstore. They had entered the twentieth century at the same time as their fellow Americans, an impossibility had it not been for the automobile and their acceptance of it.

HELEN FRYE

THE AUTOMOBILE AND
AMERICAN FASHION, 1900–1930

In his seminal book, *On Human Finery*, Quentin Bell argues that "the study of clothes is of capital importance in any consideration of human behavior." Whether a person's choice of raiment is interpreted as a form of self-expression, a means of status differentiation, a response to powerful cultural changes, or (most likely) all of the above, what Bell calls "sartorial morality" forms a highly visible part of any significant social activity. This is especially true in the twentieth century, a time when new clothes were introduced at ever-shortening intervals in response to technological innovations, like the automobile, that mimicked the parade of fashion itself.

Clearly the fundamental effect of the car was to accelerate the demise of those objects of "conspicuous consumption" that Thorstein Veblen derided in his *Theory of the Leisure Class*, especially late Victorian women's fashions. One does not enter an automobile in a crinoline or bustle or encaged in such unyielding fabric that sitting, not to mention enduring bumps, is a medical hazard. The vogue of bicycling had inaugurated more rational dress, but only as a sub-category of sporting attire. It would take the car to help establish a normative pattern of reformed dress, because in everyday life, even among the upper classes, the car quickly became part of routine leisure existence. If the cardinal rule of fashion is that "beauty" is more or less incompatible with "efficiency," it is no less true that the standard of beauty will change to accommodate desirable objects of everyday use. And this is just what happened at the turn of the century.

In the infancy of the automobile, male drivers of necessity chose clothing that allowed them to "get out and get under" to make baling wire and chewing gum repairs, fix frequent flats, and withstand gasoline, flying grease, and mud. By the time a woman dared to trust herself to such a contraption, she most likely just tossed on the old plush cape from the entry and climbed aboard. The carriage and train provided appropriate models for comfortable, or at least tolerable, dress.

Naturally, as the automobile became socially acceptable, the dressmakers and tailors could not ignore this golden opportunity and got to work. As early as 1902, *Butterick-Delineator* was offering coat patterns with a choice of automobile length. An article in *Cosmopolitan* in 1903 suggests a car ride as a diversion for a weekend house party where ordinary country clothing would be a la mode. Some very charming overgarments were devised for the ladies to protect the delicate gowns of the period. These were usually made of mohair, linen, taffeta, or pongee trimmed with pipings or bandings of color or leather and often had attached hoods. Men wore country clothing of tweed and leather and adopted the linen duster with cap and goggles.

Country Life in America stated in 1906 that "clothes designed in the infancy of autoing lacked grace and simplicity, but the models being offered now have none of their grotesque features." The reference might be to the odd headgear and masks seen in the European press. The article continues,

> Durable and modish garments may be had at small cost, with no extra charge being entailed for having them made to measure. Approved styles follow closely the lines of ordinary clothing. A three-quarter coat of corduroy for hunting or driving is double-breasted with four pockets, the flaps of which fasten with pearl buttons and is lined with worsted. Danish kidskin leather coats can be short and plain, Norfolk style, or reach below the knees. An expensive suit for rough wear is available, loose enough to be worn over conventional dress; both coat and trousers of rubber are faced with tan jean cloth, reversible and waterproof.

The ordinary Norfolk country-suit buttoned leggings were also worn by drivers, and in the event of roadside repairs were considerably more convenient than trousers. Caps needed to fit tightly, offering the least resistance to the wind. They could be of the same material as the suit, or of leather, and often had flaps to pull down over the neck and ears. The small peaked golf cap was often used, and in many catalogs caps were designated for either golf or auto for some years. In short, the specialized outfit of hunting and other demanding outdoor activities was adapted for the road.

For real warmth, male autoists looked to fur, and there were many pelts from which to choose: Manchurian dogskin, buffalo calf, goatskin, Russian pony, and the more expensive raccoon and beaver, for example. Wool coats lined with fur were popular, and a black broad-

Romantic paintings like this one by Harrison Fisher early in the century glamorized the typical costumes of drivers and passengers.

cloth coat lined with muskrat and collared with Astrakhan or Persian lamb was the epitome of luxury for years. Women, too, wore fur and fur-lined coats, ponyskin, otter, muskrat, and sealskin. A mail-order catalog offered ladies fur-lined coats with mink collars for $17.50. The coats came with fur-lined wristlets. To prevent wind blowing up the sleeve, driving gloves became gauntlets and developed cuffs that reached halfway to the elbows. The final necessities were goggles and the lap robes from the one-horse shay.

Gradually the car began to dictate styling specific to its own unique character. Suitable raiment for the motoring woman required the long, loose, protective coat called a duster for obvious reasons, but a car like the two-cylinder Reo was not the cleanest machine to climb into with yards of skirt. Skirts obligingly shortened. Artists such as Harrison Fisher often portrayed the classic duster that remained popular with men and women for many years. It was a long coat of linen crash, sometimes single-breasted with patch pockets, but better if double-breasted with pearl or brass buttons embossed with an auto design or make. It had deep flapped pockets, and under the flap was an opening through which a driver could reach the pockets of the suit beneath. The collar could be worn turned up or down, and, like the cuffs, it had straps to tighten against the wind. With increasing speeds a large hat, even when covered with a large veil and scarf, became impractical, and many women chose small-brimmed hats with the three-yard scarf. Others liked to perch a man's cap atop a pompadour with a short hatpin, tie on a wool scarf, add gauntlets or muff in cold weather, and happily defy the criticism of increasingly "old-fashioned" aunts.

Before long the totemic quality of the automobile sponsored a wide range of paraphernalia. Clothing accessories for extra warmth were in demand, and fancywork books and magazines instructed readers how to make auto sweaters, auto hoods, auto mufflers, scarfs, and caps, including one cap with a cuff that could be pulled down over the face to form a helmet with a slit for the eyes. Jewelry and button manufacturers produced small personal accessories such as leather coin purses with automobile-decorated tops, one constructed like a driver's leather cap. A straightedge razor from Germany in ivory was carved with a motoring scene. A car-embossed silver-cased pencil made a watch charm, and there were lockets for the same purpose. Watch fobs depicted auto motifs or emblems, and at least one pocket flask had a large, deeply embossed motor car racing across the front. Fancy buttons, some very large and ornamental, were legion; they came in

Women drivers ca. 1911 insisted on safety as well as distinctive finery. This advertisement appealed to both desires.

Duster buttons served an iconic purpose in the religion of automobility.
(*From the collection of Dan R. Post, publisher of Post Motor Books.*)

brass, silver, cloisonné enamel, jet—even a brass car on abalone shell. All vaunted automobiles or automotive designs.

It is always risky to give a reason for fashion, but the automobile surely added to the popularity of conventional men's styles in the years 1907 to 1910, which called for peg-top trousers and widened shoulders. Any style that presented the American as a he-man out-door type had to keep an eye on his status as driver and mechanic. Women of course made even more significant changes in style, soft-ening the blouse lines, easing the collar, but particularly in skirt design where a little shortening and a lot of slimming became essen-tial. After all, it would have been difficult to maneuver gearshift, brake, and pedals in a skirt five yards around and reaching the floor, not to mention several petticoats. Probably the most practical and comfortable attire for everyday use under the duster was the costume popularized by Charles Dana Gibson in the Nineties and worn all over America during the early years of the century. This was the dark skirt, usually of mohair or tweed, and the white linen shirtwaist. (One style commentator suggested carrying an extra waist in the handbag to wear at journey's end in case one arrived disheveled.) The choice of linen, which requires constant washing and pressing because it is so easily disfigured, reminds us that the history of fashionable dress is tied to the competition between classes, for in this early period the car is predominantly the instrument of the privileged.

And then came the Model T Ford. Inexpensive and technically efficient, it made the roads accessible to almost everyone, if only on a Sunday afternoon. Not that the fashion world became democratic at once. On the contrary, according to an article in a 1911 *Collier's*, "when once the problem of [inventing a] car that would go and keep going under all conditions was solved, the manufacturers gave their attention to giving the traveler by motor car greater comfort, *luxury*, and independence" [emphasis added]. Because the automobile now had a windshield, side front doors, top and side curtains, occupants were less at the mercy of the elements, and so regained some measure of choice in garments. High fashion rushed in to make itself available. Nineteen-twelve fashions for women show a variety of dusters and the new motor coats, accompanied by the French motor bonnet of shirred silk with rosettes over the ears and long scarf ends. *Dress* magazine recommended the utility coat, smart as well as practical, to wear over a light silk dress; its high collar could be worn with overlap-ping revers for extra warmth when motoring in town. Also shown was an automobile coat of red cloth with loose-fitting shoulders, wide

The sporty look suggested the carefree spirit of automobility itself. This status-appeal advertisement is directed at a fashionable clientele.

cuffs, and opossum collar. Men's wear showed the heavy wool ulster for cold weather instead of fur, with any preferred hat for driving, although the cap was still worn. Because the young country-club set and its imitators were discovering raceabouts or sports cars, summer wear became fashionable. White flannel skirts and trousers (ice-cream pants) were topped by the notched lapel jacket of white flannel wide striped in vivid colors. Girls wore headbands in bright colors for windblown locks, and men wore no hat at all or wore the stiff-brimmed straw hat sometimes called a boater. Both men and women wore the polo coat, a loosely belted garment, and the balmacaan, a raglan-sleeved three-quarter coat of tweed, unbelted and flared at the hem.

The National Trails Highway opened in 1913 and the Lincoln Highway in 1923. Long distance touring adventures, a new fad of the leisure class, required appropriate clothing. After World War I, many women found the women's volunteer uniforms suitable for long rugged trips. Pictures taken in the national parks at that time show outfits of this kind. Men seemed to wear mostly tweed and corduroy garments, comfortable and able to withstand hard driving and hiking. Overnight accommodations were scarce and emergency breakdowns caused by infirm cars or bad road conditions were common; consequently some drivers carried running-board gear for camping. Luggage was designed to carry extra clothing, and car trunks were built to hold two or three suitcases that slipped in one above the other for easy access. The outside case was covered with stormproof and dust-proof material and fitted with brass catches and locks. Another handy innovation was a wardrobe trunk with built-in clamps for attachment to the running board. The trunk opened up to garment hangers and a separate case for small articles. For refreshment along the road there were lunch boxes with food containers and tableware, baskets with ice compartments, and, adopted from England, tea baskets with alcohol-heated tea kettles. Best of all the newly invented thermos bottles, encased in leather, insured a supply of water or milk en route—a blessing to traveling mothers.

Heavy-duty clothing for the automobile was no longer necessary now that the car itself gave so much protection. Current styles for men seemed to fit the cars they drove, for example the pleated-back plaid suit with set-in belt looked just right for the 1919 Saxon chummy roadster. Women's wear had become even more adapted to the car. Skirts were more manageable, garments in general looser, especially waistlines thanks to the new unboned and flexible corsetry. Jackets hung straight down from the shoulder, and were loosely

John Held, Jr.'s depiction of the raccoon-coated sheiks and shebas of the 1920s is still the standard image of that generation. (*Courtesy of Mrs. John Held, Jr.*)

belted for greater comfort in driving and riding. Soft crushable hats of felt or velours often accompanied the costumes, though due to the increasing use of the closed car, larger hats could be worn if desired.

Despite woman's suffrage, the skirts of the early 1920s remained ankle length. The most significant postwar styles were associated with the exciting convertibles chosen by the young fashionable crowd, the flappers, sheiks, and shebas. The car itself with rumble seat, fender steps, and small door for golf club storage over the rear fender no doubt had some effect, for the longer skirts could not have navigated the fender step into the rumble seat. Along with the sophisticated flapper dress went a short wraparound coat of wool or perhaps seal-skin if cold. This was topped by the ubiquitous cloche hat pulled down tightly over bobbed hair showing only a spit curl or two—a hat that rendered unnecessary the long long chiffon scarf of the type that strangled Isadora Duncan. Women now wore a three-piece suit of matching knickers, skirts, and belted jacket, usually in tweed but available in linen for cross-country touring, hiking, or golf. Country club men had reinstated the knicker, adding four inches in length and a bit of width to create the plus fours. They came in woolens or linen and were worn with argyle-patterned sweaters, golf socks, and fringed-flap saddle shoes. This dashing outfit ensconced in a classy cabriolet became so popular that some men wore them who had never driven either a car or golf ball. But the twenties fashion that became a signature of the period was the huge raccoon coat worn by both young men and women. Graphics by John Held, Jr., and the song "Doing the Raccoon," recorded by Paul Whiteman and others, contributed to this item's legendary status.

Without a doubt fashion was influenced by the early automobiles. In later years, however, there is evidence that fashion had considerable effect on automobiles. Certainly the example of the fashion industry with all its ingenious methods of selling class pride and self-esteem tutored the auto industry in how to market its product. If, as Quentin Bell remarks, "the sexual impulse is a constant affect upon clothes," designers would find ways to imitate the suggestiveness and seductive qualities of fashion apparel. The aesthetics and erotics of clothes were gradually transferred to the machine, sometimes by the same engineers of public taste, in order to enhance the desirability of another consumer object Americans could wear like a second skin.

MICHAEL L. BERGER

THE GREAT WHITE HOPE ON WHEELS

The only thing that can beat Jack Johnson is an automobile. Judging from past performance, the machine stands every chance of taking up the white man's burden . . .

Philadelphia Inquirer

It is October of 1910. The Philadelphia A's and their manager Connie Mack are basking in the glory of having defeated the Chicago Cubs four games to one in the seventh World Series. Martin Sheridan has just set a world's record in the discus of 142 feet, 2 inches. And Barney Oldfield, who had established a world's automobile speed record of 131.724 mph in March, is preparing to meet Jack Johnson, heavyweight boxing champion of the world since 1908, in the new sport of motor racing.

Although an Oldfield-Johnson race could be expected to generate excitement as a Battle of Champions, it soon achieved symbolic social dimensions. Pitting as it did the first black heavyweight champion of the world against the white speed champion, the contest was seen by many as a skirmish in the continuing war of racial supremacy. Barney Oldfield found himself cast in the somewhat dubious role of the new "great white hope." The race was also significant in the development of the emerging sport of motor racing, which by 1910 was being organized and regularized by the American Automobile Association. Such a contest, involving a true champion and a rank amateur, was bound to be viewed by many as a threat to the sport's best interests. Would motor racing remain purely entertainment, a sideshow attraction at country fairs, or would it evolve into a serious spectator sport? Finally, the Oldfield-Johnson race became a "media event," in which rival factions battled to control public opinion through the newspapers and magazines of the day.

Jack Johnson had won the world's heavyweight boxing championship from Tommy Burns in 1908. The mere fact that Burns had been willing to fight a Negro had broken a cardinal rule of American boxing. Since the championship was seen as the embodiment of masculinity, a member of an "inferior" race should never be given the opportunity to hold it. Johnson's status as champion was difficult at best for white Americans to accept. It was made considerably worse by the boxer's "sinful" personal life. As one of his biographers has observed, "much of the controversy and discussion surrounding the champion stemmed from the fact that he was unlike any publicized black man America had ever known."[1] In an age dominated by Jim Crow laws, Social Darwinism, and the belief that blacks should know their place in American society, Jack Johnson broke all the rules and seemed to "get away" with it. He drank to excess, dressed in flashy clothes, drove expensive cars speedily and recklessly, and was not above engaging in public brawls. Johnson also was defiant in posture and appearance. In an era when cranial and facial hair were in vogue, his shaven head was shining and unconventional. His ever-present smile, which novelist Jack London immortalized following his fight with Jim Jeffries, glittered with gold-plated teeth. Standing six feet one inch and weighing over two hundred pounds, he presented a formidable, if not forbidding, figure to white America.

Johnson's appearance might have been forgiven had he stayed within the social boundaries of his race. In the early years of this century, to cross the color line, to establish any degree of intimacy with a member of the opposite race, was to run the risk of social ostracism and physical punishment. Johnson ignored this threat. He flaunted his desire to be with, and marry, white women. American whites could accept his ownership of nightclubs, sports cars, and diamonds, but it could not stomach his possession of a white woman. "No brutality, no infamy, no degradation in all the years of southern slavery, possessed such villainous character and such atrocious qualities as the state laws which allow the marriage of the Negro Jack Johnson to a woman of the Caucasian strain," railed one Congressional supporter of a bill to ban miscegenation.[2]

In sum, Jack Johnson was increasingly viewed as an affront to white civilization and to everything it supposedly represented. The fear also began to spread, in both white and black America, that Johnson, despite his "antisocial" attitudes and behavior, was becoming a role model for many young Negroes. As a result, the white press did its best to insinuate that the victory over Tommy Burns did

[1]Al-Tony Gilmore, *Bad Nigger!: The National Impact of Jack Johnson* (Port Washington, N.Y.: Kennikat Press, 1975), p. 9.

[2]Cited in George F. Will, "Joe Louis, Without Complaints," *Washington Post*, August 6, 1978, p. D7.

not entitle Johnson to the heavyweight crown. Jim Jeffries, who had retired in 1905 as the unbeaten champion, had voluntarily relinquished the title to Marvin Hart, who in turn had been beaten by Burns. Consequently, the idea developed that Jeffries was still the real champion, though temporarily retired.

Jack London, one of the chief proponents of this idea, is credited with starting the movement that eventually brought Jeffries back into the ring. London had covered the Johnson-Burns match in Australia and, according to one writer's judgment, "wrote a vivid, not to say lurid, account of the fight for the *New York Herald*, an account calculated to chill the blood of every member of the master race—that is to say, he appealed to the deep-rooted prejudices of the vast majority of white Americans."[3] Referring to the fight as one between "a colossus and a pigmy," London accused Johnson of toying with Burns and concluded his piece with a clarion call: "Jeffries must emerge from his alfalfa farm and remove the golden smile from Johnson's face. Jeff, it's up to you!"[4]

Overweight, aging by boxing's standards, and five years removed from his last ring appearance, Jeffries knew that a comeback was ill-advised. Yet it was difficult for him to resist growing public pressure to become the "great white hope." Therefore, he reluctantly agreed to return to the ring in a match scheduled for Independence Day, 1910. He did so "at the request of the public, which forces me out of retirement. I realize full well just what depends on me, and I am not going to disappoint the . . . portion of the white race that has been looking to me to defend its athletic superiority."[5]

Whereas press coverage of the Johnson-Burns contest had been routinely handled, with little attention to the race of each combatant, the Jeffries-Johnson match was built around the issue of racial supremacy, with the approval of the fighters who were convinced that the publicity would enhance the gate. As a result, the championship fight became national, not just sporting, news. The outcome was what might have been expected. Johnson had little trouble handling

[3]Nat Fleischer, *The Heavyweight Championship: An Informal History of Heavyweight Boxing from 1719 to the Present Day* (New York: G.P. Putnam's Sons, 1961), p. 141.

[4]Quotations drawn from contemporary newspapers and periodicals which refer to the Johnson-Jeffries fight are from editions published during July of 1910. Quotations related to the Oldfield-Johnson motor race appeared in newspapers and periodicals published during the period October 5-November 3, 1910. Readers desiring specific citations may secure them from the author of this essay.

[5]Cited in John W. Blassingame, "Introduction," in Gilmore, *Bad Nigger!*, p. 4.

the ex-champion, and in the fifteenth round Jeffries was knocked out for the first time in his career. Johnson's triumph was bitter medicine for the white population to swallow. Nineteen deaths and scores of injuries were attributed to violence erupting after the fight.

Public interest in the sport of boxing suddenly diminished. It was as if many whites hoped to dethrone the champion by ignoring him. The *Chicago Tribune* observed: "It is apparent that for a few years at least the white portions of this free republic are about to lose all interest in pugilism. . . . It is apparent now that prizefighting is an ignoble pursuit." Perhaps for this reason Johnson began to explore the possibility of getting into serious motor racing. He had always been attracted to cars, the faster the better, and may have hoped to combine this interest with his considerable physical abilities to achieve success in another sport. On the eve of the race with Oldfield the *New York Times* asked Johnson why he became involved with motor racing. "He stated that he could not remain idle," reported the *Times*. "He said that he saw nothing promising in the future in the fighting line, so he decided to choose another and more exciting competition to consume his spare time."

It was later revealed that Johnson had raced in private match contests in Southern California during the winter of 1909-10, and that he had fared well against reputable drivers. It was after these races that Johnson issued his first challenge to Oldfield. But the latter turned him down, according to the *New York Times*, because of his "previous engagements and the objection to racing a colored man."

Although Johnson continued to challenge and even bait Oldfield, the racing champion ignored him. Shortly thereafter, Johnson applied to the Indianapolis Motor Speedway, which had opened a year earlier, for permission to enter several of the upcoming September races. When he was turned down, he applied to stage an exhibition. When this request was also rejected, Johnson immediately challenged Barney Oldfield, Ralph De Palma, or George Robertson to meet him in a match race, and posted a $5,000 bond to that effect. Oldfield accepted this challenge, most likely because of Jeffries's defeat. Oldfield and Jeffries were old drinking buddies. The latter frequently commented on the number of barroom scrapes from which he had extricated the "King of Speed." Oldfield, in turn, had accompanied Jeffries on the Colorado fishing trip that followed the latter's humiliation at the hands of Johnson. Thus, he may have seen himself as duty-bound to accomplish what his friend had nobly tried, but failed, to do—reestablish the physical superiority of the white race.

By October 9, 1910, Oldfield had arrived in New York ostensibly to begin training for the race scheduled for the 20th. Asked to explain the origins of the curious race, Oldfield told the *New York Times*:

> I agreed to race Johnson only after I realized he was in earnest about such a race and really had the idea he could beat me at my own game. At first, I looked upon the proposition as a joke and scheme to advertise Johnson's theatrical connections, but in dining cars, hotels, and on Pullmans the colored attendants invariably asked me if I was going to race their idol. Then intelligent business men and friends among the sporting writers wanted to know how much longer I was going to let Johnson "get away" with his challenge to me.
>
> I realized that I would have to race Johnson some day to stop all criticism and comment just as Jeffries had to fight him, so why wait till he has a chance to acquire a thorough knowledge of the track racing game! I get a lot of money for racing him, and I will win a lot more from him and his supporters, and that is the reason why I agreed to participate in what I consider an unusual and remarkable match.

Several aspects of this statement are interesting. The mere fact that someone was "serious" about racing would not have been sufficient justification for Oldfield to engage in such a contest. Nor is it likely that Oldfield was motivated by a desire to eliminate early a rival who might later become more troublesome. Both money and the implied racial issue would seem to have been more important. Barney Oldfield's barnstorming career and his showmanship made informal contacts with Negro servants of the day likely, and talk probably did include the ever-present Johnson challenge. For many whites, Johnson's desire to compete in motor racing was just another instance of his not knowing his place. Oldfield had an opportunity to be the great white hope on wheels, and to make good money at it.

Oldfield's evaluation of the seriousness of the race and Johnson's future as a motor car driver were not shared by the Contest Board of the American Automobile Association (AAA), the era's primary racing organization. Soon after Oldfield's arrival in New York, the Contest Board announced that the driver would be disqualified from future AAA-sanctioned races if he actually competed against Johnson. In a related development, it revoked the boxer's license to participate in AAA events, claiming that it was unaware of the identity of the John Arthur Johnson who had applied for the certificate. The official reason given for the revocation was that Johnson's "entrance into the sport would be detrimental to its best interests" because the challenger engaged in boxing, a sport banned in many states, and also was an inexperienced driver. Johnson indignantly issued a statement showing that he had complied with all the conditions expected of other applicants, and he threatened to sue if his license was not restored.

Johnson had no reason to worry. Oldfield recognized the publicity value of the AAA actions, and the probable increase in gate receipts and motion picture royalties that would result. The *New York Times* may have been taken in by a publicist when it reported on October 13 that "Oldfield, it seems, would like very much to get out of the race, but he is held to the terms of his contract with the promoters. The moving picture privilege has been sold by Oldfield, and he says it would be impossible for him to withdraw at this time. 'It's a case of race or be sued,' he said last night, 'and I'll have to race whether I like it or not.'"

Although it is difficult to document the real motivations for the AAA's actions, they would seem to have been based on a concern for the development of motor racing as a sport, and the belief that the sport would be enhanced by keeping it all white. On several occasions in the past, the AAA Contest Board had denied approval to races it deemed unsafe, including the 1907 Vanderbilt Cup, or in which a nonlicensed driver or car was involved, including Oldfield's celebrated races against Lincoln Beachey in a Curtiss airplane. (Oldfield, naturally, remained on the track while piloting his car.)

On the other hand, *Horseless Age*, one of the pioneer automobile weeklies, commenting on the proposed Oldfield-Johnson race, introduced the possibility of a racial reason: "Of course the contest board will not register a negro driver, much less sanction such a meet, and the white man in question probably will not care to participate in an outlaw meet."

The idea that Oldfield would not participate in an outlaw event was wishful thinking. Friction between Oldfield and the AAA went back to December, 1902, when Oldfield was racing for Henry Ford and set a speed record for the mile in the 999. The AAA had refused to recognize the record for obscure technical reasons. Without the official sanction, Oldfield lost out on prize money. Several years later, the AAA suspended Oldfield for participating in outlaw races with his Peerless *Green Dragon*. To prove the superiority of the machine, Oldfield engaged in competition against all comers without attention to the niceties that the AAA had established for sanctioning such races. His suspension seemed to have no effect on his popular appeal, and he continued to barnstorm from coast to coast for months.

Oldfield's manager, Bill Pickens, apparently did not believe that the AAA would again suspend Oldfield, given his importance to motor racing, because he urged Barney to go ahead. It was also becoming clear that the AAA's actions were giving the race an air of respectability. The *New York Times* thus, on October 16, reported that: "At the outset the race was regarded as little more than a farce, and was considered in many quarters merely as an advertising affair for both Oldfield and Johnson. The events of the past week have put an entirely different aspect on the matter." The *Times* then went on to recite the AAA's refusal to sanction the meet, the indefinite suspension of Oldfield, the revoking of Johnson's license, and the revelation of the boxer's California racing experience.

Meanwhile, both Oldfield and Johnson began to practice for the match, which was to consist of three five-mile heats. On the day of the race the *New York Times* stated that "While Johnson has had no experience as the driver of a racing car in competition, those who have seen him say that he will make Oldfield use all his skill as a track driver to beat him." And as if to prove his sincerity as a racing driver for once and for all, Johnson made it known that if Oldfield should beat him, he would go to Europe to secure the fastest car in the world and return to challenge Oldfield in a rematch.

Daily newspaper reports regarding the upcoming race tended to be factual or based on promotional press releases, and thus lacked the racial content that had accompanied the Johnson-Jeffries fight of the previous June. But at least one trade publication spewed racism. *Horseless Age* stated on the day of the race that "B. Oldfield has embarked in the coal business in colossal style. Not only has he added Mistah J. Arthur Johnson to his all vaudeville and county fair engagements on the kerosene lamp circuit, but he is catering especially to that class of 'sporting persons' interested in such elevating pastimes as cakewalks, craps, ragtime, chicken dinners and policy." The article then went on to report that Oldfield had been booked to race at the Colored State Fair in Richmond, Virginia, later in the month.

After rain forced two postponements, the Oldfield-Johnson race finally was run on October 25 at the Sheepshead Bay Track in Brooklyn. A racially-mixed crowd of 5,000 to 7,000 people viewed a match that was, by all accounts, very boring. The *Brooklyn Daily Eagle* termed the race a "miserable fiasco"; the *New York Sun*, "a burlesque affair that was not even amusing"; and the *New York Times* referred to the "ridiculous ease" with which Oldfield won. In the first heat, Oldfield bested Johnson by a half mile. In the second heat, he again scored an easy victory, though by a lesser distance, apparently slowing down for the benefit of motion-picture photographers. Given the fact that Oldfield was driving a 60 h.p. Knox; and Johnson a 90 h.p. Thomas, the outcome was even more impressive.

The ease with which Oldfield won raises several questions. First, why did the great showman, who had often allowed complete unknowns to defeat him in the second heat to add to the excitement of the third and final heat, go for two straight victories in this particular race? Did Barney "tease" Johnson by slowing down in the second heat, as the *New York Times* claimed? Second, why was Oldfield so concerned about the quality of the filming? Was it simply a question of the royalty payments, or was something more important involved? Finally, since Oldfield had brought the 200 h.p. *Blitzen Benz* with him to Sheepshead Bay, and in fact drove it in a race against time between heats, why did he not use this car, in which he had set the world's record, in the race against Johnson? Tangentially, why did he elect to put on a speed exhibition that day?

The answer, or at least a partial one, to the first question may be found in Oldfield's statement to the press on the eve of the race. "I did not enter into the race against Johnson for gold or glory," he said, "but to eliminate from my profession an invader who might cause me trouble in a year or so if I ignored him now. If Jeffries had fought Johnson five years ago when the white man was in his prime, he would not have had to return to the ring and suffer the [July 4] Reno defeat."

This statement would seem to support the contention that money was not the most important consideration for Oldfield, but rather the defeat of a black challenger. However, it is difficult to accept Oldfield's contention that Johnson represented a future threat, or that defeat at this point would eliminate Johnson from contention. In fact, it can be argued that Oldfield, by accepting Johnson's challenge, especially when the AAA Contest Board had ruled against him, was abetting the boxer's racing aspirations, not ending them.

The most telling aspect of Oldfield's press statement is his reference to the Johnson-Jeffries fight. He not only claims that the outcome would have been different had the fight been fought earlier, he also specifically refers to Jeffries as the "white man." Thus Oldfield ran the kind of race calculated to embarrass his opponent, but one which would not diminish its value to the media. And the media were important, for given the "outlaw" status of the contest, Oldfield's best hope to publicize the victory, to show racial superiority in action, lay with the motion picture films that would emerge. He therefore decisively defeated Johnson in the first heat, and toyed with the pugilist in the second heat, making it clear to all that he was in total control.

This also helps to explain the lack of a third heat, which had been expected by the more skeptical pre-race commentators, who figured that with Johnson, Oldfield would be up to his old country fair antics. The first heat of his staged match races invariably resulted in a close victory for Oldfield; Barney would lose the second heat, and then come back to win the third—sometimes by the margin of a tire. Each spectator went away feeling he had seen the ultimate in motor-car racing. A third heat in the Johnson match might therefore have lent credence to the idea of a rigged race. If that idea became commonplace, the competition would have had no sociological significance. Oldfield wanted, and got, precisely this kind of headline (from the *New York Sun*): OLDFIELD SAVES WHITE RACE.

Finally, Oldfield may have realized that the AAA, and groups like it, were slowly transforming motor racing into an organized sport. To maintain his premier position, it would be necessary to downplay the circus-like antics of the past and to concentrate on defeating worthy opponents. Picking up on this idea, the *New York Daily Tribune*, in reporting the results of the Johnson race, noted that Oldfield "refused to take any chance of losing his prestige or a lucrative contract to tour the world."

The question of why Oldfield took the filming of the race so seriously has been partially answered. He was, with Johnson's unknowing help, producing a film in support of white supremacy, and he intended to determine the plot, if not the direction, as much as possible. The New York dailies carried numerous reports of motion picture crews at the track during the practice sessions. Although they maintained they were simply exploring the best shot angles, allegations abounded that actual filming was taking place. It was claimed that the footage would later be mixed with that of the race to make a more exciting product. There is no denying that on the day of the race several events were staged solely for the benefit of motion pictures, including a series of "false starts" and hysterical crowd reactions after an Oldfield victory. Johnson apparently believed that films of the event would further *his* career as a racing driver, assuming he made a good showing. One hesitates to impute the most mercenary motives to public figures, but in this case we are clearly dealing with celebrities whose hunger for publicity and respect from a mass audience appeared to be boundless. If nothing else, we see in this contest how technological innovations such as film and automobiles enabled vanity and ambition to thrive as never before. Racism itself seemed to take second place, though it informed the event from start to finish as a primary cause.

As to why the *Blitzen Benz* was not used in the race, Oldfield simply had no need of it. Why run the risk of damage to the vehicle in an easy match race? (Johnson, an amateur, might cause an accident). The *Benz* was on hand though, because Oldfield was eager to show that he was still "King of Speed" and the "Daredevil Dean of Auto Drivers." Not only would he defeat Johnson handily, but he would exert so little energy in doing so that he could attempt to best the world's speed record between heats.

In sum, Oldfield's atypical conduct during the race can be largely explained by his desire to make the black heavyweight champion look bad. Many whites may have hoped for more. Unable to find a man who could defeat Johnson in the ring, some whites hoped that an "unfortunate" accident might deprive the boxer of his ability to defend his title. In its account of the race, the *New York Sun* reported that "a lot of white men [were] feeling somehow cheated because Jack Johnson had not had an accident." Similarly, the *New York Daily Tribune* noted suggestively that Johnson "did not break his neck or even his leg at the Sheepshead Bay racetrack yesterday."

Two weeks after his victory over Johnson, Oldfield went to court to fight his AAA disqualification, with particular reference to a series of forthcoming races in Atlanta. Although Oldfield's legal arguments were diverse, his lawyers tried, among other things, to convince the judge that the Johnson contest was justifiable, even if Oldfield did break the Contest Board's rules and regulations. According to the *New York Times*, Barney's counsel argued that the "outlaw" meet was good for motor racing "because it would tend to discourage Johnson from future competition with white sportsmen." The defense attacked that argument, produced affidavits purporting to show that Oldfield raced Johnson for money, and won the case. Although the suspension was upheld, Oldfield was eventually permitted to reenter AAA-sanctioned races including the Indianapolis 500 where he placed fifth both in 1914 and 1916. Nonetheless, his suspension came when he was in his prime, and perhaps limited the honors he might have won.

As for Johnson, his defeat was so humiliating that he limited his future racing to the highway. Years later, in his autobiography, he claimed that he "never had an ambition to be a real speed demon, but I must confess to having a weakness for fast driving. I decided, however, that I was not cut out for a race driver, when on one occasion I entered a race with Barney Oldfield. The manner in which he out-drove and outstripped me, convinced me that I was not meant for that sport."[6] In 1946, Johnson was killed after his automobile went out of control in North Carolina.

Placed in the context of the times, the Oldfield-Johnson race was significant for at least three reasons. First, racial attitudes associated with it mirrored to a large extent the prejudices of American society in general and professional sports in particular. Oldfield saw himself as a savior, less than half a century after the Emancipation Proclamation, of an embattled race. The first active challenges to racism had been mounted by 1910, and the culture was sensitive to threats of legislative change. One has only to think of D.W. Griffith's exaltation of the Ku Klux Klan in *The Birth of a Nation*, released four years later, to appreciate the tensions underlying Johnson's "uppity" challenge to the masters of the new automotive technology. Oldfield was sworn to prevent Johnson from becoming the king of racing as well as boxing, and to keeping car races segregated, if possible.

Secondly, the Oldfield-Johnson contest may have represented a watershed in the history of car racing. Up to this time racing had been viewed largely as a novelty act, to be offered in conjunction with fairs or other local extravaganzas. Even when presented alone, the emphasis was more on establishing speed records and creating match races between "name" drivers than on establishing a professional sport governed by enforceable rules and regulations. By maintaining its suspension of Oldfield, for a time at least, the Contest Board of the AAA showed that the organization was more important than the man. It could disqualify the best-known driver in the country and the sport would survive, even prosper, as others arose to take his place. Together with the construction of stadia such as the Indianapolis Motor Speedway and a trend away from road races to

[6]Jack Johnson, *Jack Johnson Is A Dandy: An Autobiography* (New York: Signet Books, 1970), p. 104.

track contests, these developments signaled that motor racing was coming of age as a professional sport.

Finally, the Oldfield-Johnson race revealed the degree to which the media could "hype" a sports event. The race might have amounted only to a local, novelty exhibition, but it was transformed into an event of national interest through press coverage. The lesson of the thrilling automobile race between the champion pugilist and the speed king was not lost on promoters of almost every future sports contest.

IMAGES OF THE
EARLY CAR

Out to Pasture
Courtesy, Ford Archives, Henry Ford Museum, Dearborn, Mich.

John Sloan, *Gray and Brass*, 1907
Collection of Arthur G. Altschul, New York

Actress

Bruce C. McCombs, *Billboard*
Courtesy of the Artist

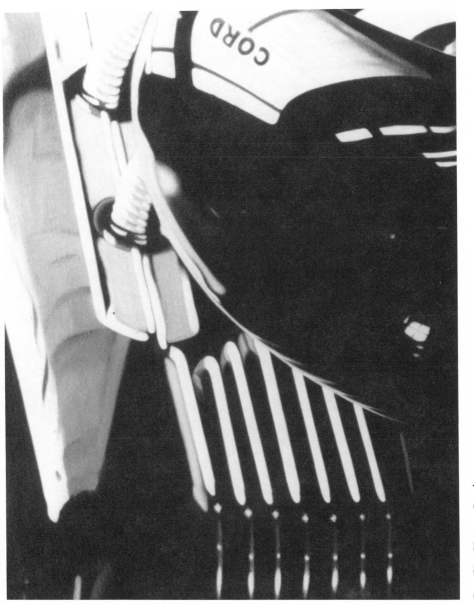

Jose Vaz Vieira, *Cord*
Courtesy Orlando Gallery, Sherman Oaks, Calif.

William Crutchfield, *Model "T" Ford*
(from the "Americana Suite")
Courtesy GEMINI G.E.L., Los Angeles, California

Giacomo Balla, *Speeding Automobile*, 1913
oil on board, 73 × 104 cm
Balla Collection

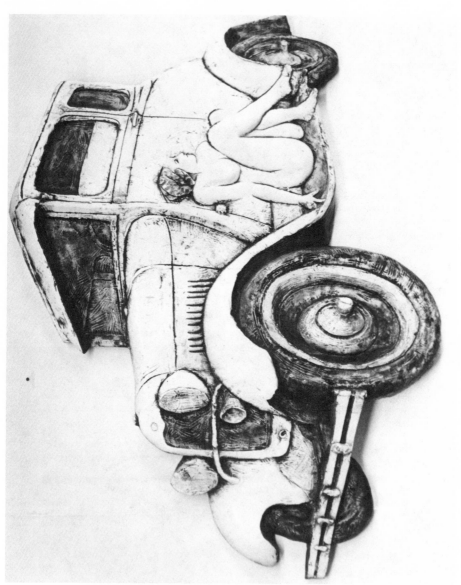

Richard Parsons, *Fantasy Machine, Model A*
Courtesy of the Artist

WILLIAM S. DOXEY

VANISHING AMERICANA

So many of you guys have bugged me about the first runner-up to Miss America that I'm gonna set it all down once and for all and send two notarized copies to the Americana Collection in the Library of Congress.

ITEM: Yes, Miss Kitty Blackburn at the time was the runner-up to the reigning Miss America.

ITEM: Yes, she was (note *was*) not the warmest, friendliest twenty-year-old in the nation, although she was then (and still *is*) the best-looking.

ITEM: Yes, she found me irresistible (*after* she got to know me).

Which brings me, finally, to what we cultural anthropologists call "The Record."

SITUATION: Professor Rogers Edward McBride's seminar titled: "Relevant Problems in Modern Anthropology." The class is a mixed bag—several grad students, the rest seniors chosen by the prof because of their "dedication." Miss Kitty Blackburn and I are among the chosen. You'd think the presence of a beautiful young woman such as Kitty, who is to top it all the runner-up to Miss America, would blow the class mind. But you'd be wrong. Most of the dudes are so hung up on academics that they hate Kitty because they think she's a dumb broad who plans to deal herself an ace by conning McBride. That's what I thought, too, at first. After the second meeting I gave her a chance to have a beer with me. She fixed me with a frosty stare and said, "Who the hell are you?" It was a question that didn't call for an answer—right then.

By the time a couple more meetings passed Kitty knew I was a quiet, serious sort of guy, who showed by his I-don't-give-a-damn looks that he was interested in her as more than a passing fancy. By this I mean she went out of her way to ignore me.

"Okay, runner-up to Miss America," I told myself, "your time will come."

And it did three weeks later. That was when Professor McBride came to class so excited he broke the chalk twice trying to scrawl the good news on the board.

What happened was he got this grant he had applied for. It was a pretty simple deal. He called it the "Vanishing Americana Project." He explained it to us like this: "Two-man teams will go out into the field and record those bits and pieces of American culture which will be lost when their eyewitnesses die."

The grant would pay field expenses—transportation, room, board —for one week. Each team would carry a tape recorder and camera. The whole thing was, in McBride's own words, "One hell of a chance for the beginning cultural anthropologist!"

And, thought I, one hell of a chance to get to *know* the runner-up to Miss America (in the Biblical sense).

PROCEDURE: The first order of business was splitting the class into teams. All the scholars had already paired off. The only two oddballs left were me and, you guessed it, Miss Kitty. The intellectuals avoided her like the plague.

"Well," said I, "are you game?"

"*Game* is not the proper word," she replied. "If you mean can we be partners, my answer is yes, if you don't forget I am a liberated woman who knows the score, one who is not about to take any shit off the likes of you."   .

"Me, I'm strickly business myself," I said, not without the hint of a worldly smile.

And that settled it. Kitty and I formed this partnership. We traveled in my car; she kept the records of our expenses and reminded me, by jamming herself against the door on her side, that as far as she was concerned, our deal was purely academic.

Our territory was a real nowhere, I mean like mudhole smalltowns where (honest-to-God) one ancient woman said she wanted nothing so much as a speedy end to the War and the execution of Kaiser Bill. In another place the flag they flew over the coffin-like post office had five stars fewer than fifty. Man, going down those steadily narrowing roads reminded me of H. Schliemann burrowing into the hill called Hisarlik in search of the remains of Troy. It was a time machine effect, one which took us back, back beyond the eras of which our parents spoke into the realms of American myth outlined by fireball history profs.

Not that it wasn't interesting—it was. Somebody's great-great aunt allowed us to record her secret method for making lye soap, which, she said, had been in her family ever since hands got dirtied. Another old-timer was at San Juan Hill. He had the rusty, nicked saber to prove it, with which he sprained hell out of his wrist demonstrating the proper way to decapitate a "spanyard."

For four or five days it went like that. We stopped here and there and picked up maybe a dozen bits of "Vanishing Americana," which to my mind couldn't vanish fast enough. Of course, cultural anthropology wasn't my main concern, not with Miss runner-up Blackburn at my side. I made several attempts on her person—nothing overtly physical, exactly—just high schoolish remarks like, "Press much harder against that door and you'll fall out," or "God, got a crick in my neck. How about giving a massage," or (last resort) "Yawn—gee I'm sleepy. Why don't you drive and I'll sort of lay down here on the seat and rest?"

In answer to the first move she tightened her seat belt; to the second she said, "Tough shit, Jack": and to the last—well—she ignored me completely.

And was I disappointed, was I upset, was I put down?

Damn right!

Especially when, as they say in the flicks, *the sun sank slowly in the west*. When night comes I'm like any normal human being—I think about going to bed. And that meant first finding a bed. Which was sometimes a problem, being so far from the interstate and all.

I mean we stayed in places that might've posted signs reading: "Dan'l Boone rassled a matress here—an' lost." Talk about *primitif*. I thought chamber pots were only used by lovely matrons to arrange flowers in.

Still, I didn't complain openly. I thought that if all this nostalgia bugged me, well it must be driving Kitty wild. Soon as she had enough she'd soften up, because, hell, I might not be much to her, but I was something from the civilized world.

As usual I let horniness screw up reason. Which is to say Kitty thrived on this diet of boondocks and, if anything, got colder.

Well, by the next to the last day of our search and record mission I was ready to cry "Uncle" or "Comrade" or fly the white flag. It was then that something of a cultural nature occurred which—. Wait, let me tell it like it was.

We stopped at this one-pump filling station and general store. While I was under the hood checking the oil, Kitty started talking to this rustic who was handling the gas. It was one of those old pumps, with a glass tank at the top. You worked a hand lever to fill the tank and then gravity moved it through the hose to the car. Well, she talked to him and when we were back on the road again, she said, "We're going to a place called Paradise Springs."

"Great," I said, "and where the hell is it?"

The fellow at the station had given her careful instructions. We turned left down a really narrow gravel road and must've gone twenty miles through some pretty rough country. As I tried to keep the bouncing car on the road as much as possible, Kitty said, "Mr. Snavery—he runs the filling station back there—said we should talk to Mr. Beau Chester. His people have lived in Paradise Springs longer than anyone. If there's anything worth knowing, Beau Chester will know it."

Well and good—all in the interest of anthropology, I thought. But as the country got wilder, the trees bigger, thicker, the shadows through which I drove got darker—as this happened the idea came to me that maybe it was a trick. Maybe this guy Snavery had set us up. Yeah, pretty soon a gang of rednecks would stop us, relieve me of my city shoes and cash, and then—the bastards!—force me to watch as they made—yummy—mincemeat out of Kitty. I stole a look at her tightly crossed legs. Smooth, tanned, skin you'd love to touch. Her gold anklet winked at me. Damn!

Cursing the fickleness of fate (I could've been a redneck!), I gripped the wheel tighter, squinted into the darkening shadows, and brought the car over an iron bridge. We passed under an arch of flowery vines. There *was* a town. The sun was bright. The buildings were one and two story. The streets were shady, quiet, but not deserted. Small shops were open for business.

The road into Paradise Springs led to a four-story gingerbread hotel, set in the midst of a smooth green lawn with spewing fountains and glassy reflecting ponds. Close by a church pointed its finger-like white spire above the maples.

Kitty said, "Drive past the church and take the second left. Beau Chester lives at the end of the street."

I drove by the church. On the porch of the house next door sat an elderly woman, who smiled and waved a pink handkerchief. Kitty waved back and I nodded.

Mr. Beau Chester's house was a setting for one of those girl-boy small-town flicks. I expected to see the young Mickey Rooney peeping through the white picket fence, waiting to put a spider on unsuspecting Ann Rutherford.

We parked under a sycamore tree and went through the swinging gate up the flagstone walk to the front porch which was equipped with several wicker rockers and a swing. On either side of the door were large brass lamps, so highly polished that the whole scene was visible in their curved sides.

Mr. Beau Chester was like the town. He was a small fellow, slender, neat, who wore sharply creased dark trousers and a crisp white shirt buttoned at the cuffs. I would've pegged him a typical duffer, conservative to his kidneys, except for his tie and his eyes. The tie was something else—six inches wide, a study of the most fantastic ways in which red, yellow, and green can be screwed up together. His eyes were—well—let me put it this way: when he looked at Kitty he didn't just *look*. Got it?

Anyhow, I stared at the tie and he said, "If this'uns too quiet I got plenty more upstairs."

We all smiled, even Kitty, who shot me a "screwoff!" look while her moist lips curved so sweetly. She told him what we were after—the Americana bit—and he said set down on the porch and let's talk, which we did.

We started in on the interview only it didn't go right. He interviewed us. Wanted to know where we were from, exactly what we did. I tried to go into detail on the Americana Project. But the old goat was interested in Kitty, not culture. He gave her a once-over I wish I could've recorded for posterity. And when I ended my spiel, he allowed it was "curious," and then gave almost-Miss America's leg a husky squeeze some four inches above the knee. When Kitty squirmed, he laughed and wanted to know if we "was hitched, or what?"

You better believe I laughed! Kitty scowled. I swear she moved her leg just enough so the old guy's fingers edged under the hem.

"Well now," he said, "if you two ain't hitched are you in love?"

"All the time," I answered.

Kitty smiled sweetly and said we didn't give love much thought because we were totally dedicated to the project.

Beau Chester gave her leg another little squeeze and replied what a shame that was. He hoped a handsome young fellow like me and a really sweet—I know he said "piece" but since the recorder wasn't on I can't prove it—like Kitty would get together. "Be a real waste if'n you don't," he said.

When she heard that, Kitty moved away and tugged at her hem. She became all business. "Mr. Chester, you've lived a long life. What can you tell the future about the past?"

As I flipped on the recorder he asked did she want him to begin at the beginning. Kitty nodded and gave him the mike. "Well," said he, looking over the porch rail into the distance, "I was born in this same house way back there in 1877. In them times Paradise Springs was a booming place, famous all over for its curative mineral waters. There was millionaires and kings and queens laid up at the hotel. Every once in a while a few wild Californians'd show up and shoot out a few windows. Yes sir, Paradise Springs was some town to grow up in."

He paused for breath and to squeeze Kitty's leg again. Then, "My father was a doctor. Had his office in the hotel. Directed the whole operation." He smiled. "Nowadays you'd call him a Red Cross swimming instructor, 'cause his only remedy was immersion, no matter what the ailment. Course, lots of the so-called sick were healthy as horses." He chuckled and winked at me. "They came for the he-and-she fun 'n games."

Hell, I winked back. If this was Americana don't let it vanish!

But practical Kitty wasn't enthusiastic. Whoops! There she went, out of fondle range again. She asked Mr. Chester to be specific, to speak only of his experiences.

Kitty's attitude set the old guy back a notch. He quietly said, "Guess you're in for a big letdown. My life's pretty average. Oh, I didn't run from adventure. Not much came my way. I joined the army in '18, but before we got finished training it was over."

His hand crept toward Kitty's leg again. What about your sex crimes, old-timer? I wondered to myself, visualizing on that porch woman after woman in disarray.

Kitty said, "But you must've had some memorable experience? Did any presidents visit Paradise Springs? Were there royal intrigues?" Now her eyes sparkled. "What about murders? With all that hanky-panky someone must've gone crazy from jealousy!"

"Hanky-panky?" Chester said, his voice revitalized. "There was plenty. Guess that's why there were no crimes of passion—too many easy outlets, if you know what I mean?"

Kitty did, perfectly. She stood, said, "Sorry we wasted so much of your *valuable* time. We have other people to interview. Goodby."

Mr. Chester ignored her extended hand and concentrated on her perky breasts. His face lit up like one of those cartoon light bulbs. "Now don't get excited," he said. "Come to think of it, I might have something after all."

He patted the swing seat beside him. Kitty sat down and he slipped his arm behind her. "Would your professor like to hear a first?"

"First? You mean like a discovery?"

"That's right. Nothing like Columbus, but it's still a record, I'll bet."

"You bet? Can't you be sure?"

"Well, no I can't, 'cause I never heard anyone else claim the distinction. That's not to say a lot of folks still don't damn the automobile. They do, yes sir!"

I said, "Let's get this straight. You discovered the automobile?"

"I never said that. I reckon I discovered a very popular use for it though." He grinned from ear to ear, and when Kitty tried to say something, he held up his hand and went on.

"The way it was, a lot of folks used to swear the decline of American morality was due to Henry Ford's devil-inspired invention. Why they'd say 'he turned the country's roadways into lovers' lanes when he took boys and girls out of the parlor and put 'em in those damned rolling beds!' "

Beds? I increased the volume level and gave the old guy an encouraging nod.

"Maybe they was right about the morality," he said, "but far as I'm concerned they was dead wrong about the start. Didn't begin with Henry Ford. No sir, it all began with Beau Chester, *me!*"

Kitty said, "You mean you manufactured cars here in Paradise Springs?"

He shook his head. "Me, I couldn't even change a spark plug. But you see autos came to Paradise Springs long before they appeared in other parts of the country. My father bought the first one, an 1893 Duryea. What a car! See them lamps by the door? They're all I managed to save. The Duryea brothers used to come here regular for the waters. It was a strange contraption, not much more than a buggy with an engine. Steered her with a tiller like a sailboat. Just about as easy to navigate. When you hit a bump—which was most of the time—tiller'd jump out of your hand. Driving that Duryea was some experience."

Kitty frowned. "Let me get this straight. Your *first* was driving the first car in Paradise Springs?"

"No ma'am, my daddy did that."

He rared back and laughed from deep down inside. "I was the first man to put the automobile to its good and proper use."

"Good and proper—?" said Kitty. Her face turned white, then a hot pink.

"That's right, honey. I'm the fellow who got the *first* piece of nookie in a motor car."

I wanted to give him a standing ovation! By God, this was *real* Americana! And to think it began with him! Of course, like Edison and the light bulb it would've happened without him. History was ready. But just like Edison, Beau Chester had done it. So he was unique. Our interview would make his name a household word.

But details were needed. While Kitty fumbled for her composure, I led him on. "We need facts. What happened?"

"Thought you'd never ask." He smiled. "It was a right pretty day, kind of like this one. Daddy's car was parked about where yours is." He sighed.

"And now I bet you're wondering who the lady was. For the sake of history I'll tell you. Her name was Jeannie DuPree. From Paris, France. Father managed the hotel. She was only fifteen but some beauty. Had flaming red hair down to her shoulders and a figure that looked good even in the godawful dresses of those days.

"I'd been sweet on Jeannie for some time. But she wasn't interested in me. She liked my daddy's Duryea though. So it wasn't too hard putting one and one together. On this particular day I was sitting here on this same swing when she came by and admired the car. So by golly I strutted out the gate, gave it a crank, swung up, told her to hop in. Let me tell you one thing: didn't have to ask her twice."

Mr. Chester gave Kitty's arm a little squeeze. She must've been sort of stunned by the old guy because she didn't try to pull away.

"In those days," he said, "roads were for farmers' wagons, not autos. It was a rough ride—bouncing, slipping, lurching, not to mention lots of plain jiggling. I think it was the jiggling that did it. Stirred the blood—hers and mine. By the time we cruised two miles to the logging road round the lake she was whispering French things in my ear."

Kitty's mouth was open. She watched him in wonderment, as though he might be a visitor from another planet.

"Well, we reached the lake and went on a bit till we came to a little clearing in the pines. The air coming off the blue water was cool, sweet-smelling. It was what you'd call romantic. I threw her in neutral and pulled the hand brake. Jeannie knew what I was thinking—she was thinking the same. We let down the Duryea's curtains, then pulled down our own. It was somewhat pinched on that narrow seat. But I always did like a challenge." He looked straight at me. "What about you?"

"Right on!" I said.

"That's exactly how it was—right on, and then some. Jeannie was very helpful, yes sir. We sort of let that two-stroke engine set our pace."

He winked at Kitty. "That's my *first*. Can you use it?"

"Can we ever!" I exclaimed. "Man, that's *real* Americana!"

"Don't forget it happened in 1893," he said. "In a Duryea; that's D-u-r-y-e-a."

"We've got every word on tape."

"Good, he said. "Wouldn't want any misunderstanding." He turned to Kitty. "Would you?"

But Kitty was for once remarkably silent. She nodded, and then Mr. Chester rose and walked us to our car. Every inch the gent, he opened the door for her—and gave her bottom a farewell pinch—while I stowed the recorder in the trunk. As I slipped in the driver's side, he was saying, "Your car's a fine piece of machinery. Upholstery's soft as a goosefeather bed. Don't make 'em the way they used to, thank the lord. But they haven't changed girls, thank the lord for that, too."

Kitty smiled—made a sort of Mona Lisa twist—and said, "Thank you for the interview. We'll send you a transcript."

He wasn't impressed. "I've got all the record I need. But I suspect you aren't convinced. So why don't you interview Jeannie?"

"She—she's still alive?" said Kitty.

"You bet. What we did's rarely fatal. She's still pretty as a picture."

"Where can we find her?"

"She married a Mr. Wilson when she turned seventeen. He's been dead thirty years at least. Jeannie lives with her grandson, the preacher at the church you passed coming in. Most days she sits on the manse porch watching the cars go by."

Now it was my turn to grin from ear to ear.

"Stop by," said Beau Chester. "She likes to talk over old times."

Kitty said, "You mean she'd tell us about *that*?"

"Well now, I suppose she would. It was a pretty historical event. Besides, even years and years ago it was tremendous fun, but then I guess you folks know all there is to know about that?"

We turned around and started off to see Jeannie.

We did—but—well—the runner-up to Miss America moved away from the door and suggested it might be more interesting if we investigated that place at the lake Mr. Chester mentioned. "We need to check his story completely," she said.

CONCLUSION: Report filed with Prof. McBride, coordinator, "Vanishing Americana Project."

COMMENTS: Mr. Chester's story did check out, *completely*.

II. THE TRANSFORMATION OF AMERICA

JOSEPH INTERRANTE

THE ROAD TO AUTOPIA:
THE AUTOMOBILE AND THE
SPATIAL TRANSFORMATION OF
AMERICAN CULTURE

In the 1920s, Robert and Helen Lynd, in their classic study *Middletown*, found that the automobile had become "an accepted essential of normal living." It had become the primary focal point of urban family life, and had made leisure activity a customary aspect of everyday experience. Indeed, the car had become so important to Middletown residents that many families expressed a willingness to go without food and shelter, to mortgage their homes and deplete their bank savings, rather than lose their cars. "We'd rather do without clothes than give up the car," a working-class mother of nine told the Lynds. "I'll go without food before I'll see us give up the car," another wife said emphatically. Other observers found that rural families were similarly attached to their cars. When a farm woman was asked by a U.S. Department of Agriculture inspector during the 1920s why her family had purchased an automobile before equipping their home with indoor plumbing, she replied, "Why, you can't go to town in a bathtub!" For these urban and rural Americans alike, the car had become a basic social necessity. This essay will examine the nature of that need in the context of changes in urban and rural space during the first half of the twentieth century.

More generally, this essay offers an alternative perspective for understanding the history of Americans' "love affair" with the car. Previous scholarship on the automobile has examined our consumption (purchase and use) of cars in terms of the car itself and the effects of its use. Authors may disagree over the relative importance of air pollution and traffic congestion versus privacy, freedom of movement and "democratic" access to consumer goods like the car, but all authors discuss the automobile strictly in those terms. This kind of cost-benefit analysis (which to a great extent ends up trying to compare apples and oranges) avoids the basic question, why people use cars. In examining the social and historical basis for our use of automobiles, scholars generally choose one of two explanations. Some writers talk about the "intrinsic appeal" of car use, its flexible and individual form of movement, as if this appeal were something which could exist outside of history. Such accounts focus on the car in isolation from a social context. Other writers explain the origins of automobile consumption in terms of corporate manipulation of consumer needs. At its most simplistic level, this argument echoes Vance Packard's "hidden persuaders" thesis—that automotive companies have abused the public trust through false advertising and government influence. More complicated versions attribute the success of corporate manipulation to people's social isolation and feelings of powerlessness. However, both versions assume that our need for cars is a "false" need created through the manipulation of consumer desire.

In contrast to these interpretations, this essay begins with the premise that our consumption of cars satisfies a real need for transportation—a need as basic as food, clothing and shelter—but argues that this need has changed as the social and spatial patterns of American culture have changed. In other words, it looks at the automobile as an historically specific form of transportation, one appropriate to a particular stage in capitalist development. It examines the automobile as simultaneously a cause and consequence of the rise of consumerism—that is, the corporate development of new markets designed to provide new goods and services to an enlarged buying public. When the automobile first appeared as a mass-produced commodity after Henry Ford's introduction of the Model T in 1908, people bought automobiles because they met old transportation needs better than existing alternatives and offered new possibilities for movement. But use of the car also altered urban and rural life in important ways, some of which I shall describe in the following pages. These changes were part of a general reorganization of the physical and social urban and rural environments which changed people's needs for transportation. This reorganization had already acquired a distinctive geographic form by 1933, when the Hoover Commission on *Recent Social Trends* christened it "metropolitanism":

> By reducing the scale of local distance, the motor vehicle extended the horizon of the community and introduced a territorial division of labor among local institutions and neighboring cities which is unique in the history of settlement. The large [urban] center has been able to extend the radius of its influence . . . Moreover, formerly independent towns and villages and also rural territory have become part of the enlarged city complex. This new type of supercommunity organized around a dominant focal point and comprising a multitude of differentiated centers of activity differs from the metropolitanism established by rail transportation in the complexity of its institutional division of labor and the mobility of its population. Its territorial scope is defined in terms of motor transportation and competition with other regions. Nor is this new type of metropolitan community confined to great cities. It has become the communal unit of local relations throughout the entire nation.

"Metropolitanism" became, in other words, the geographic configuration of a consumer society based upon car travel. Initially made possible by the automobility of the car, metropolitan consumerism in turn made the automobile a transportation necessity. This essay will explore the growth of metropolitanism in pre-World War II America. In the history of these developments can be found the origins of our dependence upon automobiles.

I

Between 1900 and 1940, changes in the structure of business enterprise and the strategy of industrial and market relations drastically transformed economic life in general and the urban economy in particular. Business firms extended their existing lines of goods to a greater number of customers at home, sought new markets and sources of materials overseas, and created new markets by developing new products for different kinds of customers. The expansion and diversification of markets occurred through the combination and consolidation of firms into single multidivisional corporations like E.I. DuPont, General Motors, and Sears, Roebuck and Company. These corporations were distinguished from older industrial firms by their integrated structures and coordinated functions. Decisions and information flowed through a hierarchy consisting of a general office, divisional offices, departmental headquarters, and field units. Changes in business structure, which were designed to plan effectively for long-term and short-term market exigencies and to insure an undisrupted flow of production for those markets, substantially altered, in turn, the quality of industrial work experience. A new class of professional and managerial workers was distributed among the various strata of the corporation to transmit instructions and information and to supervise directly the work process. The work process itself was broken down into numerous separate tasks, and synchronized through technological innovations like the automated assembly line as well as through the "scientific management" of individual and group worker behavior. As the work process intensified, the length of the work day was shortened and wage rates increased. The reorganization of factory work served the double purpose of rationalizing and increasing production, and of investing workers with the financial capacity and the opportunity to consume the goods which they produced. Together, these changes—what the Federal Trade Commission called in the early twentieth century the transition to a "maximum production economy"—radically transformed people's everyday experiences. They especially altered life in cities, where most industry had been located at the turn of the century.

Paradoxically, as multidivisional corporations integrated industrial and business relations, the spatial organization of manufacturing became decentralized. Corporations began to establish factories outside major urban centers in "industrial satellite cities" like Gary, Hammond, and East Chicago outside Chicago; Lackawanna outside Buffalo; East St. Louis and Alton across the Mississippi River from St. Louis; and Chester and Norristown near Philadelphia. Industrial growth in these satellite cities occurred at a faster rate than central city manufacturing: between 1899 and 1909, employment in the outlying districts around cities grew by 97.7 percent, while central city employment increased only 40.8 percent. Thus, while urban industrial employment continued to increase in absolute terms, the *proportion* of factory employment located within these cities declined. Between 1920 and 1930, it fell from 46 to 35 percent in New York City, and from 65 to 54 percent in Detroit. Indeed, every city with a population of at least 100,000 experienced this proportional decline in industrial employment. The decline was part of the increasing diversification of business functions, a diversification which manifested itself in specialized use of urban space. For as manufacturing declined in central cities, the proportion of communications, finance, management, clerical and professional services located there increased. Reflecting this specialization, downtown office space in the ten largest cities increased by 3,000 percent between 1920 and 1930. Tall skyscrapers mushroomed over the urban landscape: by 1929, there were 295 buildings 21 stories or taller in the five largest cities alone. These skyscrapers housed the general and divisional offices of the new corporations, as well as the banks, law offices, and advertising agencies which served them. They replaced and displaced factories, small retail businesses, apartments, and tenements. Thus cities became financial and administrative centers at the same time that they lost their older manufacturing functions.

Many residents displaced by the reorganization of economic activity and urban real estate within the city moved to outlying districts. This "suburban" boom, which began after World War I, peaked during the 1920s, and slowed but did not disappear during the 1930s, was based upon car travel. It was not simply an accelerated version of late nineteenth-and early twentieth-century streetcar movement into suburbs. Unrestricted by a need for access to mass transit facilities, real estate speculators located subdivisions everywhere around the central city. By 1922, 135,000 suburban homes in 60 cities were already wholly dependent upon cars for transportation. Most of these suburbanites were wealthy families, but during the 1920s and 1930s the movement out of the central city expanded to include the middle class (who located in exclusively residential suburbs) and the working class (who located closer to work in industrial suburbs). These outlying districts together grew during the 1920s at a rate twice as fast as the cities around which they were located. Even though the rate of increase slowed during the depression years, it remained impressive when contrasted with the absolute decline of population in central cities during the same period. By 1940, 13 million people lived in communities beyond the reach of public transportation.

Moreover, the socio-economic relationship between suburbs and the central city changed. As downtown shopping districts were transformed into central government and corporate headquarters, small retail services—which could not afford skyrocketing rents and were losing customers unwilling to face downtown traffic snarls—relocated in the suburbs near their customers. (One Atlanta drugstore owner, forced out of business in 1926, lamented, "The place where trade is, is where automobiles go . . . A central location is no longer a good one for my sort of business.") Likewise, large department stores set up branch stores in these satellite communities. Mail-order firms like Sears, Roebuck and Montgomery Ward turned into suburban chains. Banks also established branches in suburbs. Dentists and doctors opened offices near their clients' (and their own) homes. In short, many formerly centralized institutions and services were relocated outside cities. These outlying districts became the retail business centers of urban space—especially in smaller cities which had never developed extensive trolley networks. Indeed, the Hoover Commission noted in 1933 that the old "star" pattern of nineteenth century urban development (a star whose rays ran along streetcar tracks) had been transformed into a veritable "constellation" of interdependent centers within a single metropolitan region. And the National Resources Committee declared in 1937 that the whole east coast from New York to Philadelphia had become a single "conurbanized" band of metropolitan settlement.

The dispersion of manufacturing and residential settlement was based upon car travel. The importance of the automobile varied, it is true, with the size of the city and the availability of public transportation. But even in cities with elaborate mass transit systems, like Boston, Chicago, Philadelphia, and New York, observers in the 1920s and 1930s noted that car travel was necessary for much of the business and recreation which took place in and around them. Moreover, the car's importance increased as streetcar service declined through mismanagement, overextension of services, and competition from jitneys and buses. Indeed, planners in these cities were deliberately reshaping the central city landscape by the late 1920s and 1930s in order to facilitate commutation by car. In these large cities, cars accounted for 20 to 32 percent of the daily traffic into the central business district (CBD) by 1930. Cars became more important earlier in smaller cities like Kansas City, Milwaukee, and Washington, D.C. There car travel during the 1920s accounted for 50 to 66 percent of the daily commutation into the CBD. By 1930, 222 cities with at least 10,000 residents were entirely dependent on motor transportation.

Urban space was enlarged through automobile use. The further one lived from the city, the more advantageous car travel became. A 1930 traffic control study of Kansas City illustrated the savings in time during the evening "rush hour." In the downtown area, trolleys and cars moved bumper to bumper. But outside the CBD, the car rapidly moved ahead of streetcars. Two miles from the CBD it had gained a five-minute advantage; at 7½ miles, it had gained 15 minutes. Along secondary trolley lines, on which service was less frequent, cars traversed the 7½ miles with a 35 minute advantage over streetcars. The same advantages were documented in Detroit in 1930. In addition to this daily flow of traffic into the city, automobiles made possible crosscurrents of movement throughout the outlying district—something streetcars could not do. In Los Angeles, this movement superseded commutation into the downtown area. The number of people entering downtown Los Angeles between 1923 and 1931 declined by 24 percent despite a population boom in the metropolitan area. But the most important point was that the reorganization of urban space made these crosscurrents of movement not only more possible but more necessary as well. Goods which families had purchased in old downtown shopping districts now had to be purchased at stores scattered throughout the suburbs. Many employees had to drive to decentralized workplaces, or from decentralized residences to the CBD. If the automobile first appeared as a convenience which permitted more frequent, faster, and more flexible transportation movement, metropolitanism gradually made that movement an inescapable feature of urban living.

II

As metropolitanism reoriented urban areas, it also reorganized rural space. But while the distinguishing characteristic of urban metropolitanism was decentralization, the principle transformation of rural space was a centralization of institutions and activity. Moreover, rural society was affected earlier and more deeply than urban society, in part because farmers bought Tin Lizzies sooner and in greater numbers than urban residents during the prewar period. In 1910, 0.17 percent of farm families owned 0.50 percent of the 450,000 registered motor vehicles in the United States; by 1930, 53.1 percent of the rural population owned 50.3 percent of the nation's 23 million cars. The reorganization of rural space which widespread car ownership facilitated changed farmers' needs for transportation. Within the specific context of those changes, the automobile was transformed from a rural convenience into a rural necessity.

From the 1890s through the farm depression of the 1920s and 1930s, the growth of large-scale agriculture, the use of tractors for field work, and the collapse of many mid-sized farms brought about a new rural economy. The recomposition of agricultural capital was reflected in the loss of 72,854 farms between 1910 and 1930. Simultaneously, the number of farms smaller than 100 acres and larger than 500 acres increased. The shift in size represented the increasing specialization of agricultural production. Grain producers moved further west on the Great Plains; citrus growing on the Pacific and Gulf coasts increased by one-third; dairy farming also increased by one-third; and the number of truck farms, located around and supplying produce to urban areas, doubled. Along with these changes in agricultural work, the farm population declined numerically and became more stratified. Farm tenancy grew. The proportion of farms operated by tenants had remained at about 38 percent between 1910 and 1925, but it rose dramatically by 1930 to 42.4 percent of all farms. And a growing number of tenant farmers were actually share-croppers who possessed little capital and rented their machinery and, in some cases, livestock. Finally, during the 1920s farm labor changed from an all-male occupation organized around the social milieu of rail-riding and hobo camps to one comprised of poor families who used automobiles for travel.

At the same time, the spatial organization of society changed. Many families who lost their farms and did not sink into tenancy or migrant labor moved, not to cities, but to rural villages and towns. Between 1920 and 1930, these towns gained 3.6 million people while the farm population decreased by 1.2 million. Furthermore, farm villages changed in socio-economic operation. Small crossroads centers lost their general trade and service functions to neighboring towns; some disappeared, while others became specialized agricultural supply depots. Small towns located on highways developed facilities catering to tourist traffic. Many formerly localized institutions and services—education, health care, postal service, general stores— and other formerly urban institutions—libraries, chain stores, gas stations—were relocated in and around the larger rural villages. These larger villages became the centers of rural space.

Rural space was not so much enlarged with automobile use as it was reshaped into a centralized and hierarchical form. Studies of automobile travel support this conclusion. Although rural people could travel greater distances with cars, most trips occurred within a previously demarcated local area. Studies of rural villages in 28 states in 1924-1930 found that the socio-economic hinterland of two-thirds of them did not expand by as much as two square miles. And studies of car travel in five states between 1926 and 1928 found that one-third to one-half of all automobile trips measured under 20 miles. This was the approximate distance of a horse and wagon, but cars took less time to traverse it. Automobile use encouraged not longer trips, but more frequent ones. Families that traveled to a nearby village only one or two times per year before the car, traveled every three or four weeks with one. They traveled during the week and in the evening as well as on Saturday. And they traveled throughout the area to several different towns, instead of merely to the village located nearest to them. Meanwhile, they were going less frequently to crossroads centers, which were themselves disappearing or losing their retail business functions.

As in the urban case, the most important point was that the reorganization of rural space gradually made this movement both more possible and more necessary. Goods which the family had purchased at a crossroads store or by mail order now had to be purchased in town. (Mail-order houses, it may be recalled, were turning into department chains.) This centralization of services in rural areas was part of metropolitan organization. Metropolitanism changed the structure of rural society so fundamentally that by the Depression a family without a car faced special difficulties in satisfying its transportation needs: it took longer to reach relocated services in village centers by horse and wagon; and barns, liveries, harness shops, and blacksmiths had dwindled as their owners converted them into auto dealerships, garages, gas stations, and parking lots. As a result of these and similar changes, the car became a rural necessity.

III

The geographic reorganization of urban and rural areas drew these regions into closer and more interdependent relationship with each other. This relationship was most evident in the cities and towns which lay in the outlying districts around urban centers. These towns attracted people from both central cities and the surrounding countryside. For example, a 1931 survey of 4,000 families that moved to Evanston, Illinois during the 1920s found that 47 percent came from Chicago, while 46 percent had moved to Evanston from rural areas outside the immediate metropolitan region. Indeed, small towns like Chana, Illinois, were beginning to advertise themselves "as a wonderful home for someone who wants to live in a small town away from high taxes and still have the conveniences of the city." In addition, farm families that converted to truck farming were tied more closely into the urban market and urban culture. Many families held onto their farms during the Depression by taking advantage of the work opportunities in cities and satellite towns. A study of farm families living near Seattle, Washington, discovered that 25 percent of the members of those families worked in nonfarm occupations: men worked as carpenters, machinists, shipyard workers, railroad and highway laborers, salesmen and deliverymen; women worked as domestic servants, clerical workers, teachers, telephone operators, and nurses. All of these activities necessitated new patterns of commutation based upon use of a car.

This change in people's habits of movement was a change in daily routine. Many of the goods and services—food, clothing, education, health care, entertainment—which people bought in village centers or suburban retail centers had formerly been produced or performed by members of these families, especially by women. This shift from the direct production of goods to the purchase of them in metropolitan markets changed people's habits of consumption. These new habits were a central aspect of life in metropolitan America.

In the 1920s, metropolitanism began to change household activity and consumption habits by drawing women out of the household and into the marketplace. Robert and Helen Lynd observed in their study of *Middletown* (1929): "The great bulk of the things consumed by American families is no longer made in the home and the efforts of family members are focused instead on buying a living." Middletown families bought more canned and prepared goods as well as fresh fruit and vegetables, more premade sweets, more women's dresses and hosiery, more cleaning and beauty products, more "personal accessories," and new household appliances like radios and washing machines. Families also spent more money and time on recreation outside the home. Both urban and rural families consumed these goods and services. A 1930 study of bread consumption, for example, found that most families everywhere had shifted to store-bought goods: 66 percent of farm households, 75 percent of village homes, and 90 percent of urban households. These figures meant that most housewives were now traveling by car to a local baker or A&P to buy what they used to make in their own homes.

Use of the car did not lessen women's household work; rather it helped to change it into many consumer duties. Six studies of the uses of time by farm women during the 1920s concluded that increased conveniences did not decrease their workday: instead of making free time for reading or recreation, they generated more work, such as more laundry, more housekeeping, and—although the studies did not list this—more frequent car trips to town to purchase household goods. Similarly, a study of housework in residential suburbs in 1925 found that women who moved from city apartment houses with centralized heating, elevator, laundry, incinerator, and janitor service now had to take care of these things in a single-or two-family home with independent furnaces, stairways, and washing machines, as well as lawns outside which required constant care. For these women, the study concluded, "the residential suburbs represent the decentralization of consumption." And for rural and urban women alike, changes in consumption represented the other side of the geographic reorganization of the metropolitan landscape.

If the automobile did not lessen women's work, why did women and their families accept these changes so readily? The automobile originally offered new possibilities for movement. It especially liberated women from the home. The automobile was a *private* vehicle, and that characteristic made it safer and more acceptable than public streetcars or trains. Even the most genteel women began traveling alone; some wealthier women took cross-country trips together unescorted by male relatives. This "freedom," as many women described the experience of driving, was the positive side to the transformation of women's lives. An Ohio farm woman's day was described this way in 1919:

> Half a dozen years ago when only a few had cars, a farmer bought a Ford, and his wife soon learned to run it. One morning she hurried through the morning's work, had the car brought to the house before the men went to work, and after the partly cooked dinner was stowed away in a box of hay in the cellar to finish cooking itself she got into the car at a little before 10 and drove 41 miles to her daughter's home; getting there just as the family were sitting down to lunch. The route led through Cleveland, and in mid-afternoon she took her daughter and child and they did some shopping at a great department store, where she could buy better and cheaper than at home. The daughter went home on a suburban car, and the mother reached home in time to put a late supper on the table.

In the days before the automobile, this woman would have been taken to the nearby railroad station, a distance of 3½ miles, and back the same evening, which would have consumed at least 5 hours time in hitching up and driving. In Cleveland she would have had to transfer from the railroad to a suburban trolley. Automobile travel saved her time, as well as the time of the husband or son who would have driven her to the railroad depot. But, more significantly, the time "saved" would not have been "spent" in this way before the automobile. As the metropolitan market expanded to include commodities formerly produced at home, the necessity for finding them in village and town centers increased. When the farm woman told the USDA inspector that she couldn't go to town in a bathtub, she was describing the changes in her life which made shopping in town part of her work. And when Middletown women told the Lynds that they would sacrifice food and clothing before they gave up the family car, they knew that giving up the car meant sacrifices in family consumption.

IV

What began as a vehicle to freedom soon became a necessity. Car movement became the basic form of travel in metropolitan consumer society. However, there was nothing inevitable about metropolitan spatial organization or people's uses of cars upon that landscape. The car could have remained a convenience used for recreation and cross-movement outside areas serviced by railroads and trolleys, while people continued to use mass transit for daily commutation. Car travel could have remained an option offering certain distinct advantages; instead it became a prerequisite to survival. Moreover, this dependence upon automobiles was not the outcome of a corporate manipulation of consumer needs. Rather, it resulted from the *reconstitution* of transportation needs within the spatial context of metropolitan society—a reorganization of the physical and social environment which the car facilitated but did not require. Within this spatial context, automobile movement became the basic form of travel.

The Depression did not loosen the relationship between Americans and their cars. "If the word 'auto' was writ large across Middletown's life in 1925," the Lynds wrote in *Middletown In Transition* (1937), "this was even more apparent in 1935, despite six years of Depression." People clung so tenaciously to their cars, the Lynds observed, because car transportation had become a "must" close in importance to food, clothing, and shelter. Hence, "car ownership in Middletown was one of the most Depression-proof elements of the city's life in the years following 1929—far less vulnerable, apparently, than marriages, divorces, new babies, clothing, jewelry, and most other measurable things both large and small." Automotive statistics reflected this dependence on car travel. Although annual car sales declined 75 percent, from 4.5 to 1.1 million, between 1929 and 1932, car registrations decreased only 10 percent, from 23 to 20.7 million, during the same period. People stopped buying new cars, but they gave up car ownership entirely only under the gravest economic circumstances. Moreover, both sales and ownership began to rise sharply after 1933, while the country was still in the depths of the Depression. Annual automobile sales increased to 3.7 million by 1940, and car registrations rose to a new high figure of 29.6 million in 1941. This rapid growth beyond the levels of 1920s consumption reflected people's social needs for car transportation.

Yet if automobile ownership and use had become a basic need by the 1930s, the Lynds also found that people experienced that need and valued car ownership in very different ways. The working class saw the automobile as "their great symbol of advancement . . . Car ownership stands to them for a large share of the 'American dream'; they cling to it as they cling to self-respect." The business class, in contrast, viewed the car as a luxury item which "it is more appropriate for well-to-do people to have . . . than for poor people." Indeed, the business class "regard it as a scandal that some people on relief still manage to operate their cars." These different attitudes reflected a structural dynamic in modern capitalist society. For if the mass production of goods had *democratized* consumption by enlarging the potential market for goods like cars and making ownership contingent solely on the ability to pay, it did not *equalize* consumption. A range of social and economic considerations—for example, the proportion of family income which could be spent on a car—shaped people's identities as consumers and their uses of cars. In other words, inequality continued to affect the ability to consume even though the opportunity to consume became more widespread. The Hoover Commission in 1933 pointed to this inequality and even a growing rigidity in the American social structure. "The increasing fluidity of the metropolitan community seems to tend toward a local leveling of culture," it wrote, "but at the same time it seems to encourage a system of social stratification."

As both the Hoover Commission and the Lynds noted, these variations in consumption were social rather than individual differences. Take, for example, the experience of suburban residence.

Although movement to outlying districts involved both middle-class and working-class urban residents, as well as some rural inhabitants, suburbanization was a differentiated movement. Working-class suburbs and rural villages remained centers of work as well as residence, while middle-class suburbs were strictly residential areas. Indeed, this difference was protected through the use of housing covenants and zoning restrictions on land use, as well as through less formal factors such as the need for workers to remain within commuting distance of their scattered workplaces. In concrete terms, the difference was manifested in the kinds and quality of institutions located within the particular suburb: the presence or absence of noisy and sooty factories, the proportion of single- versus multi-family dwellings, the location of a highway next to or even through a working-class community, and even the kinds of schools available for children. These institutions shaped the experience of everyday life in suburbs: the relation between work and leisure, the character of domestic life and the kinds of household goods purchased by a family, the senses of privacy and autonomy one felt in one's life, and the opportunities for and definition of personal achievement. In short, the degree to which suburban and village residents were able to exert over their social environments infused these residents' attitudes toward their cars. It was the promise of such autonomy which lay behind the Middletown working-class association between car ownership and the "American dream." It also lay behind the Middletown business class's concern that widespread car ownership threatened their privileged status within the community.

The experience of suburbanites and village residents differed from that of farm families. Suburbanites used cars for work and consumption. For farmers, the car was more strictly a means of consumption. Car use encouraged a new and unique separation between field work and "domestic" family life. Before the car, farm families had to allocate carefully their use of horses; a two to twelve hour trip into town would exhaust the animal which had to be used for field work the following day. The automobile made such allocation unnecessary by providing a separate vehicle for trips into town, and thus relegated the horse to the field (where it was eventually replaced by the gasoline tractor). Cars thus increased farm families' opportunities for leisure. Yet it was this very separation between farm work and family/recreational activity which distinguished farmers from suburbanites who used their cars to commute to work. And this distinction was grounded in a different relation between work and leisure:

farmers lived on their farms/workplaces, while suburbanites travelled from their homes to their offices and factories. These differences affected the experience of automobile use: the distance to be travelled, the purposes behind travel, and the experience of the trip itself.

Of course, the significance of this separation varied for farm owners, tenants and sharecroppers. The difference was not necessarily one of car ownership itself. As many tenants as farmers owned cars: for example, 89 percent of the tenants and 93 percent of the farmers in Iowa in 1926 had automobiles. More important than ownership per se was their use of the car. Economic status affected these different households' consumption of ready-made goods, their use of recreational facilities like movie houses, and their participation in social activities like the Grange, women's clubs, and state fairs. Family activities outside the farm were also affected by the size of the village center and the kinds of services which it offered to the surrounding community. These factors affected farm households' reliance upon and uses of cars, and thus the degree to which they viewed it as another farm machine or as a pleasure vehicle.

Despite these variations, farm owners and tenants all used the automobile to commute from their farms to town. This relation distinguished them from the migrant labor family. A migrant family's car was not only a means of consumption, it was also the necessary basis for the migrant household's survival as a unit. As migrant labor reorganized around automobile movement, it became necessary to use a car to find work and reach that work as a family unit. The automobile thus dominated the lives of migrant families in a unique and deliberate way. As John Steinbeck wrote in *The Grapes of Wrath* (1939), "the highway became their home and movement their form of expression." Reflecting that relationship, Steinbeck had the Joads always feed the car before they fed themselves.

In both urban and rural areas, then, automobile use was shaped by social and economic considerations which lay behind class status: control over income level, workplace location, work hours, job tenure, choice of residence, consumption of household goods, and participation in leisure activities. (And it should be noted, although there is not room here to examine the differences, that these considerations were also affected by race, sex, and age.) These differences characterized people's different needs for transportation within metropolitan society. They remained in the forefront of automobile use because the automobile was a private vehicle which people fit into the fabric of their day to day lives. Thus, if the automobile promoted the reorganization of American space, it did not homogenize the experience of automobile ownership and use within that space.

V

As we begin to reconsider our relationship to automobiles, it is important that our development of public policy be informed by an awareness of how social inequality has shaped our needs for and uses of automobile transportation. Contemporary scholarship on the automobile focuses exclusively and abstractly on "the car." There is a dangerous tendency in this scholarship to believe that the problems "caused by" the automobile will disappear with the automobile. The tendency is not "wrong" in any technical sense—who would deny the car's destructive impact on landscape and ecology? But it nonetheless constricts our attention to a few issues which, although they may be momentarily palliated, will not resolve the larger issue of social inequality which shapes our uses of all forms of transportation. Solutions guided by a tendency which ignores the fact of inequality will inevitably place the greatest burdens of adjustment on those least able to carry them. In considering solutions to the current automobile and gasoline crisis, our goal should be not only an environment freed from dependence upon cars—itself a revolutionary undertaking—but also a society which is more just and more humane for all of us.

WARREN BELASCO

COMMERCIALIZED NOSTALGIA:
THE ORIGINS OF THE ROADSIDE STRIP

Before World War II, car use was primarily recreational—whether for a short drive to visit a friend, to see a movie, to buy an ice cream cone, or, as is the subject here, for a longer vacation to a country park, to another state, or even to another region. In the history of the American love affair with the automobile, the initial flirtation came with that first independent journey through unfamiliar territory. As in any romance, infatuation followed the discovery of differences, of contrasts, of new perspectives. Even after the erotic excitement settled into a more prosaic marriage of convenience, the aphrodisiac of early touring guaranteed a lasting emotional attachment to automobility whose consequences distress us today.

In addition to assuring our now troublesome entanglement, motor travel spawned many new business enterprises along the roadside. In designing their sales strategies, highway entrepreneurs paid close attention to tourist fantasies and needs. As such behavior and expectations changed over the years, the roadside adapted accordingly. Autocamping, an inexpensive, individualistic sport with rebellious, antiestablishment implications, evolved into the motel, a nationally standardized roadside institution. The evolving motel thus reflected the domestication of the touring romance itself. What started out before World War I as an adolescent infatuation, a passionate celebration of fresh experiences and unprecedented intimacies, developed by 1940 into a tamer, more restricted concern for comfort, efficiency, security, and privacy.

More than a register of changing motorist interests, the roadside hotel of 1940 also reflected the emergence of a leisure-based economy. Indeed, this essay might be appropriately subtitled "The Rise of an Entertainment Industry," for the job of highway entrepreneurs was to cater to an audience who viewed the road as a combined theater and amusement park. The history of this recreation-oriented industry can be divided into four main stages: (1) a liberationist peri-

Pioneer motorist for AAA, Colorado, 1912. (*Courtesy National Archives.*)

od of vagabonding; (2) a period of expanding participation and small-scale commercialization; (3) a search for middle-class respectability and stability in the late 1920s and early 1930s; and (4) the growth of tourist camps in the late 1930s, and a final period of mass production and nationwide distribution by large corporations.

1. GYPSYING, 1900–1920

The commercial roadside originated in an entirely uncommercial, spontaneous activity called autocamping. Several hundred thousand middle-class families toured the countryside, camping each night in a different spot along the road, sleeping in cars or in tents, cooking their meals over smoky campfires or even over their car radiators. Some towns allowed summer tourists to camp in their vacant school yards; farmers might grant permission to camp in a pasture; or campers simply pulled off onto the narrow shoulder between someone's fence and the road. Many campers never did seek permission, for the emphasis in motor camping was on complete self-reliance and independence. "You are your own master," one enthusiast explained, "the road is ahead; you eat as you please; sleeping when you will under the stars, waking with the dawn; swim in a mountain lake when you will, and always the road ahead. Thoreau at 29 cents a gallon." These early nomads initiated roadside self-service, for many simply helped themselves to land, water, scenery, and, all too often, a farmer's corn, apples, and milk.

Autocampers called this squatter-anarchist stage "gypsying," "vagabonding," or "motor hoboing." The name richly suggested the sense of unconventionality, adventure, and excitement that early motorists expressed in their diaries and travel magazines. As legendary nonconformists, gypsies, and hobos had long stood for that part of the human spirit which refused to be tied down. Similarly, motor gypsying seemed to liberate human will. Tourists could go almost anywhere they wanted, when they wanted. By carrying camping equipment, they maximized their spontaneity and mobility. Autocamping was to 1910 what backpacking is to the 1980s: a chance to leave the crowd.

The historical context of motor gypsying is very important. Motor camping was part of a wider turn-of-the-century revolt against late Victorian institutions. Seeking alternatives to tiresome gentility, many middle-class Americans went primitive. Following Rough Rider Theodore Roosevelt's call for a revival of the "strenuous life," they supported the establishment of national parks, idolized cowboy heroes and football players, pushed a more aggressive foreign policy, and began to move to surburban homesteads. In search of vitality, they discovered the coarse energy of the ethnic theater and working-class moving picture, and they immersed themselves in the seemingly primal rhythms of African-American blues, ragtime, and jazz. In retrospect, we know that this new emphasis on nature and physical pleasure served the needs of a new stage of American economic growth, the consumption-based economy. In addition to stimulating a wide variety of new industries—suburban housing, sporting goods, Hollywood, and, of course, automobiles—the new primitivism also fostered a hedonistic focus on immediate experience and gratification that contrasted sharply with the older Victorian production ethic of thrift, sobriety, and postponed satisfaction.

At the time, however, people did not see this change as modernistic. Rather, they conceived their desire for mobility and simple fulfillment in strictly nostalgic terms—a return to the more humane pace and associations of earlier times and places. The new primitivism was an offshoot of the nineteenth-century romantic reaction against industrial capitalism. Almost from the beginning of the Industrial Revolution, artists, novelists, and social critics had decried the costs of economic progress: a loss of individuality, spontaneity, local color, community, roots, family cohesiveness, contact with nature, spirituality, and warmth. In western Europe, where these effects were first felt, the reassessment produced the strongest political reactions: in attacking dehumanizing technology, alienating work conditions, and bourgeois greed, both socialists and conservatives invoked visions of preindustrial communal traditions. In America, where industrial growth lagged, the nostalgia wave did not really hit hard until the end of the nineteenth century. When these harsh realities hit home, the reaction did not produce powerful, European-style collectivist movements. American political resilience deserves much of the credit, but another reason was that, just when many Americans were beginning to feel boxed in by modern conditions, ingenious businessmen were devising new channels for escape. Thus, among the ironies surrounding the car culture, perhaps the strangest is this: early on, the automobile industry became the backbone of modern industrial capitalism, yet it was born in a spirit of rebellion against that system.

The nostalgic impulse was particularly clear in motor gypsying. Gypsies seemed to live more slowly, more directly; they were not driven by a compulsive work ethic. Living in small wagons and easily dismantled camps, they were not tied down by the responsibilities or distracting materialism of modern bourgeois life. Just the name conjured up tribal values, traditional dress, and patriarchal authority. The aura of a tight family unit was particularly appealing to urban middle-class people afraid of losing family functions to modern institutions. The "decline of the family" was a common theme in the popular literature of the early twentieth century (as it is today). On the road, however, the touring family spent a good deal of time together. Six or eight hours a day might be spent in the car, a cramped space, with no individual privacy. Life in a small, flimsy tent put a premium on harmony and selflessness. Setting up camp, preparing and eating three meals, the evening campfire—these were all done together. As strangers in unfamiliar territory, the family had to draw together for security, subsistence, and companionship. Novelty and hardship made the trip intense and unique. Preparing for the trip, as well as reliving it afterward, joined family members in common cause and experience. Here, then, was the new companionate family ideal: the family that played together stayed together. We know now that this ideal well-suited the new, recreation-based society. Indeed, it is virtually impossible for any mass leisure industry— whether television or McDonald's—to succeed without catering to the companionate family. Yet, in early touring, the roadside autocamp—like the suburban home—seemed more like a revival of the family solidarity of the pioneer homestead.

Motorists strengthened their sense of return by contrasting the car and camp with the principal alternatives: the train and the hotel. The train, not the car, represented Modern Times: ruthlessly efficient, fast-paced, impersonal, insulated, indifferent to personal schedules and needs. Motoring, on the other hand, seemed more like stage-coach travel: slow, arduous, close to nature, more "intimate." In entering cities, trains generally passed through factory and slum districts—ugly reminders of the industrial present. Motorists, however, could enter by imposing avenues, the Main streets, through the best part of town; or they could avoid big cities altogether and stick to pastoral countryside and picturesque hamlets. Instead of being rushed along by printed schedules and clock-toting conductors, motorists could stop and start whenever they wanted, or when natural obstacles intervened—for motoring brought them very close to the landscape in the form of rough roads, impassable streams, and washed-out bridges. While train passengers sat helplessly if the train was delayed, motorists aided each other along bad roads and at con-

Colorado campsite, 1923

fusing intersections. In addition to fostering a strong sense of camaraderie among fellow travelers, the bumpy, drafty, dusty ordeal of early
motoring seemed to revive the strenuous life being threatened by
modern ways. Railroad travel was too passive, too monotonous, too
soft. Given the overall dissatisfaction with rail transportation, it was
no coincidence that Frank Norris's damning portrait of the rail-
capitalist complex was titled *The Octopus* (1901) and that the first western film was called "The Great Train Robbery" (1903).

Campers also avoided hotels, which seemed bureaucratic, overly
formal, and ill-suited for families. Instead of dressing to dine in pretentious hotel restaurants, autocampers wore khakis, sprawled on the
ground, ate out of cans, and ignored all the dictates of genteel eti-
quette. Like cowboys, they preferred fast, informal dining, in a picturesque setting, with a pronounced preference for fried food that
could be eaten without utensils. In the earliest gypsy picnics we can
find the roots of the roadside food formula that still guides franchisers
today.

In all, autocamping served a widely felt need to break with conventional manners, to restore a lost individuality, to discover new perspectives, to experience new intimacies with family members and
motoring strangers, and to resist the hectic work routines and monop-
olistic institutions of an urban-industrial civilization. To cap their case
against modernity, autocampers argued that their way was cheaper.
Notions of old-fashioned utility and thrift were thus used to smooth
acceptance of an entirely new form of leisure activity.

2. MUNICIPAL CAMPS 1915–23

This anti-institutional stage of random squatting lasted only a few
years. In a democratic society of romantic individualists, nonconform-
ism could not be confined for long to a small elite. Moreover, an
economy increasingly reliant on the sale of consumer goods needed
an expanding consumer base. Actually, the process of expansion and
elaboration began with the very first magazine articles and books
praising motor camping—around 1910. Early enthusiasts wrote with
missionary zeal. Flaunting eccentricity, they sought popularity, and
by 1920 they achieved it. With over eight million cars registered,
several million Americans took to the road and roadside. With numbers inevitably came environmental problems and commercial exploitation.

Autocampers were very careless. Autocamping was in fact a moral

Presidential autocamping trip, 1921

holiday, a brief respite from everyday morality and institutions. Its libertarian appeal translated into littered roadsides and a full-scale appropriation of crops, flowers, shrubs, and other property. Only a few orthodox wilderness types carefully left their sites as they found them. Moreover, few campers took necessary sanitary precautions. By the early 1920s, state health officials began to warn tourists about drinking unsafe roadside water. Meanwhile, police began to chase blatant litterers, and farmers posted no-trespassing signs.

At the same time, the growing numbers began to attract the attention of downtown merchants who wanted to cash in on this new tourist trade. Through their civic organizations and city governments, they pushed to establish free campsites in municipal parks. Since they assumed that these tourists would be prosperous middle-class consumers, they hoped that a small investment in camp facilities would produce good business for local stores. City managers were responsive to such proposals in part because they shared the same economic interests; in part because they hoped to regulate dangerous roadside camping; and in part because they hoped to establish a good reputation for their towns through the tourist grapevine. Travel observers noted early that the road was a medium of long-distance communication which could be exploited for advertising purposes. Tourists tended to exchange information about roads and sights when they met at filling stations, stands, and bottlenecks. News of a nice public camp would spread rapidly through the word-of-mouth road network and would certify that a sponsoring town was a good place to visit. Public parks were politically popular in the 1920s. To have a city park like Denver's or a campground like Yellowstone's was to be truly up-to-date. The smallest towns were especially anxious to cultivate such images, since literary and journalistic treatment of village life tended to be quite negative at this time. (For instance, Sinclair Lewis's view of a bigoted backwater in *Main Street*.) Booster opportunism thus combined with village defensiveness to produce over five thousand municipal camps by the mid-1920s, most of them free.

While some pioneer autocampers bemoaned the institutionalization, the free camps attracted many others who had been unwilling to try the more adventurous gypsying. Roadside camping was too difficult for many, especially for women, whose participation was essential in a family-oriented activity. The free camps offered graded sites, safe water, privies, and often a fire circle. Also, the free camps led to a basic change in driving habits. Earlier motorists had welcomed the leisurely pace of motoring, which was much slower than the train due to poor road conditions. They rationalized this as an antidote to hectic city life. Within a few years, however, as roads improved and as motorists came to take driving more for granted, many drivers experienced a definite urge to "make miles" rather than to laze along like gypsies. By staying at established campsites listed in motor guidebooks, they could spend more time covering ground, for they did not have to spend valuable time looking for a level roadside site with safe water. As farmers began to guard their property, finding a good camping site along the road became still more time consuming.

Many autocampers, then, welcomed the convenience and efficiency of the free camp, and comparing camps became an integral part of the touring routine. Concerned about keeping a good local reputation, each town tried to outdo the next with additional facilities such as electric lights, showers, and central kitchens. These improvements further maximized time on the road and attracted still more motorists to autocamping. Thanks in part to these new campgrounds, and in part to the widely publicized motor camping trips of Henry Ford, Thomas Edison, and President Warren G. Harding, autocamping became something of a national fad, with perhaps as many as ten million people trying it at least once by the mid-1920s.

Despite the loss of independence, enthusiasts continued to use nostalgic terms to describe this new stage. In particular, they welcomed the opportunity to meet all kinds of people at these public campgrounds. Huddling around campfires or waiting in line to use showers, strangers casually chatted about road conditions, equipment, or personal affairs. The novelty of the sport, the common vulnerability to rain and bad roads, the leveling informality of khaki dress—all fostered a refreshing democratic ambience. At a time of acute rural-urban tensions, nativism, and labor-management conflict, the autocamp seemed an ideal agent of national integration. Through shared contact with the timeless values of nature, Americans from different states and backgrounds discovered a sense of community that seemed impossible in everyday life. The autocamp was like an old-fashioned family reunion. Suspicious of idealistic political rhetoric, postwar Americans welcomed the car as an instrument of patriotic harmony.

To be sure, the autocamp actually represented a new stage in the commercialization of motoring tourism. Having been banned from random roadside exploration, autocampers now inhabited a segregated tourist world with its own concerns, routines, and infrastructure. To use sociologist Erik Cohen's terminology, this specialization

Yellowstone Campground, 1923

was part of the process by which individualized "drifter tourism"—
gypsying—evolved into institutionalized "mass tourism." And, as in
other culture industries—movies, radio, professional baseball—public authority played a crucial role in paving the way for widespread
acceptance and elaboration. Government intervention channeled a
possibly disruptive movement into more socially acceptable lines.
Autocamping was now safe.

3. PAY CAMPS, 1923–28

Yet the free municipal camp was even more short-lived than the
roadside campsite. The autocamps became too popular. They grew
large, crowded, and noisy, and sponsors had trouble keeping up
maintenance—especially at camps in the smallest towns. Fleeing urban problems, tourists created the same ones on the road. Moreover,
as automobility spread to the lower classes in the 1920s, many of
these new travelers stopped at autocamps not for romantic or nostalgic reasons, but because they needed to save money. The free
camps also attracted migrant workers, peddlers, and even real gypsies and tramps, all of whom began to move around in used cars
during this period. For ordinary middle-class tourists out on a two
week vacation, this colorful mixture of different classes and styles
proved a bit too diverse, and they began to avoid camps that har-
bored too many so-called undesirables.

Free camp sponsors now found themselves in a bind. In order to
maintain their town's good name, they had to upgrade their facilities.
By the mid-1920s, the "latest" meant hot showers and community
lounges. Yet, in order to justify the added expenditures, they needed
to point to increased revenues in downtown stores. But tourists were
not spending enough—certainly not the new crop of low-budget tourists. By the mid-1920s, therefore, camps began to impose daily fees—
usually fifty cents a car—with the dual hope of screening out the poor
campers and of financing the maintenance and improvements needed
to attract the "better class" tourists, i.e., the middle- and upper-
middle-class recreationists who are the target of all leisure industries.

The backlash against "undesirables" was part of a wider revaluation of the automobile's role in the mid-1920s. Given the rising death
rate, increased traffic problems, and roadside clutter, some Americans began to worry whether automobility had gone too far. Moralists
worried in particular about the bad effects on the working class.
While American culture was beginning to adopt the consumer ethic,

it was only *beginning;* the idea of mass consumption was still very new. The attempt to limit access to autocamps reflected the persistence of older notions that only the "respectable" middle class deserved to consume leisure. With working-class income lagging through the 1920s, this restriction also made good business sense. Indeed, the imposition of camp fees paralleled moves in other neo-primitivist industries to upgrade their product to suit a more affluent market. Filmmakers replaced neighborhood storefront theaters with garish movie palaces and established the Hays Office (1922) to quiet middle-class objections to vulgar film content. The recording industry confined the most raucous, subversive jazz to the "race" market and produced a more slick, sentimentalized "symphonic jazz" for the white middle class. Similarly, in search of respectability, owners of professional baseball teams established the commissioner system and erected elaborate ball parks.

The fee did not save the public camp, but it did produce a new business: the private campground. There had always been a few private camps, especially in resort areas, but because they had not been able to compete fairly with subsidized free camps, most of them remained poorly maintained sidelines to a restaurant or filling station. Once the public camps began to charge for services, however, private operators could now compete more equally. Indeed, they often had an advantage, for they could screen guests more carefully. Resident owners might also take a greater interest in camp upkeep than a paid caretaker at a public camp. Also, speeding motorists preferred to stop at a private camp along the main highway than to venture downtown through strange streets and local traffic. Thus, by the mid to late 1920s, the advantage turned toward the private camps, and public camps either closed down or turned over operations to independent proprietors.

4. CABINS, 1928–40

In a sense, the history of private camp ownership between 1928 and 1940 recapitulated the earlier evolution of autocamping from democratic access to restricted respectability. The earliest private camps were relatively easy to set up, and almost anyone with highway frontage could enter the business. Competition soon grew fierce as gas station operators, hot dog vendors, farmers, and café owners opened camps. Instead of one centrally located municipal camp, an area might have three or four along the main approaches to town.

Such competition, combined with a strong personal drive for success and legitimacy, led many camp owners to look for ways to attract more tourists, especially the ever-beckoning "better class." The most important innovation in the late 1920s was the dollar-a-night cabin, which appealed both to noncampers and to autocampers, who began to tire of the daily set-up routine. After several seasons of lugging heavy equipment around and struggling with cumbersome tents every night, many former motor gypsies decided that they preferred the convenience of the established cottage. Also, autocamping was now associated with the poorer class, and to call oneself a "motor hobo" in the late 1920s was to risk being taken for an "undesirable." At the same time, cabins were cheaper than hotels and retained the self-service convenience and homey, nostalgic, quasi-democratic aura of autocamping. The plain-speaking vernacular of Mama-Papa proprietors contrasted favorably with the suave officiousness of hotel clerks, and guests still chatted informally among themselves while waiting in line to use communal facilities. This nostalgic, populist image received much favorable journalistic attention in the early Depression, when Americans looked to their road culture for comforting evidence of national solidarity. Writers, photographers, and film producers visted tourist camps, gas stations, and diners, where they attempted to interview the "ordinary American." Widespread participation in roadside rituals assured an insecure public that indeed there was a common American Way of Life, the economic crisis notwithstanding. Perhaps the most heartwarming example was Frank Capra's film *It Happened One Night*, in which Clark Gable and Claudette Colbert hobnobbed with "The People" at a cottage camp. Yet this was at best a middle-class populism, for the $1.00–$2.00 cabin excluded the hard strapped, who generally had to camp surreptitiously along the roadsides if they traveled at all. For the hotel class tourist, however, the cabin represented a significant savings in these budget-minded years—especially if it was as clean and well equipped as Capra's, which was top-of-the-line for 1934.

To suit the more fastidious tastes of these "desirable" customers— as well as to head off hotel industry charges that tourist cabins were unsafe, sinful, and uncomfortable—most camp proprietors further modernized their cabins in the 1930s. Indeed, all tourists seemed to want more convenience. Earlier motor gypsies had exemplified what historian Arthur O. Lovejoy has called "hard primitivism." That is, in rejecting the soft, overheated, effete world of the late Victorian parlor, they had sought to return to the more ascetic, disciplined, stoic

Grandview Cabins, Holyoke, Massachusetts, 1940

simplicity of primitive nomads. By the late 1920s, however, the mood turned toward "soft primitivism"—a hedonistic, effortless, luxurious retreat. The former model embodied the Spartan ideal; the latter longed for the Garden of Eden, a place where people lived easily off nature's bounty. For roadside entrepreneurs, this meant conveniences that were "up-to-the-minute," and in the relentless tourist grapevine, it was disastrous to fall behind. Serving comparative-shopping consumers who viewed the roadside both as an extension of the annual model change and as an elongated cut-rate bazaar, operators added innerspring mattresses, steam heat, private baths and kitchenettes, and overstuffed parlor furniture.

Yet, unlike diner and gas station owners, they did not favor ultra-modern, streamlined architecture. In part, the marginal nature of most camps precluded such expensive, nonutilitarian investments. But there was another reason. Motorists were still nostalgic for old-fashioned customs. In diners and gas stations they could get their fill of folksy manners simply by interacting with fellow customers. In the increasingly private, anonymous tourist camps of the late 1930s, however, such interactions were minimized, since travelers did not have to leave their cabins to use bathrooms or kitchens. Democratic nostalgia was therefore relegated to the realm of style and advertising: New England, Virginia, or Spanish colonial architecture; innlike signs and names; homey lace curtains, rocking chairs, and window boxes with flowers. The tourist camp was still a "home away from home," but it resembled more a suburban bungalow than a humble farmer's cottage. A similar contrast between style and substance characterized the first successful roadside food chain of the late 1930s. In business methods, Howard Johnson's restaurants were as scrupulously efficient as an automobile assembly line, but architecturally, Johnson's orange-roofed "roadside cathedrals" caricatured an early colonial New England town hall.

Anxious to distance themselves from their lowly cabin origins, industry leaders formed trade associations of "tourist courts" and "motor hotels," or motels. By 1940, the industry had won the hotel-class customer. Having achieved national respectability, it was almost ready for hotel-scale management and national mass production, i.e., the motel chain. A few oil companies had contemplated "motor hotel" chain development as early as 1929, but the Crash had ended such ambitious plans. Moreover, regional variations kept the business in the hands of Mama-Papa operators through the 1930s. Given the better climate and year-round touring, only far western and southwestern camps could afford the most ambitious improvements. In the rest of the country, touring was still too localistic and seasonal. The motel industry thus lagged behind the music and movie industries, which achieved national standardization in the early 1930s (through radio networks and centralized film distribution). By 1940, however, better roads and cars, along with steam heat and sturdier brick cabins, allowed year-round touring all over the country, and the best northern camps equaled those of California and Texas. Motel chains began to appear during World War II—the first was California's Travelodge. But large-scale mass production awaited the arrival of the automotive equivalent of the national network—the limited access highway. The postwar expressway put most of the remaining camp pioneers out of business, for they rarely could afford to relocate to the more expensive land near highway interchanges. Reflecting the no-nonsense, businesslike nature of interstate highway travel, these new motel chains tended toward the efficient, ultramodern architecture that pleased corporate accountants.

If we refer to the love affair metaphor with which this essay began, it seems clear that by the 1970s our involvement with the car had more or less settled down into a rather stolid, middle-aged marriage, a relationship cemented more by obligation and habit than by passion. Yet, as in such utilitarian relationships, there were occasional sparks of the original romance. Certainly, there was still the nostalgia factor—that hunger for premodern adventure, contrast, and community. Turning against the now all-too-modern motel/expressway complex, millions of Americans took to backpacking, recreational vehicles, and off-road jeeps.

And on the suburban strip itself, one could discern preindustrial longings. Catering to a hunger for the intimacy, coherence, and convenience of the village center—a center destroyed largely by automobiles—real estate developers created suburban malls that resembled old-time small towns. Even the most unregenerately up-to-date mass franchisers seemed to sense that they could not sell all those burgers, fries, and slurpies unless they subliminally reminded customers of Ye Good Olde Days. How else do we explain all the inns, shoppes, huts, pubs, lodges, grilles, and townes; the neo-colonial 7-Elevens and neo-Tudor Jolly Oxes; the residual steeples of Long John Silver's and Howard Johnson's; the Wild West motif of Arby's, Rustler's, and Roy Rogers's? Like the generation of the 1890s, Americans of the 1970s still saw motoring as a way to recapture the rugged self-reliance of the frontier West. (It was no coincidence that the first American-made car appeared on the streets of Springfield, Massachusetts, in 1893, the same year that Frederick Jackson Turner bemoaned the end of the frontier in his important paper, "The Significance of the Frontier in American History.") Would it be too extreme to interpret the interstate highway landscape contruction of the period after World War II as an attempt to bring back the old western landscape? Certainly, both the Old West and the interstate shared the same vistas—huge expanses of flat, unpopulated land and uncluttered blue sky. Or would it be too extreme to interpret McDonald's famed Golden Arches as inverted horseshoes—covert reminders of the gloried days when cowboys roamed the Golden West?

Indeed, the need for the mythic innocence of bygone days appeared to be so desperate that architects even turned to late Victorian models that would have disgusted our early motorized pioneers. Witness the plastic Tiffany stained glass of Wendy's, or the mansardized roofs of McDonald's. Even the train station was back. Like revolution, nostalgia appeared to be devouring itself; and there were some who, by the late 1970s, were looking ahead for a change. As of 1980, however, with the election of a former movie cowboy who rivaled Henry Ford in carefully cultivated folksiness, novelist Wright Morris's lament still held:

> For more than a century the territory ahead has been the world that lies somewhere behind us, a world that has become, the last few decades, a nostalgic myth. With our eyes fixed on the past, we walk, blindfolded, into the future. In the eyes of the world we are the future, but in our own eyes we are the past. Nostalgia rules our hearts while a rhetoric of progress rules our words.

DAVID L. LEWIS

SEX AND THE AUTOMOBILE:
FROM RUMBLE SEATS TO ROCKIN' VANS

Every form of transportation has played a part in American courtship and romance. Pedestrian locomotion, horses, boats, trains, bicycles, streetcars, automobiles, buses, and airplanes have brought lovers together, or sped them to the Elysian fields for idyllic pleasures. Before the auto age, the horse and buggy provided the most effective vehicle for romance—and even offered one advantage over the motorcar: horsepower that knew the way home. If on a familiar road, a rural Romeo could tie the reins lightly about the whip socket, and expect Dobbin to maintain a steady clippity-clop down the middle of the road. And two hands then, as now, were better than one. Moreover, some of the buggies, especially those equipped with canvas tops, side curtains, cushions, and comforters, could be cozy; and none was encumbered with bucket seats, gear shifts, consoles, and other Berlin Wall-type features that keep couples apart in modern cars. But the horsedrawn conveyances had disadvantages. The buggy admitted mosquitoes in the summer and the cold in the winter, and the horse sometimes made noises incompatible with romance. Efforts were made to have horse push, rather than pull, buggies. None proved successful.

Cars fulfilled a romantic function from the dawn of the auto age. They permitted couples to get much farther away from front porch swings, parlor sofas, hovering mothers, and pesky siblings than ever before. In motor vehicles, couples could range far afield for picnics and swims in the summertime and to dances and other forms of entertainment year-around. Courtship itself was extended from the five-mile radius of the horse and buggy to ten, twenty, and fifty miles and more. Sociologists duly noted that increased mobility provided by the motorcar would lead to more cross-breeding and eventually improve the American species.

Autos were more than a mode of transportation. They were a destination as well, for they provided a setting for sexual relations including intercourse. The earliest cars offered little improvement over buggies insofar as courtship was concerned. Most models were open, and couples, seated on "high-rise" seats, were highly visible to onlookers and exposed to the elements except when tops were put up and curtains fastened around. Heaters were nonexistent, or as primitive as heated bricks. But by the early 1920s most cars were enclosed; and passengers were less illuminated and rode lower, half-hidden by doors and side panels. Efficient heaters provided wintertime comfort. Seats, front and back, became progressively longer, wider, and more comfortable. Most seats also were detachable, and thus could be removed for ground action. In addition, many cars were equipped with long, wide running boards, and, starting in the mid-1920s, increasingly long, sloping fenders, some of which gained reputations as automotive chaise lounges. When covered with pillows or blankets, running boards and fenders provided an emergency or novelty setting for sexual encounters. Running boards were phased out in the mid- and late-1930s, and fender love tapered off in 1941-42 as fenders were extended into front doors.

Early in the century many couples made love in cars because—in an era in which many young men and women lived with their parents—they had no better place to copulate. But others made love in cars because they found it exciting, sometimes dangerously so, and a change from familiar surroundings. Lovers' lanes abounded in parks and off lesser streets and roadways in and around most communities. Ideally, police officers did not harass lovers, yet provided a sufficient presence to discourage bushwackers, Peeping Toms, and worse. Most communities officially ignored sex in cars, but some passed laws which prohibited intercourse, even kissing, in vehicles. To this day, Chicago, by legislating against any "indecent act in public" and defining sexual intercourse as "indecent" and a car as a "public place," forbids lovemaking in cars. Deerfield, Illinois, prohibits kissing within part of the dropoff zone at its commuter station, while sanctioning kissing within the other part. Signs which picture a kissing couple, one with a stripe drawn through, indicate which zone is which. In any event, laws against sex in cars are so rarely enforced, that any attention paid to them makes national news. Police officers, on the contrary, are more likely to be amused by romantic interludes they discover in cars.

The link between cars and courtship was immediately evident to everyone not wearing blinders. Songwriters, Valentine and post-card sellers, cartoonists, advertisers, and others rhapsodized endlessly on the connection. Tin Pan Alley, always attuned to the times, mixed passion with gasoline in scores of such songs as *Take Me Out for a Joy Ride*, *Take a Little Ride with Me Baby*, *In Our Little Love Mobile*, *Riding in Love's Limousine*, *On the Back Seat of the Henry Ford*, *I'm Going to Park Myself in Your Arms*, *Fifteen Kisses on a Gallon of Gas*, *When He Wanted to Love Her He'd Put up the Cover*, and *Tumble in a Rumble Seat*. Most of the lyrics, simple and syrupy, spoke of the joys of having (or being) a queen for one's machine, or motoring off for a lark to spark in the park. Many songs had couples embarking on auto honeymoons, and several automakers commissioned tunesmiths to make sure that the honeymooners used their models. A few songs were provocative, and likely would have been banned on radio had the medium existed at the time. In a 1915 tune, a "ladykiller," foxy Johnny Miller, at the slightest hint of rain and over the feeble protests of his queen, would put up the cover and fasten the side curtains around. The song, when played in parlors and at dances, invariably produced guffaws. Other songs, such as *I'd Rather Go Walking with the Man I Love Than Ride in Your Automobile (You Cad)*, consoled motorless males, or warned girls to *Keep Away from the Fellow Who Owns an Automobile*. Cars themselves occasionally were described as sex partners. *Mr. Packard and Miss Flivverette* have a fling, then, after getting married, conceive a Buick. In another song, a Tin Lizzie Mama bedazzles a Rolls Royce Papa.

Most of the love tunes were eminently forgettable, and only one, *In My Merry Oldsmobile*, the best known song ever written about the automobile, endures. Almost every reader should be able to plug the melody into these lyrics:

> Come away with me Lucille,
>   In my merry Oldsmobile,
> Over the road of life we'll fly,
>   Autobubbling you and I,
> To the church we'll swiftly steal,
>   And our wedding bells will peal,
> You can go as far as you like with me,
>   In our merry Oldsmobile.

Every auto-related Valentine, many in the shape of cars, inspired visions of romance. Most were no more complicated than the line, "You auto be my Valentine," but some waxed poetically on moon, spoon, and love-in-bloom. Picture post cards, highly popular through the 1930s, ranged widely in theme. Many were as innocent as a picture of a couple on a joy ride, the lady waving her handkerchief to onlookers. But many others were provocative, even risqué. Out-of-gas cards, many tied to romance, always sold well, as did cards which linked romance to auto parts, especially the starter, crank, and spark plugs. A female motorist-in-distress hopes the mechanic will "start something," and not necessarily the engine; a lady asks her escort to "crank up"; a pretty girl, standing next to a car, "gets the brakes." Car repairs also lent themselves to blue humor. A mechanic, looking up from beneath the rear of a lady's car, assures his nearby client that "your rear end is in great shape." A best selling post card of the 1930s shows a female hitchhiker, babe in arms, asking a motorist pulling up beside her if he "wasn't the fellow who gave me a ride about a year ago?" Other post cards, reflecting a popular theme, show a picture of a lithesome hitchhiker standing beside a jackass she had been riding, and flagging down a motorist with the words, "Can I have a ride? My ass is tired." Still other post cards center around holding one's girl, or steering the car, depending on one's point of view. A girl wants her beau to "use both hands." He'd gladly oblige, if "only the car would steer itself." Other cards focused on cars and couples in romantic settings. A pair picnics beneath the legend: "The best place for lovers/Where nobody hovers." The gentleman pictured in the card plies the object of his affection with an alcoholic beverage, but his car's detachable seat remains in place. "But for how long," chortles a sender of the card, "given the effects of that bottle of Demon rum?" Another post card simply shows a car parked in the countryside sans picnickers, its legend admonishing readers that evil comes to those who think evil thoughts.

The auto inspired more newspaper and magazine cartoons than any other artifact during the first three decades of the century, and many had sexual connotations. Parking/sparking and out-of-gas themes were perennially popular. Many jokes also centered around detachable seats. The most famous of them, appearing in the *New Yorker* in 1931, shows a bedraggled couple carrying a rear seat cushion, and informing a police officer of a stolen car. Other cartoons were highly diverse—a highway sign reading "soft shoulders"; a flapper, accompanied by two escorts, explaining that she always carries a "spare"; a boy telling a girl, as they neck on a sofa, that he's using only one arm because he's practicing for the day he'll own a car.

Sex, especially as related to masculine virility, has been emphasized in auto ads since early in the century. Pierce-Arrow's 1910 ads make no mention of price or anything else about the car; just show a sketch of a brutish machine and a couple of strong, handsome dogs whom every father's daughter had to hope were accessories that came with the car. Oldsmobile's most famous advertisement pictures a dashing figure hunched over the steering wheel of a huge 1911 Oldsmobile Limited, in the foreground, racing alongside an onrushing train. Ads featuring masculine virility eventually gave way to campaigns showing pert girls at the wheel or seductive women draped over the hood.

Automakers, according to some psychologists, not only advertised their cars as sex objects; they also consciously or subconsciously designed dreams of sex into their vehicles. As cars became longer and lower, they were pointed to as male phallic symbols; and their long, sleek radiator/hood ornaments the more so. Buxom headlamps and bumper guards and radiator grilles (notably the Edsel's) were perceived as female sexual symbols. On the other hand, Henry Ford, according to widespread rumor, sought to discourage sex through car design. The auto king allegedly limited his Model T's seat length to 38 inches so as to inhibit lovemaking in Tin Lizzies. If that was Ford's intent, he failed, for a thirty-eight-inch seat was ample for determined couples, the more so when the seat was removed from the car. Besides, said wags, given the Model T's seven-foot height, short couples could have intercourse standing up.

If carmakers sought to design and sell their vehicles as sex symbols, they have succeeded in doing so in the minds of psychologists Dr. Joyce Brothers and Dr. Herbert Hoffman. Dr. Brothers maintains that cars, to many men, have been "an extension of themselves and a powerful symbol of masculinity and virility. The more immature the male, the more his sexuality is apt to be linked to . . . cars. In their minds," she adds, "there is a link between horsepower and sexual prowess. They may also equate driving with sexual function which leads to the assumption that the bigger the car the better." Dr. Hoffman, director of a New York guidance center, maintains that a man's hidden sexual fantasies may be determined by the kind of car he wishes to own. Thus those who want jazzy sports cars have fantasies involving sexually aggressive females; those wishing to own luxury cars dream of romantic affairs in exotic surroundings; would-be owners of four-wheel drive vehicles are admirers of healthy women with well-developed bodies and physical endurance, and dream of making love in scenic spots; and one-of-a-kind custom car fanciers have sexual fantasies in which they lead the life of a playboy, having more affairs than any other man on earth.

Whether or not automakers have tried to design dreams of sex into their products, they have incorporated features which have lent themselves to sex. Long before the van era, manufacturers designed beds into their vehicles by folding front seatbacks into rearseat cushions. The 1925 Jewett, typically, slept two persons in comfort, as long as neither stretched out more than six feet, one and one-half inches in length. Nearly all automakers advertised their "sleeper cars" as a means of saving on hotel bills; none alluded to beds as a sexual convenience/comfort option. Nonetheless, knowing people winked at owners of "rolling dormitories," and inquired how fast the seatback could be folded back, whether the springs squeaked, etc. Nash president George Mason, usually a dour man, invariably chuckled as he described his firm's post-World War II Statesman, equipped with a many-splendored bed, as the "young man's car." Today no American-built auto is equipped with a seat bed, although some have tilt seats. A number of foreign-made cars have seat beds, giving them, in the minds of some, yet another competitive advantage.

Albeit short on beds, American carmakers offer many accessories which are a boon to courtship and romance. Air conditioners, along with heaters, have made sexual relations a more pleasant year-around diversion. Tilt-steering wheels provide for additional front-seat maneuverability. Lighted vanity mirrors facilitate freshing up in the event of battle fatigue. Radios, supplemented by stereo units, help set the mood for romance. Citizen Band radios enable couples to arrange get-togethers. But the use of CB radio could backfire. "Brown Eyes" was shot to death by her husband in Adamstown, Pennsylvania, last year after her husband heard her call for "Flying Angel," her lover. CB also helps prostitutes attract customers. In 1980, hookers with such handles as "Tons of Fun," "Chocolate Kisses," "Hot Lips," "Pussy Cat Sally," and "Joy to the World" lured scores of truckers to motels in Port Jervis, Washington, and Lexington, North Carolina.

Autos have done more than enable couples to meet and make love and to inspire songwriters, Valentine and card designers, cartoonists, and adsmiths. They also have influenced American culture by abetting prostitution, creating the "hot pillow" trade in tourist courts and motels, providing an impetus for drive-in restaurants and movies, and inducing many motorists to wear their hearts on license plates and bumpers.

Prostitutes and their pimps began using cars to solicit customers and as a setting for sexual intercourse in the 1920s—as soon as closed vehicles came into vogue. Pimps, especially, advertised their profession, and their status within it, by the kind of cars they drove. Desiring distinctive vehicles, they created them. They were, in fact, the first post-World War II motorists to customize their cars with opera windows. This design feature was almost exclusively associated with pimps until the mid-1970s, when Detroit began offering the feature on its tonier models. Car buffs disparagingly referred to the vehicles as "pimpmobiles."

It was common knowledge for years that tourist courts and motels trafficked heavily in the "hot pillow" trade. But the scope of that trade was not revealed until the Federal Bureau of Investigation's J. Edgar Hoover publicly assailed "camouflaged brothels" in 1940. Hoover cited a Southern Methodist University study which found that many big-city motels refused accommodations to anyone from outside their home counties because they could make more money with the faster turnover of the "couple trade." Some Texas cabins, said Hoover, had been rented as many as sixteen times in one night, while cabins in other cities were rented by the hour, "and there was a knock on the door when the hour was up." Many of these establishments, added Hoover, were closed to the traveling public on weekends and provided prostitutes in the guise of entertainers, hostesses, and waitresses.

The first drive-in restaurant, Royce Hailey's Pig Stand, was opened in Dallas in 1921, and thousands of its brethren sprouted around the country during the 1920s and 1930s. Most of the drive-ins were located at the edge of town, served inexpensive sandwiches and soft drinks, and were patronized by all manner of people. But drive-ins had special appeal for youthful, impecunious motorists, who were attracted by the prices, carhops, and other customers like themselves. Few youths stayed long at any one drive-in; they cruised endlessly and mindlessly from one to another in search of action.

The number of drive-in restaurants peaked in the 1960s, and has declined steadily since. Teen-age patrons helped kill them, their rowdiness turning away older customers and reducing the volume of business. Many property owners, moreover, found they could make more money by leasing or selling their lots to fast-food franchises. Only a few hundred drive-in restaurants remain. One of the survivors, Delores Drive-In, which opened in Beverly Hills in 1946, was proposed for historic landmark status, in 1980 a sure sign that the species is endangered.

The drive-in theater almost seemed to have been created for sex in cars. The first of them was opened on June 6, 1933, in Camden, New Jersey. It accommodated 400 cars arranged in seven inclined rows from which motorists viewed films on a 40 x 50-foot screen. Successive drive-ins grew to such size that some of them featured as many as nine screens offering 18 films per evening. Many establishments were equipped with individual heaters and air conditioners. Drive-ins quickly gained a reputation as "passion pits," and patrons generally agreed that there often was a better show in the cars than on the screen. Humorists complained that the sound track sometimes was drowned out by the unzipping of zippers, and observed that many a male patron had come of age while unhooking a bra clasp with one hand. The more amorous the couples, the more likely that they would gravitate to the theater's back rows. Some patrons had to be informed by the management that the film had been concluded, the lights had been turned on, and almost everyone else had gone home. Although some drive-in owners instructed their personnel to prevent couples from "making a scene," others had the attitude, "you pay your money, you get what you came for." Management occasionally helped matters along, hiring "ushers" who served as "auto pimps" and providing prostitutes to make "car calls."

The number of drive-in theaters reached an all-time high of 4,063 then began to decline slowly, starting in the 1960s and more rapidly in the late 1970s. Drive-ins' problems are manifold: competition from television and shopping center theaters; universal adoption of daylight savings time; a waning number of family films; and much higher fuel bills for establishments offering winter fare. Today there are fewer than 3,500 drive-ins, most of them in the Sunbelt states and California. The falloff rate in northern cities has been precipitous. In metropolitan Detroit, for example, only eleven drive-ins are now operating, as against twenty-seven in 1977. Among these eleven, only three are open in wintertime, as against eighteen in 1977.

Many motorists express their romantic feelings on their license plates and bumpers. LUV 1 and LUV 2 and LUVU and LUVU2 share Michigan driveways. Two Texans advertise themselves as SEXY and having NO WIFE; Pennsylvanians sport X-RATED, KISS ME, and WICKED; Ohioans LOVE, LOVING, and AGAPAO (Greek for love); and a Michiganian pleads Y-NOT? Californians have formed a waiting line for plates bearing the letters GAY. But more than 100 of the 1,000 Iowans issued GAY plates in 1978 paid a $4.00 exchange fee to get rid of them. Many bumper stickers are "cutesy"—"Ford Drivers

Make Better Lovers"—while others are obscene to the point that they cannot be printed here.

Two car models have especially appealed to romantics—those with rumble seats and convertibles. Rumble seats made their appearance during the 1920s, and were quickly identified with agile young lovers. Most rumble seats were lacking in roominess. But they made up in coziness what they lacked in comfort, and could offer privacy as well, if equipped with a canvas top and sides. Rumble seats were a passing fancy; all were phased out before World War II.

All of the earliest cars were convertibles, and even as late as 1919 more than 80 percent were open models. By the end of the 1920s, however, closed cars made up more than 90 percent of the car population. Meanwhile, the sleek convertible sedan with a lowerable top—the true convertible—appeared. It also appealed primarily to youth, and to those who wished to appear young. During the long convertible era, "hardly anything," according to columnist Sidney J. Harris, "seemed more romantic or glamorous than gliding through the night with the top down. One's dates," adds Harris, "pretended to adore them—until they were married—even though their hairdos, makeup, and clothes were ruffled out of recognition by high winds, dust, and the trailing exhaust of other cars."

Convertibles' popularity peaked in 1973, when the model comprised 6.4 percent of all sales. Their popularity waned with the increased popularity of air conditioners and hardtop coupes with vinyl roof styling, and high-speed expressway travel. The last domestic convertible was produced by Cadillac in 1976. But several thousand sedans are customized into convertibles each year. "People who drive convertibles don't care about the energy or any other crisis," declared a customizer. "To them, the convertible is sex, romance, wind in your hair—hey, man, it's the American dream."

During the 1970s, the van came to the fore in mobile lovemaking. Vans, described by auto analyst Arvid Jouppi as a "love affair within Americans' love affair with cars," provided young people with the best of two worlds: a way to break away from home, yet remain tied to a home. Vans undoubtedly are the most sexually-oriented vehicles ever built. Even the exteriors of many vans leave no doubt as to their owners' motives. Many feature surrealistic murals, ranging in taste from Early or French Bordello scenes of nude women to portraits of club-bearing "cave men" holding females by their hair. Many vans also bear naughty bumper stickers along the lines of "Sin Bin," "Do It in a Van!," "If It's Arockin', Don't Come Aknockin'," and "Don't

Laugh, Your Daughter May Be in Here."

Most van owners are single men between the ages of twenty-one and thirty-five. They and other owners equip their vehicles with such amenities as one-way windows, shag carpeting, soft lights, mirrored walls and ceilings, revolving flashing globes, wine racks, stereo units, color TV, bathrooms, bars, refrigerators, fireplaces—and almost inevitably—beds. "Why do I like vans?," said a vanner in response to a question. "You can puzzle people with vans. You can suck beer or smoke dope and just raise pure hell in vans. And you can score in vans."

Vans also are a prostitute's motorized dream. In them, they can cruise in search of clients. After taking in a John, they entertain without fear of police interruption. Officers cannot get inside without a search warrant.

If vans represent the ultimate in mobile sex, they also have an Achilles' heel: they are gas hogs. Their popularity has waned as motorists have become more miles-per-gallon conscious. But they remain the best way to go for the dedicated lover on wheels.

Just as the golden age of the auto is receding, so the salad days of sex and cars are on the wane. Cars, because of the high cost and potential shortage of fuel, are getting smaller and smaller, Although couples can make out even in the tiniest of cars, a point of diminishing returns sets in about the time they begin to cuddle, much less copulate, in subcompacts—except for those with reclining seats (the light at the end of the tunnel). As for the electric pygmies looming on the horizon, heaven forbid that normal-size people ever have to find the way in them. Even the most determined, ingenious and acrobatic of lovers will find them an all-but-impossible challenge.

Downsizing isn't the only problem confronting car Casanovas. The number of safe trysting spots has been drying up at an alarming rate in recent years. Big-city parks often are off-bounds to lovers after sundown, and urban sprawl, farmers' no trespassing signs, and logs and chains strung across lovers' lanes have conspired to reduce the number of car-accommodating lovenests to a small fraction of those once available.

But perhaps problems associated with lovemaking by car are beside the point. Most people no longer want or need cars for sexual relations anyway. Older people (those over thirty years of age) have beds at home, and lack the spirit of adventurousness and/or agility required of car loving today. High schoolers, who in times past counted on cars for sexual relations, now can make out at their or their partners' homes while mother and dad are at work. Collegians can have at each other in the rooms of their unsupervised dormitories. Who needs cars when beds are so readily available?

Still, lovemaking in cars is unlikely to disappear completely from the American cultural scene. It still represents pleasurable excitement and a change of pace. As a Chicago woman wrote Ann Landers in 1978, "My fiancé and I wish to add an extra dimension to our lovemaking by extending our sexual environment to God's beautiful out-of-doors—including the car." Her sentiment is one that can be shared, at least appreciated, by all of those who have made love in a car—including perhaps not a few readers of this essay.

ROBLEY WILSON, JR.

SOMETHING OF LOVE

I remember we were driving
in your mother's old blue Chevy;
it was near three in the morning,
summer, the sun still far below
the horizon but morning birds
beginning to creak and whirr like
familiar comfortable machines
in an unheated shed. I rolled
the windows down; the damp air
smelled contradictory and green.
We had left the cemetery
where we knew all the gravel roads,
every bronze flag and flower pot,
every faucet leaking to be
St. Francis for thirsty squirrels;
we had played all night—nothing
serious—on the slant of lawn
by the mausoleum, the house
with no one home, mussing ourselves,
laughing that someone's ancestors
were clenching bony hands, saying
frantic prayers in whispers cold
as wind under a broken door.
Between our sweet lives and death
was immovable Nature—its roots,
weeds, insoluble masonries;
sweaty and quick we had hugged,
melted into each other's clothes
pretending to manufacture
children who might witness to us.
Now we shook off the print of grass,
the temperature of earth, even
the shamefaced cemetery ghosts.

Love, I said, *oh love, oh good love,*
how I hurt for you and from you.
That was true. It hurt to breathe,
hurt to put my foot to the brake,
hurt me to turn the wheel; it hurt
when I inhaled a cigarette,
and if I coughed I died. You said:
Oh dear dearest darling, what can I do?
So I told you, and stopped the car
on Laurel, this side of the old
tennis courts, and you did it. *Love.*
We never accustom ourselves
to love's lineaments. Woman, wife,
mother, lover too good for me—
that was twenty-five years ago.
How many flowers we have brought
to our parents, how many cars
we have bought and traded away . . .
We have manufactured real sons,
have felt the space separating
us from the underworld shrink (roots
withering and letting go, earth
washing away, spring after spring),
hear—louder and louder—voices
under the doors of every house
we live in. The best of it is:
Now we are always together—
so close that I have noticed how
when I do something important
you are suddenly in my way
and are part of the importance.
How I love to quarrel with you,
to swing in your rage as if in
some hammock under bending trees;
how I love to put on your scorn
like a coat I cannot make fit;
how I love your kindness, which sits
close to my face, curling its paws,
and makes me tremble with purring;
how I love your patience—it is
a children's orchestra waiting

to be told what to play. *Oh dear*
dearest darling, what can I do?
And I tell you, and stop the car
on Laurel, this side of the old
tennis courts, and you do it, *love.*
Then when I start the car we drive,
away from the graveyards, forever.

CHARLES L. SANFORD

"WOMAN'S PLACE" IN
AMERICAN CAR CULTURE

During the twentieth century, the automobile became the chief
carrier of the American Dream of freedom and plenitude. If the
academic study of cars were given space relative to their importance
in American life, according to Professor-emeritus Linwood Bryant of
M.I.T. in 1975, it would fill at least 40 percent of our libraries.
Bryant also ventured the observation, perhaps partly in jest, that
cars and money rate higher than "girls" in our national scheme of
values. In a lighter vein, a writer for *Motor Trend* in 1967 cited a
survey of 1100 marriages showing that "nearly 40 percent of the
nation's reluctant males are driven to pop the question while riding,
wheeling or parking in a car."[1] Such thoughts provoke a legitimate
question: what about women in the context of car culture?

We receive little information on this subject from the few books
that might be expected to treat it. The noted historian of American
automobiles, John Rae, hardly mentions women, while women are
conspicuously absent where they should be most present, from James
Flink's more recent crusading *The Car Culture*. Although a woman,
Cynthia Golumb Dettelbach, has written the classic study of how
cars have influenced our literature, art, and music—which is to say,
the American mind at work when it is most profoundly in touch with
its feelings—her *In the Driver's Seat* clearly leaves women's voices
in the back seat, with writers like Flannery O'Connor and Eudora
Welty almost lost in an all-male chorus up front. The result is not
much better in books about the feminine image in popular culture
and advertising, where we find much about possible careers, jobs,
children, medical items, household helps, clothes, cosmetics, food,
schools, even cigarettes—but little about cars. To borrow from the

---

[1]From Bryant's talk at Rensselaer Polytechnic Institute. James Joseph, "Sex and the
Single Car," *Motor Trend* (April, 1967), p. 45.

historian John Keats, the national Ad and the Id would seem to be masculine.[2]

Car culture, briefly defined, is the cluster of beliefs, attitudes, symbols, values, behavior and institutions which have grown up around the manufacture and use of automobiles. Its economic base is an enormous, many-faceted industry which leads the business cycle and has profound implications for domestic and foreign policy. It has its own subcultures which specialize in customized vans, sports cars, trailers, professional racing, hot rods, antique cars, and the like. As an "American way of life," it invests a machine with values transcending in importance that of efficient, economical transportation. It fosters, for instance, a neo-frontier spirit, evident in the many popular films which feature cars in exciting chases, bouts with the law, daring escapes and escapades. It has its own rituals, taboos, folk songs, and legendary heroes. The most important puberty rite in the United States occurs when the young man or woman passes the driving examination, presses down the accelerator, and feels an answering surge of power, as if—some highway poet has written—"wolves howled from extinct caves in the bloodstream." Each stage of human life begets its own characteristic kind of car, one that hopefully signifies an upward social progress as well as advance in age. Exemplary cars mark rites of courtship, marriage, death, and great public occasions; and romance has never been quite the same since the advent of America's "love affair" with cars. Toy cars and car games wait in the wings for children, children who grow up to buy real cars—"most delicious of adult toys"—and exchange Halloween for the annual showroom display of next year's models to celebrate the harvest season. The high priest of this car culture, where cars sometimes seem to breed cars, is the American Adam. But where is Eve?

We catch glimpses of her in the literature of professional sociolo-

[2]James Flink's *The Car Culture* (Cambridge, Mass.: M.I.T. Press, 1975) offers a technological synthesis of 20th-century American history, succeeding to the older frontier interpretation and replacing recent interpretations that have concentrated on political administrations like the Progressive Era and the New Deal. Flink also takes issue with John Rae's optimism about cars in American life, especially in Rae's book *The Road and the Car in American Life* (Cambridge, Mass.: the MIT Press, 1971). Cynthia Dettelbach, *In the Driver's Seat* (Westport, Conn.: Greenwood Press, 1976). John Keats, *The Insolent Chariots* (Philadelphia: J. B. Lippincott Company, 1958). Trevor Millum, *Images of Woman* (Totawa, N.J.: Rowman and Littlefield, 1975). This last work documents British experience, but see Erving Goffman, *Gender Advertisements* (Cambridge, Mass.: Harvard University Press, 1979); Kathryn Weibel, *Mirror Mirror* (Garden City, N.Y.: Doubleday Anchor Books, 1977).

gists, who argue variously that the car has helped to liberate her and that she has not been liberated at all, with or without cars. President Hoover's Commission on Social Trends in its 1933 *Report* first gave public notice of the automobile's revolutionary impact on American life, "transforming even habits of thought and language." This confirmed the Lynds' famous studies of Middletown (Muncie, Indiana), where some upright citizens regarded the car as a "house of prostitution on wheels," and where the family car was the most cherished belonging during the Great Depression. Since then, a growing number of studies, largely influenced by the pioneering work of William F. Ogburn, have investigated the broad subject of technology and social change. In these studies, there seems to be considerable agreement that the car contributed significantly to important changes in the woman's roles within the family and in society. To summarize some of their major findings: the car helped loosen family ties, reduce parental authority over children, introduce women to new opportunities for recreation, romance, and work outside the home; and, in general, expand social contacts between the sexes. Charles Kettering's automatic self-starter for cars, invented in 1912, was not called "the ladies' aid" for nothing! The qualitative meaning of these and related changes, however, was a matter of some dispute.

As the divorce rate increased, many Americans became alarmed, but others welcomed these changes as leading to a freer, more relaxed and more equitable democratic society. Among the latter group, two leading sociologists concluded that culture had reduced the biological advantage of the male: "Technology has benefited women even more than men." But more recent studies stimulated by a revivified feminist movement during the 1970s do not altogether confirm such a sanguine view, and at least one female sociologist has repudiated it, arguing that the position of women has actually declined with industrialization. In fact, Arlie R. Hochschild maintains,

> Many studies [of women as a minority] draw the parallel with blacks, ranging from similarities in discrimination and prejudice to subjective traits such as passivity and helplessness to similarities in such things as the meaning of consumption; in the case of blacks, it's the Cadillac and magenta shirt, and in the case of women, the proverbial expensive new hat.[3]

[3]Arlie R. Hochschild, "A Review of Sex Role Research," in Joan Huber, ed., *Changing Women in a Changing Society* (Chicago: The University of Chicago Press, 1973), p. 256.

In other words, a traditional pattern of male domination-female subordination would seem to be affected by technological advances in a way even more detrimental to women. To such anti-technologists as Lewis Mumford (in his later work), Ivan Illich, Theodore Roszak, and Philip Slater the feminist issue is fairly irrelevant, because they see high technology hurting everybody—men, women, and children. In any case, car culture has entered a debunking stage.

Women appear in such literature as abstractions, if at all. What is needed is both an intimate feminine viewpoint from several perspectives about women's experience with cars and fairly objective, even statistical, studies of the same experience. The earliest literature that I know of which might have appealed to women, particularly of the upper class, was an article published in the *Independent* for June 2, 1904, by William F. Dix entitled, "The Automobile as a Vacation Agent." It belonged to the current back-to-nature movement, as did a later article in *Harper's Weekly* for May 6, 1911, by Eugene Clancy entitled "The Car and the Country Home." These attempts to accommodate the new invention to the aristocratic custom of preserving distance from the masses were not prophetic, because the green-belt notion that led to suburbia had already been published (in 1898) by Ebenezer Howard and activated by streetcar companies. The venturesome new idea was that of extending civilized horizons. Edward Field's novel, *A Six-Cylinder Courtship* (1907) suggests resistance to the new culture, however. In this novel, the hero is a bumpkin whose automobile explodes and so delivers into his arms a high-born woman who has always preferred to walk.

The resemblance between that woman and our own seems remote. A recognizably modern woman, also upper class, announced herself in 1911 as a champion of the horseless carriage, which she called "the finest product of civilization" (a phrase to be repeated in Sinclair Lewis's *Main Street* with epic allusions), regretting that horse lovers would "miss much of the exhilaration that goes with speed."[4] Her remark is worth noting, because women have acquired

---

The preceding quotation comes from Ogburn and Nimkoff, *Technology and the Changing Family* (Cambridge, Mass.: Houghton Mifflin Company, 1955), p. 180. But see also Francis R. Allen, ed., *Technology and Social Change* (New York: Appleton, Century, and Crofts, 1957); Elizabeth Faulkner Baker, *Technology and Women's Work* (New York: Columbia University Press, 1964).

[4]Mrs. A Sherman Hitchcock, "The Social Side of Motoring," *Suburban Life* (July 1911), pp. 9–10. She was one of many nonprofessional authors who reported their car-faring experiences to this magazine.

a reputation for not enjoying speed in transport or caring about cars as passionately as men. Certainly the author Gertrude Stein, a pioneer of modernism in literature, cared passionately about cars. During the Battle of Verdun in France, where she served as a volunteer for American relief of wounded French soldiers, she spent much time in talk "mingling automobiles with Emerson." Her account of World War I is interlaced with adventures in her beloved Model T Ford, which often bogged down in snow or mud. According to Ernest Hemingway, her famous reference to a "Lost Generation" originated with a mechanical breakdown of her car: when her mechanic was not adept in fixing it—so the story goes—the garage owner called him a member of a *génération perdue.* "That's what you all are," she was supposed to have told Hemingway. "All of you young people who served in the war. You are a lost generation. . . . You have no respect for anything."[5] Her love affair with cars also extended to the movies, where she noted a kind of traffic interchange. Her major contribution to literature was to develop a language by which to express the American habit of converting space into motion.

Although the first World War almost stopped the production of motor cars for civilians, it increased the involvement of women in industrial work and other activities usually associated with men. In 1918 a popular handbook on *The Care and Management of the Modern Motor-Car* devoted unaccustomed space to women drivers and mechanics. Although its tone was jocular and patronizing, it praised 400 female graduates of a YMCA school for mechanics who were as apt as men in "mastering the mechanical and technical details of a car" and warned professional chauffeurs, all men, to expect an invasion of women drivers, especially housewives who met their commuting "hubbies" three stations up the line:

> They are expected to lose their heads and "go up in the air," but they do not. They are not so reckless as men, are quicker to grasp a situation, and do not "take a chance" as men do. Alertness is an attribute of most women, also intuition, and these are qualities needed by an auto driver. . . . in the suburbs, where there is an almost total absence of men during the daytime, every car you meet has a woman at the wheel.[6]

[5]Gertrude Stein, *Wars I Have Seen* (New York: Random House, 1945), *passim;* Ernest Hemingway, *A Moveable Feast* (New York: Bantam Books, 1965), p. 29. About this mechanic, one is reminded of the many discussions of *value* in Robert Pirsig's *Zen and the Art of Motorcycle Maintenance* (New York: William Morrow and Company, 1974).

[6]H. Clifford Brokaw and Charles A. Starr, "Women as Drivers," in *Putnam's Automobile Handbook: The Care and Management of the Modern Motor-Car* (New York and

This tribute was presented, however, to "Wife, the Chauffeur!" and not to women as equal partners in car culture across the social classes. During the 1920s, with few exceptions, this situation did not much change. As cars became cheaper more women drove them, and so did their children; while fathers tried to hold tight to their authority. The 1920s were probably crucial for the American car culture.

In 1920, Americans owned more than twice as many horses as cars; by 1930, the reverse was true, approaching an average of one car for each family. During the 1920s, the car seemed to rule family behavior, both in families which owned one and families that didn't. Thus, the car was the major source of friction in the middle-class Babbitt family of Sinclair Lewis. Daughter Veronica and son Ted constantly vied for its use. When it came time for a new car, Mrs. Babbitt held out for a *closed* sedan, because everybody else, she claimed, had one. In rebellion, Babbitt himself took off for the Maine woods.

A character in a recent movie, *The Gumball Rallye* (1976), says, "You're nothing in this country if you got no wheels." The car has become a measure of failure as well as a symbol of success. Nowhere is this connection so direct in the national psyche as in our fictive dreams of a romantic or sexual paradise. F. Scott Fitzgerald, who once said that the richest man gets the prettiest girl, firmly documented this axiom in his novel, *The Great Gatsby* (1925). Since other readers than myself have commented at length upon the important role played by cars in integrating this novel, I shall only make a few observations. The first is that Gatsby's yellow Rolls-Royce functions not merely as a symbol of his golden dream associated with Daisy but as a death car foreshadowed by a funeral procession of limousines. In a novel which stresses motion of all kinds, Gatsby counts on the car more than on his mansion and parties, to win Daisy. Knowing her love of wealth and status, he expects Daisy to respond favorably. When she admits uncomfortably that she and her husband Tom Buchanan, who is about to buy a new car, might have loved one another at one time, Gatsby remarks that if so, it was "only personal." He presents himself as a superior provider of trans-personal, expensive symbols of his passion. By letting Daisy drive his car back from

London: G. P. Putnam's Sons, 1918), pp. 306–7. I thank Mr. Kenneth Blaisdell for bringing this work to my attention.

the fateful Plaza encounter, Gatsby again counts on his car to salvage victory from almost certain defeat. The gesture is both intimately personal and ceremonial; it leads to his undoing when Daisy proves to be an inept driver. That few readers have felt it as a mere contrivance necessitated by Fitzgerald's plot suggests that the connection between cars and sexual success or failure is deeply ingrained among Americans of both sexes.

Daisy is typical of 1920s women in her attraction to the automobile. During that decade women took their place with men as drivers of cars, though seldom as owners or mechanics and almost never as aficionados whose very identities were wrapped up in cars. Yet the movement of automobile manufacturers after 1928 away from an emphasis on engineering to one on *styling* was undoubtedly prompted by women, who were supposed—correctly, as it turns out—to have great influence over the husband's consumption of cars. Thus, George Romney, president of American Motors and prophet of the sensibly-sized small car, remarked during the inglorious tail-fin episode of 1957, "The automobile business has some of the elements of the millinery industry in it, in that you can make style become the hallmark of modernity."[7] The irony in this remark should be self-evident: it both acknowledged the influence of women and diminished them according to a male stereotype. Nothing of the kind was said by any man when European high-styling merged with performance in Chevrolet's famous Corvette. True, this styling has remained as constant as the old Model T, but largely restricted to monied people of the male sex. A woman's personal viewpoint about cars, until very recently, has not been asked about or explored in a serious way. In fact, according to sociologist Erving Goffman in his recent *Gender Advertisements* (1979), (which did not focus on car advertisements, but whose thesis I have found to include them), women tend to be treated like children, not to be taken seriously.[8]

Something is wrong in logic apparently: either non-serious women have influenced car sales or serious men would like to think so. Both are true: women are less serious about cars, and men are more romantic. That is, men tend to impute to cars more value than women tend to feel, yet have increasingly selected cars to please

---

[7]Quoted in the *New York Times* for October 16, 1977 (Automobile section).

[8]Erving Goffman, *Gender Advertisements*, pp. 25–83.

women. That is a conundrum which I cannot explain except by a faltering of male ego. The subject is worth pursuing. Marshall McLuhan noted in 1964 that a man's car was as much an item of his dress as a vehicle of motion. And who but men have made cars over into art objects and converted many Sundays into an almost religious ceremony of "polishing the car"? (Indeed, the Car Wash has become a national institution, even a kind of club for young men who work inside, preferably, to be sure, with a few women workers.) Another version of the stylistic revolution in cars credits changing times coupled with advertising: both men and women have wanted to keep up-to-date with "modern progress," and Alfred P. Sloan, Jr.'s style designers at General Motors were selling progress. But Sloan, who started it all, seems not to have had his eye so much on women as on Europe, where Americans have habitually looked for culture, style, and examples of prestigious consumption. He imported European designers to help give the box-like American car the long, low European look. Later, he wrote in 1964, the firm employed women as automobile designers, "to express the woman's point of view. We were the first to do so," he believed, "and today we have the largest number of them in the industry."[9]

The woman's point of view in car culture was heard more frequently as increasing numbers of women entered the American work force. By 1970, one of every two adult women was gainfully employed, constituting some forty percent of the total work force. Although most of these continued to occupy inferior positions at lower pay than men, some of the old stereotypes about women began to disappear. The one about speed, for instance, had been perpetuated into the 1960s. A writer for *Road and Track* once observed that "most females don't like hairy driving." Stirling Moss, a racing champion who, as he said, "never found a woman who . . . enjoyed speed for its own sake," thought women would do better, though not as well as the top men, at rallying, which ran against the clock and valorized the kind of minute detail and patience that women were good at: "But women will not compete, as the Spanish say, *mano-a-mano*, hand-to-hand." Hardly ten years later, this view was seriously challenged by both men and women. A 1978 study of professional rallying in *Sports Car* magazine found that women held top positions

[9]Alfred P. Sloan, Jr., *My Years with General Motors* (New York: Harold Matson Company, 1964), pp. 264–278, 273. See also Paul C. Wilson, *Chrome Dreams: Automobile Styling Since 1893* (Radnor, Pa.: The Chilton Book Co., 1976).

in organization, planning, and driving; further, that they tended to be competitive over-achievers who desired to be accepted for their ability and responded to the thrill of "flat-out insanity averaging 70 mph over fields, through forests and into trees."[10] Meanwhile, Janet Guthrie was qualifying for the Indianapolis 500, gem of male speed-sters.

Women now hold responsible positions in the car culture that formerly would have gone to men. One that partially confirms a feminine stereotype in its concern for automotive safety as opposed to speed is presently held by Joan Claybrook, who heads the national Highway Traffic Administration. But Martha Lorini has been the automotive editor of a sports magazine read mostly by men. Women have virtually swarmed into the car repair industry, mostly as me-chanics to be sure, some as fans of the do-it-yourself movement, a few as widows who have taken over their dead husbands' small garages. Anne Duncan of General Motors' mobile training van, stationed in Tucson, Arizona, says, "I'm going to get promoted, and some day have a big oak desk and about 50 men working under me."[11] Such evidence as we have suggests that, for better or worse, not only are more women than ever before aspiring to executive positions in the design, manufacture, care, and regulation of cars, but they share with men a visceral attachment to cars. Chevrolet recently revealed that nearly seventy percent of its racy Camaros were sold to women.[12] These cars, preferred for automatic transmissions and other conveniences, have been called "secretary specials." More astounding as a trend, however, has been the frank expression of feminine libido and identity linked with cars.

Thomas Pynchon, in his novel *V* (1961), satirizes this connection. He has Rachel Owlglass fondling, caressing, addressing her car as a "beautiful stud" while Benny Profane, observing, becomes jealous. It is no mere male fantasy. The talk-show host for KGBS in Los Angeles, Bill Balance, was surprised that so many women callers "dreamed about having Porsches or Mark IV's . . . They dream about

---

[10]Dick O'Kane, "O'Kane, on Love," *Road and Track* (August 1968), pp. 84–5; Stirling Moss with Ken W. Purdy, *All But My Life* (New York: Dutton, 1963), pp. 161–163. Steve Nickless and Tim Cline, "An Introduction to SCCA Pro Rallying," *Sports Car* (March 1978), pp. 28–9, 36–7.

[11]"Women in Auto Mechanics," *The Motorist* (July and August 1978), p. 11. There have been a number of such studies recently.

[12]In *Automotive News* (August 1978), p. 9. I thank Mr. Richard Tice for this information.

cars, man!" Much as men, he reported, they cruised the freeways looking for pickups. "If you see a man driving a VW," said one, "you know he's not much of a stud. But if you see a guy cruising around in a big Buick, you know he's got to be a virile swinger."[13] Some women, according to Balance, spent their whole lives on the freeway looking for amorous adventure. We have no reason to believe that such behavior is restricted to the Los Angeles area, because we have seen it elsewhere. Women have written odes to their cars, set up monuments for a "faithful car," and wanted to be buried in a car, seated in the driver's seat.[14] In a recent poem (1980), Nikki Giovanni settles for a high:

> i love the aloneness of the road
> when i ascend descending curves
> the power within my toe delights me
> and i fling my spirit down the highway
> i love the way i feel
> when i pass the moon and i holler to the
> stars
> i'm coming through
> Beep Beep

Nothing has done more to upset stereotypes of women as passive receptors of men's will than the entry of women into the last male stronghold, at least in peacetime.

Men have understandably been slow to acknowledge this truth, for it means relinquishing power. A source of irony, nevertheless, is that although women have greatly influenced the purchase of family cars for many years and have bought their own cars by millions during the last twenty-five years, car advertisements directed to women have seldom appeared in women's magazines, and then only very recently under the stimulus of the feminist movement. Since 1977, students at Rensselaer Polytechnic Institute under my supervision have taken note of this situation. We ran Rokeach value surveys in our classes containing almost as many women as men, followed by car questionnaires; and we monitored magazine advertisements. This

[13]Quoted by Steven V. Roberts, "Ode to a Freeway," *The New York Times Magazine* (April 15, 1973), pp. 38–40.

[14]This information comes from various news reports for which I have notations but not source references. The poetry below comes from Nikki Giovanni, *Cotton Candy on a Rainy Day* (New York: A Morrow Quill Book, 1980).

was a modest experiment from which few generalizations can be made, but is nevertheless suggestive. The students in the survey numbered 32 women and 47 men, mostly from the Northeast with a sprinkling from the rest of the nation. They were mostly middle-class, with women slightly older, ranging in age from 19 to 52 because of their heavier enrollment in a graduate class for technical writers. The control group was a small class of 17 men and one woman in my seminar, *On Wheels*, that best represented the typical engineering student.

In the car questionnaire, the control group came out as expected, with but a single surprise: it rated romantic love higher than cars. But so did men in the other classes. In the other classes women rated cars higher than romantic love! As one woman technical writer said, "I give highest priority to my car since I am family breadwinner." The male vote for romantic love in a resounding majority is easily explained, since cars follow a close second above all else. The control group owned more cars, drove them farther, belonged to more car clubs, subscribed to more car magazines, paid more attention to car ads, and objected more bitterly to government regulation than did the other groups. But the women who rated cars high did not follow through in this way. They did not join car clubs, for instance, or follow ads; and to a woman they favored government regulation.

Several studies of women's magazines during the same period, 1977–1979, turned up relatively few car ads designed expressly for women. That there were any ads at all caused one male student investigator to write, "It's not a male-dominated society anymore" [sic].[15] He found reprints of car ads from family and men's magazines, but also a few that were different. To understand the full meaning of these ads, however, it is necessary to place them in some perspective. In 1977, although three-fourths of the domestic cars in the United States were owned by men, over 42 percent of their principal drivers were women. In the same year 63.7 million women were licensed drivers, their percentage having almost doubled since 1940. In 1977, they bought 25 percent of domestic cars sold and 30 percent of the imported.[16] That was a considerable chunk of the

[15]David Abrams, "Just for Her," R.P.I. student essay.

[16]This data was compiled in *Buyers of New Domestic Cars, 1977* and *Buyers of New Imported Cars, 1977* (Copyright 1977, Newsweek, Inc.). Cited by Peter Miranda, "The Concept of Women in Automobile Advertisements," an R.P.I. student essay. Miranda also interviewed a number of women students. I am indebted to him as well for my next citation.

market, quite apart from the more indirect influence women had on total car sales. Nevertheless, one would never guess this importance from an inspection of general commercial advertising which included car ads. A variety of marketing studies about this time found not only that masculine/feminine roles were always represented in commercial advertising, but that the following sexual stereotypes were dominant:

1. Woman's place is in the home.
2. Women do not make important decisions.
3. Women are dependent on men.
4. Women are to be thought of primarily as sex objects.
5. Women do not drive in cars except in the company of men.

This was the scene, then, that greeted car ads for women.[17]

The first such ad to be examined, from *McCall's*, shows a rather jaunty young housewife in slacks unloading a bag of groceries from the back of her new AMC Pacer, which is parked in front of her colonial-style suburban home. Two children, a boy and a girl, wait at the entrance. The accompanying text stresses practicality without loss of individuality. The source of individuality is not explained, for the framed display ritualizes a familiar event in almost any prosperous American family: the housewife's shopping expedition. The woman's subordinate role is implied in subtle arrangements. Her pose is somewhat puckish, that is, lacking in seriousness or childlike; and she is associated with children. The children, as in the traditional family pattern are two, a boy and a girl. Another ad in the same magazine celebrates "Mom's Omni" with a similar family triad, this time standing close together in front of the car, the young mother's hands protectively clasped around the two children's shoulders. The car display, with its ritualization of motherhood, is almost completely surrounded by print extolling the car's low gas consumption, low sticker price, fine mechanical features, standard equipment, and options. Several things about this ad are noteworthy. The woman's

---

[17]William J. Lundstrom and Donald Sciglimpaglia, "Sex Role Portrayals in Advertising," *Journal of Marketing*, XLI (July 1977), pp. 72–9; also Phyllis Haberman and Donald E. Sexton, "Women in Magazine Advertisements," *Journal of Advertising Research*, III (August 1974), pp. 41–6; Alice E. Courtney and Sarah W. Lockeretz, "A Woman's Place: An Analysis of the Roles Portrayed by Women in Magazine Advertisements," *Journal of Marketing Research*, VIII (February 1971), pp. 92–5.

hands are important as part of the parent-child complex, as is her smile. Women are pictured smiling more often and more broadly than men. This woman, although she receives the compliment of being expected to know something about the car's engineering and to care about the energy crisis and the family budget, is not expected to go to the Dodge dealer unaccompanied. The ad ends: "And bring dad along. If things go the way they should, you and he will end up buying . . . the car. . . ."[18] Magazines for housewives like *McCall's*, *House and Garden*, and *Ladies' Home Journal* do not avoid sexual stereotyping in their car ads.

A woman is not expected to give testimonials for cars, but Lauren Bacall has done just that, both on television and in women's magazines. In *Cosmopolitan*, for instance, she is pictured standing slightly behind a Ford Fairmont Futura with a hand holding her coat tight to her waist. The lead caption reads, "I like cars that look good on me. Like the new Fairmont Futura." A small box below the large display reveals a lush interior, and below that we see Lauren's personalized ignition keys. Her hand, of course, calls attention to her slimline waist and fashionable coat. It is a sexist ad, because it evokes the stereotype that women care only for appearances, style, and comfort. The fashion magazines *Vogue* and *Harper's Bazaar* also cultivate this image. For departures from standard sexist roles in advertising, one must look chiefly to the feminist magazine *MS*. A recent ad shows Wendy Turnbull, the tennis star, poking her disheveled locks up through the open sun-window of a VW Rabbit parked on a tennis court. She carries a tennis racket in the crook of her arm. The caption reads, "She's not called Wendy 'The Rabbit' Turnbull for Nothing." The text points out that both car and woman are like their animal namesake—fast, sprightly, and agile. While this ad is not unique in presenting the car as an identity machine, it is quite clever in the way its photography merges the body of the woman with that of the car; and its testimonial, relaxed and chatty, is aimed at women in a nontraditional sports role, vying with men.

The last ad worth looking at, also from *MS*., completely reverses traditional roles. Traditionally, when men and women are shown together, the woman is made subordinate in a number of ways: by relative size, by function-ranking, by ritualized behavior with hands,

---

[18]These ads were culled by my students between 1978 and March 1980 as being typical. The analysis, however, is my own, based on the dramaturgical method of Erving Goffman, *op. cit.*

feet, and posture, and by what Erving Goffman has called signs of "licensed withdrawal": childish expressions of fear, shyness, distraction, and the like. In this ad, however, a young woman executive is standing boldly in front of an Oldsmobile Omega carrying plane tickets and a briefcase while three male garage attendants busily prepare her car for travel. She seems to tower over both the car and the men, yet is attractively feminine, dressed in longish skirt and lighter-colored open jacket. The sun beats down, causing her to stand out from the strong shadows. A student who analyzed this ad wrote that it fitted *MS*. magazine's image of the liberated woman: "This advertisement depicts the women's desired sense of identity and prestige."[19] But the same student thought that a hot, sexy Ferrari was not likely to appear in *MS*.; the liberated woman was not ready for anything hotter than the rather staid Oldsmobile Omega. Perhaps he is right. Nevertheless, women have been owning and driving Ferraris and other foreign sports cars for a long time. If there is anything traditional about this ad, it is the pledging of women to the same kind of success symbols that have characterized men.

The magazine *Woman's Day* has recently taken the lead in examining this whole situation. In 1979, in cooperation with the National Automobile Dealers Association it commissioned Audits & Surveys, Inc., to study the habits of dealers and consumers in the car-purchasing process.[20] There were 489 completed dealer interviews nation-wide and 1,002 completed interviews with new car buyers. Interviewers discovered significant differences between how dealers saw their women customers and how women customers really acted. The dealers, for instance, seriously underestimated women's incomes and influence in the purchase of cars. The belief that women were influential in purchasing cars for their style, color, and comfort turned out to be mostly a figment of male imaginations. The study found that when women were interested in buying cars, they considered first such things as economy, reliability, durability, and handling. Moreover, 62 percent of the women who shopped with a man were "very influential" in the ultimate selection—50 percent more than the dealers believed! Compared to individual male buyers, indi-

---

[19]James Spicer, "Farrah Fawcett Comes to R.P.I.," an R.P.I. student essay.

[20]*Women and Automobiles: A Study of Dealers and Consumers in the Car Purchasing Process* (A Joint Project of Woman's Day Magazine, National Automobile Dealers Association and Audits & Surveys, Inc., 1979).

vidual women had little brand loyalty in new car purchases. Some 90 percent said they would replace their old cars with different makes or models. In the matter of customer treatment, a large majority of dealers thought they treated women equally with men. Only 52 percent of women agreed; and most of the rest considered that they were treated unfavorably: dealers didn't take them seriously, or acted as if they didn't know anything about cars, or avoided discussion of price. In short, these same dealers, much like advertisers, have overlooked a major market.

It should now be possible to say something authoritative about the American Eve's position in the car culture. Of course, the American Eve is not a singular entity. In this essay I have not been able to survey all her sisters at every age and in different parts of the country belonging to different races, different social classes, and different churches. One thing that can be said with certainty, though, is that whether she considers the car a chariot of the gods or a devil-machine in her lovely garden, this mythical Eve has been far more important to the development of the car culture than men have wanted to believe. Peg Shiro, an automotive editor, has recently painted a dire picture filled with statistics of "what life would be like with no automobiles." A more interesting question, to my mind, is "what would the automobile be like without women?" Without women around, I'm sure, the automobile would soon have lost its savor and speed its thrill, for the automobile has always served and expressed power, but mainly the power to attract the opposite sex. The great irony is that the more women have come into this domain of power, the more begrudgingly have men been willing to recognize or accede to their ascendancy.

An important issue raised early in this essay, whether the position of women has improved or declined because of their involvement with the automobile, probably cannot be settled conclusively here. If Henry Adams were still alive, he might conclude that women have exchanged the power of the Virgin for the blind, corrupting power of the car. Certainly, he thought that their exposure to machinery, working and competing with men, robbed them of femininity and somehow sapped that awesome mystery in their being that made them a fecund, unifying life force in art, religion, and society. The supreme importance young men attach to romantic love suggests that such has not happened. On the other hand, we have met too many examples of unsatisfying, shallow sexuality associated with cars and cheap success to have much faith in this kind of magic. Undoubtedly, the car has greatly helped to make women more independent, but too often at the cost of their sense of identity and community. And the nature of this new independence needs more looking into, because it may be largely illusory.

NOT FROM THE BACK SEAT

The car is America and America is the car. The car is the myth and metaphor for America. We've all heard this since Henry Ford, back in the Dark Ages, invented the thing.

Yet like everything else in this country that involves speed, power and a lot of reckless insanity, the car has always been associated with the male: he got drunk in it and usually wrecked it and miraculously survived (or didn't), he used it to augment and bolster a failed ego, he made it into a dangerous weapon, he transformed it into a substitute for the penis he wondered if he had (enough of), he used it to ensure upward mobility, he went on the road to escape in it, and he made time, and babies, with as many women as he could persuade to explore the back seat with him.

But just as there were women in covered wagons, there have also been women in cars. The car was not invented, hasn't existed, solely for the purposes of the American Adam. Not if I am an example. My past life is riddled with memories of the car. I'd feel like a kid brought up with six hours of television a day who then has it snatched away if the car were taken from my life—how else could I have survived, what would I have done without it? So the car was omnipresent. Only my need for it and my attitude toward it changed.

This may partially be due to having been raised in the red hills of Mississippi, in Faulkner country, where if you didn't have a car you didn't move around much. A farm woman who does not drive always has been and continues to be a prisoner of her home. But I am quite sure that the car has not meant the same thing to me, a woman, as it meant to a man. For a man it is an extension of the self. For a woman it is generally a means to an end, a method of most expeditiously getting from one place to another. It is, rather than an extension of the self, a means of adornment, like a designer's dress. It is one of the primary means of setting female off from male.

I grew up on a farm four miles from a town of 2500 people. I remember when we did not have a car. My father bought and sold cattle, and transported us in his huge rattling truck wherever we

153

went: to Memphis to visit aunts and uncles once yearly (we took the sideboards off, carried a picnic feast, and swung our legs off the sides of the bed all the way down and back), to church and the yearly summer revival meetings, to town on Saturday afternoon for the week's groceries.

Then suddenly we had this spiffy new Pontiac, a lumbering tank of a car. I was ten years old, and this first car meant freedom and pleasure. I later learned it meant, to my father, status, but nobody I knew thought of such a thing then. It meant Sunday afternoon drives to relatives and friends, a double feature plus a serial at the only picture show in town, a trip to Memphis even in the winter. It also meant hours of working alongside five brothers when the damned thing got stuck in the red clay, which was any time you went out in the winter, since most of the roads weren't gravelled and lay like red gashes through the countryside.

I was raised quite differently from most American women, and certainly differently from the (myth of the) southern belle with her mint juleps and debutante balls and inclinations toward utter helplessness. A farm girl, I was expected to "pull my weight." And did. I plowed, picked and hoed cotton, fed the farm animals, milked, shucked corn for chickens and hogs, and did all of it as well as my brothers. I had to or risk being unmercifully teased for being a sissy. I played baseball with the best of them, asked no handicap in fights with my brothers, claimed no sympathy at "that time of the month."

But one thing did set me apart from my brothers. The car. As far as my father was concerned, women rode in cars and otherwise didn't go near them. Boys? Growing old enough to learn to drive, getting behind the wheel for the first time was a rite of initiation into adult American society. The myth of the automobile, from that point on, engulfed them and swept them along as if their individuality were beside the point. One had to make out in it. One had to roar down narrow, crooked country roads like a "bat outa hell." One had to groom the old Pontiac (later the Plymouth and finally the Chrysler) as a horsetrainer groomed a champion. And, before one left home, one had to have had at least one tremendous wreck driving while drunk or flaunting one's life as a daredevil, and survive it. Otherwise, one was not a man.

I watched each of my brothers demolish a car and walk, grinning like one of God's Chosen, away from it. I watched my father—a man who made Scrooge look like a philanthropist—almost smile when yet another son came home alive, while yet another car was wrapped around a tree or in a creek somewhere, waiting to be towed to the junkyard.

I remember being angry only because I was not allowed the same privilege. I associated nothing with my being a female. I didn't even notice that my mother and older sister didn't drive and seemed to feel they shouldn't want to. All I knew was that my father wouldn't let me get behind a wheel and that it was grossly unfair. I *did* learn to drive, though. And not because I realized it would give me the freedom my mother and sister lacked. No. I absolutely intended to do everything my brothers did. If I could keep up with them in farm chores, I could sure as hell drive a dumb car as well as any of them. (How did I learn? My brothers taught me. They thought it was a gas balancing me in their laps and letting me steer and then, my God!, even working the brakes and the clutch.)

My father tells his story through a car, too. He had, for one thing, a sense of taste. The Pontiac gave way to the sleeker Plymouth. Many Plymouths, actually, since he insisted on buying a new model each year, and since I had those brothers to wreck at least five along the way. Handing the keys to a son was serious business, man's business, and always accompanied by the sternest of lectures: don't you drive over 55, don't you git drunk, don't load the thing up with roughneck boys whose daddies couldn't make enough money to buy a horse much less a car, and don't let nobody else git behind that wheel but you.

After a while he didn't even bother to get out of bed when another car was wrecked. He would just groan, almost in pleasure, then turn over and go back to sleep. This was, in a sense, strange, too— because his car, whatever it was, always got more attention and open affection than any other thing on the farm (including children) except for our old shepherd dog Smoky.

After he switched to Chryslers one of the biggest pleasures of his old age was to go to Memphis dressed in his faded overalls, khaki shirt, and manure-covered brogans and to walk into a dealer's show-room. Salesmen, of course, ignored him. He poked around the showroom until he found the car he wanted and then, astounding an embarrassed salesman, plunked down the three thousand or so the thing cost. (And he would come home and laugh for weeks at the look on their face.)

But it remained a male's prerogative to drive. The last Chrysler that he bought had an automatic transmission. The salesman had started it off for him in Memphis. When he got home he wanted to drive it around and show it off to his sons and son-in-law. But he couldn't get the damned gears to "do right." I knew how to drive by then and happened to be at home. I went out, started the car, and showed him how the shifts worked—but he never let me get behind the steering wheel again. And would not admit to a soul that a woman, a daughter, had served as his tutor.

So my brothers grew up and moved out into society. The car, of course, was their symbol of success, and always the first thing they bought after marriage. Those who identified with my father bought Chryslers; those who unconsciously rebelled bought Buicks or Continentals.

There were no established rituals to help me through my own initiation into adulthood rites. But the car, serendipitously, nevertheless was there. I wanted to go to college and had to fight my father for the privilege. He finally found it necessary to admit I could drive, and insisted I go each day to a community college twenty miles from home and major in home economics. I refused. I wanted to go to a sort of Vassar of the south, downstate 110 miles, and major in art. I had my first and only screaming battle with him, and got my way. But I had to finance my own education and steel myself against his cold green eyes when, a painter, I came home (always of course in a car with a man at the wheel).

When I got to college, I had (caught, whatever one does) anorexia nervosa. I graduated in three years and took a train out of the south to Philadelphia. Then, when I wasted away to 76 pounds, I had to go back home.

My father drove the car that delivered me for a three-month stay in the state mental hospital. He did not want to spend the money required to send me to a private institution (shades of Eugene O'Neill!), so he enlisted my entire family as well as the only doctor in town and pressured me into agreeing to go, on the condition that after their first visit, when a month had expired they would drive me away if I couldn't stand it. I couldn't stand it, but I had gained no weight and though I begged my father, on my knees, to sign me out, he refused. I stayed three months. And was taken home in his newest Chrysler.

I left home as soon as possible to take a job with the Air Force in Memphis. And bought my own car. It saved my life. It saved my life because, suddenly, something depended upon me for its well-being and upkeep. It became my baby, and I was able to lavish upon it the care and love I felt no human would accept from me. It was a white

Plymouth Fury III with red upholstery. It had a style and dash that, at the time, I sadly needed. Whenever I felt the institutional past and its depression moving to take over my life, I simply got into it and drove until I could live with myself and until the thoughts had gone back to sleep.

But I was a woman and women were not, then, supposed to own cars that they had paid for out of their own earnings. The fates were therefore against me. The brass at the air base discovered I had been in a nuthouse and relieved me of my job. Humiliated, I got into my carriage and made an escape back to Philadelphia. I couldn't find a job. I had paid three-quarters of the installments on the car, but one month couldn't meet a payment. I phoned my father, begging him to meet just this payment, as he had met payments for my brothers. He refused the $75 and, on a bitter winter morning, the Household Finance Company sent out a cracker-type yokel who dug my Plymouth out of four feet of snow and drove it away.

Finding my way by train to New York, I settled there, and, unexpectedly, found pleasure in being rid of the American car. I came to curse people who drove their smoking exhausts through my front yard, poisoning me with their selfish egomania and dulling my brain with horns that blared madly at 3 a.m, as if they were drag racing on a lonely country road in Mississippi. I joined anti-pollution groups and resented each and every engine that passed on the street below my apartment. My dormant Methodist fervor for justice again reared its sleepy head, and I directed a long-forgotten Lord to banish the automobile not only from the city but also from people's minds.

Then I was offered a job teaching at a community college on Long Island. I needed a car. To produce the $2500 I needed to buy a good used one, I sold my rights to our farm in Mississippi. My brothers gloated and had a great laugh. They'd ripped me off and both parties knew it, but we both knew I was pretty much caught between a rock and a hard place. Another Plymouth, this time a convertible, red with black top and white interior.

I kept it for three years. The job on the Island became a college in North Carolina, and I drove back and forth between North Carolina and a New York apartment I wouldn't give up, five times a year. When I returned from North Carolina, I took a job in the city schools to be near theatres and publishing houses. And my baby became a nuisance. Because my apartment was rent controlled, I spent more to house the car than myself. There was no way I could park it in my midtown neighborhood. If I left it at an up or downtown garage, I still had to bus to pick it up. It was stolen by kids who smashed up the rear and left it filled with empty bottles of cheap beer. Many times I got in to drive to work, only to find that someone had "borrowed" a part during the night.

So I drove it back to Mississippi, to what I believed was the safekeeping of my sister. I am not sure exactly what happened, but I am told my brother-in-law called the local scrap metal dealer to come out and clear the front yard of the destroyed cars that my nephews collected to work on when they weren't in the fields—and that somehow my baby was also flattened in the process. So much for a birthright.

I have neither had nor wanted a car for many years now. Gas and rental have become so expensive that I cannot even escape to the country when the city gets too much for me. I have again come to hate the huge hulks that gorge and prey on the city, and the insensitive bastards who roar through red lights, sit on horns, screech to a stop two feet from my person, and send great clouds of death into my unsuspecting face.

But the car is still with me. It has become my enemy only in an external, physical sense. Internally, psychically, it continues to mean to me what it once meant physically: the most expeditious method of moving from one point to another. My psyche chooses cars to signify inner growth or movement. I dream, in short, of cars. In one dream, there is a long and precipitously steep mountain which must be driven up. I am always driving when I start up. I go up a quarter of the distance, then one half, then three-quarters. But the road is narrow and quite crooked, and there is no railing to prevent the car from plummeting off into empty space. As the terror of driving off, falling off, sliding off, becomes too much for me, I turn the wheel over to a man. Usually my father, sometimes a brother. He drives over the crest of the mountain and part of the way back down before I again take over the wheel.

The dream is repeated until one night I get three-quarters of the way up, stop and get ready to turn the wheel over to a man. Then, my heart raging with terror, I grit my teeth. "Damn it, I'm going to do it myself!" I do. The dream, the repetition, seems to be gone forever. Until I am ready to move again. And then back into the car I go, up the crooked road.

ROBERT M. LIENERT

MOVING BACKWARD

My parents were products of their time and place, and when they were married early in 1906, the automotive age had not yet reached Nebraska.

My father farmed with horses and gave them up reluctantly when tractors took over, much later.

As a bride, my mother had her own horse. It was a "buggy" horse. That is, it was not so big and awkward and cumbersome as a draft horse. When she wanted to visit a neighbor or go to town, she'd whistle for her horse and he'd come to the barn.

She could harness him and hitch him to the buggy and be on her way. As a result, she was more independent than were many farm wives.

My parents were married about fifteen years before they bought their first automobile. For my mother, the car did not lead to freedom or open the way to a mobile society.

As the family acquired cars and the "modern" age burst upon her, the private "buggy" horse was displaced. And my mother never learned to drive a car. I never asked why. But I recall that riding in a car made her nervous; and it would have been in character for my father to feel that only men drove cars.

My mother thus had to depend on someone else to take her when she wanted to go anywhere. And since my father often didn't wish to go places, my mother spent a lot more time at home in her mature years.

The automobile, rather than freeing her, confined her more than ever.

FOLKE T. KIHLSTEDT

THE AUTOMOBILE AND THE TRANSFORMATION OF THE AMERICAN HOUSE, 1910-1935

We in the United States have been living in the era of the automobile ever since September 1893, when Frank Duryea tested a one-cylinder carriage on the back streets of Springfield, Massachusetts. Within four years, America had an auto industry, as the Pope Manufacturing Company, the Stanleys, Ransom Olds, and Alexander Winton turned to automobile manufacturing. By 1908 General Motors was founded, Henry Ford began production of the Model T, and car registrations were nearing 400,000.

Fifteen years later, William Showalter reflected upon the rapid development of the automobile and wrote, "In 1898 there was one car in operation for every eighteen thousand people, each of them [the cars] a hybrid creation secured by crossing a bicycle with a buggy. . . . Today there is one motor vehicle to every eight people, and the worst of them is a marvel of silence and service." By 1920 the automobile was no longer merely a pleasurable pastime, it was a practical necessity. To serve it, an entirely new architectural infrastructure developed. Gasoline stations, bus terminals, roadside diners, motels, fast food restaurants, and urban parking garages were designed to meet the demands of automobile and traveler. By 1935, the architectural style of these new building types had developed from exotic and eye-catching forms to functional, efficient, and often standardized forms. The relationship between roadside architecture and the automobile is direct and obvious, since, in the words of one contemporary observer, "The thing that makes and marks The Machine Age is *The* Machine—The Car, The Automobile." Less obvious is the fact that equally radical changes reshaped our most basic and established building type, the private house.

In the mid-1920s, the car began to complement the house as an indicator of social position and prestige; at the same time, the functional plans and external forms of American houses changed. Such

160

social spaces as the parlor and front porch fell into disuse and atrophied. The garage, hidden at first at the back of the lot, merged into the house itself. The garage, or sometimes a carport, began to dominate the main facade by 1935. It displaced the traditional entry portal, usually centrally located on axis, and introduced a note of informality into the home.

These architectural changes were symptomatic of a new way of life that developed around the automobile. Though not as evident as the rapid development and changes in roadside architecture, alterations in residential form perhaps say more about the degree to which the car has affected our way of life. In fact, changing relationships between the garage, the front porch, and the parlor clearly underscore a major alteration in social and cultural patterns.

The function of the parlor and the porch was already shifting by the beginning of the century, and the car promoted this shift. By the time the Lynds made their first study of Middletown, they observed that "auto riding tends to replace the traditional call in the family parlor as a way of approach between the unmarried." They also noted that the family and neighbors no longer "spend long summer evenings and Sunday afternoons on the porch or in the side yard since the advent of the automobile and the movies. These factors tend to make a decorative yard less urgent; the make of one's car is rivaling the looks of one's place as an evidence of one's 'belonging.' "

The parlor and the porch were victims of the social and physical effects of the car. Socially, the personal freedom and mobility offered by the car offset the need for a large house with many rooms into which one could escape and seek privacy. The Lynds, in their follow-up study, discovered that Middletown residents had begun to place more value on an automobile than on home ownership during the 1930s. One social critic commented in 1932 that "the increase in ease of transport makes people look upon the home as little more than a dormitory." Though this judgment may seem exaggerated to us today, it did reflect a common attitude at the time. The European architect, Walter Behrendt, noted that modern man, "bent on his new freedom for moving around, made possible by the spread of the automobile . . . feels the excessive extent of his permanent residence as a constraint. . . . and therefore as a burden rather than as a comfort." The American designer Paul Frankl put it more bluntly when he said, "The accelerated tempo of contemporary living has swept away the home of the past."

As the car and its garage became integrated into the house proper, it rearranged the plan of the house and displaced the front porch and the parlor. In the earliest years of the automobile, the front porch still functioned as the buffer zone between the privacy of the house and the communality of the neighborhood. It was the place where family, friends, and neighbors communicated in an easy and informal way. Likewise, the parlor was always the front room of the house—the next important zone between the public and the private worlds. It was in this formal living room where members of the family met and entertained visitors who were not close or accepted intimates.

The parlor and the front porch supported a formal style of life. This style was built around an accepted social hierarchy in which a progression of architectural spaces, from front porch (or veranda) to hall to parlor to library (or sitting room) and to dining room, were related to increasing degrees of intimacy. Such a formality was hardly appropriate to what William Leuchtenburg has called the "hedonistic mood" of Americans in the 1920s, who preferred "driving in the country in the afternoon instead of sitting stiffly in the parlor."

The automobile, and the individual mobility it provided, contributed to a less formal life-style in many ways. For example, after 1910, families often picnicked by the side of the road rather than dining at the Sunday supper table; by 1930, barbecues and other roadside food stands would provide a meal to customers who never even stepped out of their car. Again, after 1910, auto-tourists, dirty and disheveled from the day's ride in an open car, increasingly avoided hotels and the disdainful glances of hotel staffs and chose the more welcoming informal environment of the motorcamp, and eventually of the motel. Moreover, owners of private houses chose to accommodate the growing number of auto-tourists by turning their houses into tourist homes and admitting strangers regularly as overnight guests. Aimless wanderings on a Sunday drive, unplanned sallies into the country after dinner, unannounced visits to a relative or friend were other automobile-inspired habits that contributed to a spontaneous and informal way of life. In a broader sense, the car broke down formal barriers, acting as a leveling force by bringing into intimate contact sections of the population which normally would never meet. It also aided in that grand escape from the formal life of the city—the exodus to the suburbs.

The suburban house, first called the country house, was the setting for this breakdown of the formality of late nineteenth-century life. The shift is best seen by comparing the plans of typical suburban houses of the decade before and the decade after our study. In contrast to a turn-of-the-century house, the house of 1945 has no hall, no parlor, and a mere vestige of a porch. The garage was moved from the back of the lot to the front of the suburban house, and adjacent to the front door, for purposes of convenience and efficiency. Entry is directly into the living and dining rooms, or into the kitchen through the adjoining garage. The element that projects farthest toward the street to greet the passer-by is no longer a shaded and generous porch. It is the large, prominent surface of the garage door. Visually, the house has lost the sense of volume when seen from the street. It has become flat and abrupt, and even the vestigial porch is usually omitted. In effect, the garage has replaced the porch in prominence. It has even replaced it in function, for most American families leave the garage door open all day and enter through the kitchen.

The early garage was, as J. B. Jackson has noted, physically and psychologically isolated from the house. The object it sheltered, like the horse, produced noxious fumes, smells, noise and dirt (and, in addition, the potential for explosion). Thus, the natural place for the car was in a stable toward the rear of the property.

For patrons who owned both horses and cars, architects designed individual structures serving as stable, with hay loft, and as garage, with gasoline storage. By 1910, however, the car had become reliable enough to replace rather than merely to supplement the horse and carriage. Many estates boasted extensive garage-houses, providing space to store, repair, clean and recharge the automobiles, as well as to accommodate the chauffeur and his family. These garages were substantial, architect-designed buildings; more often than not, they harmonized, in style and materials, with the main house. The partners of one Boston architectural firm caught the prevailing attitude about garages when, in 1911, they remarked that they sought to provide the patron with "a well developed building which will be an ornament to his place as well as mere housing for his machine." They offered the owners a choice of styles and materials, but only within the traditionally accepted eclectic modes of the period. A garage such as the one for W.K. Jackson in Buffalo (Fig. 1) is nearly indistinguishable from a house. One might say that the garage was a house well before the house contained a garage.

But the process that led to the suburban house of today was no mere transformation of the garage-house of 1910 from chauffeur's quarters to owner's dwelling. Rather, the process was complicated by an aesthetic conflict between radical architects, intent upon

Fig. 1: Garage for W. K. Jackson, Buffalo, New York, by McCreary,
    Wood and Bradney, before 1911.

integrating the garage into the house, and conservatives, committed
to maintaining the visual and physical purity of the house. The
conflict transcended any distinctions between nonpedigreed vernacular architecture and sophisticated architect-designed buildings. It
began around 1910 and lasted for about twenty-five years, ending
with the acceptance of the integrated garage and house around 1935.

For people of moderate means the chief concern was not housing a
chauffeur, but affording the garage, which was necessary mainly as a
protection for their open automobile. They built this accessory structure at the back edge of their lots, often accessible from an alley.
Many of these garages were "portable" prefabricated structures of
modular construction. Lacking any aesthetic merit whatsoever, these
garages were camouflaged with trellises and plantings. "The majority
of owners are really ashamed of their garages and therefore endeavor
to keep them from view," lamented an architect in 1924, who
proceeded to implore his readers to "build a garage that may be
worthy of standing alongside your house."

More substantial and permanent garages did just this. Henry
Saylor, in a pattern book on homes of moderate cost written in 1911,
welcomed the garage, which "lends itself delightfully as an architectural element in planning the group of buildings of a country place or

The
STUDEBAKER
Garage

THIS beautiful half
timbered stucco ga-
rage is designed not only
to comfortably accom-
modate two cars, but to
match up with similar
types of stucco homes.

SIZES:

Plan No. 1 . . . . 20' x 20'
Plan No. 2 . . . . 22' x 22'

The PAIGE
Garage

A THREE-CAR ga-
rage which will
match almost any type
of home. Provision is
made for plenty of work
room around each car.

SIZES:

Plan No. 1 . . . . 30' x 20'
Plan No. 2 . . . . 32' x 22'

The CADILLAC
Garage

A GARAGE substan-
tially designed in
brick with tile roof.
Will comfortably accom-
modate three large cars,
with plenty of work
space.

SIZES:

Plan No. 1 . . . . 32' x 20'
Plan No. 2 . . . . 34' x 22'

Fig. 2: Selection of detached garages, by Home Builders Catalog
Co., 1928.

town house." He saw the garage as one of a number of building elements to be used in composing the grounds of a country estate. Between the two extremes of "portable" garages and elaborate custom-designed structures, an infinite number of garage types served the middle-class house. The popular 1928 Home Builders pattern book illustrated at least sixty different garages in wood, brick or half-timbered Tudor, for example, to complement its varied house designs (Fig. 2). Whether architect-designed or prefabricated, the garage, as the editors of *House and Garden* observed in 1925, was assuming architectural importance.

By the end of the second decade of the twentieth century, the existence of separate garages was commonplace with most new homes. In densely populated areas with narrow lots, the garage was necessarily placed in close proximity to the house, its access drive defining one side of the property line. In more elegant suburbs, it was related to the main house by a large service yard, or actually connected by a roofed walkway. In all these cases, the house and the garage retain their separate identities. They are still physically and psychologically isolated from each other.

Physical isolation was often enforced by zoning regulations, building codes and fire laws, which prohibited any direct opening between a garage and a house. There were some interesting exceptions to this rule, however, both on the level of *ad hoc* alterations to existing houses, and on the level of sophisticated architectural design. On the one hand, stories were told of zealous new car owners, who dug trenches under their front porches and called them garages, or who built drawbridges from the attic of their houses to the adjacent hillside and parked their car directly below the eaves. Of these *ad hoc* solutions, basement garages were the most common mode of integration. A finished basement would normally have a fireproof concrete floor, and the lower level would contain and isolate fumes from the living quarters. On the other hand, a particularly good example of an architect-designed basement garage is the residence of T.S. Estabrook in Oak Park, Illinois. Designed in 1908 by Tallmadge and Watson, members of the Chicago Prairie School, it takes advantage of an intersecting cross plan to give the car its own access wing to the rear (Fig. 3).

Four years earlier, Frank Lloyd Wright had planned to incorporate a basement garage in a similar fashion on the Edwin H. Cheney house, also in Oak Park. However, such early examples of integrating house and garage were the exception. They demonstrate unusual

Fig. 3: House of T. S. Estabrook, Oak Park, Illinois, rear view
showing garage entrance, by Tallmadge and Watson, 1908.

foresight and willingness to adapt to new conditions on the part of
specific architects and clients without being evidence of a nationwide
trend. As late as the 1930s, traditional architects were still reluctant
to incorporate the automobile into the house.

Nevertheless, such an integration was inevitable. A 1937 study in
Architectural Record could claim, "The garage has become a very
essential part of the residence"; a year earlier, a study on low-cost
housing sponsored by Purdue University listed a garage as a necessity for all projects submitted; while in the previous decade architect
Charles White had claimed that "the garage has come to be quite as
much a part of the requirements of a home as a cellar, the porch, or
the kitchen." Moreover, consumer demand for a garage was so
prevalent that by 1925 real estate dealers agreed that "the house
without a garage is a slow seller." Still, until the Thirties, a garage
was generally kept separate, if only to maintain lower home insurance
rates which increased if a door connected garage to house. In fact,
during the 1920s, the garage was often referred to as an "accessory"

to the house, implying that it was considered separate or added on, rather than integral.

The aesthetic shock of large, blank garage doors was the primary hindrance to integration for many architects and homeowners. They felt that the garage should be invisible, and should camouflage its function. The *Architectural Forum* exulted over a garage in Norwalk, Connecticut in 1927 because it "so successfully . . . tied into the design of the house that it is not only an integral part of it but also from the front its purpose is not evident." When a separate garage is being planned, suggests Gilbert Murtagh in *Small Houses*, it can be made to resemble a pergola or shelter, and thus blend in with the garden.

Landscaping a garage, or designing it in a picturesque mode could effectively subordinate it to the house. Yet, to do this was to avoid the creative challenge of designing a totally unified dwelling for the Machine Age. A car is a large object, and a two-car garage requires an area close to 400 square feet, or about one-third of the total area of a small house by today's standards. Multicar families existed very early, and in 1911 architects Kilham and Hopkins spoke from experience when they urged a client "to provide more than enough room for his actual needs, for the second car follows easily after the first." Some architects balked at the challenge, claiming that "to attach two or three car stalls to a house of modest size is to distort it, to make the tail wag the dog." Other architects attempted to design houses that could absorb the addition of a garage with no noticeable damage to their aesthetic balance. One found that adding a garage onto a house created a "low, rambling character which is so often desirable in a country house"; while in the same year, 1925, another architect claimed to make a standard practice of building the garage into the house, thus improving "the appearance of a small house by giving a larger ground area and therefore better proportions to the house." In this case, the architect used the garage as a status symbol, enlarging the house and declaring that the car was part of the family.

In 1930, the architectural periodical, *Pencil Points*, announced a nationwide competition for an eight-room house with a two-car garage. Written into the program was the statement that the hypothetical owners preferred "that the garage be directly connected to the house." The more modernistic entries, clearly inspired by the European International Style, brought forth some vituperative responses from conservative readers. In particular, architect Hedley B. Sevaldsen railed at "garage doors on the front of a residence facing a street or public highway." They were offensive and aesthetically inappropriate. The car, he argued, "is not an interior ornament." He declared war on "this onslaught—the garage in the house and to the front" which "has swept the country like the other pestilence, jazz-music, and is now enthroned in the high seat and termed 'modern!' "

Defenders of the new arrangement were not armed with the rhetorical skills of Sevaldsen, nor did they have to be. Progress was on their side. Responding to Sevaldsen's attacks, E.V. Austin, an architect from Texas, concluded a letter simply by invoking the future: "I believe with Norman Bel Geddes that remarkable changes will appear in the next ten years."

The changes to which he was referring, and which had inspired the futuristic work of Bel Geddes, an industrial designer, were embodied in the new spirit of the machine proposed by European architects such as Erich Mendelsohn and Le Corbusier. The latter's book, published in 1923 and translated in 1927 as *Towards a New Architecture*, claimed that "modern life demands, and is waiting for, a new kind of plan, both for the house and for the city." Inspired in part by Frederick W. Taylor's *Principles of Scientific Management* and the American industrial examples of efficiency and mass production, Le Corbusier referred throughout his book to the house as "a machine for living in." Such aesthetic shifts in value and perception were bound to threaten a majority of practicing architects, especially those as conservative as Sevaldsen. In Le Corbusier's vision of a functionalist machine-age architecture, "the exterior is a result of the interior." Applying this dictum to the design of a house with integrated garage, modernist architects were obliged to expose the garage and its enormous blank doors. Le Corbusier's Villa Stein at Garches provided a perfect model (Fig. 4). The entry facade is dominated by the garage door on the left (painted red in at least one early color rendering). It balances a ribbon window on the right and a window of equivalent area in the center, to form a three-part major division on the facade. The entry door to the right of center is a secondary element by comparison. In this design, Le Corbusier has recognized the garage as a functionally and aesthetically valid component of the house. Such European buildings, and the theories behind them, influenced American architecture through the work of émigrés such as Richard Neutra, Rudolf Schindler, and William Lescaze, and by an increasing appearance of modernist theories in our architectural periodicals. In 1929, following some similar statements by Lescaze, Chicago architect Howard T. Fisher stressed the need to reconsider

Fig. 4: Villa Stein, Garches, France, entrance facade, by Le Corbusier, 1927.

the garage as an element of house design. Corbusian influence evidently gained general acceptance by 1934, when William B. Weiner built a weekend house in Louisiana (Fig. 5). Essentially a concrete box with large window areas, and raised off the ground on *pilotis* to provide car parking underneath, Weiner's house was a direct response to Le Corbusier's landmark Villa Savoye in Poissy (1928-1931). Earlier, Lawrence Kocher and Albert Frey had designed a prototype all-aluminum house with garage, *pilotis*, and roof deck, and in 1927 Kocher had called on architects "to include it [the garage] in the house and express it externally." Thus European theories aided the process of accommodating the American house to the car.

By mid-1930, progressive-minded architects were designing houses for clients of all social levels with integrated garages, which they made no attempt to conceal. Conservative architects such as Sevaldsen had lost their battle. Unlike the modernists, they could never agree that "it is only when we enter our garage that for a time we are in contact with reality, with clean honest design and healthy aesthetics."

As we have already seen, European functionalist theories were a contributing factor to an American architectural aesthetic which gave prominence to the garage. However, certain social and architectural factors, indigenously American, contributed equally to the general acceptance of an integrated garage. It would seem that Prairie School architects, Frank Lloyd Wright in particular, were receptive to designing for the car in the first decade of this century. Wright's Robie house in Chicago, designed in 1906, demonstrates a strikingly advanced relationship between house and garage. The only entrance into the house is through a portal in an eight-foot high wall. This leads into a service yard with three automobile garages straight ahead. The entrance to the house is to the left. Although the garage is not integrated into the main body of the house, a cantilevered roof from the second floor extends to the plane of the garage wall, offering a protective covering for the motorist. More significantly, the garage doors dominate the view as one first enters the yard. Wright also played down the entrance into the house. Recessed far back because of the splayed end wall of the playroom, and enveloped in the shadows of the cantilevered roof, the entrance is almost secretive rather than explicit. This visual subordination of the main

Fig. 5: Weekend house, Cross Lake, La., by William B. Weiner, 1934.

entrance to the garage would not begin to find its way into any other architectural syntax until the late 1920s. Almost all domestic architecture of the period made the entry the dominant focus of the street facade by centralizing and ornamenting it.

In planning the Robie house at the outset for the automobile (Frederick Robie, by the way, was an early member of the Chicago Automobile Club), Wright discarded all the conventions of accepted architectural design and created a powerful new statement of domestic life. In his later years, his house designs continued to reflect new technology. For example, his first Jacobs house of 1936 and most of his other "usonian" houses developed the carport in response to the weathertight closed cars that had become so common a decade earlier. Again, one must walk down the driveway and underneath the carport roof before finding the door into the house. This mode of entry reflects the less formal mode of living that increasingly dominated American life. Gone is the classic formality of the traditional house, with its imposing centralized entry, meant to be approached on axis. Instead, the entry is subdued, deformalized. No longer being the dominant motif of the street facade, it correlates perfectly with the informality that the automobile brought to American home life. As Wright himself remarked, "Inasmuch as this car is a feature of the comings and goings of the family, some space at the entrance is the proper space for it." Recently, architect Karel Yasko remarked that the carport was one of a number of Wright innovations which has since been "incorporated . . . into the mainstream of American home construction."

Wright's anticipation of the changes in the structure of family life brought about by the automobile, and his recognition of the need to design for the American family's increased "comings and goings" was picked up around 1930 by other progressive American architects. Modernists, such as Howard T. Fisher and A. Lawrence Kocher, called for locating the garage adjacent to the front door. Kocher even boldly claimed "the house garage should be considered as the entrance to the house." These statements underscore the radical shift in values that had occurred among architects who were willing to respond openly to the new demands created by the car. The stage was set for a new domestic architecture. In 1934, *Pencil Points* illustrated a project that met these demands. The result of a collaboration between E. H. Lovelace and M.R. Dobberman, a landscape architect and architect respectively, this project was called the "Motorcentric House" (Fig. 6). The axial center of the street facade

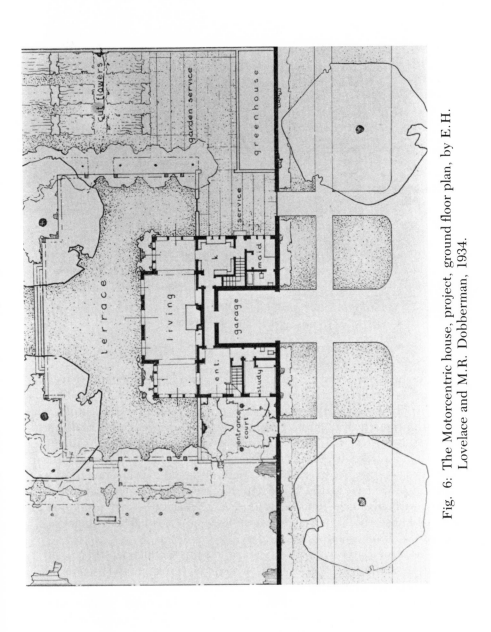

Fig. 6: The Motorcentric house, project, ground floor plan, by E. H. Lovelace and M.R. Dobberman, 1934.

Fig. 7: "Motorcentric" house for C. W. Stephenson, West Hartford,
Conn., by Adams and Prentice, 1935.

of this house was the garage. There were no other openings on the
front face of the house. Thus, the garage doors were flanked and set
off by blank two-story walls. The owner entered the house from a
door in the rear wall of the garage. For Lovelace and Dobberman, it
was only logical to "drive into the middle of the house without
making any architectural apologies." After all, they argued, "the
motor car is at present as handsomely designed and finished as any
furniture we have in the house and deserves the kind of housing that
goes with advanced thinking in design." What they were proposing
was a house "built for people whose lives, if not yet air-flown, are at
least synchromeshed."

The term "Motorcentric" caught on during the following years, at
least in architectural circles, as a general designation for garage-
centered house plans. Such plans were adopted by conservative as
well as progressive architects. As just one example, Adams and
Prentice, conservative architects who typically designed in a restrained
classical mode, built a Georgian residence in West Hartford, Connecticut on a "motorcentric" plan (Fig. 7). While managing to retain

a sense of traditional elegance from the exterior, they admitted that the front door of this house "is not so much the tasteful entrance on the first floor level, but the garage. And it is from the garage that the main stair begins."

Although all of the houses mentioned above are individual examples of the assimilation of the car, they had a profound effect on later suburban developments, in which the use of the car was planned for *en masse*. One of the earliest and best known of these developments was Radburn, New Jersey. Clarence Stein designed Radburn in the late 1920s expressly for the motor age. Although he totally separated vehicular and pedestrian traffic, he also incorporated garages below the living quarters of each house. Working from the Radburn plans, the editors of *Architectural Record* proposed their own "house for the motor age" in 1929. It also was "motorcentric" in concept; they stated that "when we enter the garage of our proposed schemes, we, in reality, enter the house."

All of these proposals were serious attempts to incorporate the automobile into our domestic architecture. By 1935 the outcome of the process was no longer in doubt. In 1933 the President's Committee on Recent Social Trends made note of an "automobile psychology" in which "the automobile has become a dominant influence in the life of the individual and he, in a real sense, has become dependent upon it." For better or worse, an old way of life, represented by the deep front porch and the parlor, had succumbed to such new forces and new cultural values as personal freedom, individualism, increased mobility, and greater opportunities to extend one's interactions with the larger physical and social environment.

Today we feel surrounded by atmospheric pollution and the visual blight of shopping centers and Levittowns; therefore, we tend to see the social and architectural changes brought about by the automobile during the First Machine Age as containing the seeds of our problems. But to the innovators who sparked the transitions, the change was seen as positive both for individuals and for society.

Funding for the research of this paper came from the Committee on Grants of Franklin and Marshall College. I am grateful for its support, and also for the support of the staff of the Avery Library at Columbia University where I worked as a visiting scholar this year. For their critical comments and editorial skills, I am greatly indebted to my colleagues Sol Wank, Sarah White, Joel Eigen, and David Schuyler.

JOHN HILDEBIDLE

THE TRUE MALL

You cannot walk to the True Mall. Roads there are, in intricate patterns all built on the same tire-squealing arc. Signs and arrows there are, with bright colors and messages so slender that you miss nothing speeding by at 80. Sidewalks there are not, nor footpaths; instead there are landscaped banks too steep to walk, high rounded curbs which offer no footing except the most temporary, and that only to an acrobat. And trip wires disguised as low fences which clutch at your trailing heel as you try to climb across. And hopeless, spiky trees, barely man-tall, which offer no shade when it is 90° and you, poor derelict, must hike into the Mall to keep cool and sane. The True Mall knows whom it wants, and it is not those who walk outdoors.

There are things you cannot buy in the True Mall. Maps, for instance. Maps, that is, of anything but the Mall itself. Those are at every turning, bright plastic screens with stars and arrows to tell you You Are Here and a roster of shops on plastic strips that change like leaves with the season and the tide of Economic Forces, and symbols for the many comforts and eleemosynary services to be found there (Function Rooms, Interdenominational Meditation Chapel, Comfort Station) all identified by tokens alone, without the need of words, so that a Slavonian religious with a kidney condition could safely come to the True Mall without fear of committing an Indecency or suffering a misdemeanor of the Faith. But maps of the city or the state, there are none. Nor maps of Brazil with the rain forest blotched in deep humid green, nor maps of the explorations of Vasco da Gama or the migrations of the Celtic tribes or the streets of Lisbon in 1565 or the crusades of the Teutonic Knights or the Great Trek of the Mormons. None of these can be purchased in the True Mall. The Mall knows where it is. Those who deserve the Mall know where it and they are, and feel no hunger to be elsewhere.

The True Mall as an artform is the Realization of the lifeforce made manifest in Nervous Energy. There is no place to sit, comfortably, although the resilient beings who flock there find places to sit momentarily and even longer, remembering somehow the infantine skill of resting in the most impossible place at the most unlikely angle and contortion of body. There are benches but they are so stiff and hard that even mothers worn down beneath the weight of plastic freezerware and small children look upon them with no joy. To relax there is impossible, you immediately slide from the varnished seat to the floor which is always being swept and is always dirty. The law of the True Mall is Movement. Move. Look. Move. The natural pace of the Mall is a steady amble, almost a prowl, like the pacing of a timber wolf slowed by cold and age.

The True Mall, like the life of a species, is never finished, although it may end. Always there is a place for Renovation to Serve U Better. Always there is An Exciting New Shopping Experience Coming Here Soon. Always there is the future promised to us and to our children, announcing itself politely but with absolute conviction: Pardon Our Dust.

The True Mall does not reveal its shape. There is no front, only corners arranged in a perspective more clever than the invisible widening of the columns of the Parthenon. The True Mall is a miracle of boxes. Its inside is betrayed by its outside no more than a skeleton is betrayed by its body. There is in the True Mall an endless deployment of turnings toward new delight.

The True Mall has its cinemas in bunches, the timing carefully staggered, seven and nine, sevenfifteen and ninefifteen, seventhirty and ninethirty. The True Mall pleases everyone. Or nearly so. No X here. Sex and Violence cannot live too boldly in the True Mall. The crowds will not stand eagerly in line if embarrassed; the very air of the True Mall will not support embarrassment. But there are films enough, and each night at just seventhirty all up and down the Eastern seaboard people settle in their seats eating from the same batch of prepopped buttercorn as the automatic projection device clicks to life and a brisk theme announces Our Feature Presentation.

These are the people of the True Mall: sleek young buyers, tightbellied windowdressers, fullmuscled tightjeaned boys whose voices still break, desperate lovers in clogs, sharpfaced twentyfiveyearold floormanagers in glossy suits wearing the moustaches of middleaged men, lean security guards in overpressed uniforms, lithe bowlegged young women with the grease of carburetors ground well under their nails, poutfaced housewives in pantsuits that fit when they were married, thinchested deliverymen with clipboards, retired gentlemen in snapbrim hats and pleated trousers, largebreasted teenagers selling French fries, fat energetic old women in lime pants and frostblue hair lugging string bags full of cotton scarves. These are the people of the True Mall. All others (do not so hastily say "I" or "we") are only visitors, on sufferance.

The True Mall is never quiet. At night, when everyone is gone, the music still plays. The music reaches its perfection when at last there is no one to try to listen. The music has the astounding property of being impossible to pay attention to. No act of will or concentration can focus the mind on more than a song or two before the sound sinks incontrovertibly into the hiss of white noise. The music is in a key that cannot be whistled or sung. The music is in a tempo that cannot be danced or clapped to. The songs are ones you never knew more than the first seven, or last five, words of. Japanese Sandman. Fly Me to the Moon. I'm Putting All My Eggs in One Basket. All through the dark hours the music proceeds, grandly indifferent. They Call the Wind Maria. Wichita Lineman. The Last Time I Saw Paris. How Long Has This Been Going On. And then the morning comes and the True Mall reawakens, with the sound of gates clattering across the empty bounce of prebottled music. Where Is Love. Volare. Blue Moon. A Nightingale Sang in Berkeley Square. Bali Hai. Green Dolphin Street . . .

III. THE MIRROR OF ART

JULIAN SMITH

A RUNAWAY MATCH:
THE AUTOMOBILE IN THE
AMERICAN FILM, 1900-1920

When American filmmakers first looked at the products of the infant auto industry, what did they see, and what uses did they make of what they saw? An analysis of the themes associated with the automobile in early films should contribute to a fuller understanding of how the first generation of motorists looked upon its vehicles and upon the notion of automobility. It will suggest one of the ways in which the automobile was "sold" to a mass audience before that audience actually entered the ranks of the motoring public.

Research for this essay was conducted at the Library of Congress, where I read copyright descriptions, plot summaries, and reviews of approximately 20,000 pre-1920 films, and where I viewed several hundred films in the motion picture collection. Of these thousands of films, about five hundred made significant use of the automobile in terms of plot, theme, or characterization. After random viewing of some thirty features for which the descriptive material does not mention any use of the automobile, I concluded that important automotive images have often gone unnoted (two examples, *The Apple Tree Girl* and *Putting the Bee in Herbert*, will be discussed later in this essay). Thus, the percentage of early movies employing significant automotive images may be much higher than the 2½

179

percent indicated by my survey of printed sources.

About a third of the auto-intensive images appear in films made before 1914; the remaining two-thirds occur between 1914 and 1920. I call attention to 1914 because it is the year the film industry shifted from one-and two-reelers to feature production. Though many thousands of shorts were made after 1914, I made no attempt to survey them other than to satisfy myself that the car's image in these films was primarily comic, as in the Mack Sennett slapstick chases. It is not surprising that the incidence of automotive images is much higher in the 1914-1920 films, because longer running time and larger budgets made the presence of cars more likely within the narrative, and because the automobile itself had by then become more commonplace on American streets.

The first celluloid images of the automobile and its new age fall into two categories: simple documentary records and trick films. In the Library of Congress film collection, the testimony begins with about a dozen "nonfiction" shorts made in 1900 by the two companies that controlled the early industry. Biograph and Edison. The first seems to have been Edison's *Automobile Parade*. A single shot in length, this 1900 film opens with two policemen on bikes pedaling into frame escorting a parade of about three dozen horseless carriages full of high-hatted gents and plumed ladies. Midway in the parade, a horse-drawn cab gets cut off by the motor traffic and has to wait while nineteen or twenty motor vehicles pass. At the end of the film, the cab is still waiting and there seems no end to the parade.

A year later, when Edison released *Automobile Parade on the Coney Island Boulevard,* the parade had grown to at least fifty cars in length. In search of novelty, Biograph staged *A Unique Race between Elephant, Bicycle, Camel, Horse, and Automobile* in 1902 (the winner is not established), then sent a camera crew to cover an early reliability run up the carriage road on New Hampshire's Mount Washington. The rather dull result was *Automobiling Among the Clouds* (1904), which was not improved upon by Edison's *Auto Hill-Climbing Contest, Mt. Washington* (1905). In *New York Athletic Club Games, Travers Island* (1905), the Biograph cameraman slowly panned across the "parking" area to reveal a hundred or more big touring cars full of spectators, while in *Exploded Gas Tanks, U. S. Mint, Emporium and Spreckels' Building* (1906), the Edison cameraman pans across earthquake-desolated San Francisco to discover a single automobile moving in the same direction as the camera.

While American cameramen seemed content to provide an almost boastful documentation of the large number of motor cars to be seen on American streets, fields, and mountainsides, English and French cameramen were supplying trick films with titles like *How it Feels to be Run Over* (1900), *How to Stop a Motor Car* (1902-03), and *The Delights of Automobiling* (1903). Full of stop-action photography, these films stress comic mayhem and dismemberment; in the last example, for instance, the delights of automobiling are for the moviegoers, not the motorists who are blown to pieces when their vehicle explodes.[1]

Though documentaries and trick films account for the bulk of automotive images available to the viewing public in the first few years of this century, they represent formal extremes that would ultimately prove less appealing to a mass audience than narrative approaches combining and subordinating realistic and expressionistic elements to the demands of telling a story. To put it simply, the earliest documentaries witnessed an uncomfortable truth about automobiles (that they were primarily the toys of the rich) while the trick films gave false testimony about motor cars in order to show off the possibilities of film form itself.

As the mechanical novelty of both motion pictures and motor cars wore off, the two infant industries faced essentially the same problem: how to get the greatest number of potential customers to buy the vehicle they offered. In 1903, the year of the first transcontinental auto trip, and the year the Ford Motor Company was organized, filmmakers made a breakthrough when the popular success of *The Great Train Robbery*, now considered the first important narrative film, demonstrated that moviegoers would respond more readily to films that involved rather than excluded them, as had the documentaries and trick films.

Probably the first true narrative film to depict an automobile is Biograph's *Runaway Match* (1903). The title supplies a happy opportunity for metaphor: movies and motorcars seemed made for each other. Not only did the automobile supply filmmakers with a natural subject for romance, comedy, and adventure, but the narrative conventions that soon sprang up around movie automobiles helped intensify popular interest in the automobile itself. It was

---

[1]These early trick films are not available at the Library of Congress (though some later ones are); my comments are based on contemporary descriptions.

more than a simple runaway match—it was a lush triangle of love affairs: America fell in love with both movies and cars, while Hollywood and Detroit fell in love with each other. The star-in-the-car soon became a staple of publicity within both industries; movies popularized specific cars; and car dealers were called upon to help advertise movies that featured their models.

The love affair begins in *Runaway Match*. Barely five minutes long, this flight of fancy establishes a number of themes that would become important in many other films treating the car: the motorist as rebellious romantic hero, the chase, and the use of the car to both precipitate and resolve conflicts. In nine shots, *A Runaway Match* tells the story of a young couple eloping in a hired car. The bride's rich father gives chase, but his chauffeur-driven car breaks down. By the time he arrives at the church, the wedding is over. Reconciled to the match, the rich man invites the wedding party (bride, groom, priest, and best man) to get into his big touring car and they all drive off together; order having been threatened by one car, it is now restored in another.

It is significant that the first auto-centered narrative film is about an elopement, for elopement itself is a result of the same kind of emotional movement that is at the heart of the power and appeal of movies (and perhaps, even, of cars). Although the automobile has usually been perceived as a mode of *transportation* in the primary and ordinary sense of the word (physical movement of objects through space), and although most political and legal accommodations to the car have been justified on the basis of the utilitarian sense of "transportation," automobility has been consciously marketed and both consciously and subconsciously embraced by the American public as a form of emotional *transport*, the state or condition of being transported by ecstasy, of being enraptured. As Hollywood and Detroit came of age, they both learned how to supply dream vehicles that would carry us away from danger or boredom, transport us to better times and bigger adventures.

Cars and movies are, in short, transports of delight. As early as 1905, in Biograph's *Lifting the Lid* and Edison's *Boarding School Girls*, automobiles were used to transport characters—and the audience—into new realms: the low-life of the New York underworld in the first case, the delights of the Coney Island amusement park in the second. That same year, an entrepreneur tried to combine the motoring and movie-going experience via the Tim Hurst Auto Tours, in which the audience sat in a theater designed to look like a huge touring car and watched motion pictures photographed along the main thoroughfares of famous cities. "The cars carry 60 people, are terraced-seated, so that every passenger has an unobstructed view," the ads in one of the trade papers proclaimed in an effort to make the reader think he would be buying a huge motorcar. "The ACME of MECHANICAL INGENUITY. . . . No jarring, no jolting, no bumping, no discordant noises—simply the correct combination of the vibratory and gently oscillating motions of a high-grade touring car. A perfect illusion without an objectionable feature. . . . Can be installed anywhere for $400.00."[2]

The Tim Hurst Auto Tours, which got their start at the Rockaway Beach, are a reminder of the early recreational use of the automobile. But though these recreational uses would appear dozens of times in films made before 1914, moviemakers, like many other Americans, were discovering the utilitarian value of the rich man's toy. One of the earliest film discoveries was that automobiles were wonderful tools for seducers and criminals; a collateral discovery was that audiences tended to prefer stories in which the automobile proves to be ultimately beneficial rather than threatening. The criminal use of the new transportation technology seems to begin in 1905 with Biograph's *The Gentlemen Highwaymen*, in which the villain in a big motorcar tries to overtake and rob a young couple in a little runabout on a lonely road. But not only is automobility useful for the criminal, it is equally useful for the intended victim, who employs his little car as a weapon to knock the villain down. The little runabout, a more "democratic" vehicle than the villain's expensive touring car, outruns the larger car (which breaks down), drives into town, returns with police, and in the last shot is seen towing the disabled touring car full of cops and robbers back to justice. A year later, both the law and the outlaws commandeer motor vehicles in Biograph's *A Daring Hold-Up in Southern California* (the cops win). By 1913, in Universal's aptly titled *Traffic in Souls*, the criminal use of the automobile reaches a low point when a recruiter for a prostitution ring uses a closed car as a private mobile hideaway for drugging an innocent young woman and transporting her into white slavery. The police, however, are equally up-to-date in their technology: in the last minute rescue they pile into a row of big open cars and dash off to break up the ring and save the heroine's sister from rape.

---

[2]This ad appeared in *Views and Films Index* throughout 1906; my thanks to Charles Musser for calling it to my attention.

The chief utility of the automobile suggested by the early American film is its role in the greatest adventure of all: the Darwinian struggle to create the best possible gene pool. In dozens of elopement films, poor but worthy young men demonstrate their adaptability and vitality by hiring or borrowing motorcars in order to carry off the daughters of rich men. In countless other films, tourists motor into strange love-encounters which lead to unexpected genetic mixtures between regions and classes.

Again and again, the automobile was employed by filmmakers as a means of proving who was the better man. A typical example is Edison's *Dashed to Death* (1909), in which a beautiful young heiress is forced by her parents to marry an old Italian duke instead of the poor young American she really loves. This uneugenic and unAmerican situation is resolved when the duke flees from a well-deserved beating at the hands of the American by jumping into his automobile and dashing off. Let the *Moving Picture World's* reviewer tell the rest:

> [The American hero] manages to secure the services of a passing auto and is soon hot in pursuit. And here ensues a sensational and thrilling automobile chase. Up and down hill and around sharp curves with unslackened speed the heavy machines are driven, the American gaining on the Duke with every turn of the wheels. The distance between the two is rapidly closing up, the tense expression on the Duke's terror-stricken features in marked contrast to the triumphant mien of his pursuer. The speed limit of both machines has been reached and but a few yards separate them when, in turning a sharp curve on the very edge of a steep cliff, the Italian loses control of his machine which crashes through the guard fence before he can jump to safety. A moment it pauses on the brink of that dizzy height, and then, turning completely over, plunges down, smashing, crashing toward the rocky bottom 300 feet below! Half way down the great car strikes a projecting rock—the boiler bursts with a terrific explosion—the gasoline tank ignites and bursts into flame—and thus it goes plunging down, with its human freight obscured by the volume of smoke and flame, until it reaches the bottom, where it lies an unrecognizable mass of smoking wood, iron and rubber. (V, 289)

One of the most difficult problems facing early filmmakers was that of managing to tell a romantic story built around the production values inherent in an expensive car while at the same time developing a male character who was handsome, young, and representative of the egalitarian values considered appealing to the mass audience. *Dashed to Death* presents one solution: give the villain a motorcar. But how could the democratic hero be put in the driver's seat? A popular celluloid solution was to focus on the chauffeur. Another problem grew out of this solution: how, in Darwinian terms, could it be explained why the possessor of great male beauty and mechanical aptitude was filling a menial position? In *The Girl and the Chauffeur* (Yankee, 1911), a rich girl elopes with the family chauffeur who becomes, by virtue of his practical skills, a rich garage owner and saves his father-in-law from economic ruin during a Wall Street panic. In other words, the young man was on his way to the top and drove part of the way. For unfathomable reasons this motorized version of the basic Horatio Alger myth was not repeated. Instead, in about a score of films between 1913 and 1920, rich young men pose as poor chauffeurs in order to get close to (or to test the love of) young ladies both rich and poor. A good example is Vitagraph's *Over the Garden Wall* (1919): once rich, now poor, the heroine meets a young man who is working on a stalled car; because she is practical and friendly, she helps the "chauffeur" get the car running, not knowing that he is actually the son of the rich woman who owns the car. They fall in love; presumably they will marry and breed a better race of Americans not afraid to get their hands dirty.

Other films tried to work the same tricks with rich young men who choose to express their democratic bents by working as traffic cops, cabbies, ambulance drivers, or other servants of the new culture growing up around the automobile. In Bluebird's *The Car of Chance* (1917), a playboy is forced to prove himself automotively when his father leaves him a seven-passenger motorcar and unlimited credit for gasoline. The father's wisdom is demonstrated when the reformed playboy turns his "car of chance" into a jitney bus, organizes other jitney drivers into a rapid transit company, and wins the daughter of a rich man and a job as assistant general manager of a traction company. *The Scarlet Runner* (1916), a twelve-part Vitagraph serial, is about another "car of chance." The hero, born with a silver spoon in his mouth, avoids being disinherited by selling his household belongings in order to purchase the "Scarlet Runner." Hiring out his red car as a public conveyance, he makes so much money in the first episode that he wins his inheritance and sets out on an automotive tour of Europe in search of love and adventure (naturally, when he falls in love it's with a girl who drives her own car).

Movies about the utility of the automobile in bringing happiness and success are of almost infinite variety. Take a pair of Edison "Conquest Pictures" from 1917, *The Apple Tree Girl* and *Putting the Bee in Herbert*.

In the first, Charlotte, the Apple Tree Girl, is transported by limousine from her rustic life on a New England farm to the magic kingdom of a rich relative's estate, where she is to serve as companion to her spoiled cousin. Soon after her arrival, Charlotte and her cousin go to school together; after school, the snobbish cousin gets into a flashy roadster with two of her admirers, leaving Charlotte to walk home with Neil Kennedy, a poor but ambitious lad. Along the way, they spot the roadster in front of a soda shop. Rather than being envious of the car, Neil admires it and seems to say that one day he'll have one. Years pass: Charlotte becomes a school teacher and Neil returns as a country doctor who makes his rounds in a Model T, that instantly recognizable film symbol of the ordinary man. Out for a drive, Neil proposes to her, but she runs away because she wants to be famous and marry a millionaire. More time passes: Charlotte becomes a famous golfer and is seen riding a horse beside a millionaire who wants to marry her. Ah, but she still loves Neil. How can this dilemma be resolved? How else but automotively? The horse runs away just as Neil, now a successful doctor, happens to drive by in an opulent, sporty roadster. He jumps from the roadster to the horse and saves Charlotte while the roadster rolls obediently to a halt, providing a backdrop for true love's embrace and Charlotte's final words: "Take me home."

Whereas *The Apple Tree Girl* uses one fancy roadster to show Neil's youthful ambition and a second, more luxurious model to document his success and resolve the plot, *Putting the Bee in Herbert* uses one new car as an inspiration and a second as a reward. Nell, the daughter of middle-class comfort, marries beneath her station to Herbert, a bank clerk who lacks ambition. After four years of marriage and no raises, Herbert is making only twenty dollars a week and the marriage is heading toward trouble. We see Nell sitting in her grim little apartment, darning a shirt, when a sound distracts her. She looks out the window and sees a big Packard touring car pulled up across the street and a fashionably-dressed lady climbing in beside the driver. "A new car!" says Nell to herself, "And that was her husband at the wheel!" Now the bee is in Nell's bonnet, and we see her bitter thoughts: the dreary image of Herbert at his desk, herself at her drab chores, and the contrasting image of the neighboring couple out for a spin in the middle of the day. That night, Nell tries to put the bee in Herbert. When he refuses to listen to her appeals, we see her thinking about that objective correlative for all she desires—the neighbor's new car. Rather than remain bitter, Nell embarks on a series of Horatio Alger schemes to turn Herbert into a success. Four weeks later, Herbert has been promoted to an important bank job at ten times his old salary—and comes home in the middle of the day to take her out for a ride in a sleek, streamlined new touring car. The film ends with a title card proclaiming "THE ROAD TO HAPPINESS" and the iris closing around the final image of the car driving away from us down a tree-lined boulevard, thus putting the bee in all of us.

Beyond the many films about the romantic and inspirational utility of the automobile, probably the largest single category of non-recreational uses to which the auto was put in the early American film is summed up in the title of a 1912 American Film Manufacturing Company melodrama, *Saved by an Auto*, which opens with a flighty middle-aged woman badgering her old-fashioned rancher husband into buying a big touring car after she gets her first taste of automobility in the big city (while visiting her younger sister, whose husband takes her for a ride in his new car). After showing the comic misadventures of the old rancher and his cowboys as he learns how to drive the fool contraption, the filmmakers get serious, ending with a strong reminder of the car's usefulness as the younger sister jumps behind the wheel of the car to save her own husband from a lynch mob. (Along the way she almost providentially runs over the real villain and delivers him to the mob—thus is justice served in the New West.)

The "saved by an auto" theme seems to have been introduced in D.W. Griffith's *The Drive for a Life* (1909). In this Biograph thriller the leading man discovers that his ex-mistress has sent poisoned candy to his present fiancée. He jumps into his car, breaks speed laws, crashes through a toll gate, and demolishes a farm wagon in a mad dash to prevent the fiancée and her four girl friends from biting into the candy. Griffith, credited with so many other innovations, may have been the first to hit upon a socially acceptable motive for a high speed chase. Within a few years, the race for a life would be so common that comic versions appeared in which desperate calls for help turn out to be false alarms. In 1915, Griffith's protégé Mack Sennett recycled *The Drive for a Life* as *Those Bitter Sweets*, a Keystone farce in which the Sennett bathing beauties must be saved from a box of poisoned candy sent by a jilted suitor.

Griffith, meanwhile, continued to look for (and find) excuses for automotive rescues. Nowhere in the history of film is the *extraordinary* life-and-death utility of the automobile clearer than in Griffith's

Intolerance, in which the last forty minutes dramatize the efforts of a young woman trying to save her husband from the fatal effects of civil intolerance. Luckily, the Dear One has ready access to four different automobiles. She dashes across town in two taxis, first to plead with the governor, and then to confront him with new evidence that will prove her husband's innocence. She then races against a locomotive in a commandeered racing car, and finally, pardon in hand, she races against the hangman in another taxi. Intercut with the Dear One's automotive adventures are three other stories: the Mountain Girl's race toward Babylon in a chariot to warn King Belshazzar of the Persian attack, Christ's progress toward Calvary, and Prosper's wild horseback ride to save Brown Eyes, his Protestant loved one, from the St. Bartholomew Day's Massacre.

Intolerance was released in 1916, the same year that James Doolittle published *The Romance of the Automobile Industry*. Beautifully printed and heavily illustrated, this expensive volume was imposingly subtitled: "Being the Story of its Development—its Contribution to Health and Prosperity—its Influence on Eugenics—its Effect on Personal Efficiency—and its Service and Mission to Humanity as the latest and Greatest Phase of Transportation." Transportation, indeed. From his very first words, "The automobile is the most important device ever made by man," to his last,

> The mission of the automobile is to increase personal efficiency; to make happier the lot of people who have led isolated lives in the country and congested lives in the city; to serve as an equalizer and a balance.
>
> Elegant in lines, powerful in action, wide in service, the modern automobile represents the incarnation of the transportation art—the silent, always-ready servant that has more strength than Aladdin's genii, and that already has accomplished vaster works for mankind's betterment than anything that has gone before.

Doolittle reveals that he has been totally transported by the invention he calls "the only improvement to road transportation since Moses, and the most important influence on civilization of all time."[3] *Intolerance* "reads" like a gloss on Doolittle's book, and the book itself seems a gloss on the early film image of the automobile.

[3]James Rood Doolittle, *The Romance of the Automobile Industry* (New York: Klebold Press, 1916), pp. v, ix, 441-42.

If a writer of Doolittle's apparent intelligence could be swept away by the new motor age, what was the ordinary viewer of the time to think when he saw *Intolerance*'s three "ancient" stories end in death and defeat while the modern one ends happily because of the ready availability of cars to even the most humble citizen? To be sure, only a simple-minded viewer in 1916 would have assumed that Babylon would not have fallen, Christ not been crucified, nor Brown Eyes been raped and murdered if only they and their friends had automobiles to flee in. And yet, what message was left in the subconscious? What little seeds were planted by this free advertising for the value of the automobile in a world full of danger and intolerance?

If the automobile was frequently useful in saving lives in movies, how about its obvious dangers in the early days of motoring when bad roads, inexperienced drivers, and uncrashworthy vehicles (lacking safety glass, seatbelts, rollbars, and padding) made the death and injury rate per mile much higher than today? If early films were to be trusted, no honest citizen had anything to fear from getting into an automobile. Of more than 110 films depicting crashes or physical injury, only three or four seem to have results that are not somehow fortunate or positive. This fact brings me to what is probably the single most common automotive theme or situation: the "happy accident."[4] Occurring in about 150 films—nearly a third of the total containing significant auto images—these crashes, mechanical breakdowns, and other misadventures lead almost invariably to happy outcomes: rich motorists, stranded in the country, fall in love with beautiful farm girls; villains are punished in last minute crashes (as in *Dashed to Death*); inconvenient spouses die so true love can triumph.

What follows are a few examples from 1908 alone. In *An Honest Newsboy's Reward* (Lubin), the poor newsboy is hit by a motorcar when he attempts to return a lost wallet. The owner of the wallet, impressed by the suffering brought on by the boy's honesty, gives him a good job and eventually makes him a partner. In *After Midnight* (Vitagraph), when a young woman slips on ice and falls in the path of an automobile, a gentleman dashes into the street, saving her not only from the car but from a life of crime. In *Through Darkness to Light* (Lubin), the heroine elopes by car with her young lover after her father tries to make her marry an older man. In the midst of

---

[4] I take this term from Edison's *A Happy Accident* (1909), a Christmas story about a rich girl who plays Santa after her present-laden car breaks down near a humble cottage. (Early breakdowns were often referred to as accidents.)

hard times, the heroine is reconciled with her parents after her little girl is run over by their car (and rides home in style in the instrument of reconciliation). The "happy accident" theme's popularity is illustrated in Vitagraph's 1908 film, *Making Motion Pictures*, which showed a day at the Vitagraph studio and the filming of a street scene. The finished product is a melodrama about a young woman who marries a poor soldier against her father's wishes. She becomes an outcast until the father's motorcar runs her down, thus effecting a reconciliation. Note that all four examples from 1908—with others not discussed—involve threats to nonmotorists. As movie audiences became increasingly middle-class and enjoyed increasing access to automobiles, the accidents tended to injure or threaten sympathetic motorists.

This concentration upon success, reformation, and reconciliation in the films of a single year suggests that the automobile is an ultimately benevolent *deus ex machina*. Indeed, the connection between fate, justice, divine will, and the automobile is stressed in the titles of three films released in 1915: Vitagraph's *Wheels of Justice* ends with convicts escaping in a commandeered auto which bears them (on wheels of justice) to doom in a fatal plunge; Lubin's *Whom the Gods Would Destroy* involves a villain who escapes in an automobile, only to be hit by a train (the moral was not lost on one reviewer who noted that "retributive justice comes to the murderer *through the hand of fate*"); and Universal's *The Threads of Fate* finds its resolution when, according to another reviewer, "either by intention of the driver or *because of fate*," a car runs wild, killing adulterous lovers and sparing the "innocent" husband who was driving.[5]

And so it goes in these happy accidents. Women are turned into vamps or nymphomaniacs by the trauma of crashes—or punished for being vamps or nymphomaniacs by other crashes. Artists find their ideal models when pretty girls are run down by autos—and in Selig's *The Empty Studio* (1913), an unsuccessful painter wins an art contest by capturing the facial expression of a witness to the death of a child under the wheels of a car.

So much for the most commonly employed themes: the happy accident, the race for a life, the car of chance, the auto elopement, and all the rest. To these one could add others that reveal the ability of the automobile to bring happiness, success, excitement, and ful-

[5]The first quote is from *Moving Picture World*, 3 July 1915; the second from *Motion Picture News*, 20 February 1915. In each case, the emphasis is mine.

fillment. Equally significant, none of the early films is clearly biased against the automobile—and none makes any kind of clear and systematic analysis of the social impact of the automobile. Indeed, only one early film even touches on the changes brought by the automobile: Edison's *A Baby's Shoe* (1912). According to the copyright synopsis, this lost film opens with Doctor Wilton's annoyance over the lateness of his buggy, an annoyance compounded when he sees a rival physician "gliding by in a new automobile." Tired of the inconvenience of being a horse and buggy doctor, Wilton invests in the new horseless technology and fires his coachman. The story then follows the technologically unemployed coachman as he looks for work until "slowly it dawned upon him that the horse was becoming a thing of the past." Despondent, the former coachman is saved from turning to crime by his sentimental discovery, at a crucial moment, of his baby's shoe. He is spared poverty by Doctor Wilton's offer of a job as chauffeur. The auto taketh away—and the auto giveth back.

Considering the usually simple nature of early film narrative, and given the preoccupation of filmmakers with individuals rather than with society, it should not be too surprising that there is no analysis of (or attention to) the broad spectrum of social changes brought about by mass personal automobility. And yet, a source for such a film appeared in 1918, when Booth Tarkington's best seller *The Magnificent Ambersons* won the Pulitzer Prize for telling the story of the impact of the auto age on one city (a nameless "Midland" town resembling Tarkington's Indianapolis), one family (the Ambersons), and one individual (George Amberson Minafer).

Listen to Eugene Morgan, Tarkington's fictional pioneer motorcar magnate, as he muses upon what he has helped to create. George, the last of the once magnificent Ambersons, curses the newfangled contraptions that have lowered the downtown property values upon which his family's wealth was based. Eugene responds:

> With all their speed forward they may be a step backward in civilization—that is, in spiritual civilization. It may be that they will not add to the beauty of the world, nor to the life of men's souls. I am not sure. But automobiles have come, and they bring a greater change in our life than most of us suspect. They are here, and almost all outward things are going to be different because of what they bring. They are going to alter war, and they are going to alter peace. I think men's minds are going to be changed in subtle ways because of automobiles; just how, though, I could hardly guess. But you can't have the immense outward changes that they will cause without some inward ones, and it may be that George is right,

and that the spiritual alteration will be bad for us. Perhaps, ten or twenty years from now, if we can see the inward changes in men by that time, I shouldn't be able to defend the gasoline engine, but would have to agree with him that automobiles had no business to be invented.[6]

Though this speech appears almost unchanged in Orson Welles's 1942 film version of the novel, such a speech would have been too long for the conventions of silent dialogue. And yet, the highly cinematic iconography of the novel, the constant visual opposition of the arrogant and impractical man of the horse (George) against the romantic, unassuming, and pragmatic man of the wheel (Eugene), would have worked very nicely on the screen. After all, Tarkington's novel builds toward that most common of movie auto-resolutions, the happy accident. George, impoverished, regenerates himself as a hard-handed servant of the new gasoline age by becoming an expert on "shooting" oil wells with nitroglycerin—and is then run down on the street by one of those motorcars he so despises. Note the description of this car of chance: "Fate's ironic choice for Georgie's undoing was not a big and swift and momentous car, such as Eugene manufactured; it was a specimen of the hustling little type that was flooding the country, the cheapest, commonest, hardiest little car ever made" (489). And thus is George reunited with the woman he loves—Lucy Morgan, the only child of the motorcar magnate. Truly, the auto taketh—and it giveth back.

[6]*The Magnificent Ambersons* (New York: Grosset and Dunlap, 1918), pp. 275-276.

KENNETH HEY

CARS AND FILMS IN AMERICAN CULTURE, 1929-1959

Cecil B. De Mille, the famous and flamboyant director whose garage housed two Locomobiles, a Lincoln limousine, a touring Cunningham, a Cord roadster, a Model A, and an odd assortment of unrecognizable machines, thought automobiles and movies shared cultural origins. The two industries rose to popularity together, De Mille explained, because they both reflected "the love of motion and speed, the restless urge toward improvement and expansion, the kinetic energy of a young, vigorous nation." Beyond this cultural interconnection, each industry found use for the other's products. Quite early in the century, location shooting in southern California made automobile transportation necessary for film crews, while Henry Ford, seeking to promote interest in his new Model T, established his own film unit. Whereas Hollywood stars preferred unusual and costly machines to match their cultivated on-and off-screen images, Ford's films emphasized rural and simple tranquility which could be reached with aid of his car. In tandem, the two industries reflected the glamorous and practical dimensions of a modern and mechanized American lifestyle.

According to Robert and Helen Lynd in *Middletown* (1929), an examination of life in Muncie, Indiana, automobiles and movies "revolutionized leisure time." Automobiles altered the sense of what leisure should be because free time with a car meant movement and change rather than the casual stability of family meetings in the parlor. Likewise, movies revised the pace of life by injecting vicarious thrills into daily experience and by subverting the reassuring conventions of dinner conversation at home and church. "Like the automobile and radio," the Lynds commented, "the movies, by breaking up leisure time into an individual, family, or small group affair, represent a counter-movement to the trend toward organization so marked in clubs and other leisure-time pursuits."

Middletowners preferred Harold Lloyd comedies and Ford cars, both of which fused traditional values with an upwardly-mobile mentality. In Muncie in the late 1920s, stability and movement were not inconsistent ideals because cars and movies had edged their way into the center of family activities. One Middletown businessman explained that he never felt closer to his family than when they were "all together in the car." A neighbor gladly sent her daughter to the movies because a young girl had "to learn the ways of the world somehow." With such an intimate relationship between family life and industrial product, there is little surprise that value inconsistencies disappeared before an unembarrassed enthusiasm for leisure-time pleasures. For sure, the one-time gadgets of the rich had become, as the Lynds explained, "an accepted, essential part of normal living."

By the time *Middletown* appeared, the industrial systems of automobile and film production had solidified. Detroit's Big Three oligarchy emerged and henceforward restricted competition to established companies capable of absorbing losses and sustaining interest. In 1920 over one-half of all automobiles in the world were Fords, but in 1927 production and management reorganization as well as yearly model changes moved General Motors ahead of Ford. Despite power struggles at the top, the remainder of the industry, which altogether earned less than one-half of auto profits, scrambled for consumer leftovers. Chrysler, the third largest, lagged considerably far behind the leaders, but enjoyed a comfortable lead over Durant Motors, the fourth largest company.

Major production realignments occurred in the film industry as well. The ubiquitous film companies of 1910 had by 1930 dwindled to a significant few: Lowe's Inc./MGM, Columbia, Paramount, United Artists and Warner Brothers. All of these companies cloistered around Hollywood, a comfortable terrain which promised year-round shooting weather, numerous types of natural settings, nonunion labor, and convenient isolation from the Eastern business establishment. While Detroit car companies maintained local franchised dealers to market cars directly to the consumer, increasingly powerful film companies owned nearly all of the nation's first-run theaters and controlled a sizable portion of the second-run houses. With stars insuring audience appeal, intercompany competition dwindling, and vertical corporate structures facilitating distribution and consumption, the film industry seemed isolated in a dream world of economic success. Thus when the Depression broke the nation's economic strength, both the film and automobile industries enjoyed a real albeit thin insulation from its early effects.

The 1930s proved that Americans would go without a lot before they would go without movies and cars. Total admissions to movies dropped from their peak in 1929 to their lowest in 1933. After that they rose again, reaching another peak in 1940. Yet more people went to the movies in 1933 than any *two* consecutive years from the late 1950s through the 1960s. Meanwhile, *The Grapes of Wrath* (1940), directed by John Ford, revealed the inflated importance of the automobile in Depression society. When evicted from their homestead, the Joads, exploited sharecroppers, headed West to a mythical land of milk and honey. Although their wanderings caused family disruptions and proved futile besides, the Joads still benefited from the advantages of spatial movement—a horizontal movement to ameliorate the failings of social, vertical mobility. The automobile operates as a symbol of the economic system which produced it. Constantly in need of repair and adjustment, the Joads' machine transports them from one transient community to another. As long as they accept mobility as their fate, organization and mass protest elude them. Meanwhile, benefactors of migrant labor drive new cars which show no outward signs of wear. Only when Casey and Tom leave the confines of the mechanical culture and start walking does serious protest congeal. In a curious twist of social concern, wealthy film producer Darryl Zanuck turned the Okies' misery into an instructional and profitable product for nationwide consumption. The Joads did indeed get around.

The wider effects of automobility appeared in visual materials outside the movies as well. James Agee, a poet and film critic, and Walker Evans, a photographer, released *Let Us Now Praise Famous Men* (1939), a penetrating look at life in the rural South. Evans included a photograph which captured the impact of the car on small towns. Dominating the photograph is a large, diagonal Main Street lined with cars. Most of the picture space is consumed by the roadway, which, at the moment the picture was taken, carried only one car. The town serves as a parking lot with advertisements, a hard, cement space where humans must walk in the alleyways left empty by bulky cars. The message seemed obvious: proliferating automobility had rendered anachronistic the small town of nineteenth-century America.

The effects of this change from small-town individualism to industrial nationalism served as central focus for John Ford's *Tobacco Road* (1939), a story of the people "left over" from the past. The main character, Jeeter Lester, owns a dilapidated but practical car. Its potential range seems limited, but it matches Jeeter's indifference to

In *The Grapes of Wrath*, sleek Packard convertibles serve the managerial class and separate the viewer from farmers on the "other side" of automobility. Tractors will destroy the Okies' home and make the road their new address. Courtesy The Museum of Modern Art Film Stills Archives.

efficiency, progress, and increased productivity. He refuses to trade his old car for a newer, more stylish model because his happiness does not depend on product consumption. He can laugh at his car's shortcomings, whereas his half-sane son, the next generation personified, idolizes newer cars and actually marries an older woman as a means of acquiring a sleek convertible. When he and his new-old wife return in the car, they bang into trees, knock down fences, and eventually push Jeeter's car into the ditch. Rural tranquility, nature, and even the family have been permanently invaded by hostile forces.

The characters' lives change when the car appears. Jeeter's daughter rubs dirt from the metal body and stares at her reflection, a narcissism born of fanciful and stylish interests. The car actually redefines her self-image, and she runs away to the city and presumably a "new" life. Jeeter's son next careens the car out the driveway, nearly ramming his own mother. She staggers to her feet, a symbol of the ravaged family structure which remains behind in a shroud of dust stirred by the machine's advance. *Tobacco Road*, the dirt path of traditional society, submits to scientific cultivation, while the new cement highway bypasses the Lester home and runs straight to the city. Eventually the car and the highway will transport Jeeter to the city's Old Folks Home and complete immobility.

Despite the ravages of an economic disaster, automobiles and films maintained their commercial appeal. In 1940, 35,153,000 family units in the country produced 80,000,000 moviegoers each week—2.28 visits per family per week. Meanwhile, Detroit in 1940 produced 2,717,385 new cars, or roughly one for every ten families in the country. The weekly attendance-per-household figure and the new-car-per-household figure both had increased over one-third since 1924. However, they had both reached peaks in 1929 which neither surpassed until after World War II.

During the war, machinery and propaganda, baseline essentials in any military endeavor, flowed steadily from Detroit and Hollywood, and reaffirmed the industries' status as defenders of an American lifestyle they helped create. As the war edged into the realm of recent history, however, the bourgeois world on screen returned to the glamor of its pre-Depression glory, and with good reason. After a momentary postwar lull, American society found itself in the midst of an economic boom, the proportions of which surprised even the most optimistic. The era's prosperity prompted historian David Potter to identify "affluence" as the single most characteristic feature of

American society and the determining factor in the American "character." The industrial system could rightfully claim much of the credit. Charles "Engine Charlie" Wilson, chairman of General Motors and Secretary of Defense under President Eisenhower, told the Senate Armed Services Committee: "For many years, I thought what was good for our country was good for General Motors and *vice versa*," and his claim seemed reasonable. As early as the 1920s, motor vehicles consumed 90 percent of the country's annual petroleum production, 80 percent of its rubber, 80 percent of its steel, 75 percent of its plateglass, and 25 percent of its machine tools. Although these figures had slightly declined by the 1950s, they continued to reflect accurately the influence of the automobile upon the nation's economy. During the 1950s both management and labor demonstrated enthusiasm for more and more production and more and more consumption. No matter what the car actually did on the screen, what part it played in the plot, its ubiquitous presence as an instrument of raw overwhelming force made the essential point. The car *belonged* to the landscape, as once the horse had dominated it. In the genre of *film noir*, in romantic dramas, in the first attempts at defining the youth culture, in sagas of truckers or cops and robbers—all of these promoted the car, subliminally when not overtly, as the objectified realization of the American self.

By 1950 the automobile had essentially reached the mechanical level it was to maintain through the next decade and a half. It did not stop changing; but most of the changes were cosmetic: smoother automatic transmissions, three-toned bodies, whitewall tires, and so on. Automobile advertising moved away from patriotic wartime appeals and the postwar "scientific" image, and associated vehicles with luscious females and sensuous pleasures. Indeed, the lines on some stylish models bore a striking resemblance to recumbent female forms. This allusion reached obvious and gaudy proportions with the tail-fin craze late in the decade. Soft, comfortable interiors reinforced the connection to "feminine" fantasies, while push-button controls, power steering, and brakes permitted the most feeble to experience the machine's powerful thrust.

Fantasies manufactured with the car as a catalyst paled next to those of Hollywood filmmakers, and yet the two remained similarly profligate in spending habits. *An American in Paris* (1951), *Singin' in the Rain* (1952), *A Star is Born* (1954), and similar films showed a surging and excessive interest in flamboyant style, glorying in color, bathing in fantasy, and idolizing star "images." Female forms from

Marilyn Monroe to Jayne Mansfield and foreign models like Sophia Loren and Brigitte Bardot bounced around the screen to reveal the supple woman as commodity. Decadent style and sexual titillation probably resulted from the increased popularity of television, the affluent society's latest individualized entertainment system, which by 1953 sat in the living rooms of 46.2 percent of all American households. The intimate experience of the living room screen supplanted the collective and social experience of the movie theater. Hollywood producers assumed that anyone who ventured out from this security sought adventure and escape on a grander scale than television could offer. In a limited sense, the lavish and anxiety-ridden movies which resulted were "escapist," but they were like the escape one made by pushing a button to close the car window, pushing other buttons to fill the car with recorded sounds and cool air, and pleasurably ignoring an ugly or bothersome world which now silently rolled past the car window with musical accompaniment.

Both the automobile experience and the film experience put barriers between their users and the social world which existed *outside*. Both experiences involved movement, and both permitted the consumer to select desirable settings or themes, offering an ecstatic experience potentially devoid of depressing connections to reality. In fact, Cinerama, the three-camera system which wrapped the visual field around the viewer, seemed like an affluent industry's attempt to imitate and exceed the automobile experience. Most sequences from early Cinerama films (*This is Cinerama*, 1954; *Cinerama Holiday*, 1956) were travelogue shots filmed from atop various forms of transportation, especially the automobile and airplane.

Both movies and automobiles increasingly reinforced personal isolation, whether in a commuter traffic jam or behind 3-D glasses, and thus they both served as sanctuaries of individualism in a world of corporate conformity. Some popular writers of the 1950s described the automobile as a machine-age "Walden," a space in which the individual could escape from the world's noises and commune with the buried self. Through heavy star-image melodramas, individual consumers could empathize with protagonists and actually "watch" themselves pass through some terrible tragedy. This paradox is what makes these two cultural icons so ambiguous: they were equally serviceable for antisocial behavior (fantasy indulgence, impulsive desires, extended solitude) *and* for traditional social rituals (dating, acquiring "discipline"). Because each member of the public craves both states of being, the industries, seemingly in cooperation, racked their brains for technical innovations, advertising slogans, *anything* that would lure consumers into their show-rooms.

It was appropriate that the two industries should meet in the 1950s—at the drive-in theater. Richard M. Hollingshead, Jr., who knew that even a Depression could not separate people from cars and films, created his first outdoor theater in 1933. Five years later, he lost a patent case in the Supreme Court, which by refusing to hear his appeal against E.M. Loew's Theaters effectively argued that the drive-in was not a patentable item. From 1954 to 1973, drive-ins earned approximately one-fourth of theater profits. The social nature of the movie experience underwent considerable revision at the drive-in because the car theater offered privacy in the midst of a crowd; it granted isolation inside the car and actually afforded the ticket buyer such alluring distractions within his car that movie viewing often became a secondary interest. Whereas the movie house audience departed with shared memories of a shared experience, the drive-in audience left the parking lot with such a wide variety of memories that sense of community seemed laughable. The theater was now one big parking lot filled with cars driven by people from no single neighborhood or group. The drive-in was an artificial community created by a consumer choice, something Daniel Boorstin later labeled a "consumption community."

These consumption communities flourished in the suburban culture, and in fact resembled a mobile tract development. Instead of the suburb's row of similar houses, each containing its own private space, the drive-in lined up similar cars, each with its private space and each with a picture-window view into the reel world. Furthermore, the popular features of the drive-in paralleled the experience of a suburban Sunday drive or an evening before television. No one had to dress up, the elderly or disabled did not need to be mobile, and everyone could converse freely without threat of being silenced from the next row. Most importantly, a young family did not need to hire a babysitter, a consideration which appealed to the postwar parents who had become Hollywood's over-thirty "lost audience." Perhaps that explains why drive-ins burgeoned in number from fifty-two in 1941 to 4,200 in 1954.

The curious combination of movies and cars rekindled the entrepreneurial fires extinguished in the nationalized production systems. In 1947, when the Supreme Court ordered major film companies to divest themselves of neighborhood theater operations, theater managers pursued their own methods of enticing potential customers out of their suburban homes. Michael Redstone in 1938 had amended Hollingshead's large front speaker system—a public nuisance which did not endear drive-ins to neighborhood civic groups—by decentralizing the sound system and putting a speaker in each car. But his ingenuity faded before the onslaught of gadgetry proffered in the 1950s. Reaching back to vaudeville, some Philadelphia drive-ins featured live stage shows prior to the feature film; patrons registered approval by honking their car horns. The Oasis Drive-In in Bensonville, Illinois, exploited a desert motif. Entering through a neon Taj Mahal, customers found their parking spot with the aid of a turbaned usher. Even though gently swaying palm trees (potted, of course) and a bubbling fountain system added a romantic touch, the Oasis may have been outclassed by a Weymouth, Massachusetts, drive-in featuring man-made moonlight. A Woodbridge, New Jersey operator issued credit cards, while a Belmar, New Jersey, colleague constructed a landing field for airplanes ($1.25 each planeload). The Autoscope Drive-In in Albuquerque, New Mexico, displayed 260 3 x 5 screens, one for each car. In Brattleboro's Lie-In Theatre, customers could line up in their car for 75 cents, or take a motel room whose front wall opened toward the outdoor screen ($16 per double room). Staying over Saturday night made sense in some Massachusetts car theaters where Sunday morning church services appeared in the mid-1950s, as did Sunday afternoon flea markets in California. In 1953, theater owner Stan Kohlberg of Oaklawn, Illinois, turned his back on Lake Michigan winters and remained open for the entire year. "I thought, if a father and mother and all the kids could go to one place and have a good time together, that could be the greatest thing in the world."

Not only did Detroit and Hollywood cross paths at the nation's drive-ins; they also met on television. The benefits to be accrued from filmed automobility dawned on Henry Ford quite early, and his company's film office delivered short and feature-length films to local dealer showrooms as well as neighborhood theaters free of charge. This same workable combination of advertisement and entertainment led the Ford Motor Company directly to television. The new visual medium could dynamically accentuate the pleasure and convenience of driving a Ford. When footage was shot at an extreme Dutch angle (*i.e.*, the horizon line made diagonal across the screen), the effortless motion seemed to defy gravity. Spatial dimensions became meaningless because the car's image filled the entire screen, and a series of quick, short shots elicited the feeling of quickness, agility, and speed. The auto industry now had a true media network. Ford sponsored the 1947 World Series and other special programs but finally settled for "The Ed Sullivan Show." General Motors backed "Bonanza," while Chrysler Corporation, which in 1955 spent 32 percent of its advertising budget on television spots, sponsored "The Best of Groucho." To see the increasingly glamorous car accompanied by its own song. "It's delightful, it's delovely, it's Desoto" interlaced among painstakingly diminished Marx humor in a talkshow format was to understand the difference between transient personalities and permanent institutions.

Like Detroit, Hollywood, increasingly involved in television production, came to realize the valuable asset its latest competitor represented and negotiated a *detente* which benefited both. General Teleradio, a division of General Tire and Rubber Company, paid $25,000,000 for the television transmission rights to 740 RKO feature films. Warner Brothers sold its films for $21,000,000, Twentieth Century-Fox for $30,000,000, and Paramount for $50,000,000. These pre-1948 'used' movies appeared on The Million Dollar Movie formats, frequently sponsored by an imaginative array of used car dealerships. Besides these 'used' shows, "77 Sunset Strip" attracted large audiences each week, and connected new cars with Hollywood lifestyles. Thus, television boosted both Hollywood and Detroit further into American consciousness.

The film and auto industries also had their detractors in the 1950s. Some "underground" filmmakers explored the medium's possibilities beyond the commercial product. One director, Maya Deren, made movies which attempted to study the nature of consciousness (*Meshes in the Afternoon*, 1943) and to portray abstract ideas like rhythm and movement (*Ritual in Transfigured Time*, 1948). Other "independent" filmmakers followed her lead, and by 1960 an organization, The New American Cinema Group, lent support to independent artists and gathered them into a community with shared interests. This group and others that followed differed from the Hollywood studio in size, purpose, and aesthetic bias, and consequently experimental films never challenged the corporate monsters' hold on market control. However, their mere existence demonstrated a growing frustration over the mindless formulas of studio production.

The automobile industry had its critics as well. Teen-agers, frequent carload patrons of drive-in movies, reworked their old jalopies, initiating a reaction against industry-wide uniformity as well as the annual model change which encouraged unnecessary waste. The young designers lowered front-ends and "raked" rear-ends; disassembled entire engines and rebuilt them with oddly-shaped "speed" parts; reworked carriage frames to permit faster cornering; softened cab interiors to create a womb-effect; and "leaded-in" exterior surfaces, molding a smooth overall body to highlight special paint which glistened in the sunlight. Similar predilections toward automotive remodeling stimulated these rebels to join together into clubs (some preferred the word "gangs"). Club members "toured" at night, "borrowing" hubcaps and pasting bumper stickers on "square" cars, *e. g.*, "Made in Detroit by Idiots!" Thus, while movies and cars decentralized leisure time and furthered cultural isolation, rebellious practitioners preoccupied with rearranging industrial styles organized clubs and groups to facilitate innovation.

By 1960, postwar trends revealed divergent paths for the two industries. The 52,772,000 family units in the country produced 40,000,000 movie viewers each week and purchased 6,674,796 new cars. Approximately 12 of every 100 families bought a new car, up slightly from the 10 of 1940. But each family averaged only .76 movie tickets each week, an astounding drop of 66 percent since 1940. Attendance at the movies, after reaching an all-time peak in 1946, started an irreversible decline, while automobile purchases continued a slow but steady ascent throughout the period.

Television, more attractive leisure activities, and higher ticket prices adversely affected movie attendance. But beginning in the mid-1950s movie audiences changed, and the former working-class entertainment became a middle-class activity. At the decade's end, those with less than a high school education said they attended movies rarely (66 percent said NEVER), while those with a college education went often (35 percent said FREQUENTLY). Furthermore, those who earned less than $7,000 attended less frequently (60 percent said NEVER) than those who made more than $15,000 (31 percent said FREQUENTLY). Perhaps film themes, subjects, and ideas, which increasingly came from the pens of highly educated, middle-class screenwriters, no longer suited working-class interests. Whatever the cause, one costly trend dominated the statistics: unlike automobiles, films were becoming a specialty industry, serving a diminishing portion of the population.

The auto industry's main problem did not relate to domestic trends such as increased prices, changing clientele, or alternative services. Detroit's biggest challenge involved foreign imports, which seemed to last longer, perform more efficiently, cost less, and even look jauntier zooming down the road. "Planned obsolescence," the practice of producing cars which needed replacement within a few years, insured a constant market for the giants. But it also locked the system into unbendable concepts such as increased production for increased profits. In the middle of the decade's economic boom and its spiraling production and peripheral frivolity, foreign cars invaded the market and attracted those people whose primary concerns centered on unique design and superior engineering. Foreign cars managed to amalgamate bourgeois respectability and value with latent teen-age rebellion. In 1955, 60,000 imported cars passed through United States customs; in 1959, 700,000. Imports in four years increased their market penetration from 1 percent to just under 70 per cent.

The film industry also faced a foreign invasion. World Wars I and II, as well as the Depression, had decimated European film production, especially in Germany and Italy. Some German directors, notably Fritz Lang, came to the United States, and some English directors, like Alfred Hitchcock, also were attracted by Hollywood's bigger budgets and public notoriety. But the disasters which gave an advantage to the American film industry did not completely obliterate innovation in Italy and France. Italian neo-realists such as Vittorio de Sica and Roberto Rossellini practiced a tighter, more evocative film style, while French "new wave" directors, among them Jean-Luc Godard, Alain Resnais, Louis Malle and Francois Truffaut, developed highly personal styles as they expanded the medium's range. These filmmakers penetrated the American markets because the increasingly elite film audience enjoyed their unique craft and provocative ideas. The educated minority which followed the foreign or "art film" (a popular misnomer) relished the aesthetic qualities of imported "vehicles." Workers once enjoyed movies because they momentarily alleviated industrial alienation; now affluent audiences looked to the film experience as either a reinforcement for their ideas or as a resource for a worldly education. Hollywood responded to the evocative foreign products by producing longer, more lavish films like *Ben Hur* (1959). An industry that had thrived on the indulgence of fantasies continued to do what it did best, and from this perspective one might say that it made a shrewd decision. Foreign films no longer lure away movie patrons, as foreign cars entice American buyers. It is *Star Wars*, an epic of hot-rods in space, that audiences desire, while the New Wave has flowed to Hollywood (Malle, Truffaut) or out to sea (Godard).

In summary, both industries closely identified themselves with the middle class, as suppliers and defenders of the "suburban" values. The industries relied on momentum, on ever-increasing luxury, but history shocked them with unexpected and almost fatal news. The middle class changed its values, of necessity, within an astonishingly short space of time, switching from big and beautiful cars to small, economical (and foreign) ones; but this same public, perhaps because of the same historical shocks, ultimately sought out the American luxury film with greater fervor than ever. Unlike the case of Jeeter Lester, moreover, this divided lifestyle spans generations. If this continues to be the case, the development of these two great American industries will diverge even further, until the dichotomy represented by the flamboyant Cecil B. De Mille and the austere Henry Ford once more defines our native culture.

GERALD D. SILK

THE IMAGE OF THE AUTOMOBILE
IN AMERICAN ART

Almost as soon as it was invented the automobile began to make inroads into the world of art. Although the major focus of this essay is the image of the automobile in American art, some preliminary discussion of European developments is appropriate because so many of the key themes of "auto-art" were inaugurated abroad. Indeed Italian Futurism was the first major art movement to adopt the automobile as a key image, and even *before* the Futurists exalted the racing car in 1909, several works of art appeared which were prophetic of the role of the car in contemporary culture. Among these were Toulouse-Lautrec's 1896 lithograph *The Motorist*, which portrays Lautrec's car-buff cousin as a supercharged extension of his fuming vehicle, and a 1904 advertisement for the Richard Brasier, a highly successful racing car, which shows a windswept mythological figure preceding the speeding coupe."

In the Lautrec, the diagonally-divided composition contrasts the vibrantly-delineated, forward-surging, explosive form of the car and its possessed driver with a female promenader and her dog, sketchily relegated to the background. Straddling the centuries, one foot in the nineteenth-century world of Impressionist imagery, the other in the twentieth-century realm of technological innovations, Lautrec achieves a dual perspective. His car's spewing exhausts, which seem about to enshroud the entire scene, suggest the dominant and ambiguous role the car would play in modern life. Toulouse-Lautrec's work, moreover, reveals his own passion for vehicles of speed, especially the bicycle and the motorcar, and his general fascination with the kinetics and rhythms of modern life, whether the terpsichorean movements of Parisian cafés or the technological motion of traveling vehicles.

The configuration of the Richard Brasier ad harks back to images of the classical theme of Aurora, goddess of the dawn leading the way for Apollo's sun-carrying chariot, now with the car as symbol of the

H. Bellery Desfontaines, *Automobiles Richard-Brasier,* 1904
lithograph, 84 × 144 cm

dawning of a new age, a modern-day chariot of Apollo bringing
technological power, energy, and light to the world. And the equation of the automobile with a classical god (or any classical artifact)
was symptomatic of a larger early twentieth-century development:
the emergence of the myth of the machine.

Since myths often arise to help explain complex and sometimes
unintelligible phenomena, it was inevitable that a mythology develop
around a class of objects felt to possess nearly supernatural powers,
objects which were both altering the environment and changing
man's perception of the world. Machines were most often used to
symbolize human power. Early in the century this "power-urge"
helped to inspire both the Futurist notion of a technological
Übermensch and the Dada practice of using machines to parody
human processes. Particularly popular was the exploitation of mechanical analogies for sexual behavior; such comparisons reveal the
Futurist obsession with machismo and sexual potency, a leitmotif
running through many of the movement's manifestoes and exemplified in the following passage from the *Founding and Manifesto of
Futurism* of 1909:

> We came up to three snorting beasts, to lay amorous hands on their scorching breasts. I stretched myself out on my machine like a corpse on its bier, but was revived at once under the steering wheel, a guillotine threatening my stomach.[1]

Or they could function totemically in Dada, à la Alfred Jarry, as a means of both elucidating or veiling processes regarded as illicit or taboo, as in many of Francis Picabia's mechanomorphic works, or even in Marcel Duchamp's famous *The Bride Stripped Bare by her Bachelors, Even (The Large Glass)* (1915–23), for the sexual activities described in the accompanying notes in *The Green Box* are often expressed in automotive terms.

Moreover, artists began to liken their creations to technological inventions. The artist identified himself with the engineer, a notion institutionalized in Futurism and perceptible in works of Constructivism, the Bauhaus, De Stijl, and other modern movements, receiving a sardonic twist with Andy Warhol, whose studio was called "the factory" and whose remark, "I think everybody should be a machine," became a Pop slogan.[2]

As noted earlier, Italian Futurism was the first important art movement to incorporate the car as a significant image. Inspired by the turn-of-the-century technological revolution, the Futurists regarded the automobile as a paradigmatic innovation. In 1909, Futurist poet and propagandist Filippo Tommasso Marinetti proclaimed in the christening broadside of the movement that

> . . . a racing car, its frame adorned with great pipes, like snakes with explosive breath . . . a roaring motor-car which looks as though running on shrapnel, is more beautiful than the Victory of Samothrace.

This analogy of a common technological object with a museum-enshrined classical masterpiece belligerently announced Futurism's rejection of the past in favor of the objects and ideas of the modern world. The selection of the automobile was based on the belief that it best expressed "the beauty of speed" and the concept of dynamism, and that these twin conquerors of space and time not only were the unique characteristics of the twentieth century, but also, as Henri Bergson concurrently suggested, the underlying forces of nature.

---

[1]F. T. Marinetti, "The Founding and Manifesto of Futurism," 1909. Quoted in Umbro Apollonio, *Futurist Manifestos*, 1973, pp. 20-21.

[2]Quoted in G.R. Swenson, "What is Pop Art?" (Part I), *Art News*, November, 1963, p. 26.

This new canon of speed and dynamism is immediately evident in Futurist representations of the automobile, which invariably depict the car in motion. For example, the work of Giacomo Balla, the Futurist artist most involved with the car (he did more than one hundred pieces relating to the theme), emphasizes its speed and motion, rather than its inherent form. By superimposing a repeating, diminishing image of the car from right to left, while overlaying and affixing lines and forms which reemphasize directional energy and activate the space that surrounds the vehicle, Balla, in his *Speeding Automobile* of 1913, initially accomplishes two things: he nearly obliterates the car's form within this network of quasi-abstract lines and shapes, and he creates the sensation of velocity and movement.*

However, these converging vectors and churning whirlpools, added to the sequential reiteration of the car's form, do more than create feelings of speed and movement; they also evoke the sensation of forces in struggle. The phalanx of V-shaped forms, which the Futurists called "force-lines" (basic units of force which all objects possess), and the coils of spiraling shapes are not simply kinetic signifiers, but also symbolize dynamic forces penetrating and scattering the static environment. Consequently, the painting can be interpreted as representing the battle between Futurism and the past. The automobile, the incarnation of speed, dynamism and forward-movement, is *symbolic of Futurism itself*, and the formerly static environment, now fragmented, is symbolic of the vanquished past. In other words, the auto becomes a kind of esthetic and cultural "getaway" car.

While the Futurists were fervently embracing the automobile as a symbol of cultural liberation, there seems to have been an ironic succession of events that conspired to exclude the car from American art in the early years of the century. For instance, the artists associated with the Ash Can school, the movement which chronologically coincided with the first flowering of the auto age in America, were avidly interested in urban life. However, for these artists the fascination of the city lay in the purely human interactions it produced. They believed machines did not enhance and perhaps even obstructed human intercourse; consequently, technological subject matter played a minor role in Ash Can art. In the mid- and late-Teens, there emerged a second generation of American artists concerned with urban and mechanical themes. Though many were strongly influenced by the Italian Futurists, these American artists were mesmerized by the

*See page 77—Ed.

overall dynamics of the metropolis. To their eyes gigantic and distinctively American artifacts such as the skyscraper and the bridge, not the car, functioned as symbols more aptly evocative of the grander energies of the burgeoning cityscape.

A notable exception to the car's ostracism in the early decades of the century can be found in the work of Ash Can artist John Sloan. A sympathizer with socialism, Sloan exploits the car's initial association with the upper classes as a means of ridiculing the rich. As early as 1907, in *Grey and Brass*, he perceived the pomp and circumstance that marked the wealthy group in their "brass-trimmed, snobbish, cheap, 'nouveau-riche'-laden automobile passing the park."3* In caricaturing the strivings of the new wealthy class, Sloan parodies the passion for fashionableness and possession symbolized by the triumvirate of good food, fine clothing, and fancy modes of conveyance transmogrified by excess. In another Sloan work, *Indian Detour*, the artist gives history a telling reversal, as tourist buses transporting well-to-do travelers encircle a group of Santa Fe Indians performing a ritual dance, inverting the nineteenth-century image of a ring of Conestogas protecting the pioneer from the Indian onslaughts. Sloan already seems to recognize the absurdity of associating car or bus travel with the frontier spirit, with the romantic notion of leaving civilization behind to explore virgin territory.

Curiously, the most significant contribution to the iconography of the automobile in American art during the first few decades of the twentieth century resulted from the contact of a European artist, Francis Picabia, with the American environment. Picabia, a Dada artist and a car fanatic (he owned nearly a hundred in his lifetime), introduced the image of car parts into his art while in America in 1915, utilizing these forms in highly personal ways. His most striking examples are his "object" or "machine" portraits. Unlike conventional portraits, they bear no likeness to the individual being portrayed, but through a string of "correspondences" make reference to the individual's personality, a procedure Picabia called "mechanical symbolism."

Thus, in his self-portrait entitled *Le Saint des Saints*, designed in 1915 for an edition of the Alfred Stieglitz publication *291*, Picabia represents himself as an automobile horn which, as various scholars have pointed out, refers to Picabia's notoriously clamorous personality and his role as a mouthpiece for modern art. It may be added that

---

3John Sloan, *New York Scene* (diaries, notes and correspondence 1906–13), 1965, p. 155.
*See page 72—Ed.

the sexual innuendoes of the drawing allude to his notoriously promiscuous behavior. Visually, the phallic nature of the automobile horn, and verbally, the inscription "Le Saint des Saints," an unlikely epithet for this rakish artist, suggest a sexual content. Moreover, the horn is not alone in the drawing but surmounts what can be identified as the cross-section of a car cylinder; Picabia superimposes and visually interlocks the tooting end of his horn with the combustion chamber, that region where the mechanical explosion erupts. These drawings, derived from advertisements and diagrams in auto trade journals, also reflect Picabia's fascination with the captivating powers of American advertising, powers he hoped to transfer to his own art.

From the microcosmic world of Picabia's isolated car parts let us move to the macrocosmic world of the automobile assembly factory in Charles Sheeler's depictions of the Ford River Rouge plant. Sheeler's paintings, done in the early Thirties and executed from photographs he was commissioned to take for the Ford Motor Company, express the cleanliness and precision that characterized Picabia's work, at the same time they forge a link with the American nineteenth-century image of the idealized and aggrandized landscape. But now the landscape is an industrial one, the myth of the wilderness replaced by the myth of industrial capacity.

The irony of Sheeler's tranquil vision is that a year after its execution the River Rouge plant was the scene of a bloody clash between striking auto workers and the police in which several demonstrators were killed. A view of the auto factory more attuned to its violent potentiality was Diego Rivera's controversial murals of Detroit industry, commissioned by Edsel B. Ford for the Detroit Institute of Arts in 1931 and completed in 1933.

Animated and complex, Rivera's two major frescoes, both devoted to auto manufacturing, are a far cry from Sheeler's serene images. Sweeping serpentine rhythms unite the quasi-mechanized men and the quasi-anthropomorphized machines into one gigantic interdependent "organo-mechanism." The sinuosity of movement and the repeating rows of workers performing identical tasks or twisting and bending in slightly different poses, which, like movie frames, document the sequential progress of the assembly line, are both dance-like and hypnotic, and consequently ritualistic in feel. Rivera, who in his Mexican works elucidated the magnificent cultural achievements of "Old America" by intertwining her ancient legends, myths, rituals, and actual historical events, presents the assembly line as a personification of the myth, ritual, and historical actuality of the "New America."

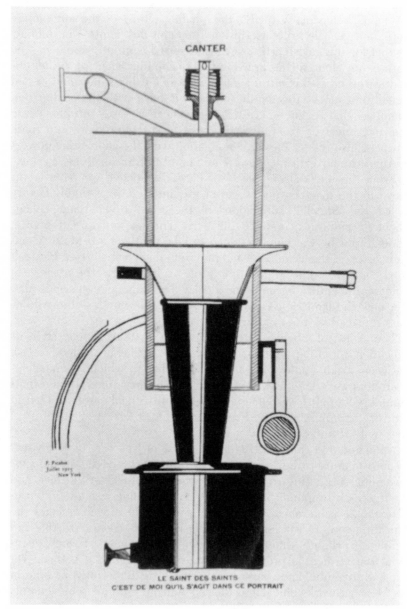

Francis Picabia, *Le Saint de Saints,* 1915 from *291,* nos. 5–6, July–August, 1915

The major theme of the mural is the split between the constructive and destructive potential of new technology. The negative side is immediately recognizable in the dehumanizing nature of assembly-line existence: man is subjugated to the relentless rhythmic demands of programmed machines. Such expressions were common in the Thirties and Rivera's murals have important cinematic and literary parallels. Charlie Chaplin's indictment of mass production in *Modern Times* of 1936 was modeled after Detroit assembly-line techniques similar to those of parts production in Rivera's murals, and John Dos Passos's *The Big Money* (1936), the final part of the USA trilogy, documents worker degradation in a passage that could easily be an analysis of Rivera's frescoes:

> At Ford's, production was improving all the time; less waste, more spotters, strawbosses, stoolpigeons (fifteen minutes for lunch, three minutes to go to the toilet, the Taylorized speed-up everywhere, reachunder, adjustwasher, screwdown bolt, shove in cotterpin, reachunder, screwdown bolt, reachunderadjustscrewdownreachunderadjust, until every ounce of life was sucked off into production and at night, the workmen went home gray shaking husks).

That technology has a positive side is made clear throughout the murals by a series of contrasting images—good on the left and evil on the right. An avowed Communist, Rivera regarded assembly-line work as a prime example of collectivism, which when properly employed could eliminate material wants and strenuous labor; therefore, it could serve as a model for a socialist society.[4]

The next decade, dominated by war, produced no automobile images as suggestive as those already discussed. The 1950s, however, ushered in a new age in automotive history. The new goal was to sell more cars in the prosperous postwar economy to a public which reasserted its purchasing power with a vengeance. The means of improving consumption were several, but most pertinent to our subject was the concept of obsolescence, both in style and workmanship. Increasingly sophisticated advertising stimulated consumer appetites for glamorous and romantic images. Fantasies were attached to the automobile which not only made cars more desirable commod-

[4]A good discussion of Rivera's murals can be found in Max Kozloff, "The Rivera Frescos of Modern Industry at the Detroit Institute of Art. Proletarian Art Under Capitalist Patronage," *Artforum*, Nov., 1973, pp. 58-64. For the most up-to-date information on both Sheeler's and Rivera's work for Ford see: *The Rouge: The Image of Industry in the Art of Charles Sheeler and Diego Rivera* (cat.), Detroit Institute of Arts, 1978.

ities, but also reflected the belief that the car symbolized a "freedom"—political, social, cultural, and economic—that had been cramped and threatened by Depression and war.

Art in the mid-Fifties responded to this shift in emphasis by commenting on what might be called the "consumer-technological" culture. The result was Pop Art, a movement which co-opted the subject matter and techniques of the mass media. Although Pop culture was strongest in America, Pop Art was launched in Great Britain in the mid-Fifties in the work of Richard Hamilton and Ed Paolozzi. The initially euphoric and exciting attitude toward Pop culture was, to a great extent, the result of observing this phenomenon through the distorted, somewhat rose-colored lenses of geographical separation. British Pop artist Gerald Laing articulated this sentiment:

> That Utopian dream of the USA which I held in common with most of my contemporaries in London, which made it inevitable that I should eventually choose to depict these gleaming exotic images and extravagant attitudes so heavily propagandized in Europe and which for us implied not only an optimistic classless society but that every American had his hot-rod and his surf-board.[5]

When Pop Art developed in America, the romantic haze of the separating ocean dissipated and American dispassion replaced British fascination as an attitude toward consumer society. Although the auto remained a symbol of consumer culture and of its transformation of the environment and its consequent alteration of sensibility, both perceptually and psychologically, the euphoria of the British outlook was considerably devalued in American Pop images.

For example, Andy Warhol's *Car Crash* series is not a glamorization of the "autoculture," but a commentary on the atavistic nature of technological advancement, and on the anesthetizing effects of American mass-produced life. In an era when the death-counts of the Vietnam war attracted less attention than the daily Dow-Jones averages, the countless number of car wrecks were shrugged off as a part of everyday reality. As Warhol stated, "When you see a gruesome picture over and over, it really doesn't have any effect."[6] This attitude toward society recurs in Jean-Luc Godard's film, *Weekend*, in

[5]Gerald Laing, statement in "Environment U.S.A.: 1957-1967," *Sao Paulo 9* (catalogue), 1967, p. 82.

[6]Swenson, *op. cit.* p. 24.

which car wrecks become symbolic of the paradox of progress. Both Warhol and Godard display the savage assault of mass culture on both the mind and the body, and the reduction of "advanced" civilization into a kind of mental wasteland and physical junkheap.

American Pop explored not only the emotional and psychological effects of the automobile and mass culture, but also their perceptual impact, often in relation to the world of "highway culture," that is, the world of billboards, strip architecture and clutter, and super-highway sterility. Trained as a billboard painter, the artist James Rosenquist, whose paintings often contain the consumer culture triad of food, sex, and cars, reflects through leaps in scale and fragmentation of images the disorientation and confusion of the modern environment. Billboards, which the writer Matthew Josephson remarked as early as 1922 "represent America's indigenous art-form containing the fables of her people,"[7] also influenced artist Robert Indiana, who adopted their hardness and precision as the formal basis of his work. His art, like the road signs it emulates, is both visually arresting and symbolic of extended information. As Pop architect Robert Venturi argues:

> Only symbols . . . can evoke the instant associations crucial for today's vast spaces, fast speeds, complex programs, and perhaps jaded sense which can respond only to bold stimuli.[8]

Alan D'Arcangelo paints the other type of autoscape—the pure geometric interstate, not the cluttered sign-and store-laden strip. D'Arcangelo responds to the hard clean surface both of the super-highway and of minimalist art, posing the question—"Is this a highway center strip or a derivative Barnett Newman 'Zip'?" A work such as *Holy Family* makes reference to the experiences of the contemporary family unit, a modern-day Mary, Joseph, and Jesus, who travel not across the desert by donkey, but speed across the desert-like Interstate Highway System. The rest stops are not shade trees and babbling brooks but Burger Kings and Best Western Motor Lodges.

Moreover, in D'Arcangelo's work, the inclusion of the car's rear-view mirror emphasizes the sensation that what is approaching is identical to what has passed and vice versa. The work suggests not only a condition of "highway hypnosis" but also the increasing standard-

---

[7]Matthew Josephson, "The Great American Billposter," *Broom*, November, 1922, p. 304.
[8]Quoted in Fran Schulze, "Chaos in Architecture," *Art in America*, July-August, 1970, p. 90.

ization of road-related experiences, a theme further explored in the work of Ed Ruscha. Ruscha's laconic *Standard Station, Amarillo, Texas (Day)* (note that he chose a *Standard* station rather than Exxon or Shell and that he geographically and temporally locates it in the title because it could be any station, anywhere, anytime) brings to mind a passage from X.J. Kennedy's poem, "Driving Cross Country":

> A room the same as last night's room,
> Exact same bath mat underfoot.
> In thrall to some unlucky charm,
> We hurtle; but, it seems, stay put.

In another *Gas Station*, George Segal frames his characteristic rough-hewn, white plaster figures in a rigidly architectonic, Mondrianesque environment, effecting a haunting dialogue between specificity and departicularity, creating an ambience recalling Vladimir Nabokov's description in *Lolita* of a roadside station with its

> stationary trivialities . . . . : that green garbage can, those very black, very white-walled tires for sale, those bright cans of motor oil, that red icebox with assorted drinks, the four, five, seven discarded bottles within the incompleted crossword puzzle of their wooden cells.

Thus, a recurring theme in American Pop art is the non-uniqueness and homogeneity of experience, the growing standardization, both perceptually and psychologically, that mass culture has produced. As a prime contributor to this state of affairs, the automobile became a standard image in American Pop.

The "Consumer-technological" society which the Pop artists explored has as one of its byproducts a vast proliferation of junk, due in part to the automobile industry's principle of "dynamic obsolescence." Like recycling ecologists, a number of sculptors such as Richard Stankiewicz, Jason Seley, John Chamberlain, and Cesar raid the auto junkyard for raw material, transubstantiating the dross of car cadavers into the esthetic gold of sculpture, a process Marshall McLuhan tellingly labeled the "phoenix syndrome," and establishing the technique known as "assemblage."

Cesar's approach is particularly intriguing. In a manner which brings to mind Claes Oldenburg's softening of objects, Cesar crushes cars in a compactor and consecrates them in sculpture. By altering the original form of the vehicle, Cesar eradicates the glamorous and dynamic associations of its once baroque fins, fenders and bumpers, creating a monolithic static hulk which sardonically foretokens the emergence of minimalist sculpture while it functions as a kind of stele to the internal combustion age.

If any group of artists explode the romantic myth of the automobile which the Futurists initiated and the British Pop artists perpetuated, it is the American photo-realists. Utilizing the automobile, truck, or motorcycle as an important image and symbol of the environment, the Photo-realists, far from reveling in speed and dynamism, work from photographic images of immobile vehicles parked in streets, auto graveyards, shopping centers, fast-food chains, or used-car lots. The inherent qualities of the inert car—shape, texture, surface, color, light—become the subject of their paintings.

Yet formalism is only half the story in photo-realist art. For instance, photo-realist Don Eddy's *Private Parking X* of 1971 depicts the way America travels—by car and by credit—in images ostensibly indicative of freedom. In all cases this freedom is illusory. The automobile, often considered the freest form of transportation, in reality is highly expensive, costing dearly in money, natural resources, and human lives. The BankAmericard in the foreground of the painting signifies credit, which superficially diminishes the pain of purchasing and creates a "false" sense of "free" money. The Blue Chip stamps sign offers the promise of "free gifts," which in actuality are paid for by the consumer well in advance of their redemption. Thus a sign, *PRIVATE Parking,* and a chain-link enclosure point up the contradictory nature of the automobile's Orwellian "free-ness."

Perhaps the most hauntingly evocative photo-realist images are those of Robert Bechtle, who has been dubbed "the poet of the parking lot." Although his paintings contain other elements besides automobiles, they invariably receive their titles from the cars in the picture. For instance, a painting that might appropriately be labeled "Family Portrait" is, in fact, called *'61 Pontiac.* The family poses in front of the car, which, depicted in stasis, is no longer a symbol of liberation, but of stultification.*

Claes Oldenburg has said, "The world frightened me. It would be great to control the world by creating all the objects in it."[9]

---

*See page 312—Ed.

[9]Quoted in Harris Rosenstein, "Climbing Mt. Oldenburg," *Art News,* February, 1966, p. 23.

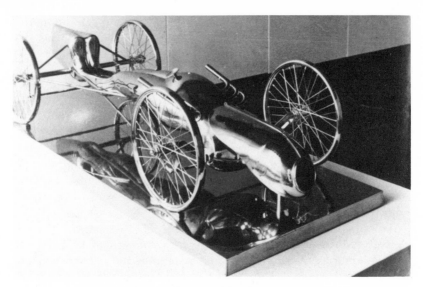

Ernest Trova, *Falling Man / Study (Carman)*, 1966
silicon bronze, 21 × 79 × 31″ (edition of six)
Courtesy Pace Gallery, New York

Oldenburg's career is a testimony to this pursuit, and like a number
of contemporaries who react against the feeling of helplessness in the
face of new technology, he has done many pieces involving the automobile. Described by Oldenburg as "his most natural subject, because of all of the doubles man has made of himself . . . the car is the
most ever-present, competitive and dangerous," the auto crops up in
his happenings, environments, proposed monuments, and in his
characteristic denatured sculptures.[10] In one series, Oldenburg selected as an icon of the automobile age the 1930s Chrysler Airflow, a
breakthrough in car design whose salient characteristic was streamlining. By softening the hard object, or by dissecting it into parts,
Oldenburg controverts the dynamic essence of its streamlining, exerting his control over it and rendering it limp and impotent. In a
democratizing maneuver, Oldenburg's *Airflow* became the cover for
Art News in February, 1966—a cardboard cut-out providing every
magazine purchaser with his own automobile voodoo doll. Meanwhile,
other contemporary artists made similar efforts to control the auto-

[10]Quoted in Barbara Rose, *Claes Oldenburg* (cat.), Museum of Modern Art, 1970, p. 97.

mobile symbolically in their art. Among them is Wolf Vostell who encased a Cadillac in concrete, thus giving the automobile, which has caused so much of nature to be paved over and *concretized*, its just desserts.

While Oldenburg and Vostell effect symbolic control over the automobile, other artists willingly document the increasing power of the car over man, as evidenced in the work of Ernest Trova and Hugo Schumacher. Trova's chilling, science-fiction image *Falling Man* seems to extrapolate theories of evolution in which man's body changes according to the use and disuse of certain parts. The dependence of man on the motorcar is reflected in a hybrid, eugenic image. Arms and legs become wheels and axles, across which is stretched a streamlined, sexless body, whose navel becomes a fuel tank (man's new umbilical cord) and to whose lungs are attached fin-like exhaust pipes, recalling man's alleged aquatic origins in an earlier state of evolution. Schumacher, in his *Frautos* series, paints women's torsos, in which flesh becomes shiny metal, bumper-shaped breasts are nipped with Mercedes-Benz symbol pasties, and hands and rib cage assume the guise of a car radiator.

As the work of Trova and Schumacher suggest, the theme of sex and the automobile gained great favor in contemporary art, a trend which has parallels in modern literature, music, and cinema. Examples abound; among the more provocative is Luis Jiminez's sculpture from his *American Dream* series, a depiction reminiscent of the scene in Thomas Pynchon's novel *V*, in which Rachel Owlglass utters smoldering entreaties to her MG:

> "You beautiful stud," she said. "I love to touch you. Do you know what I feel when we're out on the road? alone, just us?" She was running her hands caressingly over the front bumper. "Your funny responses, darling, that I know so well. The way your brakes pull a little to the left, the way you start to shudder around 5000 rpms when you're excited. And you burn oil when you're mad at me, don't you?"

Perhaps the most famous work of art involving auto-sex relationships is Ed Kienholz' *Back Seat Dodge '38*.* First exhibited in Los Angeles in 1964, the work was scandalously received, and a crusade spearheaded by County Supervisor (and candidate for Governor of California) Warren Dorn branded the piece obscene and pornographic. Unable to get the show closed, Dorn at least got the door of the car

*See page 309—Ed.

closed, except for specific tours restricted to those eighteen years or older.

In this environmental piece, the truncated car, front-seat excised, becomes a kind of "bedroom-on-wheels," recalling John Steinbeck's often-quoted remark in *Cannery Row* that "most of America's children were conceived in Model T-Fords and not a few of them were born in them." The sexually-engaged figures, a beer-drenched chicken-wire male and plaster female, fuse in a single, faceless, conjugal head, which contains a photograph of a salacious scene, suggesting the fantasy-reality interface of sexual activity, a kind of "eroticartesian" mind-body split.

Though it is voyeuristic in nature, Kienholz, by lining the interior windows of the *Dodge* with mirrors, short-circuits the pleasures of voyeurism, thus confronting the spectator with his own viewing of the work. *Back Seat Dodge '38*, temporally located by a variety of details in the mid-Forties and exhibited in Los Angeles in the mid-Sixties, exposes the true morality (or immorality) of an older generation which was presently criticizing the new morality (especially the sexual mores) of the Sixties generation. (Curiously, a hypothetical child conceived in the *Dodge* would have been about 20 years old when the work was completed.) The middle-aged protectors of the public morality are "caught with their pants down," so to speak, and this exposure is made even more embarrassing because they are revealed in that trysting spot where they felt most secure—the car.

Although a general trend seems to suggest that the initial Futurist romance with the automobile has tempered somewhat, attesting to the recognition of the abuses of technology in the intervening years, positive expressions toward the car can be found throughout the Fifties, Sixties, and Seventies. Artists such as Don Potts and Peter Harholt express a genuine fascination with the inherent beauty of the car's form, and Harholt's self-built Lotus, replete with Jasper Johns numerals and Washington Color School stripes, served both as his MFA thesis and his entry into numerous sports car races. It thus became perhaps the first officially sanctioned work of art to compete in a car race, a fitting fulfillment of Marinetti's Futurist pronouncement. Also in the spirit of Futurism are contemporary car customizers, individuals whom Tom Wolfe has called "America's true folk artists," and perhaps her "true avant-garde," working in garages rather than garrets. In their attempt to dynamize, estheticize, and personalize stodgy, mass produced automobiles, customizers carry on the legacy of Ettore Bugatti, the artist who, working at the time of Futurism, broke from conventional art and began designing cars.

Still, most of the ecstatic, automobile-related themes which the Futurists inaugurated have their negative counterparts in contemporary art, and the promises of a technological nirvana that the Futurists heralded has become instead a macadamized, bumper-to-bumper hell. The more critical attitude of today's artists toward the car reflects the reality that a future history of the automobile may cite the Seventies and Eighties as the decades in which the automobile's impact on society reached its apogee. But the auto remains a resilient artifact. So far it has survived energy crises, skyrocketing prices, sweeping recalls, and pollution alerts. No substantive alternative to auto transport has yet been realized. As long as the car is with us, providing emotional experiences, taking lives, metamorphosing the environment, and altering perceptions, art will be influenced by and comment on this most inspirational of modern inventions.

for Robert Phillips

If you stare long enough perhaps it becomes beautiful.
If you translate its colors into comely sounds—
ochre, russet, coppery-pink, nutmeg—
perhaps it becomes merely an anti-world,
another way of seeing.

An industrial slum gaily glaring
in a mid-summer squall:
porous smoke rising heavy and leaden-pale as a giant's limbs,
the sickly air heaving in gusts,
sulphurous blooms whipping in the wind.
Here, an ancient sea-bed
guarded by a twelve-foot chain link fence.
Clouds break companionably about the highest smokestacks.
Factory windows, opaque with grime, slant open
into the 100° shade.
You stare, you memorize, you do not wish to judge.
Your lungs shrink shy of the bold air.

Scars' stitchings in the earth,
high-tension wires whining thinly overhead.
What is there to say about what we see,
what is the compulsion to make judgments,
to invent visions?

This is the base of the pyramid, of course.
But it is not strewn with workers' bones:
it glowers and winks with their acres of parked cars.
If the air is noxious perhaps it is you who have weakened.

It is you who wonder what creatures gaze in such pastures,

brood beside such rancid ponds—
giant crab-spiders of wire and rust,
toads with swollen white bellies,
armoured things with spiny tails and eyes
staring unperturbed at the ends of stalks.
It is you who observe most of *Ford* obscured by filth:
And you who see again at the top of the highest smokestack
the same plastic wreath you'd seen at Christmas,
wondering if it was a joke:
Joy to the World   Gilmore Chemicals.

What is there to say about what we see,
what we cannot not see?

Reprinted with permission from *The Iowa Review*, IX:3 (Summer 1978)

LAURENCE GOLDSTEIN

THE AUTOMOBILE AND
AMERICAN POETRY

If the business of America is business, as Calvin Coolidge memorably proclaimed, then the supreme realization of national identity between the wars was certainly Henry Ford's construction of the Rouge River factory complex in Dearborn. Encompassing all aspects of the manufacturing process, from blast furnace and foundry to moving assembly line, it symbolized the self-sufficiency and astonishing magnitude of the American free enterprise system, and, by extension, of the American dream itself. As the demiurge of this industrious world, Ford built into his creation the dynamic principles of power, economy, continuity, and speed which he conceived as essential to the success of mass production, and therefore essential to the vitality of the democratic ideal he served. He added to those the virtue next to godliness, erecting giant windows to open the white-and blue-painted walls and ceilings to sunlight, in order to reveal how clean, spacious, and well-ventilated a workers' hive could be. He offered the Rouge to artists as a model of the new historical era—some, like Charles Sheeler and Diego Rivera, agreed to immortalize it—and to the public at large in daily tours. Multitudes looked upon it and saw that it was good.

But time works upon cultural symbols no less than upon their creators. A half-century after the Rouge triumphantly produced its first Model A, the energy crisis, the environmentalist movement, and the simple facts of economic life have altered, probably forever, the Rouge's public image. The poem by Joyce Carol Oates preceding this essay provides a convenient and dramatic measurement of the change. In 𝒮––– , the proud name "obscured by filth," the Rouge becomes the monumental ruin of a commercial empire. Like the Acropolis or Roman Colosseum in the elegiac poetry of other ages, the Rouge is a community dispossessed of purpose and belief. Haunted only by organic forms of the most demonic kind, in an atmosphere of smoke and grime, this "industrial slum" rebuffs the hopes once invested in it. Readers of contemporary poetry are familiar with

satirical poems about the planned obsolescence of automobiles—
Howard Nemerov's "Ozymandias II" and Philip Booth's "Maine," for
example—but the decay depicted here is more fundamental and the
tone more prophetic. "You do not wish to judge," Oates writes, but
the negative judgment is implied in the selection of detail and in the
plangent conclusion.

The function of ruins poems, aside from the pleasurable shudder
of horror they provoke, is reformist; they awaken the reader to
preservative action. A poem like 🚗 is not written with vindictive
intentions; if anything it is generous in withholding judgment, for
there are prophets aplenty in America who have denounced the
iniquity that Oates merely suggests. In the 1970s alone, such books
as these argued that the once-flourishing industry symbolized by the
Rouge had reached an end: Kenneth R. Schneider, *Autokind vs.
Mankind*, John Burby, *The Great American Motion Sickness*, Tabor
R. Stone, *Beyond the Automobile*, Ronald A. Buel, *Dead End: The
Automobile in Mass Transportation*, Helen Leavitt, *Superhighway-
Superhoax*, John Jerome, *The Death of the Automobile*, Emma
Rothschild, *Paradise Lost*, and Lester Brown, *Running on Empty*.
These jeremiads claim that history has turned against the automobile
because its manufacturers misunderstood the essential meaning and
destiny of their product, and in so doing brought ruin to themselves
and to the humane values they flaunted before being overtaken by
crisis. Though none of these authors looks to poetry for counsel,
Oates's poem reminds us that poets, as the unacknowledged legislators of mankind, are accustomed to providing just the kind of preservative service most in need at this watershed of industrial evolution.
As interpreters of the latent meaning of things, poets are likely to
offer significant guidance for the reshaping of "what we cannot not
see" into a form closer to our desire. To be sure, poets assumed this
role grudgingly in the early decades of this century, but their plenti-
ful warnings since then, as well as their imaginative prescriptions for
the car's use according to its true nature, deserve a respectful hearing. What follows is an analysis of significant American poems about
the automobile, diverse in theme and point of view but all useful in
forming a consensus for action in the final decades of this century.

I

At the turn of the century, America must have seemed a country
God-given for the automobile, a territory waiting for a means of

transportation as Eden required Adam and Eve to complete its perfection. The great poet of this continent's manifest destiny was Walt Whitman, who barely preceded the automobile age but seemed to attain a Pisgah sight of its wonders. "Oh highway . . . you express me better than I can express myself," he marveled at the eastern edge of the Open Road. By his expansive catalogues of American places he fed that hunger for restless movement and raw experience that characterizes the national identity. It is entirely proper that D.H. Lawrence imagined Whitman himself in vehicular terms:

> He drove an automobile with a very fierce headlight, along the track of a fixed idea, through the darkness of this world. . . . I, seeing Walt go by in his great fierce poetic machine, think to myself: What a funny world that fellow sees!
> ONE DIRECTION! toots Walt in the car, whizzing along it. . . .
> ONE DIRECTION! whoops America, and sets off also in an automobile.

The poets and readers who followed Whitman, however, stepped back from his bulldozing example. Perhaps the world of modern inventions he found so promising came to look merely vulgar to the next generation. Or perhaps his "barbaric yawp" put into disrepute his mode of praise. Whatever the reason, it would be many decades before a good poet granted the automobile much reality.

The curious silence can be observed in the most popular anthologies of serious verse in the modern period. For better or worse, anthologies are the chief conduits whereby a national audience is introduced to innovative texts. Their contents provide us with a fair index of public taste and of the range of contemporary writing that at once reflects and reforms that taste. The first important anthology that might be expected to notice the automobile was Louis Untermeyer's groundbreaking collection of 1919, *Modern American Poetry*, which made a special effort to champion the Whitmanian practice of lending dignity to allegedly unpoetic objects, including mechanical inventions large and small. And yet despite the emphasis on modernity in his preface, there is only one line of one poem in the whole anthology that mentions an automobile. "The rich man has his motor-car," writes the now-forgotten F.P. Adams in a bit of whimsy. This single instance illustrates the fact that the car made its principal appearances in light verse, songs, ballads, and other popular forms.

The cautious Untermeyer proved to be ahead of his time. When Conrad Aiken in 1927 prepared his anthology *Modern American Poets* for the Modern Library, he took special pride in its contemporary flavor; not one poem in it mentions an automobile. Two years later John Drinkwater, Henry Seidel Canby, and William Rose Benét produced the most comprehensive anthology yet, *Twentieth Century Poetry*, including British and American writers; not one poem in it mentions an automobile.

Poets are not obliged to take note of anything, of course. Poetry is an art of exclusion and concentrated focus; literary history tells us that the most encyclopedic poets, with a few famous exceptions, usually fail to write verse of enduring interest. But this neglect—one might almost say boycott—of the automobile *is* significant because it extends to almost every other industrial product and therefore represents a rejection of "business" as a dignified subject of discourse. The car is seen to be part of the world that "is too much with us," in Wordsworth's phrase, and the disregard of modern poets matches Wordsworth's dislike and fear of the mechanical forms which increasingly occupied a rural landscape privileged to poets for millennia. The poets' almost conspiratorial strategy to take no cognizance of mechanistic intruders—as true of masters like Pound, Yeats, and Stevens as of genteel lady poets with three names—had profound effects in modern literature. It produced a variety of unworldly reveries that rank among the greatest lyrics of all time— precisely because they *are* purified of the journalistic impulse to pounce on what is novel and newsworthy. But inseparable from the triumph is the remorse and self-doubt that flow from a reactionary consciousness. Ezra Pound laments:

> How our modernity
> Nerve-wracked and broken, turns
> Against time's way and all the way of things,
> Crying with weak and egoistic cries.

And W.C. Williams asks in a youthful romance in the Shelleyan mode, "How shall I be a mirror to this modernity?" The anxiety to "make it new," to champion modernity and yet not succumb to the vulgar appeal of new inventions, characterizes the esthetics of this century.

The one poet after Whitman who tried programmatically to bridge the abyss opening between poetry and a new generation which

increasingly looked to figures like Edison and Ford as the truest
native geniuses, was Carl Sandburg. His "Portrait of a Motorcar" in
1918 is the earliest poem on the subject by an important poet. This is
the complete text:

> It's a lean car . . . a long-legged dog of a car . . . a gray-ghost eagle
> car.
> The feet of it eat the dirt of a road . . . the wings of it eat the hills.
> Danny the driver dreams of it when he sees women in red skirts
> and red sox in his sleep.
> It is in Danny's life and runs in the blood of him . . . a lean
> gray-ghost car.

Sandburg's intention is to absorb the car back into the creaturely or
primitive world, to identify it as a totem of the industrial tribe. The
penetration of the car into remote parts of the American continent, a
fact of life by 1918, is acknowledged in the image of the eagle, the
bird of empire and the *genius loci* of the Western mountains. The
poem enacts the process of mythologizing; not in Sandburg's mind, it
must be noted, but in Danny the driver's. Using Danny as an
intermediary, Sandburg can expose the dream of speed as a desire
for male conquest, its lusty origin signalled by the red skirts and sox
of the women Danny admires in the same dream. Unfortunately,
Sandburg does not anatomize the condition he suggests, and his
failure to articulate, to join this simple perception to a larger body of
vision, makes the poem propitiatory, seemingly frightened of its
subject.

Sandburg's failure is significant, for of all modern poets he possessed the most sympathy for the capacity of machines to fulfill
human longings, and the willingness to interpret the American past
as an informative source of his belief in progress. W.C. Williams, a
greater poet, had no such sympathies, as his dismissive poem on the
car, "Ballad of Faith" ("No dignity without chromium/No truth but a
glossy finish" etc.) clearly demonstrates. Sandburg would not trace
out the ramifications of the yearning for power he describes in poems
like "Portrait of a Motorcar," but instead retreats into a reportorial
mode that gives up the field entirely. He will not challenge mechanical energy with articulate energy; he will not bring to his poem the
hard thought and complex design that characterize his resourceful
subject. Rather, he accepts his marginality amidst the modernity
pushing him to the wall. Hugh Kenner has characterized The Pound

Era, as he calls it, by terms such as "an esthetic of glimpses," a poetry of "eschewals and refrainings" in which the content remains mute and undeclared, suggested rather than studied. In fact, this withdrawal from the realm of polemics disguised an envy of the prophetic mode. Few poets resisted the call to speak out during the 1930s when opportunities for political alignment arose. Pound took his stand with the fascist cause; Sandburg as energetically defended egalitarianism and the poet's clarion function in the free world.

It is no surprise, then, to find Sandburg in his long prose poem of the 1930s, *The People, Yes,* finally turning back to the automobile to fill in the unspoken implications of his youthful "Portrait":

> One of the Cherokees in Oklahoma, having a million or so from oil rights, went to a motorcar dealer, looked over the different new makes, and in a corner of the salesroom noticed a brand-new white hearse, embellished, shining, emblazoned. "This one for me," he said, and he rode away, his chauffeur driving and himself seated inside the glittering white funeral car. They tell this in Oklahoma as a folk tale. It is.

Here is the victim's perspective on young Danny's obsession. The native Americans possessed a mystical or "poetic" kinship with the landscape and its creatures. But for them there can be no sharing the land with the new totem of an advancing civilization, the overwhelming car which, like the train in Hart Crane's *The Bridge,* brings an "iron-dealt cleavage" to the community of man and nature. The wilderness is transformed into oil fields to service the machinery that will occupy still more of the land and further dispossess its natives. The Cherokee has of necessity traded his inheritance for a white death-symbol of the historical force ruining his way of life. This is the kind of warning that a culture sensitive to the perils of accelerated social change needed to preserve it from the fate which has overtaken it in the 1970s. In the 1930s, of course, the public had troubles enough to distract it from the automobile, such as the European conflict Sandburg summons in the conclusion of the poem. And Sandburg would have been the first to acknowledge that the American ideals which later prevailed over the fascist juggernaut had been strengthened by the independence and pride of property endowed by the automobile, and by the mechanical expertise required of a car-producing and car-owning nation.

Sandburg's "folk tale" is an authentic scion of the pastoral mode,

which constantly assesses the competing claims of nature and culture. In such poems, since the time of Virgil's first eclogue, the
march of progress has been regretted by the impotent poet, whose
warnings of irretrievable loss nevertheless have helped to create an
ecological conscience in the civilization at large. One contemporary
work in a direct line with Sandburg's is William Stafford's wry poem,
"Written on the Stub of the First Paycheck," which has these first
and final stanzas:

> Gasoline makes game scarce.
> In Elko, Nevada, I remember a stuffed wildcat
> someone had shot on Bing Crosby's ranch.
> I stood in the filling station
> breathing fumes and reading the snarl of a map.
>
> It takes a lot of miles to equal one wildcat
> today. We moved into a housing tract.
> Every dodging animal carries my hope in Nevada.
> It has been a long day, Bing.
> Wherever I go is your ranch.

Here again is the demythologizing of the dream—Danny's dream—
which fuses car and animal into a single ontological shape. Bing
Crosby, that most gentle of singers, has increased his wealth by
providing an arena where people can more easily kill animals; they
simply drive in by virtue of the gasoline extracted from the same
Western lands. Even to escape this preserve of civilization one must
use the cars that symbolize murderous intentions, and, alas, murderous accidents on the road. But in fact there is no escape, for
every odometer mile extends the fence within which the wild creation is made scarce: "Wherever I go is your ranch." Nature, including human nature, encompasses the principles of Eros and Thanatos,
but the driver's perspective reveals more of death than of love.

II

If poets insisted on this division into Eros and Thanatos for a long
time—Karl Shapiro's diptych "Buick" and "Auto Wreck" will offer us
another example—it is because the industry promoted it and historical circumstances endorsed its truth. As the most ubiquitous and
ultimately the most essential industrial product of the century, the

car carried with it the idea of progress as part of its mystique. If the car could be perceived *in any sense* as an improvement of daily life, then it deserved praise for superseding the lower form of experience from which it was alchemized.* To love the car it was necessary to embrace the primacy of change in American culture, and assent to the destruction of values underlying the pre-industrial world. The implications for esthetics were obvious. The factory, and behind it the industrial tycoon, assumed the title of "maker" which had been claimed exclusively by the individual artist, and most insistently by the poet. John Burroughs asserted that "No poet ever expressed himself through his work more completely than Mr. Ford has expressed himself through his car and his tractor engine." And the poet Matthew Josephson, the chief spokesman in the 1920s for Machine Age Art, addressed a panegyric to Ford's achievements:

With the brain at the wheel
the eye on the road
and the hand to the left
pleasant be your progress
explorer, producer, stoic, after your fashion.
Change
CHANGE
to what speed? to what underwear?
Here is a town, here a mill:
nothing surprises you old horse face.
Guzzle-guzzle goes the siren;
and the world will learn to admire and applaud your concern about
    the parts, your firmness with employees, and your justice to
    your friends.
Your pride will not be overridden
Your faith will go unmortified.

This is clearly Our Ford of Aldous Huxley's satire, *Brave New World*, the transcendent demiurge of an entirely artificial world. A

---

* That lower form is thus described by Thomas A. Edison: "You see, getting down to the bottom of things, this is a pretty raw, crude civilization of ours—pretty wasteful, pretty cruel. . . . And in a lot of respects we Americans are the rawest and crudest of all. . . . We've stumbled along for a while, trying to run a new civilization in old ways, but we've got to start to make this world over." Cited in Allan Nevins, *Ford: The Times, The Man, The Company*, I, p. 531.

later version of the same sentiment is Richard Kostelanetz's concrete poem, *Homage to Henry Ford*, in which the gigantic letters A and T march across the field of the page.

It is a world in which, for a while, carmakers and modernist poets seemed to be natural allies. Who could appreciate more than poets the artful variations on standardized models emerging from Detroit year after year? Alfred Sloan, Jr., writing about dynamic obsolescence in *My Years with General Motors*, might almost be discussing the reconstitution of poetic genres in some little magazine like *transition* or *Broom*: "The changes in the new model should be so novel and attractive as to create demand for the new value and, so to speak, create a certain amount of dissatisfaction with the past model." This new version of the Metamorphoses would profoundly affect all the arts by bringing to them the anxiety of novelty that characterizes modernism itself. And yet what manic pleasure there was in the annihilation of the old time-space relations and the pedestrian art of that pre-automotive age! Poets could not help loving the strange sporting beauty of new models—their names, the names of their parts. If Persephone was to be reborn daily on the lathes of Detroit, Flint, and Lansing, then the poet's responsibility was to say so memorably, and thereby associate his making with the more glorious energies of his Promethean contemporaries.

Karl Shapiro's "Buick" is such a poem; it not only humanizes but eroticizes the gorgeous General Motors creation:

As my foot suggests that you leap in the air with your hips of a girl,
My finger that praises your wheel and announces your voices of
    song,
Flouncing your skirts, you blueness of joy, you flirt of politeness,
You leap, you intelligence, essence of wheelness with silvery nose,
And your platinum clocks of excitement stir like the hairs of a fern.

The rapturous devotion poets once gave to God, and later to Nature, can be transferred to the car without reservation. "It's a poem that has never, in my opinion, been understood," Shapiro recently remarked. "It is always mentioned, when it is, as some kind of satire or irony. It's no such thing. It's absolutely STRAIGHT, a love poem to a Buick! A big fat Buick. I was in the Army in Virginia in 1940 and hitchhiked back to camp from Baltimore. An officer picked me up in his Buick. Somewhere below Fredericksburg, at night, he opened it up to a hundred miles an hour. Equals poem."* The long lines and swaggering anapests of the poem transmit the thrill of passion to the reader. They convey too a ballad-like sense of mystery, so that the machine becomes easily confused with a siren or *belle dame* "with your eyes that enter the future of roads," carrying the excited devotion, the independence, and perhaps even the soul of her admirer into the distances.

Shapiro places this poem next to his translation of Baudelaire's "Giantess" in his *Selected Poems*, perhaps to remind the reader that the Buick—with its famous insignia of a ring pierced by a flying phallus—is also in its way a "gargantuan offspring" of Nature, who exhausts as she stimulates the desire of her temporary owner. Such foreboding is not present in "Buick" however, which has the sunny playfulness of many poems of this period melding car and girl into a rapturous unity. E.E. Cummings's "she being brand new," in which a new model is taken for a test-drive with ecstatic results, is certainly the most charming of such poems, and one for which Cummings's jerking typography seems most appropriate.

In American culture, however, the pagan has always been closely shadowed by the prophetic mode, visible in imaginative literature at least since the time of Hawthorne and Melville. So too in Shapiro's first volume "Buick" is answered by "Auto Wreck." The "silvery nose" of the Buick is replaced in the first line by the "quick soft silver bell" of the ambulance racing to rescue the mangled. If a fast drive in a new Buick conjures associations of sexual consummation, here the imagery mordantly reproves that lust: "One with a bucket douches ponds of blood/Into the street and gutter." An auto wreck represents the smash-up of the romance of progress, based as it is on the mechanization of the sexual instinct. Auto wreck is the artist's version of God's vengeance upon the multitude for its worship of false idols (including Shapiro's own apostasy). This is why Allen Ginsberg places his poem "Car Crash" at the exact center of his prophetic book *The Fall of America*, why Jean-Luc Godard uses the auto wreck as his continuous image of the secular era in *Weekend*, why almost every museum in America exhibits a sculpture of twisted auto parts, if not a graphic work like Andy Warhol's *Green Disaster*, why J.G. Ballard, perhaps our most acute modern commentator on the ontology of the machine, summons in his novel *Crash* "a new

---

* Letter to the author, 25 March 1980.

sexuality born from a perverse technology" in which the protagonist is excited by a vision of "the whole world dying in a simultaneous automobile disaster, millions of vehicles hurled together in a terminal congress of spurting loins and engine coolant." Shapiro stops short of such Spenglerian gloom, but the conclusion of his poem displays astonishment at the singularity of this entirely modern form of mass destruction:

> For death in war is done by hands;
> Suicide has cause and stillbirth, logic;
> And cancer, simple as a flower, blooms.
> But this invites the occult mind,
> Cancels our physics with a sneer,
> And spatters all we know of denouement
> Across the expedient and wicked stones.

The car Shapiro praised as a female "intelligence" in "Buick" has this Hecate form as well. The distance in modern America between *liebe* and *liebestod* has narrowed at the same accelerated pace as the giantess's growth and development.

"Buick" and "Auto Wreck" are probably the most widely-anthologized poems about the automobile in modern American poetry. Written in the early 1940s they just missed inclusion in Selden Rodman's popular Modern Library volume, *A New Anthology of Modern Poetry* (1939), a compilation that explicitly featured poems of social engagement and cultural commentary. In that collection of mostly 1930s verse I find three references to cars, all of them negative and all of them, not surprising given the leftist orientation of the volume, associating the car with insolent wealth. Horace Gregory sneers at the "nickel-plated limousine"; Kenneth Fearing expostulates, "O, executive type, would you like to drive a floating/power, knee-action, silk-upholstered six?"; Rodman himself draws a country-club scene, "the drive still congested with enormous cars."* Following these impoverished images, typical of the modern poet's inability to deal with the car imaginatively for the first forty years of its existence, Shapiro's poems established the automobile as a serious subject of modern poetry, much as Hart Crane (in *The Bridge*) and

---

* Similarly, in Harriet Monroe's revised edition of *The New Poetry*, a 1932 anthology of some nine hundred poems, the only significant reference to an automobile, apart from a few notices in city sketches, is Sherwood Anderson's sarcastic rebuke to his contemporaries: "Why the devil didn't you make some money and own an automobile?"

Stephen Spender (in "The Express") belatedly made the train a compelling image during the 1930s. After the war, poets continued to elaborate the symbology of the car in order to precisely define human personality in an age of triumphant machine technology. Robert Lowell, for example, concludes his poem on modern Boston, "For the Union Dead," with a despairing image of usurpation:

> The Aquarium is gone. Everywhere,
> giant finned cars nose forward like fish;
> a savage servility
> slides by on grease.

Theodore Roethke, by contrast, acknowledging that "the road was part of me," remembers nostalgically the joy of hot-rodding in open country as a perfect union of self, machine, and landscape ("Journey to the Interior").

My unscientific survey of recent anthologies and introductory textbooks of American poetry indicates that the most widely-reprinted contemporary poem involving a car is one that has close thematic links to "Auto Wreck." It is William Stafford's "Traveling Through the Dark" (1962), which I reprint in full:

> Traveling through the dark I found a deer
> dead on the edge of the Wilson River road.
> It is usually best to roll them into the canyon:
> that road is narrow; to swerve might make more dead.
>
> By glow of the tail-light I stumbled back of the car
> and stood by the heap, a doe, a recent killing;
> she had stiffened already, almost cold.
> I dragged her off; she was large in the belly.
>
> My fingers touching her side brought me the reason—
> her side was warm; her fawn lay there waiting,
> alive, still, never to be born.
> Beside that mountain road I hesitated.
>
> The car aimed ahead its lowered parking lights;
> under the hood purred the steady engine.
> I stood in the glare of the warm exhaust turning red;
> around our group I could hear the wilderness listen.

I thought hard for us all—my only swerving—,
then pushed her over the edge into the river.

It must be said first that the presence of a dead animal in the road
is a familiar one in contemporary poetry, as it is in everyday experience. Philip Levine notices "the smear of possum" in one poem of
traveling ("Autumn Again") as does J.D. Reed:

A possum lies splayed
on the midstripe of U.S. 12
suet-colored guts dribbling
on to Adrian.

Radcliffe Squires foresees such carnage in "Animal Crossing":

Can it be true that animals cross here from woods
To woods in some old way? No, not true. Should
They set paw upon this moving road
Then they would flow with its aluminum flood,
Drift with silent fur and burning eyes
Upon a gray river—into me, under me.

Even aquatic life is not safe, as in Donald Hall's "Swan":

Driving; the fog
matted around the headlights;
suddenly, a thudding
white shape in the whiteness,
running huge and frightened, lost
from its slow stream . . .

These examples could be multiplied indefinitely, especially from the
poetry of the 1970s, the era of the four thousand pound, V-8 cylindered,
250-435 horsepower-driven and power-steered full size models such
as the Imperial, Fury, Caprice, Marauder, and Monarch, under
whose wheels anything smaller than a cow would be crushed unnoticed.

These images set in deadly opposition the automobile and the
natural creation to which man belongs in his physical being. The
earliest hope had been that these could coexist or be harmoniously
merged, as in Sandburg's "Portrait" or the often-reprinted remark by
Henry Ford in *My Life and Work*: "Unless we know more about
machines and their use . . . we cannot have the time to enjoy the
birds, the flowers, and the green fields." Stafford continually punc-

tures this hope, as in the poem about Bing Crosby's ranch, or another well-known poem, "At the Bomb-Testing Site," in which ominous happenings on the frontier are registered through a lizard, or "Boom Town" which juxtaposes snake and oil-well engines. In "Traveling Through the Dark" the horror of the scene is heightened by the matter-of-fact tone, rendered by simple declarative sentences, which places the burden of interpretation and moral judgment on the reader. Who has not referred to the "purr" of an engine, in the spirit of reconciling animal and machine life? Indeed, this steel predator, its "exhaust turning red" as the dying deer's blood, must kill to preserve its own life. As with so much technology, killing is a condition of the car's dominance in a culture which has increasingly ceded land, water, and air, as well as creaturely life, to its hegemony. The reader is kept from smug exculpation ("*I've* never run down a deer") by the figure of the live fawn which the innocent speaker, bound to the absent killer by his identity as driver, must kill as an act of mercy, not without the one "swerving" that produced the poem. The automobile, as Walter Chrysler once said, "knows no limits except a right of way." Poetry, an art of limits, insistently creates scenes like the one in this poem to challenge that right of way, that onrushing overpowering force, with an account of the expense to the rule of right itself.

III

The imposition of limits is a conservative, or preservative activity, and though it is the special prerogative of the poet to stop the speeding automobile within the frame of the page, and thereby enable the public to focus on its debits and credits as an instrument of progress—weighing its "blueness of joy" against the dying life left in its wake—the poet cannot help but be conscious of such limitations as a boundary of vision. Perhaps the most authentic artwork about the car has to mimic the state of open consciousness created by driving, just as in the graphic arts the car achieves its proper kinesis in cinema and not on canvas. The problem the poet faces here is obvious. Traversal of the open road has the paradoxical effect of making elements of the landscape more organically related—hurled together in the field of vision at accelerated speed—and more discrete because seen by glimpses, and often *seen* only, not heard or felt or smelled. An assemblage of miscellaneous impressions recorded faithfully and randomly will induce the kind of narcotized fatigue in the reader that overcomes the driver in real life. Certainly there is a tradition of loco-descriptive poetry in the English language—the forest walk, the city stroll—in which catalogues of sights and sounds are ordered (sometimes just barely) by the poetic sensibility. Whitman's poems are the finest example of this mode, which has produced at least one great contemporary poem, Galway Kinnell's "The Avenue Bearing the Initial of Christ into the New World." But the challenge of an automotive version defeated poets until very recent times.

It was the most vociferous and daring of Whitman's apostles who entered the lists during the car's undisputed heyday, the 1950s, when cheap gas and powerful engines created an autopia for believers in the car's magical powers of spiritual renewal. The Beat Generation produced many volumes of what Allen Ginsberg calls "green auto poetries, inspired roads," each a skein of momentary sensations, small lyrics that try to capture the beat of life as it impinges moment by moment on the observer. The driver thus became a principal figure for the hipster, a mystic recreated in every mile of road. (Neal Cassady, the wild hero of Jack Kerouac's novel *On the Road* and Tom Wolfe's *Electric Kool-Aid Acid Test*, is the most notorious example.) Gregory Corso's *Gasoline* and Kerouac's *Mexico City Blues* illustrate the genre in poetry, but far more ambitious and impressive are Ginsberg's volumes *Planet News* and *The Fall of America*, sequences composed, we are to believe, mainly in cars and vans moving back and forth across the American continent.

Ginsberg's ingenious idea is to meld the maya of phenomena (as he calls it) sweeping past his car, signals from the car radio which let in another refracted version of "the real world," and the curtailed train of ideas provoked by his perceptions. The verse sounds like this:

> Lulled into War
> thus commercial jabber Rock & Roll Announcers
> False False False
> *"Enjoy this meat—"*
> Weak A&P Superright ground round
> Factories building, airwaves pushing . . .
> Trees stretch up parallel into grey sky
> Yellow trucks roll down lane—
> Hypnosis of airwaves
> In the house you can't break it
> unless you turn off yr set

> In the car it can drive yr eyes inward
>   from the snowy hill,
>   withdraw yr mind from the birch forest
>   make you forget the blue car in the ice,
> Drive yr mind down Supermarket aisles
>   looking for cans of Save-Your-Money
>   Polishing-Glue
> made of human bones manufactured in N. Vietnam
>   during a mustard gas hallucination:
>   The Super-Hit sound of All American Radio.
> Turnpike to Tuscarora
>   Snow fields, red lights blinking in the broken car
>   Quiet hills' genital hair black in Sunset . . .

The impression Ginsberg wishes to convey is of the camera-eye being bombarded by data, but he constantly selects and arranges the bits and pieces of information which serve his overall moral intention: a condemnation of the ruthless American materialism that has led to the Vietnam War and its support forces, television and AM radio. The monotony of long-distance driving corresponds to the lookalike and tastealike products of the supermarket, and the soundalike tunes carried by the "hypnosis of airwaves" that anesthetize the American mind and "withdraw" it from the unseen forms of nature. Ginsberg-in-the-automobile, then, is a microcosm of the creative individual enclosed in a technocracy or megamachine ("Amerika"), desperately trying to articulate his hard-won prophetic truth amid the standardized expressions of Moloch. If the pure products of America go crazy, Ginsberg seems to say, it is in part because their nature is deformed by a culture that sets them against the prolific variety of the natural creation. Here as everywhere Ginsberg remains a displaced pastoralist, his work a field guide to the *fleurs de mal*.

But it is part of Ginsberg's pastoralism that he will not deny to his readers the obvious pleasure he derives from the automobile. If cities are to exist, then so must transport allow access to landscape:

> Autumn again, you wouldn't know in the city
> Gotta come out in a car see the birds
>   flock by the yellow bush—
> In Autumn, In autumn, this part of the planet's
>   famous for red leaves—

The car is appreciated for its utilitarian service, much as it was in the early days of the century, the Model T era, when proponents joked that "one touch of automobilism makes the world kin." It is not as a racing machine—Danny's dream of the gray-ghost—but as moving windows upon the creation, for the sake of recreation and not for itself—that the car receives homage. The car provides Ginsberg with a vision of the minute particulars of American life that would otherwise be overlooked. His vignettes of farms, roadside cafes, communes in rural glades, and downtowns in the heartland, are among the most vivid and compassionate in contemporary literature. By propelling himself restlessly through the land, Ginsberg found a way to speak for the generation of the 1960s, nomadic in body and spirit, and to make his journeys a model of human control of the machine and machinelike in our culture.

Perhaps the most ambitious attempt to create an "auto poetry," an experience of self entirely informed by driving, is Rosmarie Waldrop's volume of experimental verse, *The Road is Everywhere or Stop This Body*. Engendered by twice-weekly round trips between her home in Providence and Wesleyan University, where Waldrop had a temporary teaching position, the eighty poems in this book treat the habit of commuting as normal or fundamental to life, and therefore usable as a paradigm of all other human activities. One might say that Waldrop surrenders the motive common to all other poems discussed in this essay: to argue a point of view, to be polemical. Rather, as the seasonal divisions of the volume suggest, Waldrop's intention is wholistic, to make a calendar of the totality of living systems, including the linguistic system responsible for the medium of verse itself. In a curious way these often obscure poems are statements even more Whitmanian than Ginsberg's, because their inclusiveness, their unwillingness to divide one part of the American experience from its opposite, carry out the great bard's doctrine of the *imperium:* "Oh highway . . . you express me better than I can express myself."

Because the poems eschew ideas in the usual sense, it is difficult to restate their thematic content, but what follows is a reasonable summary. The road is a distance between two points, and therefore all movement upon it recreates the Heraclitian flow of time wherein all matter is transported and changed into a different state. Every terminus is a simulacrum of death, and deserves the sign that Waldrop places at the end of one poem. The poem itself is a model of driving, a montage of sights and sounds, prey to the distortions of ordinary psychic experience on the highway. Waldrop incorporates such disturbances into the order of words, the grammar, which no more than matter itself can stand fast against acceleration. So a poem sounds like this:

> still
> this vehicle responds
> to the key
> words
> germinate on their own obstructions
> anywhere it doesn't
> matter
> continues
> your doubts about it
> are still words
> taste of acid gears edge into slots
> determine
> the melt into the margin
> dwindling illusion
> of going places
> on this page

Punctuation disappears along with the possibility of clear syntactical units of meaning. Every line is subject to metaphorical interruptions,

or because of the hypnagogic state induced by driving.

And because commuting is made necessary by financial need, the movement of the car is analogous to the circulation of money in a society shaped in large part by the automobile industry. Economics controls the flow and fate of cars no less than people: both are subject to what Waldrop calls the "compulsive periodicity" of generation and decay. As if to remind the driver of this connection, she notes the "pulsing in your sex" from the routine stimulus of driving, a memento of Nature's dynamic obsolescence in the Creation, which *Homo sapiens* has recreated in its economy of things. The arousal, in its positive aspect, is like the awakened desire of some giant entity (Humankind) through whose arteries flow replicating and energizing cells. (J.D. Reed likewise imagines himself as "A country Gulliver. . . . rusted Kaisers and hot/Buicks race out my limbs.") By analogy the poet makes him/herself the Promethean demiurge of a flourishing world in which poems and cars are interchangeable signifiers of the potent/fertile American genius.

In its negative aspect, the arousal remains sterile, unconsummated, a false transport. Its comprehensive demonic form is the traffic jam (e.g. poem #44), in which all systems suffer congestion. In the traffic jam is depression and Depression; desire reaches "the limits of motion" which contain and (thereby) make abhorrent life itself. As in the poem by Joyce Carol Oates, such breakdowns reveal a depletion of vision at the cultural source. The round-trip commute, like the calendar year, enacts the periodicity of our lives and can come to resemble the dull round of unproductive labor and stalled progress that Blake abhorred in the "dark Satanic mills" of industry.

In the poetry of automotive consciousness, then, we find the same misgivings, and the same premonitions, of Oates's poem on the Rouge. To assume a metal skin as a matter of habit, and experience the world like a speeding machine, is to endanger the psychic equilibrium derived from a recognition of creatureliness, of human limits. Because they themselves aspire to transcendence, poets utter such warnings to drivers and automakers with genuine sympathy. Poets are technicians, manipulators of systems who understand the perils of usurious design. Just as they strive to discipline their own craft—to keep it from monstrous rhetorical inflation—so too they denounce the antisocial in popular culture. In their preservative efforts poets imagine the car as neither on the side of the angels nor the devil, but participating in the mixed nature of humanity, an object of its affections but an enemy to its highest ideals. At this historical moment those ideals seem to be threatened at their foundation, for clearly a means of transport which depletes the elements necessary for human life—air and water—must be reconstructed if life is to continue. Carmakers must engage the problem of *style* in its most capacious sense, for style and social function are most inseparable during times of crisis.

The poetic imagination conserves every human product fresh as the day it was born. There are celebratory hymns to the car waiting to be written, when the ruins of Michigan's empire sponsor a happier marriage of culture and nature, when the groom (from OF *gromet*, servant) is a more responsible machine and the open road becomes again what it appeared to a hopeful writer in 1902, "a bride waving palms, rhythmically keeping time to some melody of gladness."

BIBLIOGRAPHICAL NOTE

The quotations in this essay can be found in the following texts, alphabetized by author.

J. G. Ballard, *Crash* (New York: Farrar, Straus & Giroux, 1973), p. 16. Allen Ginsberg, *The Fall of America* (San Francisco: City Lights, 1972), pp. 49, 56–57. Donald Hall, *The Alligator Bride* (New York: Harper & Row, 1969), p. 74. Matthew Josephson, "The Brain at the Wheel," *Broom* #5 (Sept. 1923), p. 120. D. H. Lawrence, *Studies in Classic American Literature* (New York: Thomas Seltzer, 1923), p. 248. Philip Levine, *The Names of the Lost* (New York: Atheneum, 1976), p. 23. Robert Lowell, *Selected Poems* (New York: Farrar, Straus & Giroux, 1976), p. 137. Ezra Pound, *Collected Early Poems*, ed. Michael John King (New York: New Directions, 1976), pp. 169–70. J. D. Reed, *Expressways* (New York: Simon and Schuster, 1969), pp. 10, 13. Theodore Roethke, *The Collected Poems* (New York: Doubleday, 1966), p. 193. Carl Sandburg, *Complete Poems* (New York: Harcourt, Brace, 1950), pp. 106, 499. Karl Shapiro, *Selected Poems* (New York: Random House, 1968), pp. 17, 21. Radcliffe Squires, *Waiting in the Bone* (Omaha: Abattoir Editions, 1973), p. 21. William Stafford, *Stories that Could Be True* (New York: Harper & Row, 1977), pp. 47, 61. Rosmarie Waldrop, *The Road is Everywhere* (Columbia, MO: Open Places, 1978), p. 120. W. C. Williams, *Collected Earlier Poems* (New York: New Directions, 1951), p. 3; *Collected Later Poems* (New York: New Directions, 1963), p. 131.

DAVID LAIRD

VERSIONS OF EDEN:
THE AUTOMOBILE AND
THE AMERICAN NOVEL

In Edith Nesbit's *The Magic City*, it is a law of life that if one wishes for anything one can have it. But with that law goes another about machines. If one wishes for a piece of machinery, one is compelled to keep it and to go on using it for the rest of one's life. Machines are held to be a special case, their employment subject to conditions that run the life of the contract, so to speak, and disclose themselves only in the course of time. In Nesbit's fictional world, escape from the strange fatality that haunts machines is possible only for those who resist altogether their lure and fascination. When her leading character has the choice of wishing for a horse or a bicycle, he wisely chooses the horse and thereby wins exemption. Characters in recent American fiction are not so fortunate. An infatuation with machines is with them from the start, a condition of their existence. Machines promise power, mobility, freedom, even a "poetic" space that beckons from beyond the too familiar course of things, from beyond the rush of time and time's sad waste. But in the web of circumstance in which these characters come to be entangled something like the special rule about machines begins to take effect. We sense its operation in the eventual discovery of unforeseen liabilities and losses. This essay is an account of those somber reckonings. The machine in question is the automobile and my concern is with its passage through recent American fiction, with the hopes and dreams it carries, the casualties and losses to which it is linked.

Modern American fiction reflects a society enormously dependent upon the automobile both as a means of transportation and as a source of economic activity. It acknowledges practical advantages such as speed, comfort, and convenience, which cars are bound to embody in an environment fashioned for them and in which their employment has become all but indispensable. Yet is is by means of analyzing and evaluating the various impulses and aspirations in the grip of which Americans have bought, driven, and cherished

244

automobiles that modern fiction locates its most telling revelations. Invariably linked to personal goals and satisfactions, cars in fiction measure individual self-worth; they offer a way of making the scene, a means of escape from the oppressive, conditioning forces by which individuals are threatened and against which they feel compelled to make even an enfeebled stand. Thus cars figure in a variety of schemes, strategies, and psychic maneuvers by which individuals seek to outdistance their pursuers, to fortify themselves against the drag of time, oblivion, or loss.

But there is another dimension to this analysis and here the going gets tough. A contrary impulse links cars to a misguided attempt to escape a larger social reality; they become a destructive agent, violently disruptive and confusing, a menace to the natural and the social environment. The addiction to cars is shown to be an evasion of moral and social responsibility, a bad trip that destroys community and leaves the individual wasted and alone. Thus cars run through literature in defiantly paradoxical and contradictory ways. There is the love affair with cars, the romance impulse, if you like, and there is a counter-movement in the detailed, sobering assessment of what happens when a society takes to the road. Cars blossom in a season of Edenic promise, offering enclosure, security, individual autonomy and control, freedom to do as one pleases. In such a comfortable and glowing light, they assume the attributes of a garden, an environment improved by careful cultivation, by artful manipulation. For the purpose of exposition, for whatever benefit it may afford as a convenient heuristic device, I wish to adapt Leo Marx's terms to suggest that the machine is the garden, opening the way to or itself becoming a sheltering space, free from the conditioning, shaping influences which beset the fallen world. Through various links and contacts, the myth of the automobile merges with, is strengthened by, the myth of the garden. Such an affinity exists in, for example, texts as diverse as *The Great Gatsby*, *The Natural*, and *The Crying of Lot 49*. Its acknowledgment and the exploration of its implications will, perhaps, help us to understand the dreams we have entrusted to the automobile, the imaginative, idealizing transformations in which it has figured, and, at the same time, to grasp the peculiar vulnerabilities which that idealization has incurred, the ironies which have played against it in the coercions of history.

The essential historical process is a familiar one: the sheltering space with its Edenic promise proves illusory, doomed to collapse in the movement of time, overwhelmed by sequentiality, successiveness, destination. A useful illustration is the following timely meditation on the automobile in William Faulkner's *The Reivers*:

> Even in 1905 the wilderness had retreated only twenty more miles; the wagons bearing the guns and food and bedding had merely to start at sundown. . . . Though by 1925 we could already see the doom. Major de Spain and the rest of that old group, save your Cousin Ike and Boon, were gone now and (there was gravel now all the way from Jefferson to De Spain's flag stop) their inheritors switched off their automobile engines to the sound of axes and saws where a year ago there had been only the voices of running hounds. Because Manfred de Spain was a banker, not a hunter like his father; he sold lease, land and timber and by 1940 (it was McCaslin's camp now) they—we—would load everything into pickup trucks and drive two hundred miles over paved highways to find enough wilderness to pitch tents in; though by 1980 the automobile will be as obsolete to reach wilderness as the automobile will have made the wilderness it seeks.

The passage predicts the decline of the automobile as an effective means of transport to wilderness and heralds the beginning of its awesome rule as creator of another sort of wilderness, one presumably given over to junk yards and used car lots, the urban sprawl that blights the landscape and exiles its inhabitants. That the troublesome changes which Faulkner foresees have been accomplished even in garden preserves is suggested by an article on the front page of *The New York Times* (August 3, 1980), which includes the following description of the splendors of Yosemite valley: "The field of vision is filled with hot asphalt, slow-moving lines of cars and buses, and crowds of tourists, some visibly irritated by the heat and congestion." Such, then, is the wilderness which the automobile has helped to create. In Faulkner's harsh chronology, the ends men seek to serve are not those they do serve; ends are mastered and transformed, emptied of meaning, by the means employed to reach them. In stressing that disparity, Faulkner concurs with Samuel Butler who, in his novel *Erewhon*, first published in 1872, tells us that "this is the art of the machines—they serve that they may rule." In *The Machine Stops*, E. M. Forster takes much the same view, describing the products of modern technology, the automobile included, as exerting an independent force "that moves on, but not on our lines; that proceeds, but not to our goals." More recent commentators, such as Jacques Ellul and Langdon Winner, have argued that technology imposes its own conformity to which those under its spell must adapt their previously held objectives and aims. Here, again, is an echo of the special rule about machines whose operation binds the individual to undisclosed obligations and hidden liabilities.

But before pursuing the operation of that rule in literature, something remains to be said about the brighter prospects, the promised satisfactions cars bring within the reach of their fictional drivers. There is ample witness to the thrill of life in the fast lane where motion itself can be transformed into a sense of individual power and sexual excitement. A passage from James M. Cain's *Mildred Pierce* exemplifies one kind of pleasure to be found behind the wheel: "She gave the car the gun, exactly watching the needle swing past 30, 40, and 50. . . . The car pumping something into her veins, something of pride, of arrogance, of restrained self-respect that no talk, no liquor, no love could possibly give." In Thomas Pynchon's *The Crying of Lot 49*, Oedipa Maas escapes the dull, dispiriting uniformity of a planned community by fleeing to the freeways:

> Amid the exhaust, sweat, glare and ill-humor of a summer evening on an American freeway, Oedipa Maas pondered her Trystero problem. All the silence of San Narciso—the calm surface of the motel pool, the contemplative contours of residential streets like rakings in the sand of a Japanese garden—had not allowed her to think as leisurely as this freeway madness.

Oedipa, like Echo, her mythic counterpart, struggles to find her voice. For Oedipa, any human voice, her own included, would lift her above the panic and emptiness that threaten to engulf her. In a rented car, she manages to escape not only the smooth, reflecting surfaces of San Narciso, but also the meaningless, incessant din of information flow and the electronic noise of the Paranoids, a musical group and a state of mind by which she is pursued. She wins deliverance from passivity and madness, venturing beyond the barriers of self into uncertain relationship with the world beyond, hoping to find in its "sonorous score" an authentic voice, "a cry that might abolish the night."

Thus cars furnish the stuff of raw sensation and exhilaration; they are vehicles of initiation into the riddles and perplexities which await the self in relation to the world it seeks to enter, and they are tokens to spend again in nostalgic reflection and celebration. They also furnish protection and containment, distancing their occupants from the pressures and influences that impinge upon them. Again, they nourish an instinct to self-assertion against restrictive environmental pressures, a desire to exercise power over an immediate, if limited environment, claiming it in the name of individual freedom and autonomy. Will Barrett in Walker Percy's *The Last Gentleman* is most at home in a Trav-L-Aire car, where he can at times convince himself of his own existence, a cogent, reflective self, having weight and occupying a space that "is protected, self-contained, yet open to its surroundings, mobile yet at home, compacted . . . in the world, yet not of the world." A common element in these intimate depictions of fictional drivers and their vehicles is the notion of an escape into a "poetic" space, a secret garden, a room of one's own, set off from the ordinariness of things by means of motion, memory, or encabined contemplation.

Such service can, of course, be mocked as it is in the Percy novel and, more recently, in Jerzy Kosinski's *Passion Play* with its chivalric, disciplined, and finally ineffectual display of interiority against the terror of history. Mocked, but not dismissed. In *City of Words*, Tony Tanner suggests that "the instinct to cultivate and protect an area of inner space is a recurrent one in contemporary American fiction." Manifestations of that instinct haunt the pages of our literature like ghosts. They reflect a deeper grounding in the basic psychic structures by which Americans, consciously or unconsciously, have experienced and responded to the bewilderments and confusions of modernity. Nor is the conscientious, deliberate cultivation of inner space unique to American literature or to Americans. It has its analogues and examples in other literatures and in the psychological and social history of Western civilization at least since the Romantic Period.

A modern American novel which perfectly summarizes and synthesizes that yearning is F. Scott Fitzgerald's *The Great Gatsby*. Nick Carraway observes throughout a commitment to "poetic" space. He credits Jay Gatsby with an unshakable, uncompromising faith in his capacity to draw a timeless moment from the dregs of time and to transfigure by the very energy and intensity of his commitment the otherwise drab materials of existence. For Gatsby, it is a vision of "poetic" space, dream-like, mysterious, that fortifies the self and brings a heightened sensitivity to the promises of life, conferring what Nick calls "an extraordinary gift of hope, a romantic readiness." Emblematic of that space is Gatsby's Rolls-Royce, a "gorgeous" car, "rich cream color, bright with nickel, swollen here and there in its monstrous length with triumphant hat-boxes and supper-boxes and tool-boxes, and terraced with a labyrinth of wind-shields that mirrored a dozen suns." The effect it creates is that of "sitting down behind many layers of glass in a sort of green leather conservatory." The car catches a reflection of the "fresh, green breast of the new world" of which Nick speaks elsewhere in the novel—the new world "that flowered once for Dutch sailors' eyes," and "pandered in whispers to the last and greatest of all human dreams." "For a transitory enchanted moment," Nick continues, "man must have held his breath in the presence of this continent, compelled into an aesthetic contemplation he neither understood nor desired, face to face for the last time in history with something commensurate to his capacity for wonder." We glimpse in Gatsby's hoard of enchanted objects the reflection of an idealized world of fabulous adventure and special revelation. The car, in particular, conceals and reveals the incorruptible dream under the spell of which Gatsby seeks to transcend the mundane traffic of this world. A complex, ambiguous symbol, it signifies as well the contingencies and conditions of the everyday world, the burdens of time and history. When entrusted to Daisy Buchanan, it becomes the death car, an instrument of violence and destruction, raising in its accidental course the foul dust of a moral wasteland.

The point of interest here is the depth and comprehensiveness Fitzgerald brings to the analysis of the fateful role of the automobile, the possibilities it presents, the conditions and consequences it creates. American writers subsequently play countless variations on those themes without, I think, significantly adding to the stock, already scaled and inventoried in *The Great Gatsby*. The range and prominence of that display must strike us as the more remarkable when we consider the date of the novel's publication, 1925. On October 31, 1925, the Ford Motor Company produced 9,109 Model Ts, one every ten seconds. The price of the Model T had come down from $850 in 1921 to $350 by 1925 and it was headed lower. James Flink, in *The Car Culture*, tells us that "by May 27, 1927, when the last of over 15 million Model Ts rolled off the assembly line, a new Model T cost as little as $290 and mass automobility had become a reality." And a year later in his victorious campaign for the presidency, Herbert Hoover was calling for "two cars in every garage." Fitzgerald not only draws attention to the emergence of a car culture in America, but also creates intelligent concern over attitudes and modes of behavior with which that culture was to become increasingly identified.

The novel is richly furnished with the products of a new technology. Those products and the attitudes they foster, an implicit challenge to older practices and values, shape the social landscape of the novel.

Cars flash like jewels across its glittering, shimmering surfaces. Nick is captivated by the glamor, the seemingly inexhaustible variety of the life they seem to promise. While Tom Buchanan can speak disparagingly of Gatsby's car as a circus wagon and has himself achieved a certain notoriety on Long Island by converting his garage into a stable for polo ponies, he remains intimately involved with cars. There is Nick's good-natured account of the desolation felt in Chicago when the Buchanans left for the East: "All the cars have the left rear wheel painted black as a mourning wreath, and there's a persistent wail all night along the north shore." The Buchanans, of course, own cars; Tom trades in them rather in the manner in which he trades in people, using them in some elaborate scheme that momentarily strikes his fancy. It is in one of Tom's cars, an easy-going blue coupé, that Nick and Jordan return from Manhattan one sultry Sunday afternoon. As they start for Long Island, Nick remembers that it is his thirtieth birthday: "before me stretched the portentous, menacing road of a new decade. . . . Thirty—the promise of a decade of loneliness, a thinning list of single men to know, a thinning brief-case of enthusiasm, thinning hair." Nick's contemplations are of time, the inevitable losses to which he must submit. And then, from that bleak and lonely prospect, his attention turns to his companion:

> But there was Jordan beside me, who, unlike Daisy, was too wise to carry well-forgotten dreams from age to age. As we passed over the dark bridge her wan face fell lazily against my coat's shoulder and the formidable stroke of thirty died away with the reassuring pressure of her hand.

Loneliness suddenly gives way to new possibilities, comfortable assurances; a "poetic" space beckons and Nick retires to its warmth and intimacy. But the passage continues, the moment invaded by the grim knowledge of what lies ahead: "So we drove on toward death through the cooling twilight."

The structure of that passage is paradigmatic of the whole narrative. The automobile, Manhattan, Jordan Baker, Myrtle Wilson are linked in various ways with natural beauty, sexual freedom, and romance, projecting a glowing world of infinite variety and excitement, but the effect, increasingly as the novel progresses, is to disengage the reader from the enchantments of that world in favor of a more critical, more cautious outlook. Even the benighted Nick sees the automobile in a harsher, less congenial light after the accident which follows one of Gatsby's parties:

Fifty feet from the door a dozen headlights illuminated a bizarre and tumultuous scene. In the ditch beside the road, right side up, but violently shorn of one wheel, rested a new coupé which had left Gatsby's drive not two minutes before. The sharp jut of a wall accounted for the detachment of the wheel, which was now getting considerable attention from half a dozen curious chauffeurs.

An inquiry into the cause of the accident fails to turn up a satisfactory answer. The car appears to have assumed responsibility for its own fate. When one of its occupants is asked how the accident happened, he replies: "I know very little about driving—next to nothing. It happened, and that's all I know." A bystander responds: "You're lucky it was just a wheel! A bad driver and not even trying!" "You don't understand," the suspect explains. "I wasn't driving. There's another man in the car." The confusion surrounding the accident is never altogether dispelled; the notion of dangerous, irresponsible driving here introduced gains increasing force and authority. Later on, for example, Nick learns that Tom Buchanan's first adultery was revealed when he "ran into a wagon on the Ventura road one night, and ripped a front wheel off his car." The hotel chambermaid who was with him suffered a broken arm. Dangerous, irresponsible driving is the privilege of the arrogant and the rich. Their performance on the road provokes Nick's anxious concern and disapproval, offending what he calls his provincial squeamishness. It furnishes a kind of litany for his relationship with Jordan.

> It started because she passed so close to some workmen that our fender flicked a button on one man's coat.
> "You're a rotten driver," I protested. "Either you ought to be more careful, or you oughtn't to drive at all."
> "I am careful."
> "No, you're not."
> "Well, other people are," she said lightly.
> "What's that got to do with it?"
> "They'll keep out of my way," she insisted. "It takes two to make an accident."
> "Suppose you met somebody as careless as yourself."
> "I hope I never will," she answered. "I hate careless people. That's why I like you."

With that declaration, Nick begins to think he is in love. The conversation is recalled when Jordan breaks off the relationship at the end of the novel.

"Oh, and do you remember"—she added—"a conversation we had once about driving a car?"

"Why—not exactly."

"You said a bad driver was only safe until she met another bad driver. Well, I met another bad driver, didn't I? I mean it was careless of me to make such a wrong guess. I thought you were either an honest, straightforward person. I thought it was your secret pride."

Then Nick mumblingly replies that he's thirty, five years too old to lie to himself and call it honor. He rebels at the whole deceptive, muddled business, reluctantly concluding that Jordan is a liar and a cheat.

The wreck that troubles him most however, is not the figurative one involving Jordan and himself, but the catastrophic one that ends the novel. The careless driver who meets someone as careless as herself is Daisy and the someone she collides with and kills is Myrtle Wilson. In their last encounter, Tom and Nick recall the accident. Tom barks out defiantly: "That fellow Gatsby had it coming to him. He threw dust into your eyes just like he did in Daisy's, but he was a tough one. He ran over Myrtle like you'd run over a dog and never even stopped his car." In reply to such shameless, hopeless perjury, Nick tells us there was nothing he could say, except the one unutterable fact that it wasn't true. Nick proceeds to construct his own bitter and diminished version of events stripped of the warm bright hope he once felt, instructed by the deteriorating social reality he can no longer fail to recognize. Accordingly, the machine ceases to be a vehicle of enchantment, emblematic of Edenic promise or "poetic" space. In the stark, raw light of the new world into which Nick has been delivered, the automobile serves instead as an image of a vast carelessness born of money, technology, and the modes of mercenary behavior they tend to encourage. In T. S. Eliot's *The Waste Land*, it is the sound of horns and motors that brings Sweeney to Mrs. Porter in the spring. It is the sound that Nick associates with careless people who "smashed up things and creatures and then retreated back into their money or their vast carelessness, or whatever it was that kept them together, and let other people clean up the mess they had made. . . ." In the end, it is the sound of a now "material" car—"material without being real"—that prevails over the music and the laughter, faint and incessant, that once flowed from Gatsby's house and that continues to haunt Nick's imagination: "One night I did hear a material car there, and saw its lights stop at his front steps.

But I didn't investigate. Probably it was some final guest who had been away at the ends of the earth and didn't know that the party was over."

Nick turns his back on the once glittering, dazzling world he had so eagerly sought to enter. Anguished and repelled by what he has observed of human waywardness and corruptibility, unable to shield himself from the social reality to which his quest for "poetic" space is unalterably bound and by which its meaning is so deeply compromised, he abandons it altogether. He adopts a stance of moral earnestness, a wide-eyed, unblinking vigilance:

> When I came back from the East last autumn I felt I wanted the world to be in uniform and at a sort of moral attention forever. . . . No—Gatsby turned out all right in the end; it is what preyed on Gatsby, what foul dust floated in the wake of his dreams that temporarily closed out my interest in the abortive sorrows and short-winded elations of men.

In that mood of bitter disenchantment, cars reflect the material world of spoiled success, of moral bankruptcy and careless anonymity which conspire to corrupt the values and aspirations with which that world was initially endowed, at least by the young and unsuspecting.

In more recent writing we find a deepening sense of violation and betrayal, as the possibilities and promises with which cars were once identified dissolve in the acids of experience. A white Mercedes rides like a phantom through Bernard Malamud's *The Natural,* at first a free and floating paradise and then an occupied, contaminated space where dreams are buried and nothing flourishes for long. *The Natural* is an account of the tragic career of a professional baseball player named Roy Hobbs. With extraordinary energy and ambition, Hobbs pursues a dream of heroic proportion that plays itself out against a rich tapestry of mythological allusions, triumphs, and seductions. His success with the New York Knights fires the team's dwindling hopes, cures dissension and clumsiness, returns his surrogate father Pop Fisher to bouncing good health and the parched earth of the infield to a rich, green lawn. Thus does this latter-day Grail Knight restore the wasteland to fertility. On Roy Hobbs Day, the hero is presented with a white Mercedes purchased with the donations of grateful fans. In accepting the car, Roy reveals a fatal innocence; still the prisoner of egotism and selfishness, he declares that he aspires to be the best ever and abruptly flees the community that has come to pay him homage. The car signifies his moment of glory and public acclaim and it carries him to the point of self-betrayal, isolating him from sources of strength and nourishment: "The gleaming white job was light to the touch of hand and foot and he felt he could float off in it over the stadium wall." He heads for the sea, the dark lady of his life at his side. He feels "the contentment in moving," the easy, relaxed satisfaction of a "poetic" space: "It rested him by cutting down the inside motion—that which got him nowhere, which was where he was and she was not, or where his ambitions were and he was chasing after." But the serenity and peace of the moment are short-lived, dimmed first by memories of childhood happiness—"a dog, a stick, an aloneness he loved (which did not bleed him like his later loneliness)," and lost altogether when he stops the car by a small stream running along the edge of a wood. He and Memo Paris cross a bridge to the grassy side of the stream and are confronted by a sign: *Danger. Polluted Water. No Swimming.* The entranced moment ends in a desolation; the ride brings them to a place of sickness and death. When they return to the car and Memo takes the wheel, there suddenly appears on the road ahead a strange, visionary image of a boy and a dog. "For Christ's sake, stop—we hit somebody," Roy shouts. "I heard somebody groan." "That was yourself," Memo replies. The dream gives way to nightmare, the trip ends in a wreck, and the white Mercedes becomes a haunting image of guilt and remorse. The episode marks the beginning of the end for Hobbs, who, having failed to realize his own bright hopes or even to understand the nature of his failure, now proceeds to sell out his team's chance for the pennant and to abandon himself—the deposed and wasted king of baseball—to overwhelming self-hatred.

It is finally the contradictoriness of the figure of the machine as garden that prevails: "poetic" space invaded by the foul dust of contamination and decay. In Thomas Pynchon's *The Crying of Lot 49*, the figure captures just that sense of paradox and duplicity, gaining its force as a token of ironic debasement and deflation. The familiar quest for "poetic" space, the restoration of a lost Eden, is transformed into a grotesque parody in which individuals trade in their worn-out, junk-laden cars in exchange for equally worn-out and junk-laden ones in a futile effort to escape the drabness and confinement of their lives. The process is observed by a character resolved to free himself from the bogs of frustration and despair in which he drifts and will eventually disappear.

Yet at least he had believed in the cars. Maybe to excess: how could he
not, seeing people poorer than him come in, Negro, Mexican, cracker, a
parade seven days a week, bringing the most godawful of trade-ins:
motorized, metal extensions of themselves, of their families and what their
whole lives must be like, out there so naked for anybody, a stranger like
himself, to look at, frame cockeyed, rusty underneath, fender repainted in
a shade just off enough to depress the value, if not Mucho himself, inside
smelling hopelessly of children, supermarket booze, two, sometimes three
generations of cigarette smokers, or only of dust . . . it made him sick to
look, but he had to look.
If it had been an outright junkyard, probably he could have stuck things
out, made a career: the violence that had caused each wreck being
infrequent enough, far enough away from him, to be miraculous as each
death, up till the moment of our own is miraculous. But the endless rituals
of trade-in, week after week, never got as far as violence or blood, and so
were too plausible for the impressionable Mucho to take for long. Even if
enough exposure to the unvarying gray sickness had somehow managed to
immunize him, he could still never accept the way each owner, each
shadow, filed in only to exchange a dented, malfunctioning version of
himself for another, just as futureless, automotive projection of somebody
else's life. As if it were the most natural thing. To Mucho it was horrible.
Endless, convoluted incest.

Such incest suggests an unnatural, pernicious relationship between
the exhausted, cluttered lives of one generation of car owners and
the next, a relationship entered into in the misplaced belief that the
machine might still renew, make good, the broken promises of life.
The effect of that relationship is to shatter belief and spawn a sense
of dismal failure and despair.

Emma Rothschild in *Paradise Lost: The Decline of the Auto-
Industrial Age* surveys the varied reactions of automobile executives
and others associated with the industry to the troubles which have
recently befallen the automobile in America. She recalls the plaintive,
melancholy query of Ed Mullane, head of the Ford Dealers' Alliance:
"When I grew up in New Jersey the automobile was the one product
that universally signified success in America. What has happened on
the way to Paradise?" Needless to say, Mullane's question has been
anticipated in the literature of the automobile as its pertinence has
been verified by history. The notion of the machine as a way to
paradise, the machine as garden, is a persistent one, increasingly
subjected to a scrutiny that is likely to be bitter and ironic. Writers
have tried to decipher America's fascination with cars—the dreams

in which they are entangled, the yearnings for a "poetic" space liberated and remote from time's hard truths—and to refer such matters to the seasoned norms and standards by which human endeavors customarily have been judged and evaluated. By doing so, they have prepared the ground for a more sensitive, more intelligent assessment of automobility in America. They have warned against the extravagant and errant spirit that invades the driver's seat in pursuit of paradise, privacy, status, power, even, at times, survival itself. They have labored to disclose liabilities and losses now no longer hidden and from which we can no longer hide. They have encouraged us to think of other, less destructive ways to chase our dreams, other avenues of escape, even to find ourselves at home in relation to each other and in whatever neighborhoods or garden plots remain within the compass of our unextended, merely human reach.

JON T. POWELL

CB: AN INQUIRY INTO A NOVEL
STATE OF COMMUNICATION

The recent growth of Class D citizens band (CB) radio communications has been attributed to such causes as the public's appetite for personal electronic gadgetry, low cost, accessibility, ease of operation, and advertising. Whatever the reason, it has been estimated that one out of nineteen vehicles and one in eleven families now have CB radio.

CB communication can provide a practical service. "Probably the single biggest use of citizen-band radios is for highway information—avoiding traffic jams and reporting accidents, among other things," according to Richard Cowan, publisher of the oldest and largest of CB radio publications. "Other things" include identifying the location of highway speed traps. There is also the sheer fascination of overhearing conversation. "A good many people," according to *Forbes*, "apparently just like to kibitz—on what truck drivers say to each other, for example—a kind of radio verité."

Three characteristics appear to typify CB communication, each different but equally significant. First, there is the use of the Ten-Code (originally developed by the police and other mobile units' to minimize transmission time) as part of CB language, though frequently with slight variations. Some very common examples of this adaptation include such terms as "Ten-Four" which has come to mean "Yes, Message received," or "Okay"; "What's your twenty?" (for "Ten-Twenty" referring to location of the person queried), or "Asking for a Ten-Thirty-Six" to request the correct time. The Ten-Code ranges from "Ten-One" (receiving poorly) to "Ten-Nine-Nine" (mission completed, all units secure) and "Ten-Two-Hundred" (police needed at . . . .).[1]

The second characteristic involves the use of a special jargon. This

[1]*The 'Official' CB Slanguage Language Dictionary*, edited by Dot Gilbertson (New York: Louis J. Martin & Associates, Inc., Distributors, Revised Edition, 1976), pp. 68-70.

spoken code is different from the Ten-Code and, though it is color-ful, does not appear to be concerned with minimizing transmission time. There are a number of expressions requiring frequent use of a CB "dictionary" for the novice: for example, "bear bite" refers to a speeding ticket, and "bear bait," a speeding car without a CB unit. "Green apple" means a neophyte CBer, and the question "Got your ears on?" substitutes for "Are you listening?" When the CBer is listening he is "copying the mail." Such terms can vary considerably depending on individual interpretation and the region where the transmission takes place. The language continues to evolve, thereby creating a renewable market for CB dictionaries.

The third characteristic—mandatory for any self-respecting CBer—is the adoption of a "handle," a self-appointed title to identify the speaker during a transmission. The selection of a handle is as arbi-trary as it is colorful. It might be "Ashcan," "Screaming Eagle," "Monkey Wrench," or "Carrot Top"—purely a matter of personal choice.

These three traits characterize a highly popular form of social interaction, free from the obligations of face-to-face communication. Subject to the limitations of the transceiver, the CBer can be any-where, fixed or moving, and listen or communicate instantly. He is an anonymous presence everywhere and nowhere simultaneously with a personal identity both enhanced and concealed by flashy codes and a flamboyant handle. According to Amitai Etzioni, a Columbia University sociologist:

> A CB allows you to present a false self: to be beautiful, masculine, tall, rich, without being any of those things. Like the traveling salesman who drops into a singles bar and says he is the president of his company, a person can project on the air waves anything he wants to be.[2]

Etzioni goes on to note that in a mobile society without strong social roots, there is the urge to relate but without the full investment in a relationship required, for example, when joining a church group. "With a CB, you can have personal contact with the turn of a dial. It is very controllable and protects you from getting too involved." It is the abbreviated quality of its language, in fact, which limits personal contact. This method of communication, while not completely fulfill-ing Marshall McLuhan's broad assertion that "Electric technology does not need words. . . .," does exemplify his statement that "Our

[2]"The Bodacious New World of C.B.," _Time_, May 10, 1976, p. 79.

new electric technology that extends our senses and nerves in a global embrace has large implications for the future of language."[3]

CB chatter, beyond seeking specific information about road conditions, etc., often appears as continuous repetition of code words punctuating an exchange of questions, answers, and comments which could not or would not be considered acceptable for prolonged face-to-face communication. "What're you doing now?" "What're you going to do?" "How are you feeling?" "What's happening?" are typical of the questions constantly repeated between two CBers, only to be again reiterated should either start communicating anew with another CBer. As a rule, such questions are answered in mundane fashion without much specificity. The noncommital responses and comments on those responses are highlighted by frequent repetition of such expressions as "negatory" for "no," "mercy" for all the obscene terms banned by FCC regulations, "Ten-Four," "good buddy," and others which may reflect personal and regional differences. It is a set of formulas as aimless and ritualistic as the act of driving in a circle, verbal cruising. How can this use of language be explained?

I. A. Richards describes two uses for language as "scientific" and "emotive." The scientific use is "for the sake of the *reference*, true or false, which it causes," while the emotive is concerned with the "emotion and attitude produced by the referent it occasions."[4]

Apparently, CB language has taken on a poetic function since effect appears to be more important than information when response rather than understanding becomes the primary goal. Such a literary function is described by Richards:

> When this happens, the statements which appear in the poetry are there for the sake of their effect upon the feelings, not for their own sake. Hence to challenge their truth or to question whether they deserve serious attention as *statements claiming truth*, is to mistake their function. The point is that many, if not most, of the statements in poetry are there as a means to the manipulation and expression of feelings and attitudes, not as contributions to any body of doctrine of any type whatever.

> A poet may distort his statements; he may make statements which have logically nothing to do with the subject under treatment; he may, by

---

[3]Marshall McLuhan, *Understanding Media: The Extensions by Man* (New York: The New American Library, Signet Books, 1964), p. 83.

[4]I.A. Richards, *Principles of Literary Criticism* (New York: Harcourt, Brace & World, Inc., A Harvest Book, 1964), p. 267.

metaphor and otherwise, present objects for thought which are logically quite irrelevant; he may perpetrate logical nonsense, be as trivial or as silly, logically, as it is possible to be; all in the interests of the other functions of his language—to express feeling or to adjust tone or further his other intentions.[5]

That is not to say that CB language *is* poetry, although it seems to have a poetic function. Specialized language and personal titles satisfy an urge to manipulate, to achieve response, or to create an emotion (such as sense of brotherhood) without attendant restrictions of linguistic discipline or intellectual effort beyond the use of a casual code. There is chiefly the effort to "share symbols" in order to establish rapport without conscious effort to give these symbols much definite meaning. Moreover, although the CB codes comprise a metaphoric language, there is another distinct difference from the traditional poetic function. Richards properly asserts that "mere inattention, or sheer carelessness, may sometimes be the source of misreading; but carelessness in reading is the result of distraction. . . ." The CBer might respond by pointing out that inattention or distraction are irrelevant because the effect of his communication is judged principally by a "Ten-Four," a clear signal, or the good feeling arising from a disembodied affirming response.

Such a sense of union would not have been possible without electronic gadgetry which nullifies the isolation of the automobile. The CBer can communicate conveniently without concern for face-to-face identification or the requirement to be in any fixed location. Freed from such limitation, awareness and response take on new dimensions.

CB language may also serve to circumvent the obligation for expressing private values. Whereas the metaphor has traditionally been used as a linguistic adjunct to illustrate or emphasize personal values, it has now taken on new form. There does exist, of course, some implied commentary on the state of affairs—calling a policeman a "bear," for example—but CB terminology generally reveals little beyond the most superficial expression of values, remarkably standard and devoid of negativism. The metaphor has become the norm, indeed almost the exclusive standard, for casual CB communication. The colorful language of the CBer masks personal values, while at the same time reinforcing self-esteem through the reliance on sym-

[5]I.A. Richards, *Practical Criticism: A Study of Literary Judgment* (New York: Harcourt, Brace & Company, A Harvest Book, 1960), pp. 180-1.

bols the unfamiliarity of which marks the outsider and excludes the uninitiated.

This ritualistic uniform metaphoric terminology, however, gives to the CBer more than a sense of worth and pleasure in communication. Just how far the CBer goes beyond the poetic function could be explained in the following manner. Bronislaw Malinowski has described what he terms "phatic communion" as a type of speech in which ties of union are created by "a mere exchange of words." In this form of communication words are not used principally to transmit meaning, but serve to bind the participant socially in such a way that the words "are neither the result of intellectual reflection, nor do they necessarily arouse reflection in the listener." Language thus becomes a means of satisfying the need for companionship without concern for the transmission of ideas.[6]

CB communication seems to be a form of reaching out, binding socially when, despite faithful adherence to a code, what is said seems not so important as what the participants experience while transmitting to each other in a newly-found freedom from wires, fixed positions, or visual identity. It is not what is said that is important, but what feelings are experienced in the process of saying it. A little like being in love with love, the CBer submerges the linguistic exchange of meaning in order to enhance the feelings engendered by the act of communication.

Like television, CB communication can bridge physical distances, instantly engage the participants without threat to personal identity, creating an event entirely for the sake of enjoyment. It is a form of technological speech, an inevitable discovery of the car culture. For most CB users, the medium is the message: they make statements by means of the vehicles of transportation which define them by occupation or by nature. But driving can be a lonely art. Like the solitary poet the user of CB radio speaks with a fictive voice to an unseen listener, who *answers back*, as readers do not.

---

[6]See C.K Ogden and I.A. Richards, *The Meaning of Meaning* (New York: Harcourt, Brace & World, 1965), pp. 315-16.

MOTIVATIN' WITH CHUCK BERRY AND FREDERICK JACKSON TURNER

MAYBELLENE

Maybellene, why can't you be true?
Oh, Maybellene, why can't you be true?
You done started back doin' the things you used to do.

As I was motivatin' over the hill
I saw Maybellene in a Coupe de Ville;
A Cadillac a-rollin' on the open road,
Nothin' will outrun my V-8 Ford.
The Cadillac doin' 'bout ninety-five,
She's bumper to bumper, rollin' side by side.

Maybellene, why can't you be true?
Oh, Maybellene, why can't you be true?
You done started back doin' the things you used to do.

The Cadillac pulled up ahead of the Ford,
The Ford got hot and wouldn't do no more;
It then got cloudy and started to rain,
I tooted my horn for a passin' lane.
The rainwater blowin' all under my hood,
I know that it was doin' my motor good.

Maybellene, why can't you be true?
Oh, Maybellene, why can't you be true?
You done started back doin' the things you used to do.

The motor cooled down, the heat went down,
And that's when I heard that highway sound,
The Cadillac a-sittin' like a ton of lead,

A hundred and ten half a mile ahead.
The Cadillac lookin' like it's sittin' still
And I caught Maybellene at the top of the hill.

Maybellene, why can't you be true?
Oh, Maybellene, why can't you be true?
You done started back doin' the things you used to do.

© 1955 Arc Music Corp. (BMI)

In 1893 Frederick Jackson Turner warned that the official discontinuance of the frontier had ominous implications. Turner argued that the migration westward had been responsible for American economic growth, democratic institutions, and robust values. With the apparent closing of the western safety valve, Turner worried that pent-up social tensions might find no ready release. As it turned out, Turner's fears were misplaced. In *The Moving American,* George Pierson has argued that Turner missed the key variable in the American experience: the "M-Factor." As long as we can move somewhere and somehow, it doesn't matter if the geographic frontier is closed. Even if the literal frontier was terminated in 1890 (and western historians dispute that), the days of figurative, frontier*style* movement were just beginning. Indeed, even as Turner spoke at the Chicago World's Fair, canny entrepreneurs were developing two seductive opportunities for regenerative movement: automobiles and ragtime. Both mass motoring and African-American based popular music would take over where Turner's West left off. In particular, each offered the crucial chance to "strip off the garments of civilization," to experience the "perennial rebirth, this fluidity" of American life, to reestablish contact "with the simplicity of primitive society."[1]

With cars came autocamping, recreational vehicles, suburban homesteads, and, above all, the leveling sociability of the Open Road. And with the mainstreaming of black music—first ragtime, then jazz, blues, and later rock 'n' roll—came the neoprimitivist dance party. What better place than a pre–World War I cabaret, 1920s speakeasy, or 1930s jitterbug marathon, to witness the ritualistic reinforcement of values that Turner had held central to American culture, especially

---

[1]Frederick Jackson Turner, "The Significance of the Frontier in American History," *Annual Report of the American Historical Association for 1893* (Washington, D.C.: American Historical Association, 1893), pp. 190–227; George W. Pierson, *The Moving American* (New York: Alfred A. Knopf, 1973), pp. 1–39.

. . . that coarseness and strength combined with acuteness and inquisitive-
ness; that practical, inventive turn of mind, quick to find expedients; that
masterful grasp of material things, lacking in the artistic but powerful to
effect great ends; that restless, nervous energy; that dominant individualism, working for good and for evil, and withal, that buoyancy and exuberance which comes from freedom.

Since World War II, rock 'n' roll has combined the primitivist vitality
of black blues with the agrarian, pastoral flavor of white country-
western music. Indeed, in some ways rock best embodies the frontier
process, for its principal audience is youthful and rebellious. Also,
like the archetypal frontier town, the rock business has a boom-bust
nature; fortunes are more suddenly made and lost in rock than in
other areas of music. Thus, in both consumption and production, rock
reenacts Turner's West, where "for a moment, the bonds of custom
are broken and unrestraint is triumphant."

Rock 'n' roll is also closely related to the other parafrontier: the car
culture. Like other popular musicians, rock performers live the road
life—for better and for worse. As Peter Guralnick writes in *Lost
Highway*, popular musicians are the quintessential lonesome travelers, experiencing more freedom and more despair than their more
rooted fans.[2] Also, rock is made to be listened to while on the road.
The greatest success in rock 'n' roll usually goes to those whose music
suits the hyperkinetic formats of the top-40 stations that transmit
primarily to car radios and transistor receivers. Moreover, like blues
and country music, rock 'n' roll lyrics frequently concern the road.
Nowhere are the glories and tragedies of the car culture better documented than in the songs of Chuck Berry, the Beach Boys, and Bruce
Springsteen.

It seems appropriate, therefore, that one of the first successful
syntheses of blues and country-western styles was a song about a road
race: Chuck Berry's "Maybellene." Recorded in 1955 on the Chicago-
based Chess label, Berry's song quickly rose to top-10 status, where it
outshone white rocker Bill Haley's hit, "Rock Around the Clock."
Rock critic Michael Lydon describes the impact this way:

A beat that made Bill Haley pallid, nutty words like "motivatin'" and a
story about a guy chasing a Cadillac in his beat-up Ford to catch his girl.

[2]Peter Guralnick, *Lost Highway: Journeys and Arrivals of American Musicians* (Boston:
Godine, 1979).

Oh, the triumph of the "V-8 Fo'd" leaving the "Coupe de Ville" sitting like a "ton of lead." But even more, it was the drive of the thing, the two minutes of *rock*, pure manic intensity, that sucked you in.[3]

Central to the "pure manic intensity" of the piece was Berry's guitar, which sounded unmistakably like a souped-up car engine.

Berry followed with other car songs—"No Money Down," "Nadine," "No Particular Place to Go," "Too Much Monkey Business," "Back in the U.S.A."—along with his often imitated rock anthems— "Roll Over Beethoven," "Johnny B. Goode," "Rock and Roll Music," "Sweet Little Sixteen," "Memphis," and "Carol."[4] Of all these songs, "Maybellene" may be Berry's most suggestive, especially when its lyrics are read in the context of other mobility songs, as well as the Turner thesis. As an unself-conscious folk poet, Berry would never be pretentious enough to claim "significance," and rock purists, who generally celebrate such humility, tend to downplay textual analysis. Nevertheless, it can be argued that song lyrics are rarely chosen at random; rather, successful popular songs must in some way engage in the ongoing dialogue that constitutes a culture's core language. Like Frederick Jackson Turner, Berry knew instinctively that Americans respond strongly to Open Road imagery. From the cryptanalytical perspective of the cultural historian, "Maybellene" emerges as an implicit commentary on the M-Factor. Reading carefully, yet playfully, I find three contradictory visions of mobility: nobility, fragility, and futility.

MOBILITY = NOBILITY

In its broadest outlines, the plot resembles the usual Grade B romantic formula: boy meets girl, boy loses girl, boy gets girl. Having earlier lost sight of the alluring Maybellene, our hero spots her in the villain's Coupe de Ville. After an arduous race, he catches the Cadillac—and Maybellene—at the top of a hill. Aware of the hackneyed nature of this story line, most analysts have concentrated on Berry's musical contribution, especially his guitar work and his sensuously "biracial" vocal style. Yet the seemingly banal plot deserves

---

[3]Michael Lydon, *Rock Folk* (New York: Delta, 1971), p. 11.

[4]For a general overview: B. Lee Cooper, "'Nothin' Outrun My V-8 Ford': Chuck Berry and the Automobile, 1955–1979," *JEMF Quarterly*, 16 (Spring 1980):18–23.

attention, too, for it expresses a strong faith in mobility as a guarantee of dignity, democracy, pastoralism, and equal opportunity. As we shall see later, the song also has darker implications, but the banal, most obvious level was most responsible for its success in conservative Eisenhower America. The outwardly upbeat affirmation of cherished American values smoothed this black bluesman's acceptance by white-controlled radio stations and won him fans nationwide.

When we first encounter the anonymous protagonist, he is "motivatin' over the hill." This is a rich pun, one of rock's finest. The word "motive," meaning goal or incentive, stems from the Latin *movere*, meaning to move. *Movere* is also the root of "motor." Etymologically, to Berry, the end (motive) equals the means (the motor). That is, in describing the act of driving his car, Berry suggests that the inherent pleasure of moving is enough reason for getting behind the wheel; there need be no other rationale. There is true chivalry in this sentiment: the most noble actions are the most disinterested ones; true nobility transcends utility; the best things are done for their own sake. To the road zealot, utilitarian considerations—like using a car in order to *get somewhere*—are secondary. Historically, it was the intrinsic appeal of being in a car that induced the earliest motor pioneers to endure poor roads and uncertain machines. To use a line from another Chuck Berry song, the first generation of drivers usually had "no particular place to go" when they hit the road; they simply "motivated." There is also an element of cruiser coolness in our hero. The "as" that begins the line suggests that he *just happens* to spot Maybellene while he is already on the road for a casual drive. The consummate cruiser would never drive around looking for someone, particularly a fickle female. No, the true cruiser drives because, well, that's what a true cruiser does.

Of course, it is also possible—indeed likely—that the hero's reasons for "motivatin'" may not be quite so pure and uncomplicated. When he spots Maybellene, he is somewhat "over the hill." Both geographically and metaphorically, he is apparently on a downward slide. Perhaps after a spat with Maybellene he has taken to the road not just for its own sake, but also to let off steam. As Turner stressed in 1893, the ability to hit the road has long served as a safety valve for social pressures, and the recuperative journey is a staple of classic American literature. William Least Heat Moon explores this theme in "A Journey into America: Blue Highways" (*Atlantic Monthly*, September 1982). After losing his wife and his job, Moon decides "that a man who couldn't make things go right could at least go." This need to break free of stifling entanglements and domestic disappointments has been vividly expressed in Bruce Springsteen's epic anthem to the car culture, "Born to Run":

> Baby, this town rips the bones off your back
> It's a death trap, it's a suicide rap
> We gotta get out while we're young
> 'Cause tramps like us, baby, we were born to run.

> © 1975 Bruce Springsteen (ASCAP)

In popular music, motoring frequently serves as a surrogate for human relationships. For example, in his often-covered "V-8 Ford Blues," Willie Love boasts that his self-contained, self-sufficient automobile is a refreshingly autarchic alternative to the vagaries and vulnerabilities of complicated love affairs, especially those affairs involving socially ambitious partners (like Maybellene):

> I get my gasoline in the morning,
> I get my oil checked at night,
> Then I don't have to worry
> Cause I know everything's alright.
> I'll be down at your burial,
> Ridin' in my V-8 Ford.
> You think you're so high styled and worldly,
> I declare, girl, you just don't know.

> © 1951, 1979 Globe Music Corp. (BMI)

Similarly, in the Beach Boys' insipid "Ballad of Betsy," a car—"born in 1932," the first year of Ford's V-8—is described as "more loyal than any friend can be."

As we shall see later, such restiveness may be socially disruptive, but in the case of Chuck Berry's hero, his escapist "motivatin'" actually puts him in a position to regain his elusive Maybellene, for while he is letting off steam on the road, he coincidentally spots his girl and wins her back. In the easy formulaic world of popular art, we frequently can have it both ways: we can escape problems and we can also solve them—in the very same action. In "Maybellene," driving brings both relief and retribution.

Who is Maybellene? On one level, she is simply a flighty young woman, a love object. A variant of Mabel, the name derives from the Latin *amabilis*, lovable. But perhaps there's more. A one-time hairdresser, Chuck Berry claims he took the name from a hair cream bottle. But where did the cosmetic company get it? Is Maybellene the archetypal May Queen, springtime bestower of new life and fertility? According to rock historian Charlie Gillett (*The Sound of the City*), the song's original title was "Ida May," but the symbolism is identical; "Ida" stems from the Old Norwegian Ithunn, goddess of youth. Given American iconography concerning the Virgin Land, either name is richly evocative, conjuring up pastoral images of fresh flowers, meadows, youthful optimism, endless possibility. Is Maybellene a sister of F. Scott Fitzgerald's Daisy, representing "the fresh green breast of the new world"? Like Jay Gatsby—or perhaps even like the original passengers on the Mayflower—does Berry's hero dream of Virgin Land, with its associate promises of rebirth and domestic prosperity?[5]

The villain's Coupe de Ville is also suggestive. Like another Cadillac model, the Brougham, the name dates from the days when only the rich rode in carriages, while everyone else walked. Representing cosmopolitan wealth and sophistication, the villain's city carriage opposes the hero's virtuously Spartan Ford. Like the more radical colonial rebels of 1776, our leveling hero seeks to fight off the corrupting influences of metropolitan power.

The race also reenacts the original Ford–General Motors conflict in automobile marketing. The first V-8 engine was actually developed by Cadillac in 1915. Powerful, costly, and complex, it was considered strictly a high-priced luxury—something to trade up to. In 1932, however, Henry Ford offered a simpler, lighter, revolutionary V-8 to the mass market. Easily maintained and modified, this V-8 was popular with working-class hot-rodders (like our hero?) after World War II. In 1949, GM reasserted its lead with a low-economy, high-compression overhead valve V-8 that doubled the horsepower available to pull the heavy, chrome-laden, tail-finned Cadillacs of the 1950s. The engine guzzled gas, but it allowed unprecedented conspicuous display to upper-middle-class consumers.

Chuck Berry's race between an old V-8 Ford and a new V-8 Cadillac thus juxtaposes two contending value systems: Fordist democratic mass production and Sloanist conspicuous consumption. In the real world, the race might very well have been won by the more powerful Cadillac. (Indeed, in recognition of this superiority, Ford Motor

[5]Charlie Gillett, *The Sound of the City: The Rise of Rock 'N' Roll* (New York: Dell, 1972), p. 42; F. Scott Fitzgerald, *The Great Gatsby* (New York: Scribner's, 1925), p. 182.

Company soon developed its own Cadillac-style, souped-up V-8 line in the 1950s, thus cutting its last ties to the founder's ascetic roots.) If "Maybellene" were a standard blues, where the barriers of upper-class power are rarely breached, the jilted protagonist would have to satisfy himself with bitter recrimination, self-pity, and ineffectual vows of revenge. This at least is the dismal outcome of Willie Love's "V-8 Ford Blues," where the "high-styled and worldly" girl apparently remains out of reach.

I'm gonna get my gravedigger—to make you a place,
I'm comin' along myself—and throw dirt in your face.
I'll be down to your burial, ridin' in my V-8 Ford.
You think you're so high-styled and worldly,
I declare, girl, you don't know.

© 1951, 1979 Globe Music Corp. (BMI) (Used by permission of Globe Music Company, Jackson, MS. Copr. #EU253101, 10/15/51.
Renewal #RE28-371, 6/25/79.)

In the more optimistic world of teenage rock 'n' roll, however, the disadvantaged hero reduces the privileged Cadillac to "a ton of lead."

Still, Berry senses that youthful self-reliance may not be enough. It also helps to have Mother Nature on your side. Although the race is a fair fight "on the open road," the hero needs a sudden cloudburst to gain his goal.

The Cadillac pulled up ahead of the Ford.
The Ford got hot and wouldn't do no more;
It then got cloudy and started to rain,
I tooted my horn for a passin' lane.
The rainwater blowin' all under my hood,
I knew that it was doin' my motor good.

© 1955 Arc Music Corp. (BMI)

Our hero's alliance with the rain gods has considerable historical precedent. From the beginning of the car culture, when motorists first fled cities for wilderness campgrounds and sylvan suburban retreats, cars have had a symbiotic relationship with nature. As Leo Marx shows in *The Machine in the Garden*, this idealistic harmony between technology and nature is at the heart of the pastoral ideal. In Berry's song, the immediate upshot of this lucky fusion is an almost mystical "highway sound" that suggests pure power, energy, speed, and erotic reunion.

In all, the song expresses fundamental American hopes: through a combination of rugged determination (the hero's gutsiness), democratic engineering (the V-8 Ford), fair competition (a race on the open road), and divine providence (the thunderstorm), the poor man conquers the rich man and wins back his elusive May Queen—at least momentarily.

MOBILITY = FRAGILITY

Although the nobility of mobility is the song's most explicit message, further reflection reveals less optimistic undercurrents. Just as "May Day" means both a springtime celebration of rebirth and a universal signal of distress, Maybellene connotes both May flowers and mayhem. Contradictions are common in commodity arts, for ambiguity increases potential market size. Such double speaking is particularly useful for Afro-American musicians seeking to cross over to the dominant culture while still retaining a foothold in the black subculture. The pessimism in "Maybellene" is understated and inconclusive, but it does become more clear when placed in the broader context of other songs about Fords, Cadillacs, and mobility.

"Maybellene" actually concerns two types of movement: the horizontal, spatial mobility of the road, and the vertical, social mobility of consumption. The song's optimism is reserved primarily for the hero's spatial mobility—his ability to speed along in his own beat-up Ford, outrun the villain's Cadillac, and catch Maybellene. But we must remember that Maybellene, too, is on the road, and her automobility is viewed more negatively. She is clearly "born to run," and the chorus emphasizes that this is not the first time she has taken off.

> Maybellene, why can't you be true?
> Oh Maybellene, why can't you be true?
> You done started back doin' the things you used to do.
> © 1955 Arc Music Corp. (BMI)

If Maybellene were a man, her restiveness might be taken as a sign of colorful nobility, as in Hank Williams's "Ramblin' Man":

> I can settle down and be doing just fine
> Till I hear an old freight rolling down the line.
> Then I hurry straight home and pack,

And if I didn't go I believe I'd blow my stack.
I love you baby, but you gotta understand.
When the Lord made me he made a ramblin' man.

The rambling man's wife is supposed to tolerate stoically such inborn eccentricity. But if women flee, tragedy results. Thus, the gloomiest lyrics in traditional country blues are sung by males left behind by restless females. Listening to Robert Johnson's plaintive "Love in Vain,"—popularized recently by the Rolling Stones—we are induced to sympathize solely with the deserted husband/lover:

I brought her to the station, with her suitcase in my hand
(twice).
Well it's hard to tell, hard to tell, when all your love's in
vain.

When the train left the station, with two lights on behind
(twice),
The blue light was my blues, the red light was my mind.

Leroy Carr's "How Long, How Long Blues" has a similarly bleak chorus:

Here I stood at the station, watched my baby leaving town.
Blue and disgusted, nowhere could peace be found.
How long, how long, baby,
Has that evenin' train been gone?

With his automobile, Berry's hero can at least catch up to his girl—an option not available to the train-bound Robert Johnson or Leroy Carr. But even if he can catch her spatially, can he ever meet her social expectations? Maybellene's vertical mobility is even more dangerous than her horizontal mobility. The hero is clearly a poor man. He would not be heroic if he drove an expensive car, and his assertive asceticism—"Nothin' will outrun my V-8 Ford"—enhances his populist appeal. But Maybellene wants to rise; she cannot remain loyal to her lower-class relationship. A fickle climber, she keeps getting into a rich man's car.

Oh Maybellene, why can't you be true?
You done started back doin' the things you used to do.

The postwar Cadillac's adulterous attractions are overwhelming. With its breast-shaped Dagmar bumpers, its womblike interior and watery suspension, and its sassy fishtail rear end, the Coupe de Ville is a high-priced mobile bordello. To be sure, Maybellene's treachery has historical precedents dating from the settling of the New World. Even the chaste Pilgrims on the Mayflower could not withstand the temptations of prosperity. Like the ever-backsliding colonists, Maybellene keeps prostituting herself for a taste of luxury and sensuality. The song thus hints at long-standing tensions between contending ideals of pristine democracy (the Ford) and bourgeois success (the Cadillac).

Although the former certainly has populist appeal, the latter is not entirely condemned in the song. After all, what is so wrong with the desire to rise? Is Maybellene so bad? Doesn't she pursue the American Dream? One also wonders about the driver of the Cadillac. Is he un-American? It is interesting that Berry fails to paint him as the classic, upper-class philanderer of stock melodrama. Perhaps he is simply a poor boy who has made good. For many working-class Americans the Cadillac has represented hope and aspiration. Unlike the explicitly upper-class Pierce-Arrow or Rolls-Royce, a new Cadillac is a considerably less exclusive commodity—well within the reach of the moderately nouveau riche. As an exceptionally durable used car, it is also available to more modest incomes. As Bruce Springsteen notes in "Cadillac Ranch," the vision of even an old Eldorado in the driveway makes a workingman's hard day seem bearable:

Well, there she sits, buddy, justa gleaming in the sun
There to greet a working man when his day is done. . .

Eldorado fins, whitewalls and skirts,
Rides just like a little bit of heaven here on earth.
Well, buddy, when I die throw my body in the back
And drive me down to the junkyard in my Cadillac.

This quasi-eschatological connotation is also seen in Dizzy Gillespie's whimsical "Swing Low, Sweet Cadillac":

I looked over Jordan
And what did I see?
Comin' for to carry me home,
An Eldorado, a comin' after me
Comin' for to carry me home.

© 1959 Iwo Music (ASCAP)

Is this Cadillac a limousine or a hearse? Either way, it suggests heavenly delights considerably softer and more plush than those represented by the purist's V-8 Ford.

Of course, as history shows, and as Berry implies, this pursuit of Eldorado—the fabulous golden city—has induced some to desert families and roots (as does Maybellene) and even to pillage former communities (as may be the case with the Cadillac driver). But many have been willing to pay the price of treason, and some have even boasted of it. For example, in "Speedoo," the theme song of a top rhythm and blues group of the 1950s, the Cadillacs (!), the slick tenor brags of his ability to steal numerous Maybellenes:

Well now, they often call me Speedoo,
    But my real name is Mr. Earl.
I'm known for meeting brand new fellas,
    And takin' other folks' girls.

© 1955, 1973 Big Seven Music Corp. (BMI)

Etymologically, the name Earl connotes royalty, quickness, bravery, cunning. Could it also refer to Harley Earl, the well-known designer of the Cadillac tailfin? The seductive powers of Earl's design are further explored in another 1950s song, "When I Get Lucky," where Chicago bluesman Floyd Dixon dreams of the opportunity to revenge the social slights and snubs suffered in poverty:

If anyone calls me, I'll look the other way.
Be a shame on you baby, won't hear a word you say.
When I get lucky, gonna buy me a fishtail Cadillac Car.
Gonna cruise by all you girls, just like I don't know who
    you are.

The tensions between populist roots and upward mobility have been particularly strong in the rock 'n' roll business, where countless poor boys have made it big almost overnight, with ironic, if not also

tragic results. Thus, in "Baby, Let's Play House" (1955), one of Elvis
Presley's last records on the small Memphis Sun label, the proud
country boy criticizes his socially ambitious girlfriend, who, like
Maybellene, has run away:

> You may go to college,
> You may go to school.
> You may have a pink Cadillac,
> But don't be nobody's fool.

Yet, unlike Arthur Gunter, the black bluesman who wrote the song,
Elvis did not stay close to his roots. Within a few months he signed a
contract with RCA, left Memphis, and bought the first of several pink
Cadillacs. As Greil Marcus points out in *Mystery Train: Images of
America in Rock 'N' Roll Music*, the story of Presley's jump from
"woods and welfare" to power and fame, had epic proportions:

> The Pink Cadillac was at the heart of the contradiction that powered Elvis'
> early music; a perfect symbol of the glamor of his ambition and the resent-
> ments that drove it on. When he faced his girl in "Baby, Let's Play
> House," . . . Elvis sang with a contempt for a world that had always ex-
> cluded him; he sang with a wish for its pleasures. . . . Girls who had
> turned up their noses in high school were now waiting in line, just as today
> [1975] men and women who are barely hanging on to the edge of the
> middle class wait in line to see a man who has achieved an eminence class
> can never bring.[6]

In his early art, Presley may have sounded like Willie Love scorning
the "high-styled and worldly" runaway of "V-8 Ford Blues," but in his
heart he shared the dreams of Floyd Dixon in "When I Get Lucky."

For Chuck Berry, too, the Cadillac certified success. Before he
recorded "Maybellene" Berry was a twenty-eight-year-old weekend
bluesman who was tired of supporting his wife and two children as a
GM Fisher Body assembly-line worker and part-time cosmetologist.
According to a fellow blues musician in St. Louis, "Nobody pays you
no attention 'round here til you gets your first Cadillac,"[7] and in the
semiautobiographical "No Money Down," Berry outlined the vision
that drove him to Chicago and Chess Records in 1955:

---

[6]Greil Marcus, *Mystery Train: Images of America in Rock 'N' Roll Music* (New York:
Dutton, 1976), p. 186.
[7]Lydon, *Rock Folk*, p. 8.

Well, Mister, I want a yellow convertible,
Fo' do' de Ville
With Continental spare
And wire chrome wheels;
I want power steering
And power brakes,
I want a powerful motor,
With jet off-take;
I want air condition,
I want automatic heat,
I want a full-length bed,
In my back seat;
I want short-wave radio,
I want TV and a phone,
You know I gotta talk to my baby,
When I'm riding along.

© 1956 Arc Music Corp. (BMI)

Ironically, what did he want to trade in for this dream machine? An old Ford. Berry was well aware of the dangers of such a transaction; the title alone implied that even if the status symbol could be attained on credit, eventually a price had to be paid (similarly, in Dizzy Gillespie's "Swing Low, Sweet Cadillac": "Old Cadillacs never die / the finance company just fades them away").

Qualms notwithstanding, Berry's life—like Elvis's—suddenly took to the fast lane in 1955, and he too bought numerous Cadillacs— powder blue, not pink. With fame came inevitable separation from family and home. Eventually, Berry's motivatin' brought disaster. Like the fighter, Jack Johnson, another "bad nigger" who had dared to encroach on previously all-white turf, Berry infuriated racist authorities with his well-publicized love for fast cars and good times. In 1959 he was arrested for allegedly smuggling a fourteen-year-old Mexican prostitute in the trunk of his car—was it a Cadillac? Berry's defenders argue that he was framed by an establishment out to repress integrated rock 'n' roll. Like Johnson fifty years before, he was tried under the Mann Act (transporting women across state lines for illicit purposes). When he entered federal prison in 1962, his marriage and career were shattered. Later on, he did make a modest comeback as the opening act for white musicians who rode in Rolls Royces, not Cadillacs. For Chuck Berry the move upward had brought fame and wealth, but also personal tragedy. Like another problem-plagued early rock star, Little Richard, he got what he wanted, but he lost what he had. Chuck Berry knew firsthand the fragility of mobility.

MOBILITY = FUTILITY

Berry's hero catches Maybellene "at the top of the hill," but does he keep her? The third line of the chorus—also the last line of the song—implies not: "You've started back doin' the things you used to do." Apparently this is not the first time that Maybellene has been disloyal, and, given her ambitions, it will not be the last. Indeed, one wonders what will happen in the scene *after* the frozen-frame reunion at the top of that hill. Does Maybellene get out of the Cadillac, or, like Sisyphus's stone, will she roll away down the hill, forever unattainable? Like Jay Gatsby, is Berry's hero doomed to keep running, faster and faster, after "the orgiastic future that year by year recedes before us?" Does all his "motivatin'" ever get him anywhere? Is the slippery, silent Maybellene—part pastoral dream, part facial cream model—really worth the effort?

In 1955 Chuck Berry was too young and optimistic to give much of an answer. Moreover, there has been little precedent in American popular culture for such interpretations of mobility. Most discussions have followed Turner's focus on nobility, with a weaker countertheme of fragility. Only occasionally has someone asked, What's the use? Does all this moving about have any real purpose or lasting effect? In the mid-nineteenth century, Charles Dickens quipped that the typical American would be reluctant to enter heaven unless assured that he could go further west. Similarly, Alexis de Tocqueville suggested that American restlessness was more obsessive than noble:

> In the United States, a man builds a house in which to spend his old age, and he sells it before the roof is on; he plants a garden and lets it just as the trees are coming into bearing; he brings a field into tillage and leaves other men to gather the crops; he embraces a profession and gives it up; he settles in a place, which he soon afterwards leaves to carry his changeable longings elsewhere. . . . Death at length overtakes him, but it is before he is weary of his bootless chase of that complete felicity which forever escapes him.

But Dickens's and Tocqueville's views were never popular or influential in this country. In the 1920s Will Rogers observed that "America

is a nation that conceives of many odd inventions for getting somewhere but can think of nothing to do when it gets there," but Rogers's
self-deprecating style of humor tended to obscure the full seriousness
of his commentary. At least it never deterred anyone from filling the
gas tank for a Sunday drive. Through the 1940s and 1950s, the American romance with the M-Factor was proudly hailed as an emblem of
our superiority in the worldwide contest with communism. Where
else but in capitalist America were the suburbs so extensive, the
traffic so thick, the cars so heavy? The ideological defense of mobility
extended even to the academic community. When, in 1961, historian
William Appleman Williams condemned our "frontier-expansionist
outlook," and dared to suggest that Americans would have been better off trying to build democratic communities closer to home, he was
denounced by virtually all establishment reviewers. Ironically,
Williams taught in the history department at the University of
Wisconsin—initially made famous by Frederick Jackson Turner.[8]

Only in recent years—inspired by concern for energy, ecology, and
roots—have we taken a deeper look at the efficacy of movement. This
revaluation has extended from fashion (peasant dresses), to academia
(Williams was made president of the Organization of American Historians in 1980), to popular music. For example, in "So Far Away,"
Carole King implies that the romance of the road has become a tired
cliché that actually hinders growth and awareness.

In "Born to Run," Bruce Springsteen hints that hitting the road in
pursuit of a "runaway American dream"—Maybellene?—is more an
act of self-destructive desperation than one of romantic nobility.

> In the day we sweat it out in the streets of a runaway
> 　American dream,
> At night we ride through mansions of glory in suicide
> 　machines. . . .
>
> The highways jammed with broken heroes
> On a last chance power drive.
> Everybody's out on the run tonight
> But there's no place left to hide.
>
> © 1975 Laurel Canyon Music Ltd. (ASCAP)

---

[8]Pierson, *Moving American*, pp. 48, 161; William Appleman Williams, *The Contours of
American History* (Cleveland: World Publishing Co., 1961).

And in his own self-descriptive album, "Bio" (an artistic gem but a commercial failure in 1973), Chuck Berry supplies a revealing glimpse of Maybellene's lover eighteen years further down the road. The elusive dream still holds, although it now seems considerably domesticated, indeed maudlin.

> All that I ask of this old world is just to have a
> happy home.
> All that I ask of one little girl is to be my very
> own.
> It seems just like I'm existing, aimlessly drifting
> alone.
> "Aimlessly Drifting" © 1973 Isalee Music Pub. Co. (BMI)

Eighteen years before he had boasted that "Nothin' will outrun my V-8 Ford"; now, however, he seems to pity himself for still being trapped in Maybellene's shallow game.

> I'm aimlessly drifting, looks like I live from day to day.
> Hard as I try to make a showing, something is always
> in my way.
> Even the one I truly love deals in the games that people
> play.
> "Aimlessly Drifting" © 1973 Isalee Music Pub. Co. (BMI)

Like Turner's noble pioneer, he considers heading west in search of a fresh start, yet there is a tired, déjà vu quality to the road. Perhaps the old safety valve has lost its regenerative powers.

> I guess I'll go to California, seems like I'm always on
> the run.
> Nobody ever needs a loser, we just exist under the
> sun.
> Someday, somehow, someone may need me, when
> my drifting days are done.
> "Aimlessly Drifting" © 1973 Isalee Music Pub. Co. (BMI)

For all too many rock musicians, the pursuit of new frontiers and virgin goddesses would end in drugs, booze, and death. In Chuck Berry's case, however, age and experience brought a decision to downshift and abandon the race. Retreating from the road, he returned to Missouri and played the blues, whose rewards were modest but solid.

IV. DREAM MACHINE OR AMERICAN NIGHTMARE?

DANIEL L. GUILLORY

BEL AIR: THE AUTOMOBILE AS ART OBJECT

On one of those high, dry October days when the sunlight spills warmly into your field of vision and the icy tang of winter clings to the edge of consciousness, I found myself driving over the bad farm roads of east central Illinois. The countryside was geometrically neat and planar: corn and bean fields fell in regular intervals like squares on graph paper or the blue lines of a surveyor's notebook. I was heading toward the Indiana line, and even now the land was no longer as flat as a table top but began to undulate and dip into ravines, hills, and little sandstone cliffs. The roads turned serpentine and narrow, enclosing an apple orchard here or a herd of fat Holstein there. Everywhere the sunlight was falling in big, manageable chunks, illuminating the farmhouses as formal as postage stamps and the sharp-edged red barns that must have been cut out with scissors and pasted to the horizon.

Everyone feels rich at harvest time, and perhaps that is why these farm folk who raise the corn and apples delighted in horse-trading, auctioneering, flea markets, barn sales, and open-air swap sessions. I had already passed two auctions in progress, and I would have passed up the next one except for an especially severe glint, a blister of light that emanated from the heavily chromed snout of a 1936

Packard. I half expected FDR to be sitting on the back seat. This sedan stood tall and stately, and the farmers approached it with a certain air of hesitation and respect. A 1929 Model A seemed more democratic and inviting, even though it did have traces of rust on the rear fenders. But the showpiece was a 1950 powder-blue Ford Tudor, "slick as a bar of soap and smooth as a sewing machine," according to the old farmer who owned it. Clearly, this was no ordinary flea market; serious collectors were sprinkled among the farmers in overalls, plaid shirts, and John Deere caps. Although the sermons were better, the prices were too steep for my professorial salary. "Tell you what I'm gonna do," said the owner of the blue Ford. "Feller up the road, friend o'mine, has a Chivvy fer sale," he explained, as he pointed toward a hill some two or three miles distant. "You jog left at the crossroad and follow the hard road up the hill. You can't miss it."

The crudely lettered sign *Car For Sale* was planted in the front yard of a white frame house that might have served as an archetype of the region. No one seemed to be around, so I ambled into the inviting red barn, with its rich texture of smells: timothy, alfalfa, manure, and mud. The cracks between the old barn boards were thinner than knife blades, allowing the cool October light to squeeze through like thin sheets of glass. Dust motes hovered everywhere. There was just enough light to discern the strawcovered outlines of an automobile resting in the corner like some found object. Here was no Victrola or tacky butter churn; here was a piece of pure Americana, a 1958 Chevrolet Bel Air sitting glumly on tires that were squashed flat and useless. A bale of hay had fallen on the roof. A rusty-colored chicken sat pensively on the back seat. Yet the sheet metal, lacquered in alternating bands of metallic blue and creamy white, still glowed impressively. This old sedan arched its metallic eyebrows over the four intact headlamps, and the front bumpers were puckered open and spread wide like a shark's jaw filled with numberless teeth. I was drawn especially to the turquoise blue interior, the dashboard and instrument panel composed in sweeping parabolic curves punctuated by conical knobs and switches in a style that was pure Buck Rogers. A shape reminiscent of the fabled V-2 rocket had provided a decorative motif that was repeated on the upholstery of the doors and seats.

This Bel Air was Everyman's Space Ship for 1958, an artifact from a happier and dreamier time when space ships and their telltale fins had charmed the national imagination. In the year before this

Bel Air left the assembly line in Detroit, Sputnik was launched. Eisenhower was ensconced safely in the White House, Elvis was king, and the Cold War was turning icy-hot, as suggested by the Civil Defense "Conelrad" logo on the radio dial. Somehow this car had cheated the inexorable march of time, like the strange, captured moments of a prized photograph. But unlike the photograph, the Bel Air was not a ghostly image but a three-dimensional presence, enticing and seductive in its pure physicality. I dimly understood that by possessing this car I was retrieving part of my past and—through a kind of Proustian logic—expanding my present. The good hard money of the 1950s could still be spent; the music persisted, not merely the music of lovers' lanes and hamburger heavens but the deeper strains of a past recaptured. Rock and roll pounded in my temples; the hiked-up bass lines of electric guitars ricocheted in the close, cabin-like interior of the old Chevy. Some dark-haired singer in a gold lamé suit intoned pleadingly into a microphone; the rhythms grew stronger and stronger, overwhelming in their intensity. Like so many before me, I found my virtue and good sense powerless before this onslaught. And I bought that car.

Some days later a tow truck deposited the Bel Air in the driveway of my house on Faculty Row, adjoining the grounds of the starchy liberal arts college where I taught literature and writing. Something was dreadfully out of place. The car was older than most of the students. Surely the Prof was off his rocker for buying such an old junker! A neighbor and colleague, indignant and peeved, demanded that I remove that "relic" from the driveway. Property values were going to suffer, he insisted. As if to exacerbate my feelings of guilt and squeamishness, the local Chevrolet dealer refused to touch the car. The service manager, in fact, broke into peals of laughter when I timidly admitted that the car was a '58. Apparently, Mr. Goodwrench was as phony as any other character on television. No independent garage wanted the work, either. Even a so-called "custom" shop saw no profit in the undertaking. I now owned a piece of collectible kitsch, something to frame and elevate as an art object in the manner of Joseph Cornell, the artist who spent a lifetime making glass-framed boxes which he filled with various *objets*.

But if the automotive establishment wasn't interested in a disabled 1958 sedan, many other people obviously were. The doorbell began to ring daily, and inevitably a stranger appeared, asking about The

Car. Was it for sale? How had I found one in such excellent condition? Was it a straight six or a small-block eight? Did I plan to exhibit? The most interesting visitors were those who, like the rural antique dealers, wanted to swap stories. One fellow recounted in vivid detail a trip that he and his family had taken to the Yukon in a 1958 Bel Air. Others rehearsed first dates, proms, traffic tickets, and other small moments of family and personal history. Although the stories, for the most part, amounted to trivial and corny tales, the act of nostalgic recollection and the process of retelling were genuinely impressive. An American paradox was parked in the driveway, an assemblage of insensate rubber, steel, and glass parts that somehow triggered poignant human feelings. A college dean, who usually spoke in terms of "cost benefit analysis" and "management by objective," arrived one morning, asking to inspect the ancient oil-bath air filter. He then gave me an impromptu sermon on the virtues of this 250-cubic-inch straight six engine, closing with the colloquial observation that "these here motors will run forever. You could hit 'em broadside with a bazooka, and they'd still keep running." I had never heard those tones in the official memoranda he sent through campus mail. By this time, I suspected that I had fulfilled every anthropologist's secret dream: the discovery of an authentic tribal totem. When these visitors spoke of the Bel Air, their tones shifted, and their voices fairly rose in song. One man produced a billfold in which, next to snapshots of his wife and kids, were pictures of the three '58 Chevies he had owned, including an Impala convertible, black and shiny as a hearse. The Bel Air had provided an entrée for each of my visitors, and something indisputably human in their own past had suddenly become larger and more accessible. Like the car itself, memories were being towed out of some red barn and made ready for restoration.

Buck and Larry appeared on the doorstep like all the other strangers who had come to see The Car, but from the very first moment I sensed that our association would be different. For one thing, in dress and manner they resembled dropouts from some Tantric California commune of the late Sixties. Larry was a vegetarian who sported a red beard down to his chest, and he generally spoke about the beauty of "natural and organic" ways—when he spoke at all. Buck was a dark and loquacious fellow with old-fashioned wire-rim glasses that bobbed up and down on his nose as he laughed nervously and launched into frequent jokes or sarcastic anecdotes. Although they tried to pass themselves off as young innocents, I later learned that Buck had a degree in anthropology and that Larry had completed everything but the dissertation for a Ph.D. in biology. During the time I knew them, they asked me more pertinent questions about philosophy, literature, and world affairs than did most of my students—or even my colleagues, for that matter. They read voraciously, and they fixed old cars. Lesson number one: a book is a tool.

They sized up the car with a cool, professional savvy, checking tie-rods, A-frames, wheel bearings, gear lube, and throttle linkage while petting the metallic flanks of the old Bel Air as if it were a pony about to receive its first saddle. At first I thought these automotive guardian angels fit into some convenient sociological niche, like "hippie hot-rodder" or "blue-collar car buff" or "nostalgic collector." Actually, they belonged to a more original category that I dubbed *homo mobilis*, self-reliant, Emersonian types who believed that "less was more" and that maintenance was a way of life. Keep it running, keep it running, and above it all, do it yourself. Since the age of twelve or thirteen, Buck and Larry had torn down and reassembled every kind of engine they could get their hands on: motorcycles, lawn mowers, outboard motors, even garden tillers. They had learned to trust the palpable reality of the well-tuned motor as much as they learned to distrust and despise automotive dealerships with their sinister wiles and shoddy business practices. Well, I had started off in the right direction, they assured me, by buying the car from another individual (never from a dealer, new or used) and by buying a used vehicle that was *potentially* road-worthy. At this point, I had my doubts. The thing hadn't run in years. Belts were loose, gaskets were brittle, valves and rocker arms were painfully out of adjustment. The carburetor sprayed gasoline in fan-shaped spumes over the entire engine compartment. Could this lethal, incendiary weapon be transformed into a civilized sedan, after all? As if to answer my question, Larry shuffled over to his pickup and returned with a tube of industrial-grade sealant and a small crescent wrench. After a few minutes of tinkering and a boost from the truck's oversized battery, the old Chevy fired up, coughed throatily, and began to turn over in a rough but regular rhythm. "Needs work," observed Larry.

That laconic utterance translated into six weeks of intense physical *and* intellectual exertion of a kind and combination I had never experienced before. We all had jobs, but every afternoon, Larry and Buck appeared faithfully with whatever tools, jacks, torches, lights, and meters were dictated by the task at hand. In the end, we stripped the car down to its bare bones, piece by piece, even the maddening watch-like interiors of the carburetor, speedometer, and clock. When we finished, some six weeks later, at a time when the first snow was beginning to dust the ground, the car was mechanically perfect and aesthetically pleasing, with one small exception. The electric clock proved intransigent to the very end; Buck concluded that it would always gain five minutes per week, that it was probably a design defect. I never learned if that was a face-saving rationalization on his part, but it was the only time Buck or Larry ever offered an excuse. In their view, everything on a car behaved according to immutable principles of logic and right reason. If anything malfunctioned on the car, there was always an exact and assignable cause for the problem. Unlike the world of men and ideas, where reality was surrounded by a nimbus of confusion and doubt, the systems of the automobile obeyed laws of a Platonic and Newtonian kind.

I began to appreciate the subtle meshing of one part with another and the larger coherence of whole *systems* of parts (engine, drive train, brakes). Precise articulation was the goal here as in the teaching of rhetoric. If the front wheels were out of alignment, then the tires would wear unevenly and commence to wobbling at high speeds. This vibration, in turn, would weaken the tie rods, and eventually grind down the rubber bushings until the car would be next to impossible to steer. On the other hand, if one had the precise point of alignment for every system, the whole car began to behave with a beauty that was proved in flawless acceleration, cornering, and braking—and in the knowledge that these small parts of the universe hummed perfectly. Hence, the ignition points must be separated by a gap of exactly thirty-five thousandths of an inch for reasons of engineering as well as aesthetics. So too, the timing was adjusted exactly five degrees from "top dead center." I never heard Buck rhapsodize about the special beauty of the automobile, but one splendid afternoon when the western sky was flaring and we had finally returned the last pieces of chrome trimming to their proper places, Buck caught me staring at the finished product. For once, he was speechless. His face crumpled into something like a smirk or a wink before he loaded the last of his tools on the bed of the truck. He and Larry drove away, looking for all the world like the Robin Hoods of the automotive kingdom.

Although Larry and Buck might have earned hundreds of dollars apiece for the work they performed, I knew better than to offer them money—despite the fact that the Bel Air had quadrupled in market value. Our exchange had been more educational than mercantile. Buck and Larry would have never used the word, but they surely taught me that an automobile, first, in its operating parts and, second, in its repair and maintenance, amounts to a kind of *logos*, a self-contained system of causes and effects, a wholeness of truth and reason. Automobiles, which had heretofore baffled me with their perverse and irrational breakdowns, now seemed tractable and sane. Furthermore, working on an automobile provided one with a sense of control that carried into every department of human life. No one would want to be guided by the strictures of *Chilton's Repair Manual*, but how refreshing it would be if our scholarly and political discourse approached the clarity of the manual. Words like *knurled*, *tapered*, and *pitted* were semantically pure in a way that terms such as *liberal*, *symbolic*, and *axiomatic* rarely were. One night after reading chapters on gears and ratios in *Chilton*, I picked up a recent issue of the *Publications of the Modern Language Association* and found myself translating the critical jargon into something like plain English. Other tilts occurred, also. Even though I punished my hands and arms with special soaps and brushes, ultimately I could not conceal my secret life as a devotee of oil and pistons. Immovable sludge from the heart of the old engine lodged permanently under my fingernails and cuticles. Ground-in blackness darkened the whorls of my fingerprints and the tiny crosshatchings of my knuckles. Was it sacrilege to teach Shakespeare and Keats with hands in such a state? Perhaps. But in ways that daily surprised me, I was becoming more and more sensitive to the struts and supporting members of literary creations. Any poem is infinitely more complex than any engine, but going from one to another in the intimate way I was doing proved instructive and enlightening. One did not need to lapse into the breezy generalizations of Robert Pirsig in *Zen and the Art of Motorcycle Maintenance*. Whether one called it zen, logos, or *ratio*, the inherent discipline of repair work sharpened the hands, the eyes, and the mind, leaving one with a self-sustaining sense of liberation. Once I grasped that fact, my apprenticeship was over, the *rite de passage* was accomplished, and Larry and Buck disappeared forever, leaving me with a car that stayed out of doors during the worst winter in one hundred years. It never failed to start on the first turn of the key.

The experience with Larry and Buck released a whole complex of memories which I had conveniently tucked away or repressed once I entered the rarefied atmosphere of academe. In those sacred precincts, automobiles were not a proper subject of discourse, except perhaps as counters in a game of fiscal or economic analysis. And one learned quickly to drive the right kind of automobile, namely, a foreign one. Preferences varied from one ivory tower to another, but certain makes were always in favor. For the economy-minded, a used Hillman Minx or Morris Minor might be ideal. An MG, old or new, was always popular, as was the Mercedes, particularly the diesel-powered models. But the ultimate in academic chic was the Volvo, sold in advertisements as the thinking man's car. And I believed that I shared vicariously in that cool Swedish rationality as long as I owned my Volvo 145 station wagon, despite the fact that the SU carburetors were untunable, that the points wore out every 2,000 miles, or that the camshaft collapsed after 50,000 miles (for which the factory did partially reimburse me). I needn't cite the thrown piston rod from my new Mercedes or the VW Square Back that greeted the front passenger with a cascading waterfall (via the glove compartment) every time it rained. And while my two MG's were delightful to drive, both leaked notoriously, and the electric systems were abysmally inefficient. And I did drive three hundred miles (in a borrowed Plymouth) to buy a fuel pump for the last MG. I had been duped with advertising techniques long since documented by Vance Packard in *The Hidden Persuaders*. When the Volvo left me on a snow-packed road in the middle of January, I vowed to find an American car that most resembled the one I had almost forgotten: my father's pride, a 1950 Chevrolet De Luxe.

That Chevy had been my father's first new car, and I knew it as our family car, as well as the car on which I learned to drive. My first lesson on the correct operation of clutch and brake pedals ended with the destruction of our wooden garage doors and a few flecks of white paint permanently embedded in the front bumper of the Chevy. The car cost $1,800 new in 1950, and except for tires, batteries, brake linings, belts, and hoses never cost another penny. We performed all the work on it right in the driveway, with a few simple tools and the jack as provided by the factory. The car came with a service manual, no radio, and a "lap robe" for chilly evenings. I don't recall ever thinking of it as anything but transportation or work since I held the wrenches, pumped the pedals, or cleaned up the mess while my Father did the interesting jobs. Once a month we checked every fluid, bulb, and belt, changed the oil and greased everything. No one ever touched the car except me or my father. When I inherited it, that old Chevy had 99,000 miles on the odometer. When I sold it five years later, the total was up to 133,000—and I sold it to a service station owner who used it to haul wrecks and boost batteries on cold winter mornings. The luminous days with Larry and Buck may have allowed me to relive these days from the past, and perhaps the restoration of the '58 Bel Air was a strange way of reclaiming the lost '50 De Luxe. Sometimes I would be driving late at night across the prairie during the dead of winter. The world had turned glacial; time and distance melted into one another. The radio cracked and fizzed as station signals faded in and out from all over the country: WABC (New York) . . . WSM (Nashville) . . . WLS (Chicago) . . . WWL (New Orleans). The wheel vibrated ever so slightly through my thick gloves, and for an instant this car was every car I had ever owned. I thought of grandfather's Model A, bought new in 1929 and kept running for twenty-five years. The thing rocked and pitched like a buckboard through the cotton fields. The roof was kept tight with yearly applications of tar. It came to be a part of him, like a horse or mule. I half expect to find it one of these days, waiting at the edge of a green pasture, where he left it over twenty-five years ago.

All this telescoping of time and distance seems especially ironic since the American automobile is the supreme example of planned obsolescence in the world's largest consumer economy. What had been designed as a piece of ephemera, something to be forgotten as soon as the annual models appeared, became instead a preserver of the past and the trigger mechanism for a whole cluster of nostalgic feelings and associations. Automobile travel became a species of time travel; we found ourselves going backward in time while moving forward in space. Aristotle was deprived of the opportunity to define the exact nature of the automobile, but I suspect that with his keen concern for causation and movement generally, he might look at the automobile as the art of movement in the machine age. In *The Poetics* Aristotle described the plot or mainspring of action in a play with the Greek word *dunamos* (English "dynamic"). Perhaps we have thought of automotive dynamics in rather narrow and unimaginative ways. The term "dynamics" is a staple in the critical vocabulary of disciplines as diverse as engineering, psychology, and aesthetics. In ways not yet fully understood, the automobile belongs in all three areas of inquiry. As such, it represents a nexus of many human skills and undertakings.

Precisely because the automobile can be viewed from so many different perspectives, it possesses an unusually high visibility within American culture. Automobiles are probably the most recognizable and identifiable artifacts shared by most Americans. Literary critics might call this charismatic power "resonance," while an anthropologist might see the auto as our source of *mana*. But the copywriters seized upon and enhanced this mythic potency almost from the outset. Here is a representative sample from a 1951 Ford advertisement:

> Today the American Road has no end: The road that went nowhere now goes everywhere. . . . The wheels move endlessly, always moving, always forward—and always lengthening the American Road. On that road the nation is steadily traveling beyond the troubles of this century, constantly heading toward finer tomorrows. The American Road is paved with hope.

It isn't the Ford as such that is being sold here but a sort of Whitmanesque dream of the future. In an analogous way, the central importance of the automobile today is suggested by a recent Chevrolet Chevelle spread in which a gallery of American types (hardhats, housewives, and professionals) are grouped around the car which is parked conveniently in front of the neighborhood Roxy. The marquee proudly announces "A Fresh New Slice of Apple Pie." Even though the photograph is clearly staged, the overall advertisement is clever and convincing because we all recognize ourselves in it. The movie is over; the car is parked at the curb, waiting for its driver. Any member of the crowd might hop in and drive away. That intoxicating promise of power, that irreducible pleasure in moving from here to there is what the automobile finally means.

There isn't a Roxy in my town, but there is an architectural clone called The Cinema, and nearby lives an old gentleman who owns two 1965 Chevrolet Corvairs. One is "Sea Green," the other "Fathom Blue." If the old fellow has heard of Ralph Nader's *Unsafe at Any Speed*, he won't admit it—at least not to me. I've been eyeing the blue one, always discreetly and with no apparent haste. In matters like these timing counts for everything, so I'm waiting for another one of those high-domed October days. When the conversation hits a lull and the light softens on the contours of the old Corvair, I'll incline my head gently toward the car and make him an offer he can't refuse.

KATHLEEN SPIVACK

AS ANIMALS

Green New Hampshire
on the road and the radio playing.
Behind each thicket
crickets like irritation

part the air.
This car divides the road.
I drive the uncombed side:
the grasses waver,

little splashes of gravel sprout.
Blue car in the blue air,
I am hurrying somewhere
fifty miles an hour while,

roadside, from each stalk of grass,
a microcosm watches, wondering.
Each froth of spittle
on the vetch hides complex

compound eyes.
Each gall, inside, is star-
shaped, cancer-weird:
a smug worm, cradled, watches.

Trees along the shoulder
stand up beside the road,
slim organ pipes,
their water driven upward.

It is soundless for them, fingering
the wind, like practicing.
And I am practicing
being independent, greedy

through the country,
swallowing the green of it
and speeding—
Where's the stop?—

to some unproven mountain top
as if to choose one view
while the ground breathes,
heaving upward,

and a sweet sunlit smell
rushes in the car windows
like small strawberries, wild,
like lying in a meadow,

parting the leaves, and finding
them. Now the mountains
bump against me,
the hills tumble together;

the trees are racing me
to the waterfalls
and the road cuts the edges
of gulleys

and the radio is twanging:
be American.
Drive forever!—
I downshift at the curves.

Live forever.
The mind is suspended.
Driving is a sensation
unending, cool as sunset,

slowing finally by some
unnamed meadow, the clover darkening,
the sun finishing, the car huddled,
watching, inert: silent as animals.

WILLIAM E. GILES

LOVE AT SECOND SIGHT

There was something about the car. Or, maybe, just something about me at the time. But instant affection occurred when I first saw the 1960 Chevy Impala —in 1960. Nothing but memory came of that dalliance. With four young children, a mortgage, and a modest salary, there was no sensible way for me to seek a match. I went on to other, less attractive things.

Twenty years later, out of the blue, my 18-year-old son Joe came rolling into our driveway with his newest acquisition: A 1960 Chevy Impala in gleaming turquoise, white rocket trim, chrome-traced wings, and real, wide whitewall tires. It was love at second sight.

Joe, who buys and sells cars with youthful abandon, tells me all about the intricacies of the motor, the "wonder bar" on the radio, and the miles-per-gallon. But I'm not really interested; the facts merely confuse fantasies. After Joe let me drive the lithe beauty to the store, I discovered the fantasies are not mine alone. The car turned more heads—and fluttered more hearts, I'm sure—than a Bo in a bikini.

I do not know what it is about people and their cars. We used to hear a lot about Americans' "love affair" with their autos. But it's not Yanks alone; people around the globe similarly see their cars as something more than transportation alone. It embraces the idea, perhaps, of freedom, status, progress. The car is—or was—an object of affection and romance, if not love itself.

I leave it to the psychologists to explain this bit of craziness which seems to affect every generation of car owners. But perhaps we ought to dwell a little these days on the notion of romance and cars amid the gloom and doom hanging over the American auto industry.

The carmakers' problems are real, of course. The gas crunch, high interest rates, federal regulations, inept management planning, growing labor costs, high prices, inferior products, foreign competition—they all add up to a depressing burden on sales and the industry's future. In the panic and passion to deal with those problems, howev-

292

er, the carmakers may be ignoring the one thing that somehow gave their product special, irresistible attraction: human affection.

Impala
Courtesy of *Detroit News*

What I'm suggesting is that American car manufacturers created a large and expandable market for their products by gearing them to a human need which had nothing to do with getting from here to there. They focused on that understood need and helped fulfill it with tangible fantasy.

I'm not sure how they succeeded in doing this. There was hype and hoopla, of course, with every model year. But above and beyond that, consumers responded to the idea of romance, if not romance itself. They even *looked forward* to being wooed and won. It was akin to the magic of the courtesan; new vistas kept opening up.

The cars today, especially the high-mileage imports, are poor fantasy substitutes. They have the stunted look and spiritual attraction of a mountain goat. They are practical, all right—small, straight, simple, not terribly dissimilar to the idea of the Model T. The point was to get from here to there cheaply and dependably.

There were, to be sure, many people who wanted only transport, and early unadorned models found a ready and significant market. But transport alone soon paled. Buyers wanted—or were led to believe they needed—more power, more comfort, more styling, more space in their autos. It was that kind of response that led to the explosion of the car market in America to its present dimensions. It took design, ingenious touches of fantasy and, yes, imaginative advertising to create the truly mass market.

The market potential endures. For all their faults and excesses, those carefully contrived beauties of yesteryear still strike a responsive chord. And it's not nostalgia. The older folks may be more sensible, more practical; they don't buy dreams easily any more, I fear. The young people, though, react to the nifty '60 Impala—and other models of similar vintage—much as youngsters did twenty years ago. The builders and sellers of those cars managed somehow to engineer imagination and glamor into metal, cloth, and rubber.

It took some touches of genius all along the line to build the American car—and the American car market. Competitive pressures obviously energized all the activity. But it was a distinctive American success story which, I believe, cannot be copied or sustained by foreign competitors.

There's no turning back the clock, obviously. But I hope U.S. automakers understand they built and sold more than cheap transportation, the rage of this day. They built and sold a great market with design and promotion, producing things of enduring beauty for large numbers of eager buyers. Despite the drive for small and bare cars, the market is still there.

If you doubt it, come drive with me in the ingratiatingly seductive Impala.

STEVEN DIMEO

SWEET CHARIOT

He was flying.

He had left the Van Buren Loop at the curve where it dropped a thousand feet to Jordan Canyon, and he was flying.

Nothing sounded beyond the closed windows of his '72 Caprice but the low soughing of the air that seemed to be holding him aloft. The car hesitated in its arcing. Light-headed from the weightlessness—the way he felt after a double martini—he wanted to remain airborne like this forever. As long as it soared, it would keep him safe inside. But if it ever started plunging toward earth, nothing could be back the way it was.

Dark air suddenly hissed through the worn rubber weatherstripping between the windows. And in slow motion, like another Phaethon dragging the sun through a watery apocalypse, it was falling.

He wrenched up uselessly on the black steering wheel, wriggling behind the seat belt at the machine's failure to respond. It welled up inside him like hot grease, more of a groan than a scream. That was finally what startled him awake.

Ken Hoch bolted upright, gaped across the bedroom at the oval mirror of the vanity table. Did he glimpse the shimmering image of a crowned beast? He shook his head, blinked, and it was gone—if it had ever been there in the first place.

"This is getting ridiculous," said his wife April who pulled back the covers he had torn from her in his sleep.

Shivering from the sweat that had broken out on his face, he said, "It was another nightmare about the Caprice."

"Why don't you do something about that high blood pressure of yours," she said, "so I can get a decent night's sleep for a change?"

Later that morning after breakfast Hoch lifted the blind at the utility room window that looked out on the carport. Damp yellow maple leaves, paper claws blown in during the night, had lodged in the cracks and cavities. Otherwise, the Chevrolet sat there unchanged. Still, he knew he would never be able to drive it to work now. Not so soon afterwards.

"It still doesn't seem real to me," he said under his breath.

The words had been loud enough for April to hear from the bedroom where she was donning her coat for work and rattling the keys to her Maverick. "It's only a car," she said as she came out.

Hoch just looked at her. "But the dream—"

Her lips stiffened. "Have *any* of your dreams come true lately?"

He opened the side door and approached the car. Cat tracks in the dust marred the hood. Looking around for the night intruder he hadn't been able to scare away for long, he tried wiping off the marks with the cuff of his shirt sleeve. "What?" he said.

"Nothing," she said from the door.

He turned. "I can't take this to work today, April. Not when I'm feeling this way. I'll have to call in sick."

She glared at him. "Suit yourself." And viciously swinging her purse, she huffed past him to the driveway.

But then how could she have understood? It made little difference to her that, after saving for months and looking for over a year, he had found an affordable model almost exactly like the kind he always wanted.

The last of a breed in an era when the luxury of big cars might be dying out forever, the two-door hardtop came equipped with power steering and disc brakes, power windows, a six-way electrically adjustable front seat, a rear window defogger, and even a dashboard clock that worked (though it tended to run slow in cold weather and fast in hot). The posh black fabric seats had been upholstered with a swirling heraldic design that he protected from spills with silicon foam and, in the front seat, with a cover since he often ate lunch there.

There were a few things wrong, of course, some of which he had already managed to correct. The horn didn't work until he replaced a faulty relay switch. An eight-track AM/FM radio he upgraded to a 10-watts-per-channel digital AM/FM cassette player the same time he substituted for the four factory-installed speakers the best quality coaxials he could buy. And whenever he filled the tank, the fuel gauge—in an unwitting sign of the times—registered only a quarter full. That he could live with as he could with the flaws in the exterior. Although the original paint job still shined like new, it had been chipped in many places, particularly on the doors despite the rubber guards, themselves loose or broken off from the chrome channels. Hoch was content merely to keep the white vinyl roof and the red body washed and waxed. Besides, to repaint the car would risk losing the tone and luster of what he already had.

He realized all too well what an incredible stroke of luck it had been to have stumbled on a car that in style, color combination and cost matched his greatest expectations. That was certainly the kind of good fortune that had lately eluded him. Never settle for second best, he had often told his first wife Lola. But that was before she took him too much to heart and ran off with an unemployed philosophy major minoring in the more lucrative pursuit of pushing grass; before he was forced into even more compromises with someone like April and that job offer from Black Distributors. The Caprice stood out as a lone exception to his own principle.

Now he owned outright something built in the days when workmanship still mattered. New cars no longer held the attraction they had when he was growing up. "Big" cars were only "big" in price any more and seldom in quality. His suspicions had proved too well-founded when a friend at work bought on time a '79 Monte Carlo and, after just 10,000 miles, had to replace the transmission where Detroit had actually used *plastic* bushings. Even if he had believed the lavish propaganda that new models were better than ever, though, he would never have wanted the burden of large monthly payments or knowing that it could not be his for good until three years down the line.

Everyone at the office, of course, thought his choice bizarre. The men who normally boasted of outrageously high gas mileage after spending five times the cost of his Caprice for foreign economy cars, couldn't understand why, in time of gas shortages and skyrocketing prices, he had opted for a gas-guzzler that averaged 13 miles per gallon. And if he was going to be such a profligate with the car allowance from Black, why didn't he pick a van instead that would better accommodate the books he tried to sell to the Northwest outlets? The highest praise he received was from a portly, tow-headed colleague who labeled the red Caprice a "nigger car."

No matter. He could live with a job on the road somewhat less than the commercial illustrator he had once hoped to be so long as it afforded him a long-awaited luxury like this.

No, he couldn't quite agree with April here either. The Caprice *wasn't* just a car.

He frittered the day away in the makeshift studio of the converted garage working on another acrylic painting he would probably never be able to exhibit, let alone sell.

That night his long-time friend Terry Williams dropped by after dinner.

"What's eating April *this* time?" he said as he entered the family room where Hoch was reading next to the fireplace.

Hoch set the book down and looked up.

Williams, who lived alone and had developed terrible eating habits and an inevitable weight problem, took out another small package of Planter's peanuts from his nylon coat pocket, downed them all in one gulp, and threw the empty foil into the hearth.

"I didn't want to drive the car today so I called in sick," Hoch explained. "She thinks it's irresponsible, that's all." That, and a little unfair. Despite her Seventh Day Adventist espousal of the "total woman" philosophy of submissiveness, it galled her as a secretary that he could make twice as much by doing so little and get away with it. She had what she thought were subtle ways of letting him know, like launching into a "See? What did I tell you?" speech about the imminent Second Coming after he brought up the day's headlines, or—as she had done tonight—by cooking tuna casserole which he hated when he had suggested spaghetti and meatballs.

"Trying to make up for all those years of academic dedication?" They at least agreed that Hoch's flawless record of attendance until college and his subsequent devotion to the intellect had been sublimely stupid.

"Not exactly. I just had another nightmare."

Williams gave a crooked half-smile. "You've always had some imagination, haven't you. Too bad nobody else appreciates it." And he looked out on the denuded birches in the back yard.

"Sounds like you had another wonderful day on the job."

"And why not? Doesn't every budding psychologist want to end up an electrical engineer working for his father?" Williams sat on the slate hearth and leaned forward, hands clasped, forearms resting on his knees. "Sometimes," he said, "don't you ever wonder what would happen if you could just throw in the towel and start over again?"

"That," Hoch smirked, "would be irresponsible." He watched his wife clear the table of the dishes and pick up the folded-back issue of *Woman's Day* she had laid on the kitchen counter before dinner. "Besides," he added, "it'd probably turn out just as bad."

"Probably," Williams said. Then, eyes reflecting the glow of the fire: "But what if just once it didn't?"

"And I thought *I* was supposed to be the dreamer!"

Williams chuckled. "But you know if somebody dangled a ticket to Tahiti in front of me right now, I think I'd actually pick up and go."

"And leave behind $30,000 a year?"

"I've been putting a little aside same as you," Williams said. He gazed off in the direction of the sunburst wall clock. Hoch thought at first he was staring at the nearby decoupage of a distant sailboat on the ocean at sunset whose serenity was disrupted only by the words, "A ship in a harbor is safe, but that is not what ships were made for." "I'll bet," Williams added wistfully, "some have already gotten away with it—disappearing then popping up somewhere else with a different name, a new identity, dying to do it all differently this time . . ."

"We know too much any more. Ashborough's our home, Terry. It always has been even the few times we've been away. In my case you'd be talking about giving up a house as well as a job. Then there's my painting, don't forget." He lifted his head to indicate the carport. "And how could I ever leave the best thing that's happened to me?"

Williams laughed in his throat at what Hoch had once said of Lola. "It's a good thing April didn't hear that."

"I meant—"

Williams, smiling, just raised his hand. "I know."

But it set Hoch to remembering again. She had come along shortly after Lola left. As a divorcee herself, she had sympathized, noting similarities between them where there were mostly differences. But she had filled a terrifying void, had given him back temporarily some sense of self-worth—and managed to make him feel guilty when they started sleeping together and she lost her job at Black because of it. What had probably appealed to her more was pooling two salaries to buy things for a home. She hadn't particularly wanted a diffident romantic still in love with the past and a frustrated painter whose love of books and fear of further unemployment had compelled him to settle for Black's modest offer. Nor had he particularly wanted a moody, uneducated secretary with simple, albeit expensive, needs.

So they had gotten married. It was like most marriages nowadays. Dependent on two incomes and dreading that they might get even less the next time out, they felt inextricably bound for life.

"It's almost enough of an escape," Hoch finally said, "whenever I get behind the wheel of that car." The only time he ever felt in control of anything, he thought.

"About like me in *my* luxury car." A past car buff who had once owned a raked 428 Cobra Jet, complete with hood scoop and mag wheels, that could do a 12-second quarter-mile easy, Williams now helmed a beat-up brown Pinto that barely got him to work and back and to singles' bars every Saturday night. Hoch could never understand why, now that his friend made so much more than he and April combined, he had become so absurdly frugal. "I mean," Williams explained, "it's not exactly a Biarritz Eldorado, Ken."

All Hoch could think to counter with was, "She is to me."

That night he had another dream. He was on his way home, following a Union 76 tanker, listening to the song "American Pie" when he touched the "Seek" button of the Panasonic to find a station with a stronger signal. The radio picked up the end of Joe South's "Don't It Make You Wanna Go Home." When he looked up from the dash, he saw only the large red hood of the car wrinkling back like the lid of a sardine can—that, and a huge ball of sun-gold flame.

He didn't go to work the next morning either. Why return for only one day with Thanksgiving the very next? And hadn't he, after all, gone three years without taking one sick day?

Much of the day he spent in the parked Caprice paging through one of the collections of classic autos he had placed in local book stores. He paused over photographs of other more impressive luxury models: the 1927 Phantom I Rolls-Royce with Brewster-built coachwork; the 1929 Duesenberg J with its dashboard warning lights; the 1935 twelve-cylinder Boattail Speedster Packard complete with compass and altimeter; the 1939 Cord Phaeton Model 812 and its disappearing headlights; the powerful but sleek 1949 Type 175 Delahaye; and the smooth 1972 V-12 Vanden Plas Daimler. Hoch's Caprice appeared nowhere, of course, but its very omission only confirmed his self-styled complacency. These other classics had always been out of reach for people like him. But he was convinced in the face of all the changes around him that what he had in hand now would become a kind of classic in its own right as well.

In the evening April wanted to make love, but he was too tired from reading all day. When she locked him out without his keys, he slept the night comfortably away in the front seat of his car.

Hoch's parents, who lived four blocks away, were having them over for the traditional holiday meal of turkey and candied yams at two the following afternoon. That gave Hoch the morning to wax the car. He had been meaning to protect its finish anyway before the oncoming winter which Cassandras other than his wife were all saying would be the worst in years. When he finished polishing the outside, he vacuumed the interior, something he had made a weekly habit since buying the car three months before. After the Armor-All and vinyl and upholstery cleaner, the car had back a clean, factory-fresh smell—something, he thought, like new, sun-warmed plastic.

"I'm beginning to think you love that car too much for your own good," said April as she started carrying the salad cruet and the half-gallon of gin out to the car.

"I don't see," he said, "why we have to drive when we live so close."

"You got a better way of getting everything over there?"

He muttered something about the spoiled generation of Americans he was so much a part of, but went on helping her load the car. She set the two bottles down on the floor in front where she could hold them steady between her legs.

When they arrived at his parents' house, Hoch did not park along the curb. Instead, he pulled up alongside and half-on the small driveway so that the car was more off the wide, well-traveled road. "You can trust cars most of the time," he had once explained to her when he first decided to protect his car from possible sideswiping this way, "but you can't ever trust the ones who drive them."

It was just as April was struggling to get out, pushing against the large door made even heavier by the slant of the car, that he heard the gurgling on the floor. He sniffed. "You spilled the gin!"

Paling, she bent down and righted the bottle. "I thought you'd put the cap on better the last time."

The stench was rank, overpowering.

"My God," he said. "It's seeping off the mat into the rug." He grabbed a terry cloth rag from underneath the seat and began sopping up some of the liquid before lifting the red mat. Not saying a word, he carried a pail of hot water and ammonia from the utility room and scrubbed with a brush at the deep black nylon pile carpeting. He stood up, his back cracking from being bent over so long, and hooked hands at his waist. The smell remained as strong as ever.

When he finally came inside, his father said, "Don't worry, son. Alcohol evaporates quickly."

"How long is 'quickly'?"

"You shouldn't detect a thing after a week, believe me. So why not just appreciate what you've got left in the bottle?"

"Why not?" he said and poured a lead crystal stem glass full of gin.

April twirled her solitaire wedding ring. "I never meant to spill it, honey," she said.

He gulped at the drink, wincing as it burned its way down. "I know, I know," he said. As its effects began creeping back up, numbing his cheeks, he thought of another way he would try to rid the car sooner of the smell. Later, when he raised his second glass to everyone in a toast, he said, "We have more than the dregs to appreciate now, don't we." And he stared out the living room window at the car. Tilted upward at the edge of the driveway, looking to him somehow like a wounded animal, it glimmered blood-red in the dusty autumn sunlight.

"If only we could be thankful for what we have," said April, stirring her own clear drink with a plastic Hilton swizzle stick.

"We haven't changed much in that respect the last 4,000 years," said Hoch, "but at least our chariots have." He felt doubly high now. "No more *deus ex machina* for us. Machines *are* our gods."

"That depends," said his father, "on where they end up taking us." And, while the women nervously thumbed through Christmas catalogues, the two men were off again on another disagreement about the spiritual vacuum and moral decadence of Western civilization.

After dinner when they retired to the family room in back, Hoch suggested a fire. As he and his father each carried in an armful of madrona from the back yard, the elder Hoch paused at the patio door. "Is everything all right, son?"

"What makes you ask?"

"April said you stayed home from work a couple days this week. You never told us."

He dropped his few pieces of wood to the concrete just outside the sliding glass door. "I was just afraid something might happen to the car," he said.

His father had often felt the same whenever his son years ago asked to drive the then new '63 Impala, even before he and his teenaged friends slammed it into an embankment on a slick Sunset Highway. Leaning back slightly from the weight of the wood still in his arms, he said, "Son, you'll lose your job if you keep this up."

Hoch had had a long siege of unemployment right after college ten years ago, knew that it had contributed to the strains placed on his first marriage. Losing another job was hardly a past experience he wanted back. Maybe the lack of sleep was getting to him. He tried to grin. "Guess I just needed to recharge my own batteries, Dad. I'll be fine now."

"It isn't such a bad job, you know. You sure can't beat the freedom."

Hoch opened the glass door for his father. The women were still in the kitchen stacking the dishwasher. His father let his armload clatter to the bottom of the wood box in front of the wall of brick.

"Even if you can't feel the same about her as you did the other one," he added, "you haven't got such a bad wife either, son. She likes taking care of the house and cooking for you. That's more than you can say about most women these days."

"I suppose so." Then suddenly he clutched at his father's arm. "This is all I'm going to get, isn't it, Dad."

At first his father looked confused, startled by the remark. Then he shook his head. "You kids today," he said, clucking. "You don't know what 'nothing' is."

"I know I don't. But can't you see why I can't risk losing again the best of what I've got?"

The elder Hoch laid a large hand on his son's shoulder. His palm still felt rough and calloused though he used it more for the arms of slot machines now than for the handles of hammers and saws. He ventured one of his Burt Lancaster smiles. "You mean April?"

His son merely knelt and, scratching a wooden match against mortar, lit the fire.

When he and April got back inside the Caprice, whose windows he had left open since the accident, the odor of gin was as pungent as ever.

The only thing she said before they went to bed was, "Well, the turkey was pretty good anyway."

The only thing he said was, "I thought it was a little on the dry side myself."

Early the next morning Hoch got up to scour out the inside of the car once more with the vinyl cleaner. He next applied upholstery cleaner to the rug. When it had dried sufficiently, he vacuumed it again. Only then did he try going back to work. An hour later, he was certain the smell had returned as bad as ever.

When April came home that night, she saw him again vigorously brushing on more detergent and hot water, afterwards saturating the carpet with Lysol.

Exasperated, she said, "It's just going to take time."

"I have to live with it all day," he snapped. "You don't."

But the stink was as intolerable on the weekend. Hoch found himself forced to read with his wife in bed Saturday night. When she became amorous, he didn't have the heart to refuse. He satisfied her but, try as she might, he was too flaccid to be satisfied himself.

During the following week the dreams at night stopped, he didn't know why.

In the car the stink of gin had changed to something else. He tried to cover it up with a pine-scented car deodorant but couldn't stand its artificiality and ended up discarding the tree-shaped ornament altogether. He started taking shorter and shorter lunches in the car and making more frequent stops every day just to get away from the smell.

When he tried cleaning out the car again the next weekend and pulled off the red mat in front, he discovered the apparent cause for the thicker smell. The dampness left behind in the carpet from his scrubbing had combined with the warmth from the heater he had kept on high all week to form a series of white speckles on the damp cardboard below. Mold. He scraped the worst off with a knife, then scrubbed until the surface underneath the carpeting began to shred.

Was the Caprice running the same now? She chugged heavily while idling at stoplights. Yet he had just given her a tune-up the month before in preparation for the coming winter. It was almost as if she knew something were wrong.

And the sounds she was starting to emit! One time Hoch had to pull off the side of the road, unlatch the hood from inside, and get out to see for himself. It had been a "whoosh"—like a ponderous sigh. The engine fan coming loose? A fan belt slipping? He hoisted the hood all the way up, the hood light flickering on and off as he did so.

Did he detect a kind of moist squirming from somewhere beneath the air conditioning unit? The breathing noise had subsided but he had an uncanny sense that something dark and flesh-like lurked somewhere beneath the steel.

That weekend he left the windows partially open and when he made his rounds on Monday, he kept the heater and fan both on high. The days were colder now anyway, but he had to make sure the mold did not return.

Neither gin nor mold now, still an odor lingered.

He tried another deodorizer, a one-drop bottle of ortho di chloro-benzene so strong the directions recommended only one drop of the liquid be placed in a space as small as a car his size. Hoch let five drops fall on a tissue which he kept in the black vinyl trash bag that hung down from the unused ash tray. It was a sweet odor, chemical yet clean, like lilac-scented ammonia. For a few days that seemed to take care of the problem. Every morning he treated the car with drops of the compound.

By the second day, the headaches began. Toward the end of the week, nausea hit. That Friday, parked off I-80 at the Bridge of the Gods exit overlooking the Columbia River, his windows shut tight against the cold east wind, he tried to finish his lunch of a tuna fish sandwich and couldn't. For an instant he feared self-poisoning—that or his ulcer starting to act up again. He decided to pull into a Dairy Queen in nearby Hood River for a vanilla milkshake, hoping that would settle the qualmishness. And as he sat there in the parking lot, the windows open for the crisp fresh air, the motor running so he could keep warm, the pain in his head and stomach eased. That's when he suspected the chemical. He had been breathing it for a week.

But now he couldn't eliminate *that* smell either. Despite the winterlike temperatures, he had to keep the windows partially lowered for air. That allayed the discomfort but it did not diminish the intensity of the tainted air inside. It felt like a fist was tightening around his heart to think he might have irrevocably vitiated the car's beauty by trying too hard to erase his wife's mistake.

By this point he no longer spoke of the accident or his desperate attempts to correct what she had done. Neither did he speak any more to his office co-workers. And he talked to the book and magazine managers at the outlets on his route only when necessary.

One very cold morning when the ice had sealed the car door's lock so that he had to jiggle the key to break through the rime, he knew what had to be done.

"I've given up trying any more," he told Williams over the phone after lunch that day. "Time will take care of bringing things back the way they used to be."

Williams, who thought his friend was joking again, said, "Spoken like a true cynic."

That night Hoch did not come home.

Before dawn April was about to call the police when an officer came to her door. Rather than tell her in-laws, she phoned Williams who met her at the scene in his Pinto.

Red and blue lights flickered like strange fires on the roofs of the squad cars lined along the edge of the Van Buren Loop.

An officer with a bony face and an incongruously bushy mustache stood by one car, adjusting the searchlight again at what they had found halfway down the cliff beyond the broken white railing.

April, shivering, looked down. Williams' arms hung limp at his side.

"Must have been the ice," the officer said.

"He was the best thing that ever happened to me," she was saying softly as though to convince herself. "It never seemed real. About as real as this." Tears came but she held back more as if the first were an oversight. She took out a clump of kleenex from her purse and noisily blew her nose.

"It was real all right," said the officer, wiping frost from his mustache. "So real the impact must have thrown his body to the bottom of the canyon."

Williams turned. "What?" he said.

"We haven't located a body yet."

"How long have you been searching?"

"All night. But I've seen stranger accidents in my time. Cars—they're the most unpredictable kind of weapon we make, if you ask me."

April stopped sniffling but kept her eyes riveted on the twisted red metal immured in the cone of misty yellow light.

"All night," Williams repeated. And, without catching April's glance in the gaudy, dream-like flashing from the patrol cars, Terry Williams gave the rest of the night beyond the ruins of the Caprice an envious half-smile.

THE HEYDAY OF
THE CAR CULTURE

William Schenck, *Cadillac Eldorado*
Courtesy of the Artist

Dixie Dunbar of 20th Century-Fox and her 1936 Packard 120
Courtesy, Henry Austin Clark, Jr. Collection

Tommy Manville, a Bride, and a Car
Courtesy, Henry Austin Clark, Jr. Collection

Edward Kienholz, *Back Seat Dodge '38,* 1964
environment, 66″ × 20′ × 144″
Mrs. Edward Kienholz Collection, Los Angeles

Gabe Kreiswith, *Black Dahlia*
Courtesy, Orlando Gallery, Sherman Oaks, Calif.

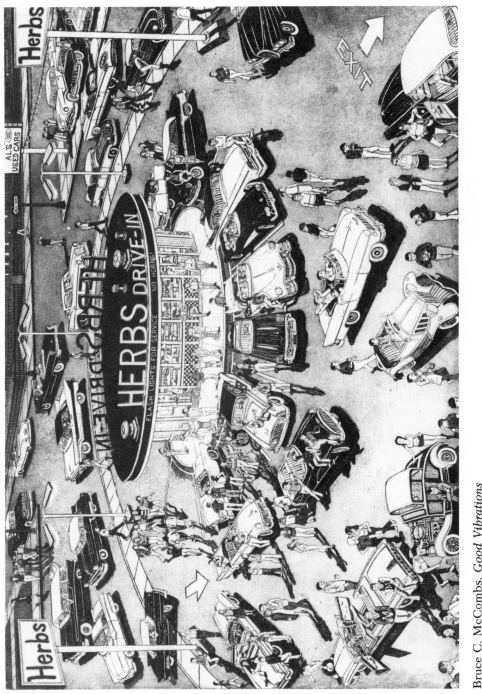

Bruce C. McCombs, *Good Vibrations*
Courtesy of the Artist

Robert Bechtle, *'61 Pontiac*, 1968–69
oil on canvas, 60 × 84"
Collection of Whitney Museum of American Art
Richard and Dorothy Rodgers Fund

John A. Chamberlain, Model for *McNamara's Band*, 1979, assembled plastic, rubber, wood, and mirrors on painted wood and plasterboard base, 23.6 × 122.1 × 94.0 cm., 1977.47.101 Courtesy of the National Collection of Fine Arts, Smithsonian Institution; Transfer from General Services Administration.

Dave Bowlan, *The Strip*
Courtesy of the Photographer

FRED SETTERBERG

CRUISING WITH DONNY ON
THE SAN LEANDRO STRIP

. . . . for all the shut down strangers and hot rod angels,
rumbling through this promised land.
—Bruce Springsteen
"Racing in the Streets"

All through the darkness, you watch them come and watch them go.

A seventeen-year-old anachronism warily circles the Goodyear parking lot, praying for cover or at least some distraction in the street. He's driving his older brother's car tonight—a Honda CVCC, if you can believe that—and he's not exactly anxious to let the news get out. Just in time a scorched-orange Firebird Trans Am burns rubber off-the-line at the corner light and the intersection explodes into life with smoke and squealing—and following that, the familiar din of hoots and catcalls as an attentive SLPD patrol car emerges from a sidestreet and picks off yet another Exhibition of Speed. The kid in the Honda slips into the Goodyear lot unnoticed. In another minute, he has joined his friends at the corner. They're all laughing now, nodding, smiling with the frosty satisfaction of the sly and the innocent. Someone jams a brown-bagged can of Old English 800 into the kid's fist. Complicated handshakes ensue and there is much talk about the Trans Am. There is a good deal of the usual talk about other cars, other cops, brew, "young ladies," carburetion problems under the stress of high-performance engines—much of the predictable shoptalk about steel-belted radial tires and seatcovers, special bargains and the places to buy. Another kid strolls over to the heavily-customed Chevy van parked conspicuously beneath a row of street lamps and opens the side gate: two portable Bogen speakers produce an ungodly loud cassette recording of Van Morrison's "Caravan." *It's Too Late To Stop Now!* shouts Van, so shrill and hoarse that even the tire screams, staccato horn blasts, and the engine revs and rumbles of passing traffic are diminished for a brief, peaceful moment.

It's Saturday night on the Strip in San Leandro, California, and according to the people who make it happen every weekend, it *is* too late to stop now. Lined-up against the Oakland border, San Leandro's East 14th Street has been promoting these late-night sideshows for as long as anyone here can remember. Tradition maintains that it all began over two decades ago, deep into the age of someone named Eisenhower. A few kids with "nothing better to do" started borrowing the keys to their family cars, gravitating naturally to a nine-block length of commercial main drag drawn around East 14th Street and 150th Avenue. Gradually, word about the new "Strip" reached a few of the town's more serious idlers. A steady stream of hot rods and custom machines began trickling in each weekend. And then, the flood. Now, twenty-five years later, they're still here, moving up and down the Strip, clutching their cheeseburgers, cruising back and forth, back and forth in an endless ritual procession that sharply declares their intention to stay. As in the "old days," they arrive around nine o'clock in family Corvairs on loan, speed-equipped 'Vets, '63 Fords lowered to scrape the pavement; they arrive on foot, if necessary. As in the old days, the cops try to stop them, but can't; their parents threaten to ground them, but don't. As we chug-a-long into the Eighties, gas prices soar to all-time highs but the halting, inexplicable traffic jams materialize each weekend just the same. You demand to know why, but the kids can't explain: their words tend to jag around the established myths, they stall short of clarity. Perhaps the clearest, fairest judgment is just to say that East 14th Street is someplace not quite like home for the average seventeen-year-old. Not like home at all, it is a liberated zone of enormous promise, one of the few places left where you can still pull over to the side for a breather, and wait to grow up.

"Now let's check it out" says Donny, owner of a classic '56 Chevy sedan ("My car's in the shop tonight" he claims) and a graduate of a local South County continuation school. "I'd say we're out here in full force tonight. Every major driver in the East Bay from A to Z, from Alameda to Union City." Donny is a knowledgeable and cheerful Strip veteran, older looking than his seventeen years, the kind of mildly-rowdy, solidly-built kid who might have played tight-end in high school until he got kicked off the team for smoking. Tonight, as usual, he's down at the Strip, checking out the action, staying in circulation despite the injury to his usual set of wheels. "I got sideswiped" he growls. "By this *black dude!*" The culprit's identity seems almost as disturbing as the fact that Donny got hit in the first place. San Leandro is a predominantly white, working-class town with a longstanding reputation for keeping its Oakland border sealed tight. "How'd he get *here?*" asks Donny, poised at the center of a half-dozen buffed and polished cars and motorcycles that form a showy crescent in the Goodyear lot at the Strip's southern edge. Donny paces to the corner, nods and then waves to a couple of drivers caught in the crush on East 14th Street. No one seems to recognize him. "Nobody knows me anymore" he says despondently. "They knew my car."

"Look!" calls out one of Donny's companions. "There goes a *bad* bike."

A fresh-faced kid in a blue stocking cap points to the mess in the street. He straddles the seat of a Honda 750. The patch on the back of his jacket claims, "God Rides A Harley."

"Shit, that one's not so bad."

"Badder than you, dink."

"You wish."

"I know."

"You blow."

"You wish."

On a good night, Donny and company are joined by hundreds of other cruisers rounding the mile from Goodyear to McDonald's. At ten, they may pull over for a bite at Arby's, Pring's, Taco Bell, or Church's Chicken. By eleven, they've popped open their hoods and have lined up along Ralph's parking lot or in the corner stalls on 150th near Safeway. There are kids out here on the San Leandro Strip who can boast an almost professional knowledge of their cars, and still others who couldn't wipe their windshields without a service manual. You can find them at either end of the Strip engaged in quarter-mile grudge races, occasional fistfights, or the usual breathless exchange of phone numbers and promises to call. At the center of this sound and fury is the automobile, and it signifies everything. In the life of the average cruiser, the Strip represents a season of heroic styles and the stubborn, absolute values of adolescence. East 14th Street is their proving ground and any deviation here from the oddly-shaped norm must be regarded as something closely related to a birth defect.

"If you've got nothing to drive" summarizes Donny, "the girls make you feel like a peasant."

A pretty blonde standing at Donny's side stamps her foot and breaks out of a long-term pout. "Now, that's not true" she says. "The guy's important too. He really is. But I got eyes, and you gotta expect me to be looking at what he's driving too—you know, just like you would."

"See what I mean?" he shrugs, trapped painfully between outrage and agreement. "You can be the best looking dude on the Strip, but if you're driving, I don't know, a Volkswagon. . . ." He laughs aloud at this absurd notion, but then his face abruptly stiffens and he turns slightly pale—perhaps as his eyes focus upon the Honda CVCC secreted away in the corner lot. "Well, let's just say they won't give you a second look."

"Anyway" insists his girl, "how you gonna get serious without a car? I mean, supposing you want to get serious." She turns to Donny with a look that might possibly be love.

"That's right. That's completely right. And I happen to know for a fact that 5 percent of all meetings down here result in marriage." He drapes an arm around the pretty blonde's shoulders. "They done surveys."

The real question—at least for any adult wage earner surfacing in Strip traffic—is how do the kids *afford* some of these cars? Take for example, the '34 silver-grey roadster with balloon tires and all-chrome intestines now pulling into Ralph's parking lot. The guy fastened proudly to the wheel is a friend of Donny's—he can't be more than nineteen—and there is no way, *no way, man*, that this kid could pay for it all. These are ordinary people here; in one way or another, they are quick to point this out. And we are talking twenty or thirty thousand dollars in the case of this '34 silver-grey roadster. Like people say around here: money talks, and bullshit walks. Donny's friend is definitely not walking. But neither is the kid talking. If you'll buy his story, he's just another simple young man with a dream and a steady job—a tomcat with the canary held behind his closed-mouth grin. He's telling no one where this monster came from, though you can bet that anyone he really cares about knows the whole story, every detail right down to his brand of spark plugs.

On the Strip, life imitates art imitating life and so on. There's not a single kid cruising up and down East 14th Street—or spirited away into Ralph's parking lot—who is not decidedly aware of the role he is playing and the responsibilities he has inherited. As a young American primitive whose image must be kept as finely tuned as his automobile, the Strip cruiser bears the weight of a thousand complicated notions about kids, cars, and the romance of "just hanging out." In this respect, Hollywood is perhaps most culpable, squandering a wealth of reference on cultural archetypes like *The Wild One*—and more recently, the denizens of *Van Nuys Blvd*. and *Boulevard Nights*. In fact, after *American Grafitti* was recently re-released (and screened shortly thereafter on network television), San Leandro's own Strip enjoyed a marked increase in traffic for many months. The legend, it seems, has created its own demand—and the kids keep coming back for more. Even that most variable social barometer—the American popular song—seems destined to resurrect Life on the Strip as a protean topic from time to time. From the mindless goo of Jan and Dean to the fire-in-the-belly of Bruce Springsteen, it is all very much the same story—all pitched toward that crucial moment in adolescence when the streets of home suddenly, and perhaps sadly, wind their way to the world outside.

And of course, there is *always* music. Loud music. Sometimes you positively have to shout to be heard—and even then, it's often too late.

"SHOTGUN!" announces Donny.

"I already called it."

"When?"

"Before we picked you up."

Scrambling without his own wheels—stranded, to tell the truth—Donny is in no position to be choosy. He shrugs and climbs into the backseat of a super-charged GTO parked behind the McDonald's lot.

"Then turn it up" he orders.

The kid in the front passenger seat reaches for the tape player and the music goes up, way up. Nobody is interested in talking anyway. Donny is certainly satisfied, happy just to be ensconced in metal. And everybody else is thinking about vital appearances—everything they've been working on, everything they've been practicing. They're here tonight to show some class, their personal style, their cars; talk is for much later after everything remotely possible has already happened.

That is, of course, if anything does indeed happen at all.

"Turn it up!"

"I did. It doesn't go any louder."

In Donny's world, on the Strip, there is always loud music. Characteristically, the tunes blasted from the passing tape decks and whiny AM car radios are seldom the current hits. Like everything else, the music of the Strip is prematurely nostalgic. A few years ago when one of the Oldies But Goodies series was released on eight-track and cassette, it was common enough to find sixteen and seventeen-year olds debating the relative merits of Little Richard and Chuck Berry—an argument steeped in false recollection, since most of the Strip regulars were not then old enough to clearly remember the Beatles, never mind the actual beginnings of rock 'n roll.

Tonight on the tape deck, it's Bob Seger and his "Night Moves"—a lament about the times when everyone piled into the back of a '60 Chevy and headed for someplace just like East 14th Street.

> We were just young,
> And restless and bored.
> Living by the sword.

The sword is not readily apparent in the McDonald's parking lot tonight. Past ten, McDonald's becomes a drive-thru and customers are prevented from pulling into the front lot and hanging out. There is more to this conversion than the expedition of fast burgers. Only a few years ago, McDonald's was the Strip's prime watering hole, and inevitably, as one San Leandro policeman put it, "someone would drive by, make a remark, and a fight would commence." Some of these fights have now grown beyond their original proportions as the years improve upon whatever really did happen at the time. There are still stories circulating about fitful kung-fu experts battling atop some vinyl service counter all for the love of a nameless teenangel. There are stories about brothers who, after unsuccessfully hitting on the same cruising queen, turned upon one another. It seems that practically everyone on the Strip has a friend who has a cousin who knows someone who reputedly witnessed the boldest, baddest, or bloodiest fracas ever to rip this sleepy small-town main street. Much in the style of old men recollecting past exploits, the adolescent regulars on the Strip fortify their positions with an appropriate mythology, one eye always turned toward the glorious and unredeemable years gone by.

Of course, there are occasionally more serious (and verifiable) incidents occurring on the Strip which arouse a predictable cycle of public concern. About a year and a half ago, a boy was run over and dragged to death in the parking lot of Ralph's supermarket. This kind of sensational event—or those not infrequent times when the Strip becomes crowded by "a whole lot of out-of-towners"—usually results in an "enforcement night" wherein the San Leandro Police Department arrives in numbers, freely handing out "taillight infractions" and checking I.D.'s for under-eighteen cruisers breaking the ten o'clock curfew. On an enforcement night, dozens of kids will spend the early hours of Sunday morning in jail waiting for their sleepy, angry parents to spring them. Rarely does this action have any effect on the Strip's traffic or traditions. "It's like a string of ants" says the SLPD Strip Supervisor, Sergeant Randy Stout. "You see them moving down the sidewalk all in a line. You step on them and they're all screwed up for about fifteen minutes. Look again, and they're back in line, moving along like nothing's happened."

Naturally, Strip regulars view the durability of their turf in somewhat different terms. "The Strip will never die" proclaimed one of Donny's companions, forcing his voice above the strains of the GTO's tape deck. "Not as long as there are still young people willing to take over what we have here."

By 1:00 AM, Donny has moved on to Pring's for a cup of coffee and a slice of apple pie. The flow of customers is still brisk, though easing up—much like the traffic outside on East 14th Street. Donny spots some friends seated at one of the corner booths. They are all older than Donny, late teens and early twenties. He nods to them with adolescent reserve and slides into an empty seat at their table. A young waitress arrives shortly with a scratch pad and pencil. It's coffee all around. One pie.

"The service around here has really improved" says one of Donny's friends, gazing out the window at a clot of traffic. "Used to be you could wait for hours."

"You could wait all night."

"You could wait until breakfast."

They all laugh. Nineteen and twenty years old; they figure they've been around.

Another elaborate machine tangled-up in chrome and brightened by an electric-lime paint job pulls up to the light outside on 150th Avenue.

"*Bad*" someone says.

Nobody disagrees. It's late.

"See any action tonight?"

Donny shrugs. "Not much."

"How'd you get here?" News of last week's accident had spread. Smart money said Donny might even stay home for an evening.

"My brother, he, uh, gave me a lift."

"Your brother still cruising?"

"Hell, no. My brother's too old for that. You know."

"I know this guy—he's twenty-four, Robert's age—he's still cruising. Every weekend. I just laugh."

Donny motions for a quick huddle over the table and points to the nearby counter area. "See that blond guy in the blue jacket? That dude sitting next to him is *his father.*"

"That's right" agrees another kid. "Forty-eight years old. He's been down here for years."

"Just imagine what that guy's seen."

The father and son are perched at the counter like salt and pepper, a matching pair in attitude if not appearance. The father is darker than his son, heavy with a thick, oily mustache and the bulky muscles and drift of middle age. In both, even from a distance, you can sense some great impatience—some shared conviction that they've been waiting far too long for something. They don't talk, they don't look at each other. The kid's bootheels tap out nervous energy on the floor; he fiddles with his coffee cup while his father stares out the window into the street. The old man looks like he's spent his best years here on East 14th Street; yes, he probably *has* seen it all. Possibly, he has weathered the Strip from its infancy, from the earliest nights during the late-Fifties when independent hot rodders were slowly edging out the car clubs and their intricate bylaws and decaled jackets. No doubt, he has witnessed all the changes in automotive style, all the cyclical definitions of "class." He can probably remember the years when kids tied surfboards to the top of their cars, miles from the ocean. And after that, the biker hordes, malign and hulking—a standing threat until the custom-van people moved in and began reclaiming territory in the early-Seventies. Perhaps he can even recall a few of the older outstanding drivers and their most curious machines: "Black Power," a '55 Ford jacked-up so high off the ground that the owner carried around a stepladder to assist exit and entry; or the roving Winnebago that everyone claimed was a pleasure palace operated by professionals—though nobody had actually been inside. The old man has probably seen it all. And now, without ceremony, like a father should, he leads his son to the edge of the world that he has known, and perhaps urges the boy to grab for anything that looks new or different. Sitting at Pring's counter, sipping coffee in the early morning, the old man is a most fluent warning about what can happen if you hesitate.

"Did you hear?" Donny asks his friends. "There were some guys here tonight from some magazine. They're going to write a story about the Strip."

"Yeah, I saw a couple of guys with cameras. Do you know what magazine they were from?"

"*National Geographic.* That's what they told me."

"Chump" grins Donny's partner. "They weren't from no *National Geographic.* Don't you know what that is? Don't you ever go to the dentist?"

"Where they from then?"

"*Hot Rod.* I bet they're from *Hot Rod* magazine."

"*Hot Rod!* Holy shit. What took 'em so long. About time they're going to write a story about us."

"Yeah. Don't they know we're famous already?"

"East Bay Grease" smiles Donny, "we been here forever."

ROCK AND ROLL

Rock and Roll split the head of Gospel, burst out
mean as Athena from the brain of Zeus,
stuck his thumb in the eye of Rhythm and Blues,
and hitched a ride up the river in a Caddy that was
w   i   d   e
and wicked as the Mississippi,
tap dancin' ALL OVER the red velvet seats.
shakin' his tight lil' punk ass out the window,
curdlin' the Dairy Queens.
He was bendin' his G-string, keepin' his back-beat,
blowin' up the city on his big long gol-den horn.
Rock and Roll was comin' to GET YOU!

He was the boogie man in the closet, shakin' in there w/yr
mittens and yr girl scout badge and yr red rubber boots,
stitchin' up the hem on yr communion dress w/Chantilly lace.
Rock and Roll was
HAPPENIN'
like chords screechin' along yr chalkboard,
like yr pencil against yr inkwell.
Rock and Roll was walkin' the dog
across yr teacher's hair-sprayed head.
The Nina, the Pinta, and the Santa Maria were bouncin' BANG
into Plymouth Rock, the Pilgrims were reelin' and
everybody rolled the Injuns.
You knew it.
You knew it was true what Rock and Roll said.
You could hear him talkin' off the windows, all those
hot radios in the school parking lot, all those pistons
comin' in at the upbeat. Rock and Roll was

OUT THERE

HE WAS WAITIN' FOR YOU! Layin' right upside the school door,
scratchin' a thick old kitchen match on school brick,
tappin' a Marlboro out of his t-shirt.

ROCK AND ROLL

all zippers and grease and black black leather
flashin' out of yr closet and gobblin' up yr mother
like some bad baaaaaaaad wolf.

ROCK AND ROLL HAS BEEN COMIN' YR WAY—cruisin' Main
    Street,
makin' an il-legal left down New Jersey, sittin' on his horn
through every red/stop in the Bronx.
Rock and Roll is steamin' out the windows, lettin' in the breeze,
comin' to curl yr locks w/hot licks, baaa-bay.

Rock and Roll is out there loungin' in the spotlight of yr
corner streetlamp, jammin' w/yr good goodnight angels,
mentionin' a groove in yr sweet little dreams.

ROCK AND ROLL IS UNDER YR BED!

He is comin' to let you dance, little sister, comin' to
put the strut in yr stuff, the bend
in yr dimpled knee. He is slittin' his wrists
to bleed yr best dress red, he is SACRIFICIN'—cuttin' out his heart
just to give you a beat.

Rock and Roll is leanin' on yr school bell, one, two, three, FOR
    YOU,
w/his hot lips wrapped around a grin big as Montana,
w/his old Ford door WIDE OPEN on that
Promised Land.

JOHN R. REED

GM TECH CENTER
Warren, Michigan

Pale orchids plume above the chimneys in the gelid air
hovering like snow-white shrouds, enormous blooms
that baffle the birds cacker cackering over the children
in vermillion, yellow, blue circle-eighting on the ponds.

Indoors the word comes down from design, made flesh
in mock-up and model rooms whose minutely polite machines
finesse their rigid lines upon the boards while blueprints
scroll with egyptian calm and terminals tell their blink-green tale.

Irreverences of engineers mimick the prim machines
whose hearts burn under the weight of human dreams.
Manifold fingers perform tiny witcheries in their gloom,
concocting codes to rub the lamp and make the genie wake
to whelp ore, oil and sand into the ingenious bibelots of man.

PAUL W. GIKAS

CRASHWORTHINESS AS
A CULTURAL IDEAL

The horseless carriage provided a means of independent mobility which captivated the turn-of-the-century public. Historians have abundantly documented the rush of eager consumers during the last days of the nineteenth century to own and drive the new mechanical wonder. Statistics of patents, production, and purchases have become part of the national folklore. Less well-known is this small statistic: the first auto-related fatality occurred in 1899 when a Mr. H. Bliss was struck by a motor vehicle after stepping off a streetcar.

During the ensuing years, as injury and death tolls mounted to epidemic proportions, the highway has been categorized as the largest arena of violence in our society. Accidents of all kinds are exceeded only by cardiovascular diseases and neoplasms as a cause of death in the United States. For those aged one year to fourteen years, highway accidents are the most frequent type of accident. Of the approximately 50,000 highway deaths per year, the largest number, approximately 28,000, involve occupants of passenger cars. The annual nonfatal injury total exceeds 2,000,000. Surely this is an unacceptable price for a system of transportation, regardless of its obvious advantages.

The gravest charge that can be made against a culture is that it is indifferent to human suffering, that it lacks the will to regulate or control the violent elements within itself. The car culture in America raises this moral issue in its broadest form. In this essay I wish to survey the history of efforts to regulate the automobile industry by means of public law. Like any reform movement, the struggle to produce a crashworthy car reflects profound social conflicts, especially those between buyers and sellers in the free enterprise system. Most observers would agree that the public interest has been served by such efforts, but the tendency to relax standards during times of economic crisis—for example, the present—must be monitored with a full knowledge of the following events.

Since automobiles are driven by people, traditional efforts in morbidity and mortality reduction were directed at crash prevention through modification of driver behavior. Although vehicular defects and the highway environment play a role in crash causation, the driver, through acts of commission or omission, *is* probably responsible for most crashes. This observation logically led to increased efforts at traffic law promulgation and enforcement, driver education programs, public and private safety-oriented organizations, and their inevitable slogans. In spite of all these well-intentioned endeavors, the price tag for the automobile transportation system, in terms of death and injury, continued to rise. This should come as no surprise, when one considers the complexities of the driving task and the variety of drivers ranging from skilled professional drivers to the mentally ill. In spite of the vast sums of money the various states appropriated to high school driver education programs over the years, there is no convincing evidence that this educational experience had any salutary effect on the problem of highway accidents. Modifications of highways, on the other hand, especially the introduction of limited access divided highways, have done much to reduce the number of crashes. The fatality rate per miles traveled on divided freeways is significantly lower than on undivided two-way traffic roads with intersections. Finally, attempts to correct for vehicular defects are dependent for success on frequent inspection programs and the enforcement of needed repairs. There is obviously much potential for abuse in such programs, if indeed they can be enacted. (It is ironic that Michigan, the acknowledged home of the domestic auto industry, has failed to enact mandatory motor vehicle inspection legislation.)

From the epidemiologic vantage point, there is another means available for the reduction of injuries to occupants of cars and trucks, namely the provision of a crashworthy vehicle. Crashworthiness, synonymous with safe packaging, is that attribute of a vehicle which provides for the prevention of serious injury to an occupant in the event of a collision. This approach is not fatalistic—it is merely realistic.

One of the rudimentary principles of crashworthiness, the distribution of a force over a large surface area, dates to the fifth century before Christ when Hippocrates contrasted the greater severity of wounds inflicted by sharp penetrating objects to the less serious wounds produced by blunt weapons. This does not imply that blunt objects cannot inflict serious injury, but it emphasizes the fact that when the force of impact is distributed over a larger area, the force per unit area or pressure is less than the same force applied to a smaller surface. Hippocrates's simple observation has significant implications for the design and construction of the interior of the automobile. A second fundamental of crashworthiness is the need to preserve the integrity of the cabin area during a crash. This fact was noted in 1917 when Hugh DeHaven was the only survivor of a midair airplane collision which killed three air cadets. He credited his survival to the maintenance of his cockpit space; his fatally injured comrades' cockpits were severely compromised.

The trauma-producing forces generated in a crash result from the sudden deceleration or acceleration experienced by the occupants. Approximately two centuries prior to the invention of the automobile, Sir Isaac Newton defined the relation between velocity and deceleration of a moving object. Simply stated, the greater the stopping distance over which the deceleration occurs, the less the force imparted to the vehicle. The two-foot deformation sustained in the front of a car which collides with an immovable bridge abutment is the stopping distance for the automobile. This contrasts to the stopping distance of an unrestrained passenger in the same car who sustains a collision (the so-called second collision) of his head with the metal header above the windshield, resulting in a one inch dent in the metal. His stopping distance is only one inch, thus magnifying the danger to his cranium tremendously. To take advantage of the greater stopping distance of the car, the passenger must be fastened to the car in a manner which precludes the second collision within the vehicle. This is where seat belts, including shoulder belts and the various so-called passive system of belts and air bags, serve their function.

Unfortunately it was not until the late 1960s that these principles of crashworthiness were applied to automobiles in a nonoptional manner. The long-overdue National Traffic and Motor Vehicle Safety Act, Public Law 89-563, passed in 1966, mandated the promulgation of safety standards for automobiles sold in the United States. The standards applied to new cars purchased by the general public beginning January 1, 1968. It was the first time in the history of the domestic automobile industry that regulations concerning crashworthiness influenced the design and construction of new automobiles. The history of the pertinent events leading to Public Law 89–563 is fascinating.

In 1967 automobiles purchased by U. S. government agencies had to meet safety standards mandated by Public Law 88-515, introduced by Congressman Kenneth Roberts (Ala.). This act was passed in May of 1964 after many frustrating years of effort by Roberts, beginning in 1956 when he conducted the first hearings of the new House Sub-Committee on Traffic Safety. These hearings included discussion of the hazards of automobile design. The Roberts bill, HR-1341, which attempted to correct these deficiencies in car design, passed the U.S. House of Representatives in 1959 and 1962, but was defeated each time in the Senate as a result of powerful opposition from the automobile industry.

Criticism of vehicle safety design had surfaced long before Roberts's hearings. Dr. Claire Straith, a Detroit plastic surgeon, notified car manufacturers of interior injury-producing hazards in the 1930s. Dr. Fletcher Woodward, Professor and Chairman of Otorhinolaryngology at the University of Virginia, complained shortly afterward about the pattern of auto-related injuries he had witnessed, injuries that could have been prevented by modification of interior design and overall construction of automobiles. Dr. Horace Campbell, a Denver surgeon and member of the Committee on Highway Safety of the American Medical Association, was an industry gadfly for many years concerning matters of hazardous design. But the advice of these dedicated physicians went largely unheeded. Their frustration finally culminated in the formation of a society, Physicians for Automotive Safety, headed by Dr. Seymour Charles, a New Jersey pediatrician who received his residency training at University Hospital in Ann Arbor. This group added dignity to indignation by picketing the automobile show in the spring of 1965 at the New York Coliseum.

The momentum for federal legislation gradually increased. Senator Abraham Ribicoff (Conn.), chairman of the Sub-Committee on Executive Reorganization of the U.S. Senate Committee on Government Operations, began hearings on automobile safety in July of 1965. The hearings proved embarrassing for the top executives of the major car companies. Invited to testify, their responses revealed the paltry sums being spent on injury prevention relative to styling and horsepower. The industry launched a defensive advertising campaign to inform the nation about its safety efforts, but each facet of the campaign created skepticism. When the industry donated ten million dollars to the University of Michigan to establish a Highway Safety Research Institute, for example, a writer in the *Wall Street Journal* revealed that "one high auto official has privately remarked that [it] was a 'public relations gimmick' intended to take the heat off the industry."

The heat continued, however, fueled in large part by state legislatures more responsive to grass-roots complaints about the lack of crashworthiness. Massachusetts had been the first state to propose a comprehensive package of safety standards for automobiles. On December 3, 1963, State Senator Francis X. McCann and the Massachusetts Division of the American Automobile Association jointly filed legislation to form a special commission to draft a code of minimum safety for the manufacture of motor vehicles sold in Massachusetts. Senator McCann explained: "There are safety codes for the construction and operation of elevators, for public building construction, even for the construction of our homes, the drugs, food and electrical appliances our families use. But so far as we can ascertain, there is no such code of minimum safety standards for the manufacture of automobiles." The bill was killed in committee. But it warned the industry of legislative interest in crashworthy vehicles, and suggested that additional legislation was on its way.

The Attorney General of the state of Iowa, Lawrence F. Scalise, on January 10-12, 1966, conducted car-safety hearings which attracted medical scientists, engineers, and lawyers to Des Moines. The legal profession was well represented by Ralph Nader and Jeffrey O'Connell. Nader's book, *Unsafe at Any Speed*, published in December of 1965, served as a catalyst for the car-safety movement. It was a major source of information for the Congressional committees and state legislative committees which would deliberate on safety bills.

In Des Moines, Nader quoted a 1965 Buick Skylark advertisement as follows: "Ever prodded a throttle with 445-pound-feet of Torque coiled tightly at the end of it? Do that with one of these and you can start billing yourself as The Human Cannonball." Nader pointed out that although General Motors offered information about available torque, it neglected to inform the purchaser that a human head would penetrate the 1965 Skylark windshield with an impact of about twelve miles per hour. His main theme was that the auto industry had enjoyed unlimited power at the expense of public safety. Power was the only language the industry understood and its power heretofore had been little challenged. Nader advocated legislation. He emphasized that law is the chief form of authority in this nation concerning public safety, and that legal authority is power. He urged both federal and state jurisdictions to challenge the carmakers' neglect of safety practices.

Although Nader emerged as the safety movement's most articulate voice, O'Connell made a significant but less recognized contribution. A former associate director of the Automotive Claims Study at the

Harvard Law School and more recently Professor of Law at the University of Illinois, he was particularly concerned about the auto accident insurance industry. His book, *Safety Last—An Indictment of the Auto Industry*, appeared shortly after Nader's volume, and consequently received much less publicity. O'Connell entitled his Des Moines testimony "Dangerous Instrumentalities," echoing a 1920 court opinion referring to the automobile. He observed that Ford President Arjay Miller had described ". . . . the car [as] the strongest link in the safety chain," and recalled GM Vice-President Harry Barr's comment in the *New York Times*: ". . . . we feel that our cars are quite safe and quite reliable. . . . If the drivers do everything they should, there wouldn't be any accidents, would there?" Detroit, according to O'Connell, saw no problems with the automobile, and identified the "nut behind the wheel" as the culprit. Auto advertisements meanwhile encouraged the "nut" to continue his anti-social behavior. A television ad urged the driver of a two-ton vehicle to "drive it like you hate it. . . . it's cheaper than psychiatry." O'Connell evoked laughter in the Capitol buildng when he pointed out that Ford had recently run a twelve-page ad in *Time* urging motorists to "cultivate a safety state of mind" even as it named one of its cars Marauder—defined as one who pillages and lays waste the countryside.

General Motors, not to be outdone, in late 1965 distributed a forty page booklet entitled, "Design for Safety," which closed with the statement: "In all aspects of producing automobiles no consideration is more important to us than safety. This has been true in the past and will continue so in the future." O'Connell, assuming this consideration included advertising, pointed out a discrepancy by quoting a recent Pontiac ad: "There's a live one under the hood. Have you priced a tiger lately? Purrs if you're nice. Snarls when you prod it. Trophy V8 standard in Pontiac GTO. 386 cubic inches. 335 horsepower. 431 pound feet of torque. Want something wilder? Got it. 360 horsepower. Then prowl around in a wide track awhile. You'll know who is a tiger." O'Connell emphasized that the industry's approach to marketing was symptomatic of a deep-seated ailment, and he closed his testimony by quoting Dr. Charles, president of Physicians for Automotive Safety: "The auto industry is sick and, for all the humor, when a manufacturer has a product that kills 50,000 people a year and injures 5,000,000 more, that has the arrogance to name those products Wildcat and Fury and Marauder, and to boast with untold millions in advertising that his product has an almost neurotic urge to get going, that manufacturer cannot possibly be trusted in matters of safety, and surely, surely they are foreclosed from blaming the nut behind the wheel. Such manufacturers long ago forfeited their right to control how safe they will make their car, and all the millions of dollars they are going to be spending urging the driver to cultivate an attitude of safety, thinking safety, or forming a partnership in the cause of safety, should never let any of us forget that stark fact."

The presidents of the four leading automakers were invited to participate in the Iowa hearings, but they refused to appear. At the conclusion of the hearings, Attorney General Scalise stated: "These are just the beginnings in this field and I think we will do a couple of things. One is we will create a Consumer Advisory Council and another is this Consumer Advisory Council will study and make two recommendations. Those two things that I am talking about are an enactment of a disclosure act wherein all manufacturers will be required to produce and file with the appropriate public department all of their service bulletins and all other communications. The second thing I think we can do is set standards. By that I mean adopt GSA standards when they are finalized because it seems to me that if federal employees driving federal cars can be protected by the federal government, then the state of Iowa and its citizens have that same right."

In New York, State Senator Simon J. Liebowitz conducted hearings of the Joint Legislative Committee on Motor Vehicles, Highway and Traffic Safety, on February 8-9, 1966. This committee, under the chairmanship of Senator Edward Speno, had met in Detroit with the carmakers in 1961. By threatening to legislate anchorages for front seat belts, the committee had persuaded the industry to "voluntarily" install the anchorages as standard equipment. Witnesses at the February hearings included, in addition to several physicians, Iowa Attorney General Scalise, Speaker Vincent Steffen of the Iowa House of Representatives, State Representative Harold A. Katz of Illinois, and Heward Grafftey, a Canadian MP. Katz had established himself as a proponent of crashworthiness while participating in hearings on the subject in Springfield in 1965. His article in the *Harvard Law Review* (1956), "Liability of Automobile Manufacturers for Unsafe Design of Passenger Cars," helped inspire Nader to launch his safety crusade.

Grafftey testified that Canadians also were concerned about the lack of crashworthiness in automobiles. He urged Canadian and

American auto companies to abstain from expensive and unnecessary style changes for the coming year in favor of safe packaging for car occupants.

Medical testimony emphasized the correlation of injury patterns sustained by car crash victims with hazardous vehicle design. The testimony showed that the most rudimentary principles of crashworthiness were being violated. The hearings produced a recommendation for immediate legislation requiring all automobiles purchased by the public in New York to possess the seventeen safety features required for federally purchased cars as promulgated by the federal government's General Services Administration. These standards were to apply to all 1968 model cars. Governor Nelson Rockefeller had advised the committee that he already had decided that certain GSA standards would be required on all state-owned automobiles. In his concluding remarks, Senator Leibowitz stated: "The program for a safer automobile is on the march. The action of the New York State Legislature is heartening. The myth that a safe car is an ugly car has been destroyed. Style and safety in automobiles are consistent and can be achieved."

The only significant hearings on crashworthiness conducted in the home state of the automobile industry were held on February 21, 1966, by the Senate Highway Committee. The hearings grew out of bills introduced by Senator Roger Craig of Dearborn which in effect would have banned 1960-63 Corvairs from the highway. Although this proposed legislation had no chance of passage, it stimulated a lively discussion at the state Capitol where the automobile companies' lobbyists were well-represented and well-received. Vice-Presidents and engineers from Ford, Chrysler, and General Motors spoke for eight hours on the safety virtues of their products. They again extolled the benefits of mandatory vehicle inspection, stiffer driver licensing, and driver education. The author was allowed one hour and ten minutes to demonstrate how the vehicle injures occupants in crashes. When I showed photos of car interiors depicting the relation of injuries to specific hazardous designs, an infuriated Vice-President John Bugas of Ford Motor Company departed from his prepared text to impugn my professional integrity. He called my presentation an "inflammatory, vindictive, totally biased attack." Committee Chairperson Rozycki refused to grant me a three-minute rebuttal to Bugas's emotional assault. It may be noted that this same presentation before legislators in Iowa, Illinois, New York, and Washington had evoked a warm reception.

The auto industry had been clearly warned by various state hearings and by the Ribicoff hearings that momentum was gathering for drastic changes involving vehicle safety design. National or international corporations can of course ignore annoying state hearings by not attending them or put on a show in a very friendly environment (Lansing). When a bill proposing safety features was introduced by a state legislator, the industry would lobby to reduce its threat. Money and arm-twisting can thus thwart the will of the people at this level of authority.

The scene of action now moved back to the nation's Capitol, however, where the going would be much tougher for the automakers. Auto safety hearings began in early 1966 on HR-13228 in the United States House of Representatives Committee on Interstate and Foreign Commerce, chaired by Representative Harley O. Staggers (W.Va.). Counterpart hearings were conducted in the Senate by the Committee on Commerce, chaired by Senator Warren G. Magnuson (Wash.). Many of the witnesses who had appeared in state houses repeated their litany before the Congressional committees, which became increasingly convinced that federal safety standards were needed. The auto industry, opposing any legislation with vigor, united behind its spokesman, John Bugas, to plead for permission to voluntarily build a safer car. In response, Senator Maureen Neuberger (Ore.) told Bugas: "With me it is to say 'ha-ha' to any industry that comes along saying 'let *us* do it.' It's lovely to have you volunteer like that but some of us are skeptical." The industry argued that it had previously made optional safety features standard items in new cars, and intensively advertised them. It again placed emphasis on problem drivers and the highway environment, rather than vehicle design, as causes of auto-related injury and death. But the industry's efforts to convince Congress not to pass the legislation were futile.

In retrospect, this period of American history, midway through the Great Society legislation which lifted public spirits shortly before the Vietnam war depressed them severely, seems an age of reform comparable to the early decades of the century. The consumer movement was feeling its first renewals of strength, not as an elitist group but as a popular crusade to take charge of the quality of everyday American life. Like the struggle for better food or better air, the pursuit of a crashworthy car dramatized a public-spiritedness that is one of our legacies in the 1980s.

As for the auto industries, they seemed best represented by General Motors' Keystone Kop harassment of Nader, which helped to effect passage of the sweeping National Traffic and Motor Vehicle Safety Act. Enraged by Nader's accusations and the unfavorable publicity provoked by his book, the giant corporation hired detectives to trail him and investigate his private life in hope of finding evidence to discredit him. Discovery of this clandestine operation led the Ribicoff Sub-Committee to call President James M. Roche of General Motors to Washington. Why, Roche was asked, was GM persecuting a private citizen and Congressional witness? Roche apologized, but the damage had been done. GM, it may be added, conceded that Nader emerged from its probe as clean as a hound's tooth.

On June 24 the Senate passed an auto-safety bill which was amended in the House of Representatives on August 17. The Senate disagreed with the amendments and requested a conference. On August 31, the House and Senate agreed to a conference report and on September 9, with President Lyndon Johnson's signature, Public Law 89-563 was enacted. The act provided for a coordinated national safety program and establishment of safety standards for motor vehicles in interstate commerce to reduce accidents involving motor vehicles and to reduce the deaths and injuries occurring in such accidents.

Meantime a considerable base of scientific data had accumulated which underlined the importance of injury prevention in crashes by providing safer packaging for occupants of automobiles. An oft-quoted study was Cornell University's Automotive Crash Injury Research project. The University of Michigan's fatal accident investigation project by the author and Donald Huelke conducted from 1961 through 1965, and a program conducted by Derwyn Severy and colleagues at the Institute of Transportation and Traffic Engineering at the University of California, Los Angeles, also contributed helpful data. The methodology of a multidisciplinary detailed study of highway crashes was first developed in the late 1950s by Alfred L. Mosely at Harvard. Both the Michigan and Harvard studies were funded by the U. S. Public Health Service.

An important forum for the presentation of scientific data from these and other studies was the annual Stapp Car Crash Conference named in honor of Colonel John Paul Stapp, a pioneer in human deceleration studies in the U. S. Air Force. The Seventh Stapp Conference had been held in 1963, which suggests that a considerable amount of data had been accumulated before the enactment of the National Traffic and Motor Vehicle Safety Act of 1966. These data were helpful in the writing of safety legislation; however, critics of the industry complained at the Stapp Conferences and elsewhere, that the initial nineteen, as well as some of the subsequent standards, were seriously diluted to satisfy industry objections. The result, said critics, was another example of regulation by regulatees. The industry consistently objected to the shortness of lead time for implementation of a given standard. Federal rule-making procedures, particularly in the case of automobile crash protection safety standards, also were frustrated by industry arguments concerned with products liability.

William I. Stieglitz, director of Motor Vehicle Safety Performance Service in the National Traffic Safety Agency and nominally in charge of the drafting of the initial safety standards, was so distressed by the industry's success in diluting standards that he resigned in protest. His comment on standard 105, "hydraulic brake, emergency brake and parking brake systems—passenger cars," presented before the U. S. Senate Committee on Commerce, March 20, 1967, reflects his concern: "The standard as issued states that following a failure of one portion of the system, the remaining portion of the braking system shall 'provide a stop of the vehicle . . . on a clean, dry smooth portland cement concrete pavement.' The stopping distance and the speed of the vehicle at the time of brake application are not specified nor is it required that the vehicle be left in drive gear. Quite frankly, I do not know how it would be possible to build a vehicle that would not meet this standard. I have never yet seen one that will not come to a stop on a level road when in neutral. In fact, even if left in gear, the vehicle will stop when it runs out of gas, without brakes."

In fairness to General Motors, it should be given credit for voluntarily introducing, in the absence of a standard, the side guard beam in car doors to attenuate lateral intrusion in side impacts.

Despite foot dragging by automakers and the inadequacies of some of the safety standards as currently written, the public has benefited from their implementation. A recent report by the National Highway Traffic Safety Administration credits the safety standards with saving more than 55,000 lives from their initial implementation through 1978. This report also notes that the number of lives saved is increasing by 10,000 per year as newer, safer automobiles replace older ones.

Unfortunately, the U.S. automobile industry and its suppliers have too often played the role of follower instead of leader. An example is the relatively recent introduction of steel-belted radial tires which are safer and provide better mileage. For many years these superior tires were available only from foreign manufacturers.

The value of the shoulder strap-seat belt system was first established by Swedish car manufacturers. Their experience prompted the promulgation of standard number 208, effective January 1, 1968, which requires, over objections from the domestic industry, lap and shoulder belts for both front outboard seats in new passenger cars in the United States. The same pattern is evident in the introduction of foreign-made, fuel-efficient cars which have taken over a major segment of the U. S. new-car market. With the exception of American Motors, U.S. car companies spurned smaller fuel-efficient models until their hands were forced by the federal government and foreign competition.

The scenario is being repeated with passive restraints. Former Secretary of Transportation Brock Adams issued a standard in July, 1977, requiring carmakers to furnish restraint systems affording automatic protection in a collision. The need for such protection is obvious inasmuch as only 12 percent or less of the driving public currently use seat belts. The phased introduction of passive restraints will affect all full-size cars in 1981, intermediate and compact cars in 1982, and all cars in 1983. In the mind of many scientists and safety authorities, including a major segment of the automobile insurance industry, the air bag is the most desirable alternative in the passive restraint field. Domestic carmakers have consistently stalled on the routine implementation of this proven lifesaving device. While the number one automaker, GM, recently announced it does not intend to offer air bags in most of its cars, even after the automatic restraint standard takes effect in 1981, a leading foreign producer, Mercedes-Benz, will equip all of its 1982 cars with front seat air bags. Mercedes-Benz is taking this step even though only one of its models is required to have passive restraints by Federal Motor Vehicle Safety Standard 208.

The late Edward Cole, when a vice-president and later president of General Motors, recognized the distinction between injury prevention and crash prevention. He became an advocate for safer packaging of car occupants. He specifically promoted GM involvement in air cushion development. Thus, it was discouraging to hear current GM Board Chairman Thomas Murphy, at the 1980 Stockholders Meeting, regress to the mentality of two decades ago in a remark about the ultimate safety problem being drinking drivers rather than a need for more crashworthy cars. Murphy fails to comprehend that in a society whose legislative and judicial climate nurtures drinking drivers, the need for passive restraints such as air bags is even more acute. Although drivers, approximately half of whom are intoxicated, cause most crashes, the vehicle produces the injuries. Because of our demonstrated inability to control the drunk *or* sober driver, we need a safer package for car occupants.

While the automobile industry was vigorously opposing the enactment of legislation which provided for safety standards, Michigan's Governor George Romney, a former auto executive with American Motors, provided a fresh, healthy outlook when he said: "I can visualize the time when the superior design of a car in terms of safety will be a definite selling point and I think that time is not far off." That time has, in fact, arrived. Historical forces have caused us to redefine the nature and function of the automobile. It is less a fantasy machine than a means of conveyance from point A to point B. In that sensible, useful role, the car's crashworthiness has become the essential feature it should have been from the beginning.

DEATH OF A COMMUTER

The windshield of the black van following him was tinted so darkly that he could not see the driver. Below it a spider web was drawn in gold paint, the extremities of the web connected to the windshield above and the grill and headlights below. He increased his speed slightly keeping a good interval between his car and the car ahead. He heard a rumbling behind him and when he looked in the mirror again, all he could see was the web and a small spider also drawn in gold. In both his side mirrors he could see that the headlights of the van had come on and, even though it was a sunny morning, the headlights were an intense yellow. He increased his speed again and heard another surge in the rumbling behind him. The yellow lights were flashing now, arrogant. *Move over you bastard!*

But where would he go? The right-hand lane was moving more slowly. If he pulled in he would have to brake hard. And besides, what good would it do for the idiot in the van to get past him? The normal morning backup at the bridge was ahead and the van would just have to wait in line with everyone else. His speedometer read fifty now but soon he and the van would both be at a crawl. What if the van hit him? It wouldn't be his fault.

He took his left hand from the steering wheel and casually draped his arm out the window, his elbow blocking the headlight in the side mirror. Perhaps he should warn the van that traffic would be stopped ahead. He would use his left foot to tap the brake while he maintained his speed with his right foot. He would be doing both the van driver and himself a service. As he lifted his foot to the brake pedal he imagined a greasy-haired punk driving the van, a cigarette dangling from his lips, a can of beer in one hand, probably on the way home from some all-night blast. When he pressed down on the brake pedal he watched the van in the mirror, no reaction. Surely the brake lights must have come on. Maybe the punk knew this trick.

He pushed harder on the pedal and when his brakes engaged he heard the rumble of the van drop off. He pressed the pedal even harder and heard the squealing of brakes. In the mirror he could see that the van had lunged sideways in a skid and had dropped back several car lengths. That'll teach him to follow so close.

He was now traveling at the same speed as the right-hand lane. He saw an opening, turned on his signal, and began merging in slowly. But before he could complete the lane change he heard the van growling in spasms like a mad dog running. The van was beside him roaring and belching through a thick chrome side pipe. He pulled his arm inside, moved his car farther to the right, and slowed down. But the van stayed with him, its vast black side inches from his face. He could see his distorted reflection in the black paint. As he steered close to the guard rail he could barely hear horns sounding above the roar of the van. He choked on exhaust gases. He could feel heat on the side of his face.

Then the van swerved away and ahead, its fat tires squealing slightly. The horns were steady now and he realized that he had stopped half on and half off the road. The van had stopped him without him even realizing it, as it gunned its engine and wedged him toward the guard rail.

He could have been killed!

As he crawled across the bridge he stared at the van that was at least a dozen cars ahead in the left lane. He glared at it, his face so hot that its redness was probably visible to the other drivers who had witnessed his humiliation.

The license plate of the van was partially hidden behind a black vinyl-covered spare wheel. He could only see the last two numbers, three-nine. The van had no windows in back, only another gold spider web, this one with fibers joining the taillights and rear bumper and spare wheel. The only windows were the ones on the front doors and the windshield. He remembered that the side window had seemed as black as the rest of the body. He remembered having looked toward this window for mercy as he nosed closer and closer to the guard rail.

Near the bottom of the bridge his lane moved faster. The light turned red and the van was stopped at the head of the line. He knew he would turn right with the green arrow and head toward the plant before the van was gone. But the van would not be moving, would not be a danger to him. The arrogant bastard was in *his* territory now. Even if the van followed him he could complain to the guard at the gate.

The side of the van reflected the morning sun orange. The side pipe sputtered evenly in idle. Probably trying to ignore him as if nothing had happened. As he reached the light he lifted his hand to the side of his face, and just before he turned the corner he lowered all but his middle finger. He sped around the corner and laughed aloud as he listened to the engine of the van being gunned behind him. He turned into the plant gate feeling like a child who, having been chased by a bully, is now safe behind the screen door of his home. The steering wheel of his car felt hot in his hands.

As he walked across the parking lot he could not see the van out on the road or near the gate. He was safe. He had had the last word. Today the levers of the fifty ton press would feel good to his touch because he would imagine that each downward plunge would be upon the black van instead of a shiny flat sheet of steel.

"Why didn't you just let him hit you? Then you could've collected from his insurance and got that rusted heap of yours fixed up some." Doyle, as usual, sat at the end of the lunch room table. The main reason Doyle sat at the end was because he was too fat to slide into a side seat. He weighed three-hundred pounds and operated the two-hundred ton press. He smoked a bent black pipe that looked miniature when he held it in his mouth. Whenever he tapped the smoldering ashes out of the pipe he did it so loud that everyone had to stop talking.

Why couldn't Doyle have been like Tony and Riley? They had been dumbstruck when he told about the van. Riley had asked if he got a license number.

Tony and Riley were sitting across from him, both sipping their coffee while Doyle refilled his pipe and kept spouting off.

"You should've just stayed in your lane. He would've run into you. It would've been his fault."

"But I was going fifty."

"I thought you said you were stopped."

"Yeah. I was stopped after he practically smashed me against the rail."

"How do you know it was a *he* that was driving? You said you couldn't see the driver."

"I just figured. Would you picture a broad doing that?"

"Maybe."

Tony nudged Riley. "Hey. Maybe she was just tryin' to get acquainted. A little kiss on the fender."

Riley laughed and spilled coffee on his fingers. "Yeah, baby. Blow into my carburetor and I'll do anything you want. I heard about a van once that had a waterbed in the back."

Though he seemed to forget about the incident while he was at the press, he remembered it all over again at lunch and then again at the afternoon coffee break. He even imagined the van waiting for him outside the gate. Maybe the van was full of guys, or maybe the driver went to get some buddies so they could wait for him after work. He should never have given the finger to the van. He got to the lunch room early for the afternoon break and told Doyle about his fear.

"Don't worry about it. People forget."

"I don't know, Doyle. I got a bad feeling about this. See, I made the last move. Now it's his turn. What if he comes after me? Or she. What if that van follows me home or something?"

"All right. If you're that worried about it I'll follow you part way home."

"Would you do that, Doyle?"

"Sure. We both go south anyhow."

When Tony and Riley came into the lunch room, Doyle started talking about baseball. He was glad to have Doyle as a friend. If the van showed up after work it would have to contend with Doyle who drove a battered Willys Jeep because it was the only vehicle he could fit into comfortably.

In his rearview mirror he could see Doyle's thick arm waving from the window of the Willys. Doyle had followed him half way home before turning off and now he wished he had not asked for Doyle's help. The van had not been waiting for him. Why should it? He only hoped that Doyle would not mention any of this to Tony and Riley tomorrow. Why had he been so frightened? He had seen other people raise their fists and fingers during rush hour traffic. He had seen the rapid movements of lips behind the safety glass that silenced the curses. He had witnessed countless reenactments of this traffic jam jousting which always ends up in a stalemate. In the past he had never joined in. But this morning when he could not even see the driver of the van he had lost control. Perhaps he was angry because a machine was harassing him, a machine just like the fifty ton press he had watched all day as it squashed sheets of steel. But machines had controls, levers and buttons and switches and wheels manipulated by human hands.

The incident *had* frightened him, so much that he had imagined the press talking today. Each downward plunge said, "Again!" Each slow hydraulic rise whispered, "And."

Again! And. Again! And. Again!
The dialogue of machines was simple. Do something and repeat it thousands and thousands of times. He wanted to be at home watching television, eating a TV dinner, because at the plant *he* was a machine. Each refrain of the press was fed by exactly the same movements of his hands upon the levers.

A semi-trailer truck was gaining on him to his right, its diesel whine seeming to slow down his speed by suction. He pressed down on the accelerator and surged ahead. His engine hummed. But beneath the hum, in those fractions of seconds between bursts of exhaust and intake he could hear the same refrain repeated at high speed.

Again! And. Again! And. Again!
As he pulled in ahead of the semi he could see the shine of its tall grille in his mirror. The grille glowed orange from the setting sun appearing hot like the grids in his oven. Tonight he would have a Salisbury steak and mashed potato TV dinner. Monday night was Salisbury steak and football night since the end of baseball season.

He looked in his side mirror and saw only the orange-blue of the dusk sky. Someone had bumped against the mirror in the parking lot during the rush between cars. He rolled down his window and straightened the mirror and saw two yellow beams like eyes riding low on a misshaped head. The van was back. The van had been hiding behind the semi.

He was on top of the overpass that bridged the Interstate. The steering wheel grew warm in his hands and seemed to thicken as if he were holding an animal that would strike if he let go. The growl beside him resonated with the truck behind. He could feel the growl on his neck. He could feel the heat. He could smell paint burning. To avoid being forced down the embankment sloping away from the highway he veered from his homeward path entering the entrance ramp of the Interstate and saw, when he opened his eyes, that the van was directly in front of him, its spider web framed by glowing red taillights. The numbers three-nine visible on the half-hidden license plate.

His tires screamed and his steering wheel became a snake. A high-pitched voice wailed wordlessly. *He* was screaming. *He* would win. *He* would watch the top-heavy van roll in flames. But the van only leaned on its thick tires as if weighted down with lead.

He turned on his headlights and saw them reflected on the black body that leaned against the banked ramp. He could smell rubber burning. He stayed with the van, could not distinguish the howl of the van's tires and his. He would force the van to go too fast. But the van hung on and the ramp began to straighten.

He glanced at his speedometer. Sixty. When he looked up the van was gone, only a single taillight veering to the left. And ahead of him he could see the words "WIDE LOAD" growing before him. His foot seemed on an endless journey to the brake pedal. Above the words "WIDE LOAD" was piled sheet upon sheet of steel. Why did it all seem to take so long?

As the bumper of the trailer pressed his hood forward in a wave he could see the fluted edges of the steel bumper where a milling machine had passed again and again and again. He closed his eyes and pushed against the steering wheel the way he had, thousands of times, pushed the double levers of the press to send the fifty tons of force downward on its journey.

OUR OFF-ROAD FANTASY

Lately, I've begun to suspect that those who write television ads for automobiles don't actually drive the things. The telltale sign is that in these ads the cars are never driven on freeways or city streets. They are either slinking pilotless down a back alley in Sorrento, floating through the clouds on the way to Mars, or chewing up dirt in some desert oasis.

If the ads are any indication of what people use cars for, then their chief calling seems to be chopping up the back country. There's the Datsun racing a Barbary sheep up a gully, the frolicsome Audis playing tag in the shadow of Mt. Whitney, the Kawasaki doing its best to squash the minnows out of a wilderness stream, and the fat pickup truck perched like an airsick eagle atop an inaccessible sandstone monolith in the Utah desert.

Even the farmers are getting into the act. A down home voice drawls out on a radio commercial: "Mah daddy plowed up the state of Kansas with one International Harvester tractor."

None of my friends can honestly say that they've used their cars to race goats up desert ravines or watch for Indian smoke signals in Utah. And while all those bikini-clad girls race their Subarus through the surf at some otherwise undiscovered seashore, no doubt they would be locked up for driving that way on almost any beach in California.

So, what I infer from these ads is that the copywriters have discovered the naked truth about driving: it's a drag. Most mileage is put on a car in the lockstep and lead intoxication of the freeway commute, or amidst a crowd of squawling kids on the way to the supermarket, or, in desperation, back to the shop for another factory recall. Driving a car means not being able to find a parking place, not being able to understand the witch doctor who shakes his rattles and chants gibberish over your sick carburetor, bearing in silence the festering insult of some jerk who just stole your right of way. Driving in a car is a form of imprisonment. It's like being caught in a huge crowd that is forever surging toward a narrow exit.

I can find it in my heart to excuse the copywriters for hiding the fact that driving is mostly aggravation. I can even wink along with them at the suggestion that buying a new Volvo will entitle me to my own clear lane on the freeway of life. But in the end, I can't help feeling that the copywriters are also manipulating our private fantasies in a destructive way.

You see, more than the flag, the eagle or the Minuteman, the automobile has become our steadfast symbol of freedom and independence. Today, when our social relationships are less than certain, the private auto allows us to get away on our own terms. It's a "flee machine" that allows us to slip out of the house in the middle of a family feud, duck out of work ten minutes early, or take a weekend off in the mountains. Manufacturers know this, and from time to time they adjust the names of their products to keep up with our ideas of freedom. A few years ago, when we thought of freedom as a villa in Italy or a castle in Spain, the brochures down at the showroom read like a directory of aristocratic memories and jet-set retreats: Monaco, Monte Carlo, Riviera, Versailles, Seville, Newport, Malibu. Buying a car was like getting a date with Aristotle Onassis.

In the late 1960s, when we were all a little weary of jet-set high jinks, the manufacturers cast about for a new set of names. They alighted in the Garden of Eden, and suddenly we were all driving around in animals: in mustangs, pintos, broncos, wildcats, bobcats, cougars, foxes, firebirds, and skyhawks. Notice that they're all images of freedom, power, and independence. There are no barnyard ducks or turkeys, nothing passive or herded to remind us what life is really like.

I like skylarks and fighting bulls just as much as the next guy. But the manufacturers, on to a good thing, didn't stop there. Having taken the animals out of the woods, they began to fill the newly vacated wilderness with Jeeps racing up hillsides and grinning starlets trenching mountain meadows in Porsches. "Grab a mountain!" advises one commercial. "Do it in the dirt!" counsels another.

A lot of viewers have taken these ads at their word and in the process discovered something powerful in the solitude and controlled violence of driving on a back-country path. Now people expect to take their cars off into the woods. The federal Heritage Conservation and Recreation Service estimates that 43.6 million Americans engaged in some form of off-road vehicle activity in 1977. That is more than the combined number of people who went skiing and sailing. More than 1.5 million motorcycles are sold annually in the United

States, and most of them are used off roads. It is estimated that there are more that 10 million off-road vehicles in use in the nation.

In some places, the off-road activity is fast and furious. As many as 3000 motorcyclists participated in a cross-country Barstow to Las Vegas race in California. Back Bay National Wildlife Refuge in Virginia hosted as many as 875 ORVs a day until the refuge was closed to them. The Santa Clara County, California, sheriff estimated that a single unsanctioned area in the hills nearby attracted 2000 users a weekend. On some weekends, 9,000 vehicles crowd onto the six miles of California's Pismo Beach. "The beach there is like an interstate," says one observer.

California, with perhaps 3.5 million off-road vehicles, leads the nation. It is first because it has an unusual combination of dense urban populations and vast tracts of unpatrolled federal landholdings. (Most off-road vehicle use in the West takes place on federally managed land, while most in the East is thought to be trespass on private land.) But other states are catching up with California. Dune buggies now crowd the beaches of Cape Cod and Fire Island. Four-wheel drives are responsible for stream bank erosion in Kentucky and Missouri. The State of Washington and the Tennessee Valley Authority have provided public ORV trails. The State of Florida has opened up old phosphate mining pits to off-roaders. The City of Pocatello, Idaho, is beginning to worry about what off-roaders may be doing to the quality of its water by causing erosion in the nearby Caribou National Forest.

All that traffic has serious effects on the land. Off-road vehicles cause erosion, destroy vegetation, banish wildlife, reduce water quality, and make wildlands unusable for other forms of recreation. According to a 1979 Council on Environmental Quality Report, "ORVs have damaged every kind of ecosystem in the United States." ORV trails near Santa Cruz, California, are gullies eight feet deep after only six years of use. At Chabot Regional Park near San Francisco, off-roaders displace 32,800 tons of soil per square mile per year. In Ballinger Canyon, near Los Angeles, benchmarks sunk in two feet of concrete at the top of a hill have tumbled to the bottom of the hill after ORVs scoured away the soil. At Jawbone Canyon, in the California desert, off-roaders have scraped away all the topsoil and are now cutting into bedrock. In parts of the desert, off-roading has removed 95 percent of the shrubbery and reduced plant and animal life by 75 percent. A total of 543 acres of Dove Springs Canyon in California is completely denuded by ORVs and is now a stark moonscape of dust and tire tracks.

Such effects do not mend quickly. Topsoil may take more than a millennium to replace. Vegetation filling in disturbed soils is seldom the native vegetation that was originally destroyed. Instead, exotics like Russian thistle and Brazilian pepper invade the area. Without the plant cover they depend upon, wildlife species don't come back.

And the effects are ubiquitous. One cannot find a hillside on the San Francisco peninsula that is without the ruts and scars of motorcycles. It is estimated that more than one million acres of the California desert are seriously damaged by ORVs. Satellites provide clear pictures of wind erosion caused by off-road vehicles in the Mojave desert.

Effects are not limited to erosion and deforestation. The noise of a trail bike can be heard by a hiker two miles away, and of a dune buggy four miles away; ORVs tend to drive out bird watchers, backpackers, picnickers and cross-country skiers. And ORV users have vandalized human artifacts. The Bureau of Land Management complains that off-roaders have destroyed archaeological relics in the Southwest. Centuries-old pictographs are shot at, driven over, or spray-painted as if they were subway cars.

A lot of managers have reacted by closing their gates to off-road vehicles. Most of the timber companies in the Pacific Northwest have banished ORVs from their landholdings. The National Forests near Los Angeles have declared 60 percent of their area off limits to ORVs and left less than 10 percent open to them without restriction. In most other national forests, where ORVs have not yet made a serious impact, the ratio is reversed. The State of Indiana has closed all its land to ORVs. The National Park Service forbids the use of trail bikes and four-wheel drives, and the Department of Defense has closed most of its 26 million acres to ORVs. San Bernardino, Riverside, and Santa Clara Counties in California have all passed ordinances prohibiting ORV users from riding on private land without permission from the owner. San Bernardino's law requires the rider to have permission in writing on his person. Santa Clara's requires the landowner to secure a permit before anybody can ride on his land. The ordinance is aimed at riders who invade the land without securing the owner's permission.

In 1977, President Carter cited off-road vehicles as a nuisance that has "ruined fragile soils, harassed wildlife and damaged unique archaeological sites" and ordered federal agencies to close seriously damaged areas to ORV use. But the federal agencies have not responded. Ballinger Canyon in the Los Padres National Forest, for example, is completely denuded of vegetation in places, and suffers from a loss of soil from some of its slopes of 54,000 tons per square mile per year. Says Howard Wilshire, a U.S. Geological Survey soil expert who studies the effects of ORVs, "Ballinger Canyon is the biggest garbage dump I've ever seen. It looks like a war zone." Ballinger Canyon is certainly one of those areas that is seriously damaged and ought, under the terms of Carter's Executive Order 11989, to be closed to further use. But the Forest Service has done nothing. When it decided to restrict ORV use to the canyon floor to reduce erosion, it could not bring itself to post signs or otherwise advise the off-roaders. Says Wilshire, "I don't think they *can* close it. Unless they call in the militia."

The heart of the problem is that driving is a self-centered activity. And so, along with the vehicles comes the driver's citified indifference to the discomfort of others. The off-roaders bring to the countryside an insistent selfishness which sweeps aside the more open manner of country life. A camper in California's Stanislaus National Forest reported that one morning, five miles from the nearest road, a motorcyclist raced right across the foot of his sleeping bag. The cyclist, lost in the speed and noise of the machine, did not stop. A desert dwelling family complains of motorcyclists and four-wheel drivers who repeatedly shoot holes in their water tanks and dump mounds of garbage in their yard. So, here we are, motoring into little muggings in the pines.

It's not just motorcycles. Not long ago, in Death Valley, a man tried to leap a desert arroyo in a rented car. He had driven around barriers raised by National Park rangers closing the road because of a recent flash flood. As he approached the rain-swollen gully, he accelerated. The car vaulted into the air and came down with one bumper resting on each bank. He tried to sue the Park Service, claiming, presumably, that the agency ought to have provided a smaller gully.

It is hard to convince the off-roader that what he's doing is destructive. He is too busy trying to express urban discontent in Old West idioms. Says a southern California motorcyclist, "Listen, I work all week at a meaningless job that I hate. My children are growing up to be weaklings and the country is going to hell. All I want to do is ride my motorcycle in the desert."

That fantasy of freedom can be overpowering. When the Bureau of Land Management ended its annual Barstow to Las Vegas race, several hundred motorcyclists, following the lead of a "Phantom Duck of the Desert," showed up and held the race in defiance of the federal government. The Bureau, with only twelve rangers to patrol twelve million acres of desert, made no effort to stop them.

Individuals who try to interfere with the off-roader's idea of freedom run risks. Last year, a southern California woman and her daughter were driving to their desert home in Yucca Valley when off to their left a motorcyclist raised a great rooster tail of dust. Perched on the seat in front of the cyclist was a young child, so the woman guessed that the cyclist was not an outlaw. It was then midway into the desert's fleeting wildflower season, and the woman, thinking of the flowers, waved the man to a stop and asked him to get back on the road. The man flashed a maniacal smile and said, "I *am* on the road." When the woman explained that it grieved her to see him doing violence to the wildflowers and added that it would be decades before his wheel ruts vanished and the flowers grew again, the man lost all self-control. He pulled the woman's hair and knocked her daughter down, and then rode defiant zig-zags back and forth across the ground in front of them.

That is why the Forest Service and the Bureau of Land Management have been reluctant to mess with the off-roader's sense of freedom. "The justification cited most frequently," says the Council on Environmental Quality report, "is that 'if we close this area, they will just go somewhere else', to quote a BLM ranger, and under current land management policies, he is right." The report adds that if some restrictions aren't raised soon, the amount of damage caused by ORVs is bound to increase. "The fact is," says the report, "most ORVs are promoted and sold by the industry on the basis of their ability to break new ground across wild land, to scale steep slopes, to ford natural streams—all of which can be ruinous to the environment."

It is the tyranny of freedom in microcosm. The automobile makes us independent of each other, and therefore careless of each other's rights. The more we impinge on each other's rights, the more insistent our demand for that freedom. Off-road vehicles take us out into the woods, but they take the woods out of us.

And in the end, what does this driving really have to do with freedom? It's not really freedom when one is merely getting away from the problems of home, workplace, and urban congestion. It is escape. In the long run, I suspect that the trafficking of the wildlands will cure itself. Either the mountains and the deserts will become one huge dusty parking lot and the off-roaders will have to find a new range to roam, or we'll run out of gasoline. The environmental aspect of ORVs may be the lesser problem. The real problem may be making the cities we all want to escape more liveable—at least liveable enough to keep us from wanting to get into our cars, shut the windows, turn up the stereo and roar out across the desert, just to get away from it all.

V. THE FUTURE

MICHAEL BARONE

OUR ROMANCE WITH
THE AUTO IS OVER

In all the discussion about the decline of the American auto industry, one factor—and, I think, the decisive one—has been left out: Americans have ended their romance with the auto. I saw that romance at its most intense moments, growing up with the children of auto executives in the suburbs of Detroit in the late 1950s and early 1960s. I remember how people would whisper about the terrible financial trouble a family must be having when it kept one of its cars more than two years. I remember how excited we would be when we saw the first pictures of the new car models—or, better yet, spotted one of them being photographed for advertisements somewhere in Bloomfield Hills. I remember too the smell of new car upholstery, and how excited I was when we picked up our new cars at the dealer's, the 1953 two-tone Pontiac Catalina or our first wraparound windshield Oldsmobile in 1955.

We are told today that one reason auto sales are down so much is that cars and gasoline are so expensive. But the $11,000 car of 1982 is equal, in real dollars, to the $3,000 top-of-the-line Chevy or Ford that so many Americans bought in 1955. And in real dollars, the $1.20 gas of today is not so much more expensive than 30-cent gas in 1955. Americans in the 1950s and 1960s were, if they were living much above the poverty line, willing to part with a lot more of their income more frequently than they are today to buy cars—and mostly American cars. In the past three years, only 7 or 8 percent of American households (not counting duplications) have bought new American cars—a figure lower than in any year, even in recessions, since World War II. American car sales per household were twice as high in good years like 1955, 1965–66, 1968–69, and 1972–73.

What happened to the romance with the auto? To understand, you have to remember that the people who were in love with cars in the 1950s and 1960s are not the same people as the potential auto buyers of today. Most people under forty-three today could not drive legally in the boom sales year of 1955, for example, and most auto buyers of 1955 are not doing much (or any) driving this year. The Americans who were buying cars then were people for whom the Depression of the 1930s was a vivid and recent experience; it was especially vivid since almost everyone—economists and politicians, voters and consumers—expected it to return immediately after World War II. We know now that instead there were three decades of fabulous prosperity, of economic growth. But even those of us who lived through those years as adults find it hard to recall how unexpected that good fortune was.

So in the 1950s and 1960s, millions of Americans found themselves affluent far beyond their expectations. What would they do with their money? Many of the luxuries we enjoy today were simply not available in large quantity then: color television, charter trips to Europe, video games, vacation houses, air conditioning. For the most part, people in the 1950s spent their new wealth on things we regard today as basics: they ate more meat than their parents did, drank more liquor and smoked more cigarettes; they bought more clothes; they bought rather than rented houses; and they bought new cars.

And on all of these items they spent more on decoration and ornament and on buying this year's new model than their parents in the 1930s had been able to afford. Not just the automobiles, but the clothes and accessories of the 1950s were characterized by a gaudiness we have since been taught to regard as excessive and hideous. The Americans of the 1950s, with their costume jewelry and chrome tailfins, seem vulgar and ostentatious to us today. But we should regard them more sympathetically: they were people kicking up their heels, enjoying a wonderful prosperity and freedom that they had never expected.

Americans today are obviously different. People under forty-five have no vivid experience of the Depression, but instead remember what seems now to have been a long period of steady prosperity. They have a much wider range of products competing, as marketing vice-presidents say, for the leisure dollar; and many different types of vehicles (campers, pickup trucks, sports cars, as well as ordinary passenger cars) competing for their transportation dollar. They have less taste for ornament in consumer products: while architects and painters are moving back toward decoration, car buyers increasingly want Bauhaus-style cars. Automobiles are not symbols of success (except for the Mercedes and Ferraris of Beverly Hills), and certainly not of a sudden and unexpected freedom from economic privation; they are just a way of getting around. The children who loved the smell of new cars now resent spending money on them and buy them as infrequently as possible. They want to spend their money on a VCR or two weeks in Europe instead.

So it's wrong to blame the American auto industry entirely for its problems. Its leaders assumed, as most adults instinctively assume, that their own behavior and taste would be replicated by the next generation, and that people somehow *needed* to buy cars every two or three years. They did not understand that consumers would end their affair with the American automobile one day and pursue romances with other products. "Fashion," says the French historian Fernand Braudel, "is a search for new language to discredit the old, a way in which each generation can repudiate its immediate predecessor and distinguish itself from it." While we mock the fashion of the 1950s and make fun of the auto executives who thought the romance with the auto would go on forever, we should pause for a moment and wonder which of our own fashions and enthusiasms, which seem so sensible and natural to us now, will seem tawdry and foolish a generation hence.

DAVID E. COLE AND
LAWRENCE T. HARBECK

THE AUTOMOBILE INDUSTRY'S
FUTURE ROLE IN THE
DOMESTIC AND WORLD ECONOMY*

The U.S. automotive industry is still strong and competitive, but it is beset by severe temporary problems that could have lasting effects. The industry also is changing faster than ever before, and the pace of rapid innovation is likely to continue or even accelerate in the years just ahead. Sudden changes create major problems. But it should be kept in mind that the industry has a record of overcoming seemingly insurmountable difficulties.

This paper, in weighing the industry's problems and future, probes probable trends in technology, industry capital requirements, the status of vehicle manufacturers and their suppliers and dealers, the effect of recent developments on labor, the place of mass transit, and—possibly the most massive factor of all—the impact of the U.S. federal government. It concludes with a discussion of industry needs.

Some of these matters were investigated in a recent Delphi Survey** of technical, marketing, and administrative decision makers in the automotive and supplier industry. The University of Michigan's Office for the Study of Automotive Transportation (OSAT), with which the coauthors are associated, participated in the design and management of this survey. Our analysis begins with a brief summary of part of the study's report.

*This paper is based in part on remarks by Dr. Cole at hearings of the International Finance and Economic Stabilization Subcommittees of the Senate Banking Committee, June 18, 1980, but reflects new developments through October, 1982.

**The Delphi technique is an iterative process in which carefully selected experts work independently and anonymously to arrive at a consensus view of the future; in this case, the automotive future. If the proper individuals are selected their prediction tends to be accurate because they have made or are going to make the decisions that lead to the results they are predicting. Many factors were examined in this study, including technology and marketing.

I. TECHNOLOGICAL TRENDS

Powerplants
    Passenger car engines of the future will be predominantly in-line 4-cylinder and V-6 designs. The engines of the 1960s and 1970s, the in-line 6-cylinder and V-8 configurations, will only play a minor role. Our forecast suggests that in 1985, 52 percent of the engines produced will be 4s and 31 percent V-6s; in 1990, 4-cylinder production may be as high as 60 percent while the V-6 fraction could drop to 20 percent. Diesel engine use is forecast to increase from 15 percent in 1985 to 20 percent in 1990. (However, inability to meet particulate emission regulations could greatly reduce diesel prospects.) Turbo or supercharging will be used extensively on both gasoline and diesel engines. By 1990, electric vehicles may account for as much as 3 percent of U.S. sales. There is a reasonable chance that stratified charge spark-ignited engines will be introduced in the 1980s. Several technical and economic problems must be resolved, however, before production can begin.
    More exotic engine concepts such as the gas turbine or the Stirling engine are not expected in the 1980s. Fuel injection will be more common on gasoline engines; single point injection could be used on 30 percent of 1985 engines and 50 percent of 1990 engines. Multipoint fuel injection for the gasoline engine is not expected to increase beyond 10 percent penetration in both 1985 and 1990. At least 80 percent of all gasoline engines will be matched with 3-way or dual-bed catalytic emission controls in the last half of this decade.

Drive Trains
    The front engine front drive concept with the engine located transversely in the vehicle will be used in 70 percent of cars by 1985 and 85 percent by 1990. This system will also be applied to some light trucks and vans. Technology experts predicted that front-wheel-drive technology will add $125 to the manufacturing cost, but will result in weight savings ranging from 150 pounds in a subcompact car to 250 pounds in a full-size car. This drive-train technology is thought to be applicable to vehicles up to 3,000 to 3,500 pounds, or essentially all of the proposed future passenger cars.

Electronics
    Electronics are expected to play an increasingly prominent role in the automobile and light truck of the future. Today, about 5 percent

of the cost of the vehicle is represented by electronic systems. This percentage is expected to increase to 10 percent in 1985 and 15 percent in 1990. We foresee on-board computer diagnostic systems that will provide the operator with a much better understanding of the state of tune and the maintenance requirements of the vehicle. Microprocessors will be used in practically all future vehicles.

Materials and Components

Dramatic shifts are expected in automotive materials in tomorrow's cars and light trucks as they are downsized and unweighted. In general, lightweight materials will come into far greater use in the never-ending drive of the automotive designer to maintain the largest possible passenger and load volume while reducing vehicle weight to minimize fuel consumption. The average weight of the U.S. produced car is forecast to drop from 3,300 pounds (in 1979) to 2,700 pounds in 1985 and finally to 2,250 pounds in 1990. The most significant material reductions will occur with steel and cast iron. Steel use will be reduced from slightly more than 2,000 pounds in 1978 to 1,300 pounds in 1990, and cast iron use will be cut from 530 pounds in 1978 to only 250 pounds in 1990. At the same time, plastic in all its various forms is projected to increase from 175 pounds to 300 pounds and aluminum from 115 to 200 pounds. Most of the aluminum increase will be in castings.

Plastic materials of many types will be used, including a substantial increase in fiber-based composite materials. Only about 35 pounds of composites are used in current vehicles but this will increase to 100 pounds in 1985 and 135 pounds in 1990. The expert panelists forecast that 10 percent of exterior panels in U.S. produced cars will be constructed of fiber-reinforced plastics or other composite forms in 1985 and that this figure will double by 1990. One of the primary factors in the decision whether or not to utilize lightweight materials is the dollar value of weight savings. Delphi panelists projected that the value of a pound of weight saved is currently in the neighborhood of 60¢ a pound, but will be $1 per pound by 1985 and approximately $1.50 per pound by 1990. There is significant concern that certain materials may come into short supply; rhodium, cobalt, platinum, and chrome are all viewed as being vulnerable.

Vehicle Operation and Maintenance

From the 1960s to today, there has been a dramatic reduction in the number of scheduled maintenance visits by car owners. Scheduled maintenance presently is required every 6,000 to 7,500 miles. Panelists predict that this interval will increase to 10,000 miles in 1985 and 15,000 miles by 1990. This adjustment will place a premier requirement on all automotive materials. Another indication of this trend is that 25 percent of the passenger cars produced in 1990 may not have a spare tire.

The many advances predicted in the Delphi Surveys will require additional work on the part of the U.S. automotive industry. But these improvements could not occur in the relatively short time frame considered if the industry had not made a major effort in recent years to get these programs started—even before the belated recognition by U.S. consumers that energy supplies and prices will probably remain uncertain.

II. CAPITAL REQUIREMENTS AND LEAD TIMES

We have seen a wide range of estimates of the capital that will be required to bring the U.S. automotive industry into compliance with the CAFE standard of 27.5 mpg by 1985. One of the better substantiated figures is $25 billion per *year* from 1979 to 1985; an annual level (although in depreciated dollars) approximately equal to the cost of the ten-year Apollo moon landing program. This figure would include $75 billion capital requirements for U.S. motor vehicle manufacturers and $50 billion for their U.S. suppliers over the five-year period. Any such estimate can be quickly reduced, of course, if poor vehicle sales or other circumstances make such enormous investments impossible. Ford Motor Company announced in early May the cancellation of $2.5 billion of its capital expansion plans. Any forced decline in capital spending delays the restoration of full competitiveness for U.S. automotive manufacturers.

Perhaps the only certainty about the industry's capital needs is that they are large beyond comprehension and will create immense financial strains. Any reasonable action that can be taken to relieve the pressure will help accelerate progress. Perhaps the best way to help would be immediate changes in depreciation regulations to allow an equally immediate improvement in internally generated cash flow. Related steps could include provisions to permit a more rapid write-off and/or increased investment tax credit for special tools needed for government mandated items and the fast refunding of taxes to companies not in a profit position. New production facilities obsoleted by recent market trends could be considered for more rapid write-off as well. Longer term, the elimination of double taxation on dividends might make it easier to raise fresh capital.

There are other actions that can be considered, but the above procedures offer the most immediate and continuing promise. Inseparable from the automotive industry's capital problems is the overall capital investment situation in the U.S. Recent estimates indicate that capital investment as a percent of GNP is 20 percent in Japan, 15 percent in Germany, but only 10 percent here. These data would indicate that investing in Japan and Germany is more attractive. Recent government policies that offer more encouragement to savings and investment and the reduction in inflation are positive developments.

In understanding the ebb and flow of small vs. large car sales in the U.S. market, it is important to keep in mind the long lead time between management decisions and production for the market. Years are required to make a major modification, to produce a new model, or—and this is very important—to produce much larger quantities of an existing model. This last point is little recognized and worth repeating. It takes years to build or modify major production facilities to produce large additional volumes of cars or trucks—even if the vehicle to be produced is already in existence.

Long lead times are caused by several limiting factors including (1) financing, (2) availability of trained engineers and other personnel to design and test vehicles and set up new manufacturing facilities, and (3) the limited ability of the machine tool industry to supply production equipment. Capital and financing problems are particularly severe today because of the premature obsolescence and underutilization of huge amounts of existing capital equipment that was designed to produce, in large quantities, vehicles that are now selling in low volume.

Major losses of capital investment hurt the U.S. automotive industry more than they would automotive industries in other countries because the U.S. industry is particularly dependent on using capital investment to offset high labor costs. The only way the U.S. can be productively competitive is by investing more per worker and per unit of finished product than do its competitors. If foreign competition continues to have lower labor costs and, in addition, is able to employ more capital per worker, U.S. industry will be uncompetitive.

III. MOTOR VEHICLE MANUFACTURERS

We can be fairly certain that the United States will still have one manufacturer producing a full line of motor vehicles in 1985. We cannot be at all sure that we will have two, and three may be optimistic. We see no advantages to the nation, no technical product advantages, and no advantages to GM employees and shareholders, if Ford and Chrysler are unable to compete across the board. Despite its troubles, however, the U.S. automotive industry today is still the most competitive and technically competent. It has unmatched engineering and manufacturing strength. But it has been hurt and needs rational assistance.

The industry has made mistakes, of course. But in judging the U.S. automotive industry, it is only fair to keep the following sequence of events before us:

1. For most of the post–World War II period the real cost of energy, adjusted for inflation, was dropping.
2. In the U.S. and Canada, the two countries most dependent on automotive transportation, the retail price of gasoline reflected this decline.
3. As a consequence of the declining real cost of gasoline, and resultant consumer perceptions and demand, North American passenger cars became large and heavy. Customers wanted comfort and safety and, with low-priced and available fuel and new materials, the most economical way to meet their demands was by making the cars heavier.
4. In Europe and Japan, where cars were not so much of a necessity, and driving habits, patterns, and needs were different, gasoline prices were kept very high by adding taxes. Also, punitive taxes were placed on weight and horsepower.
5. Because of the high gasoline costs, narrower roads, and shorter distances traveled, cars in Europe and Japan were made small and economical to meet a different customer demand.
6. Imported cars were not a major factor in the U.S. until the 1970s. In 1959 the import share of market touched 10 percent but fell back to 5 percent in 1963 and never got over 12 percent—into the teens—until 1970.
7. Between 1970 and 1972, while import sales were edging up from 1.2 million units to 1.5 million, sales of domestic cars

increased from 7.2 million to almost 10.0 million. The increase alone in domestic car sales was almost twice the level of total import sales.

8. Sales of both imports and domestic cars fell sharply in 1974, but domestic car sales were up to 9.0 million again in 1978.

9. In late 1975 and early 1976, when many of the decisions concerning 1980 model cars were being made, import sales had just suffered a tremendous drop in penetration—from 22 percent of market in March, 1975, to 12 percent in November of the same year—a decline of almost 50 percent in only eight months. During this same period, government-controlled gasoline prices remained artificially low and misled consumers to buy large cars. Chrysler, whose strength was in compact cars, and AMC, the U.S. small-car company, were hurt the most by government price controls.

10. In early 1979, just before the terrorist government of Iran made hostages of American citizens, large domestic passenger cars were selling well and import sales remained depressed at penetration levels over one-third below levels a year earlier. Dealer inventories of imports were near record highs in terms of days' supply.

When the Iranian crisis triggered the incredibly inept government fuel allocation scheme, small-size U.S. cars and imports were suddenly popular again. Import manufacturers met added demand for small cars by working overtime in large capacity small-car facilities necessitated by decades of action by their governments to keep fuel and other automotive taxes high. American vehicle manufacturers, led by many years of big-car demand based on low fuel prices, had to play catch-up ball—and it takes time and money to (1) build the facilities to do this, (2) become good at it, and (3) convince customers that success has been achieved.

Earlier we suggested ways to speed up the flow of capital to manufacturers. Increased capital flow will be a long-term need if automotive change continues on a fast track—and we see no signs of a slowdown.

For the short term, it would be desirable to relieve some of the pressure of the windfall luck of the importers who had been forced to specialize in small cars and, through no foresight of their own, were able to take advantage of the government-instigated overnight switch in consumer demand in the U.S. market.

Emissions and safety standards are expensive, and a trade-off relationship exists between emissions controls and fuel economy. Tight emission standards penalize fuel economy and add considerably to cost. It is time to revise the broad collection of regulations applied to the auto industry in the context of today and a likely tomorrow rather than the past in which these regulations were created. For example, would 90 percent control of exhaust hydrocarbons or carbon monoxide, rather than the 95 percent control, yield cost and economy advantages greater than the small decrease in emission performance?

Whatever steps the government takes to assist the U.S. automotive industry, we suggest that they be positive and undertaken in a spirit of good will. The objective should be to bring all segments of the industry up to the strength of the best; not to tear down the strong. Think of the automobile industry as a willing workman whose arm has been injured in an accident. How do we help him? Do we provide aid? Or do we even him up by injuring his good arm?

IV. SUPPLIERS AND DEALERS

The question arises as to whether the current plight of the domestic auto industry is causing irreparable and irreversible damage to the infrastructure of suppliers and dealers of a magnitude that will permanently downgrade the relative importance of automobile manufacturing in our national economy.

The infrastructure of suppliers and dealers is a follower, not a leader. When sales of domestically produced motor vehicles are poor, many suppliers and dealers are hurt even more than the vehicle manufacturers; but when sales pick up again the suppliers and dealers either recover or are replaced—therefore, the overall infrastructure is not permanently depressed, despite many individual tragedies.

However, it is indeed possible that the relative importance of automobile manufacturing in the U.S. economy will be downgraded for many years, if not permanently, because of long-term damage to the vehicle manufacturers.

In the face of their own difficulties, vehicle manufacturers are, and have been for some time, making extraordinary efforts to assist their suppliers in these difficult times. Vehicle manufacturers openly discuss many of their future plans for new vehicles, new engines and drive trains, lightweight materials, etc. This openness, compared to past secrecy, is not entirely altruistic, of course. The vehicle makers are dependent on their suppliers' ability to raise capital to match new component requirements and want to be sure that the suppliers have enough information to plan ahead and be ready to meet changes when they occur. Unfortunately, conditions and affected programs have changed so rapidly for the industry that uncertainty is greater than ever, despite careful efforts to plan ahead and share information.

We know that complete car and truck lines will be redesigned once, and perhaps two or three times, during the 1980s. Usage of some supplier-provided components, such as rear axles and carburetors, will be greatly reduced. Many components and subsystems will be radically altered by new materials, or replaced completely by new technologies.

Radical upheaval in long-standing product lines of traditional vehicle manufacturers and their parts and materials suppliers will require increased emphasis on strategic and product planning. Coordinated efforts are essential between vehicle manufacturers and suppliers to meet tight redesign schedules and avoid duplication and waste. Vehicle manufacturers' plans and objectives should continue to be communicated to suppliers and a two-way flow of strategic planning information established.

Our office, OSAT, is helping in the formation of a Motor Vehicle Suppliers Association (MVSA). The scope of the task can be understood when it is realized that the industry is estimated to have more than 40,000 suppliers. Government can assist materially in improving the ability of suppliers to plan successfully and will increase their probability of business success and survival if legislators and regulators refrain from excessive policy changes and schedule necessary changes to recognize the realities of automotive lead times.

V. LABOR

The "automotive industry" is a convenient abstraction that can stand for capital and facilities and vehicles and parts and service and a host of other components, but more importantly it represents people; millions of workers. Surprisingly, the exact number is unknown. The interrelationships of motor vehicles to other segments of the economy are too complex to define with complete understanding.

The Motor Vehicle Manufacturers Association's (MVMA) statistical department estimates that more than one of every five jobs in this country is directly or indirectly dependent on the production of motor vehicles. With total U.S. employment near 100 million, the 1 in 5 estimate indicates 20 million jobs associated with the automotive industry. Of these, less than one million are directly occupied in producing vehicles and parts, although this figure is low in the sense that it leaves out many workers who produce parts for the supplier companies.

We do know that there have been hundreds of thousands of hourly workers laid off for years from the U.S. vehicle manufacturers; tens of thousands of salaried workers out of a job, and—no one knows exactly— perhaps half again these numbers affected in the supplier industries.

These are the numbers with which to measure the impact of the OPEC oil cartel, price controlled U.S. gasoline, and the resulting import sales. Fortunately, price controls and allocation schemes have ended and, naturally, fuel prices have declined. But severe damage has been done.

VI. PUBLIC MASS TRANSIT

The question has been raised as to whether government should plan for assistance to public mass transit, or should emphasis be on assistance to the producers of private passenger automobiles (private mass transit).

The possibilities of substituting mass transit for personal cars have been studied extensively. One of the best analyses is "Energy, The Economy, and Mass Transit," by the Office of Technology Assessment (OTA), U.S. Congress, December, 1975. The study is comprehensive, but one of its conclusions is not covered in its own summary—we refer to the finding that, essentially, the U.S. has no choice except to continue the use of passenger cars.

The OTA study estimates that public transit accounts for only 5 percent to 8 percent of total trips in all U.S. urban areas and only 12 percent of the home-to-work trips in urbanized areas of 250,000 or more. The study estimates that heroic support for mass transit, combined with heavily punitive measures against private cars, might double mass transit use in 5 years. The longer-term solution was seen to require government actions that "would shape and guide [land] development into more positive relationships with transit and energy." What this means, in essence, is that until you control where people live, and also force a change in present living patterns, public transit cannot account for a major part of personal travel.

We interpret the OTA study and other related analyses as follows. American life has become increasingly dependent on and molded by convenient, affordable motor vehicles. Personally owned transportation has made the United States the most mobile society in the world and U.S. citizens are extremely sensitive to attacks on this freedom and the many other freedoms associated with it. Tractors and mechanized equipment have revolutionized farming. Motor vehicles have dramatically affected the design of homes, cities, and rural areas. And they have become a pervasive factor of daily life for nearly every person, group, business and government in the nation.

Motor vehicles have also become a fundamental factor in the American economy. Industries that manufacture, sell, maintain, and depend on them account for a large share of the U.S. gross national product. If, for example, Americans stopped buying U.S.-made automobiles, the national economic structure would collapse.

Any deliberate attempt to change the status of private cars and trucks in the economy and in the culture should be undertaken with considerable caution; any major unplanned negative impact on the entire automotive industry, such as the current sales and capital crisis, should spark positive, helpful government assistance particularly if the government was a prime factor in creating the problem.

In short, we think the better choice is to concentrate on helping the producers of private passenger cars. We do not believe that the regimentation necessary to make public mass transit "work" is in accord with the principles of *this* nation.

VII. MARKETS AND COMPETITION

It is difficult to comprehend the size of the car and truck market that is supported by U.S. consumers. No other market in the world approaches it for volume of sales, homogeneity, ease of entry, and attractiveness to competition. Figures like 12 million units per year are discussed but hard to grasp. We have broken sales down to an hourly rate to give us a number we can get our arms around.

On the average, U.S. consumers buy a combined total of more than 1,000 new passenger cars and trucks every hour of the day and night, seven days a week, all year long—even in off years like 1980–82. This sales pace has held since 1963. In record year 1978 the rate was over 1,700 per hour. Our Delphi Survey forecasts that by 1990 the average could be 2,000 new car and truck sales per hour; enough vehicles to fill a 10 acre parking lot. (Fortunately, older models will be scrapped to make room.)

In sales forecasting, it is important to concentrate on long-term trends and not be overly influenced by recent events. Marketing panelists in the Delphi Survey forecast modest sales growth for the U.S. automotive industry through 1990. The total U.S. market is expected to be in the range of 11–12 million cars by 1985 and 12–13 million units in 1990. The light truck market is expected to experience a one-third increase during the 1980s growing to between 3.1 and 3.7 million units in 1985 and as high as 4 million units by 1990. Panelists foresee a substantial increase in worldwide demand for parts.

No dramatic shift is forecast in the proportion of components manufactured in-house by the U.S. manufacturers. GM is expected to continue making 50 percent of its own parts, Ford 40 percent, Chrysler and AMC about 30 percent.

A major change in the distribution of car sizes is anticipated. Both the intermediate and full-size vehicle penetration should be reduced significantly. For example, in 1978 the full-size market share was approximately 23 percent. This could be reduced to the area of 15 percent in 1985 and to 9 percent in 1990. The general, overall, marketing trend can be summarized as a modest sales increase of more durable, efficient, and smaller vehicles through the coming decade.

If the U.S. automotive industry achieves its announced product plans, it should be highly competitive in both domestic and export markets in 1985. Whether it will be allowed to compete in foreign markets is, of course, a separate matter and beyond our ability to forecast. However, if an industry can earn the "right" to compete abroad, surely the U.S. automotive industry is doing so now as imports swarm in to feast on its ill luck.

To the extent that the U.S. government has any control over international trade, it would seem eminently sound business to take steps now, while import sales are strong, to ensure that when U.S. cars become competitive in foreign markets, they be allowed to compete. Perhaps an agreement should be reached to the effect that for any car imported into the U.S. (past, present, and future) the U.S. auto industry should be allowed to export a car to the country of origin of the import, at no greater financial or red tape disincentive than the U.S. now imposes on imports. The U.S. automotive industry should be allowed to "bank" these rights for use in future years. We might call it the "Golden Rule" of international trade.

VIII. RESEARCH NEEDS

We have said, "*If* the U.S. automotive industry achieves its announced product plans," all will be well. But it is not certain that the industry can, technically, meet all of its goals. Many product objectives, particularly for the years beyond 1985, are dependent on technical breakthroughs that have not yet been accomplished. Research is the connecting link between objectives and achievements. To provide a better understanding of the broad scope of automotive research needs, one cannot do better than the following paraphrase of part of the introduction to a report submitted to the Department of Transportation in 1979 by a panel of which David E. Cole was chairman.

Existing automotive technology is more advanced than the understanding of how automotive systems work. This may seem unlikely to the nontechnical person, but is the rule rather than the exception. Many engineering advances result in part from trial and error. An idea for a new way of doing things is tried and if it works it is used. But this is not necessarily the same as understanding completely why it works.

It is important to be aware of this "cut and try" aspect of engineering, but it should not be overemphasized. Engineers and other scientists have created an enormous quantity of well-established theoretical knowledge about engines and other technologies. This body of theory forms the basis for training the engineer and scientist and gives them a practical guide for developing ideas that are tried out empirically.

But the more we succeed the more we realize how much we do not know. Scientists and engineers are like explorers of a new world. Every mountain they climb discloses a new horizon and a dim and distant view of entire ranges of unconquered peaks that were not even visible from the previous advance.

Engineers are no more precise in their use of the English language than other scientists, but there is rough general agreement that "research" and "development" are separate activities. Through research we find out, in detail, just exactly what is going on and form testable theories as to why these things are happening. If further tests validate a theory it may be applicable in practice. Without waiting for proof, however, it is common to try out a new idea before it is completely established in theory. If it works, it can be used before the "what" and "why" are understood completely. This process is called development.

In the early stages of improving a technology, development can take shortcuts that usually save time because there is an abundance of ideas that are reasonable even if unproved. As technology improves, the theoretical limits of perfection as defined by the laws of nature are approached, but never exceeded. Development increases in cost and decreases in success as trial and error produce a growing proportion of errors. Eventually, when research has been used up, when everything reasonable has been tried, the development batting average drops alarmingly. Basic research is needed then to increase understanding and provide novel viewpoints and fresh insights.

If we had another 100 years to develop automotive systems to meet today's (and tomorrow's) efficiency and emission objectives we could probably do it as long as these objectives do not require violation of a fundamental law. But the clock is running, and we must compress a century of development into a decade of research. This will only be possible if support is comprehensive and continuing.

The automotive industry is successfully engaged in a short-term program to optimize existing technologies. Emission and efficiency characteristics, weight, ride, handling, etc. are being improved simultaneously. But the limits to this developmental phase have almost been reached. Progress is slowing asymptotically toward zero. Technology to date has run far ahead of a comprehensive understanding of key basic processes. A broader and deeper research base than now exists is required to carry development successfully into the longer term, to examine alternative engine concepts, and to prepare for substantial vehicle changes. The opportunity and challenge for research is to close the knowledge gaps which now exist and thereby guide the optimization process closer to the fundamental limits.

One of the most important aspects of research is its educational impact. The educational value of research cannot be overemphasized. The disciplines included in automotive research form a large part of the technical background which any engineer or social scientist must have. Thus a major indirect benefit of research programs is a substantial increase in the output of young engineers and scientists from the nation's universities with a background and training directly relevant to automotive technology. Without such a stream of professionals, both interested in and knowledgeable about this technology, the engineering developments required to maintain the viability of our automotive transportation system in the long-term future will be in jeopardy.

Unfortunately, at this time when research needs are at a peak, research support by government and industry is declining. The University of Michigan and other research universities are undertaking major programs to secure new funding.

A related objective of this effort should be the creation of incentives that will focus the current nonautomotive research community on automotive problems. At the present time the cadre of automotive experts is small relative to the challenge and additional researchers are needed to address the magnitude of the tasks ahead.

Finally, and probably most importantly, the U.S. must concentrate on research to offset the windfall advantages of our foreign competitors. Consider the contrast: at a time when the U.S. automotive industry is forced to lay off engineers and every other kind of employee and cannot hire new research experts, and is pouring every dollar it is allowed to retain or can borrow into new capital requirements, foreign competitors are taking billions of dollars out of America to spend on fresh research in an attempt to maintain and extend their current advantage.

The U.S. must act now to provide the research support needed to meet tomorrow's problems or the windfall luck of the imports may become permanent.

IX. COOPERATION

The title of the section sums it up. Earlier we made specific proposals to aid the automotive industry in its hour of need, but the real key lies in cooperation. The government's regulatory responsibilities may require adversarial relations between government and industry, but the government wears more than one hat and is more than just a regulator. It has also assumed a responsibility for helping to maintain productive jobs. To accomplish this objective, government must not weaken industry. In this role there is no place for antagonism.

Relative to the size, economic importance, and complexity of the U.S. automotive industry, we have very little time left to set our affairs in order. If government fails to recognize its responsibility not to harm industry, we may all witness the irreversible contraction into faltering mediocrity of the giant U.S. automotive industry, the greatest engine for economic well-being and personal freedom that has ever existed. It is time to take some lessons from our foreign competitors on how to succeed. It is time to recognize the U.S. automotive industry as the positive factor it is in the lives of the American people.

THE OBSOLESCENT AUTO

I am expecting the F.B.I. to come for me any day now. There will be a knock on the door or a ring of the telephone and my guilty secret will be made public. In fact, I *am* subversive: I am one of those un-Americans who does not own a car. It's not that we aren't a two-car family, we aren't even a one-car family. We are a no-car family. I'll tell you how it happened. When we moved to Pittsburgh we bought a car. It was our first, a secondhand "family" car. It worked for a while, and then things started to go wrong. The brakes failed when I was driving my daughter home from nursery school. The clutch expired when I was all alone in the wilds of northern Iowa. Second gear was nonexistent, and soon the reverse gave out. We continued to drive it for a couple of years, always choosing our parking place carefully so that we could roll out of it if necessary. It was finally just too much to cope with, so we sold it to a junk dealer for a hundred dollars. At that time we couldn't afford another car so we decided to get along without one. To our surprise it was easy. Not just easy—it was positively joyful. We walked more, rode the bus, took taxis when essential, and rented cars for weekend trips. Our children became more independent because Mama was no longer a chauffeur. We had one less incomprehensible mechanical monster to feed and care for.

No one in America today can really afford to operate a private automobile. But few are ready to face that brutal fact. We are only beginning to weigh the true social and economic costs of our commitment to the internal combustion engine. The automobile has dictated our way of life for the last fifty years. Our once proud railroads are now bankrupt derelicts. Home-to-office transportation by subway or trolley has been abandoned in favor of the daily rush hour and the parking headache. Prime farmlands that once produced luxuriant crops of wheat and corn now produce only the noise and stink of a cloverleaf interchange. The sidewalks our children walk to school are crisscrossed by driveways to banks, laundries, and gas stations. Our central cities have decayed as people move to the

371

suburbs, those bedroom communities totally dependent on the automobile: like the Verrazano Narrows Bridge, they don't even have
"pedestrian walkways." The graceful, if elderly, buildings that once
entranced the eye in our great cities have been replaced by the
concrete spirals of parking garages. One reason our streets are "unsafe"
at night is that no one is out walking on them. Why do we demand
that the police get out of their patrol cars and walk the beat again
when most of *us* hop in the car to drive three or four blocks?

For the typical American the automobile is today what it has been
in the past—a symbol of freedom, power, status. Our love affair with
the family car has been analyzed by Vance Packard; the hazards of
driving any car at all proclaimed by Ralph Nader (and confirmed by
the statistics on any holiday weekend). The deadly pollution generated
by the gasoline engine is illustrated periodically by "episodes" in
New York City or Los Angeles. But we now have the highest ratio of
people to cars in the world—about two to one. And the sales pitch is
still strong. Even children brought up in the most environmentally
advanced families talk wistfully of the kind of car they'll buy and
pester their families to teach them to drive.

Reacting to pressure from government regulations and foreign
competition, Detroit is beginning to produce smaller, lighter cars.
But although current advertising manages, sometimes, to mention
the EPA estimates on mpg, the accent is, as always, on comfort,
styling, and "extras." "It is . . . excitingly roadable, expensive-looking,
quiet. . . . makes six people feel very well taken care of. With many
standard amenities, . . . niceties like power windows, power seats
[what in the world are they?], air conditioning and the like." Another
new car is rated superior "on an independent test of styling, riding
comfort and convenience." Its interior "includes deep cushioned
seating, thick 20-oz. cut-pile carpeting. And much more. . . . the
ultimate in luxury for a mid-size automobile." Even the Jeep has
succumbed to the lure of elegance. A recent ad played up luxury and
waffled on the issue of gas consumption: "Never before has such
luxury and comfort been combined with the ultimate in 4-wheel
drive performance. With all these most wanted options, standard:
Rich leather seats, extra thick carpeting, woodgrain trim and . . . gas
mileage that's responsive to the times."

The automobile is a necessity of life to many people, yet it is
marketed as frivolously as shaving cream or paper towels. Who has
the nerve to ask the salesman those gut questions: Will it start when
it's ten below? Will it burst into flame if I'm struck from behind?

What will happen to the front end in a collision at twenty miles an hour? Do you remember to check that the windows can be opened manually? (On the assumption that the buyer will want air conditioning, which reduces fuel efficiency, some cars do not have handles for the rear windows.) We are influenced by the advertising, cowed by the salesman, and yet resentful about the whole transaction. A car is not a good investment—while everyone knows that buying a house is a good way to invest your money, no one points out that buying a car is throwing your money away. And for all that cash, there's no real guarantee that the car will work. They are notoriously unreliable—the digital clock may run, but does the automatic transmission? Detroit has helped to set off America's great surge of confidence and expertise in technology, but it has also contributed to the rise of cynicism. If it takes a repairman half an hour to replace a bulb in a taillight, how can one have confidence in the engineering of the more complex parts of the machine? And now they're talking about putting a computer on the dashboard that will tell you when something in the engine goes wrong. If it's anything like the computers in the Department of Defense that signal a Soviet attack when none has actually been launched, our cynicism will reach new levels.

Since the latest rise in oil and gasoline prices, American car buyers have become increasingly fuel-conscious. Their search for an efficient car has led them into the willing arms of the Japanese and Germans and left Detroit with a fleet of luxurious gas guzzlers and some outmoded advertising. The American auto industry is in trouble, and I'm not shedding any tears. Why should anyone have thought that what was good for General Motors was good for me?

Some day America will admit that the automobile is socially and economically obsolete. We will recognize that it is more important to heat our homes and run our factories than to assure each legal driver his or her personal automobile. The sleek white limousine will no longer be an enviable symbol of wealth and power, but will arouse ridicule and hatred for the greedy aristocrat who flaunts his disdain for the common good. I have my own scenario for the energy-short future. Our great urban conglomerates will break up into smaller townships as the population relocates, each worker wanting to live within walking, bicycling, or short bus-trip distance of his or her job. Neighborhoods will become friendlier because people will be visible on the streets, not just walking from front door to car door, but passing other people's homes on their way to the grocery, the movies, or the corner drugstore. They might even wave and say Hi as they pass by. We will once again know our neighbors by name, and the people we love will live around the corner, not across the continent. The houses themselves will be altered. Not only by the solar energy panels on the roof, but by the vegetable gardens front and back as people learn that it's cheaper and tastier to grow your own. Instead of bulging air conditioners that disfigure the windows and blast hot air on already overheated pedestrians, we'll rediscover natural, silent, clean ways to keep cool—shutters, perhaps, or trees. There will be more people in these houses, too. As fuel costs rise and commuting becomes unfeasible, our spatial requirements will change. Two or three people in a ten-room house will become economically and socially unacceptable. Those big old houses built when the burning of coal was unregulated and inexhaustible will once again house multigenerational families, communes, various co-operative arrangements of people eager to break out of the isolation and expense of the single-family dwelling.

We need not worry about revitalizing the centers of our cities. It will happen inevitably as fuel gives out and we are forced to live where we work. There will still be a few cars on the street, too. They will be small, economical vehicles used by the community for essential or emergency trips. Or they may be larger vehicles that will take the children to school or the elderly to a bingo game.

Of course there's an automobile in our future. But the way we use it, and the extent to which we allow it to dictate the pattern of our lives, will have to change.

STEPHEN W. WHITE

ENERGY, AUTOMOBILES, AND
THE QUALITY OF LIFE

At the risk of sounding like an "ad rep" for Mobil Oil, I want to challenge two theses frequently argued as a popular pastime among intellectuals recently. The first thesis is that there is no discernible or necessary connection between the level of energy consumption of a nation, culture, or civilization and its quality of life. (See George BaSalla, "The Fallacy of the Energy-Civilization Equation," *Saturday Review*, November 24, 1979.) The second thesis is that the demise of the automobile *will not result* in an appreciable decline in the quality of life for people in industrialized nations. Both of these theses have been defended with some degree of plausibility. However, we should certainly examine the intellectual roots of these newly emerging myths before we accept them tree, branch, and leaf.

These are myths fostered by a small band of intellectuals, mostly historians who love the past, art collectors who profit handsomely from the added esteem of things past, and some university professors who make their living from preserving the past. This group of intellectuals, upon superficial analysis, insists that there have been entire cultures, civilizations, and peoples who have been *as civilized as any of our contemporaries* while consuming much less energy and driving no cars. These denizens of the distant past achieved a level of culture unsurpassed in history without GM, Henry Ford, or Chrysler-Plymouth. Without Harvey Firestone, B. F. Goodrich, or Charles Goodyear. And they could have sustained this superior level of culture without BART, METRO, or AMTRAK. Without Lockheed, Boeing, or McDonnell-Douglas.

After all, so the argument goes, did not Homer thrive in the Hellenic period without an electric typewriter powered by Edison Electric? Socrates' philosophical ideas were spread far and wide without any assistance from satellite-transmission technology. Plato preserved in written form a tradition in philosophy without the assistance of so much as a Gutenberg press. And did not Socrates,

Plato, and Aristotle succeed in defining and classifying the legitimate parameters of philosophy for the succeeding 2,000 years without IBM computers, computer languages, or data bases?

Are we not still finding new meanings in the plays of Sophocles, Aristophanes, and Euripides—even though the audiences for which these plays were originally written had not so much as the luxury of a gas-powered rickshaw in which to travel to and from plays? The quality of life—the enjoyment of the things that really matter—will not be affected by the demise of the automobile and the decline in per capita energy consumption. We can still enjoy Shakespeare's *King Lear*, Chekhov's *The Cherry Orchard*, and Ibsen's *Hedda Gabler*. Durer's *Death and the Devil*, Monet's *Le Jardin de l'enfante*, and Van Gogh's *Starry Night* will remain stirring monuments to artistic achievement for centuries to come. And Goethe's *Faust*, Dostoyevsky's *Crime and Punishment*, and Thoreau's *Walden* will be read when the automobile goes the way of buggy-whip technology. Life will still be rich with cultural offerings. The world's monuments to Eternity—the cathedrals in Chartres, Venice, Rheims, and Paris— will still stand as lasting achievements to spiritual devotion. Since there is no necessary connection between energy consumption and civilization, the coming of the postpetroleum age and the demise of the automobile will not signal a significant decline in the quality of life.

That such arguments are often given by cultural champions who prefer Shakespeare to saunas, Beethoven to beachcombing or the Bahamas, or live plays and concerts to Home Box Office flicks and the "Boston Pops" is not to the point. The point is that this contention may, quite simply, be wrong. Energy abundance has allowed us to enjoy the trivial adjuncts of technology. In many cases these adjuncts have merely extended the range of *material* alternatives available for satisfying our craving for novelty. But I would like to argue that something far more fundamental has been made possible by energy abundance and by the automobile. Both have enhanced the quality of life by practically all measures.

The quality of life includes more than cultural offerings. Certainly the Environmental Protection Agency and the Office of Technology Assessment are predicated upon this assumption. To assume that "the quality of life" is a concept skewed in favor of high culture is a common mistake among intellectuals who believe that common folk identify it with material things while they (intellectuals) identify it with things spiritual.

But quality of life is measured by a number of indices not all of which are easy to defend or to quantify:

cultural diversity	adequate income levels
absence of sexism, racism	long life span
absence of ageism	leisure
health	travel
access to open space	educational opportunity
adequate nutrition	novelty
physical activity	freedom of movement
literacy	employment
periodic holidays	enjoyment of basic rights
environmental quality	

While it may be true that a society can enjoy high literacy levels, cultural diversity, adequate health and nutrition, etc., without following a pattern of extremely *high energy consumption*, I think that it is unreasonable to think that a society can provide a lot of travel, leisure, and high income for all of its members without a *reasonably high level of energy consumption*. How would one travel? It is an open question whether public transportation can be made more efficient than the automobile, and certainly public transportation presently requires equivalent amounts of energy to move people. Bicycles and mopeds are more efficient, but how many people prefer to attend the Met on a Moped?

Energy has served ideals of a nonmaterial nature. Equality of access to health care, to education, and to culture would not be possible without energy-driven transportation. That we frequently choose not to allow certain groups equality of access to the good life is another question. Busing would not be an issue in a postpetroleum world. Of course, the ever-present urban sprawl which promoted opportunities for "white flight" would not have been possible in a petroleum-poor society either. It is not the automobile which creates our problems. Rather, it is our decision to build an entire civilization around the automobile which amplifies existing problems. The modest amount of progress we have made in eliminating sexism in our society, in industry, and even in the home, is as much attributable to an energy-hungry technology which has virtually abolished all distinctions between "male" and "female" job places as to antidiscrimination laws. The practical elimination of malnutrition and hunger in the USA was made possible by high-technology agriculture. It is true that we could distribute wealth more equally and perhaps promote an equally satisfying life for all in a less energy-intensive way. This might be done worldwide as well. However, I think that we should not fall into the easy intellectual trap of assuming that because certain measures of the quality of life require vast energy inputs for their realization for all peoples that these measures therefore ought to be stricken from our lists of ingredients of the good life. Just because we find the vision of every citizen's driving a Cadillac repulsive, we should not assume that the automobile's absence will not detract from the quality of life. To take away the automobile—even with alternative modes of transportation available—will diminish freedom of movement, of travel, and of access to culture for the affluent and the near-poor. High technology has made it possible to distribute high culture to the masses—even if it has not always been distributed equally. We should never forget that.

NOTES FROM THE PLAGUE PLANET

thru the spring & summer
in spite of terrible odds
a host of plants
chicory queen anne's lace asters
twitch grass knotweed jewelweed
spring up again & again
tho most respectable folk
devote much time & energy
to cutting them down
poisoning them
sealing them under
with a mixture called "blacktop"
which creates a smooth surface
which with constant resealing
is more or less impervious
to living growth

another apotropaic ceremony
their most popular
is to have themselves carried
by wheeled machines
(often totemically named
after extinct predators)

they construct special ditches
for this ceremony called "freeways"
in reference of course
to the detachment from sensual experience
that is sought in these rites

the ditches are lined with a kind of
artificial stone & are made as uniform
& featureless as possible

an impoverished visual environment
is the ideal grey walls grey floor
grey sky & sets of
constantly attention demanding
straight unbroken or dashed lines

this set of remarkably acutalized abstractions
(note the telling irony of "concrete"
the name for the artificial stone)
is the largest object
of purely ceremonial nature
ever constructed
on the planet
for the delusion
(the derivation of which remains obscure)
that reducing the complexity
of one's sensory experience will
ward off the plague
is nearly unanimously believed
throughout the plague planet

indeed it is applied across
the entire sensual spectrum
so that equally elaborate
technico-social assemblages exist
for reducing the range & variety
of audial
tactile
olfactory
& gustatory
input
as well as visual input
as in the "freeway" and "blacktop"
examples
already described

a common fantasy
hints at the essential role
in the aetiology of the plague
of the confusion
between metaphor & reality

the inhabitants insist
that when one is being carried
in one of their wheeled machines
one is "moving"

all who contemplate working on the plague problem
are warned
that to contradict this fantasy
or even to attempt to subject it
to rational analysis
will invariably evoke
a defensive reaction
the "take my legs but leave me my wheels syndrome"
in effect a retreat
to a yet more severe level
of reality denial

EDWARD MORIN

FILLING STATION

Night miles force us to a self-serve
where florescents arc from yardarms.
Near the pumps we join a cluster
who pretend to bump one another
like fish in an overcrowded tank.

In this all-night diner for cars
a tousled blear-eyed couple hug theirs,
two smoking serious drinkers idle,
a thin stetsoned pimp kills time,
and the youth in the plastic cage deals.

Digital numbers click off gallons
of extinct ferns, fossilized ginkgoes,
prevertebrates battered by cracking
processes—all distant ancestors
of ours gurgling their final rage

before cremation. Myriad
internal combustion dinosaurs
line up to guzzle what remains.
They inch forth for heat and light,
waiting for their time slot to expire.

DANIEL L. GUILLORY

STAR WARS STYLE AND AMERICAN AUTOMOBILES*

If, through the magic of time travel, an anthropologist of the future had descended upon the American scene in the summer of 1982, he or she might have slipped quickly into the appropriate tribal dress (Calvin Klein jeans, Nike shoes, and a knit shirt with a curious little alligator embroidered on the breast), and, in search of authentic totems and artifacts, examined the ubiquitous face of a tiny electronic goblin, whose yellow pie-shaped presence glowed and glided through electronic mazes, alternately pursued by and pursuing Blinky, Pinky, Inky, and Clyde. As Pac Man ingested his opponents, he regularly emitted a distinctive electronic whoop, *whaaa, whaaa, whaaa.* Our visiting scientist, skulking about cities and suburbs, would have heard Pac Man wailing in shopping centers, super-markets, shopping malls, and drugstores. Children's T-shirts, greeting cards, napkins, and toys echoed the Pac Man theme; the little creature was everywhere like a *deus loci*, the god of the place. Our friend from the future would be entering these data in some tiny hand-held recording device, part-computer, part-video recorder, perhaps concluding that his future had begun, thus, on a video terminal in 1982.

This love affair with imaginary electronic beings and futuristic modes of transportation would be underscored by a visit to the local Cinerama, where a revolutionary kind of movie was being screened. *Tron*, the latest production of the Disney studios, was a milestone of animation in much the way that earlier classics, like *Steamboat Willie* (1928) and *Fantasia* (1940), had been in their days. For *Tron* was a masterwork of computer-assisted animation, an electronic calculus in which depth, motion, and perspective were created on minute digital grids, capable of every shading and positioning. The result was a stunning visual illusion that expanded our notions of travel and move-

*A paper presented at a Detroit Historical Society-sponsored conference on "The Automobile and American Culture," October 1, 1982.

383

ment and that literally turned light energy, the ultimate power source, into a perfectly tuned vehicle, the "light cycle." In the most memorable sequence from the film, Flynn, the human hero who has been "sucked" into the computer on a laser beam (after he was "deconstructed" into tiny modules) joins forces with two computer programs, represented as iridescent humanoids, named "Tron" and "Ram." This unlikely trio is forced to climb aboard futuristic motorcycles called "light cycles" and participate in a breathtaking race for life on a giant electronic grid which the Master Control Program has instantly "rezzed up" for its diabolical amusement. The Master Control has virtually an infinite number of "byts" at its disposal and the awesome power to rearrange and redefine the contours of space within its electronic domain. The light cycles *are* light: they move with an Einsteinian smoothness over the surface of the grid, making incredible stops, passes, and ninety-degree turns with the perfect accuracy of a laser beam. In spite of its somewhat lame script and relatively poor gate receipts (after all, *E.T.* was playing next door), *Tron* made a profound statement about the radical reshaping of vehicular movement that is occurring right under our feet. The implications of *Tron* are staggering, offering artistic clues and visual metaphors that we are surely moving out of the age of mechanical motion, with its clumsy mechanical controls and fossil fuels, into the age of electronic motion, with its computer guidance and the infinitely sustainable energy of light.

Americans, as a people, have always engaged in a subtle dialogue with space and time as part of their national upbringing: they crossed oceans, rivers, mountains, and prairies, harnessing energies and mastering barges, steamboats, buckboards, locomotives, and those rickety contraptions, part bicycle/part buggy, that passed for automobiles at the turn of the century. This dialogue has been a unique feature of our national profile, accounting for such artifacts as Roebling's Brooklyn Bridge, the Wright Brothers' biplane, Henry Ford's "999" racing car, and Goddard's swooshing backyard rockets. What is new and exciting but still imperfectly understood about this dialogue is the curious exchange now taking place between fantasy and reality. We live and design our vehicles as if we were *already* in the future, as if laser-powered vehicles, time travel, "warp" drives, and megacomputers were already commercial realities. The video terminals, whether we find them in arcades or in the family recreation room, are allowing us to suspend our disbelief and enter the realm of electronic movement; that is to say, these machines and their programmed games have become the gates of our future.

So the Atari becomes part of our domestic life and simultaneously part of our mental life—a totem object on many different levels. So we can enter a video arcade and "play" Pac Man, Ms. Pac Man, Asteroids, Galaxion, Zaxxon, Missle Command, Turbo, or F-1. The common denominators of all such games are the video terminals and their computer programs, assisted by computer graphics and microchips that propel imaginary space vehicles and weaponry across a lighted field. The young man next to me is wearing unlaced jogging shoes and an utterly rapt expression as he jockeys Pac Man through the chutes and mazes. The little girl in F-1 takes a Formula One/Grand Prix racing car through incredible bends and hairpin turns, alternately pumping brake and accelerator, hitting the guardrail, and racking up an all-time high score. The distinction between the past and the future is blurred into oblivion here; the windshield and video screen fuse into one. Fantasy becomes vividly real, and, even in an age of inflation, a trip to the stars can be had for the small change in your pocket.

This new world of buzzes, blips, and beeps is part of a cluster of objects that have intruded themselves into the most personal crevices of our daily life, items like LCD watches and digital clocks, microwave ovens, pocket calculators, and a series of slick television commercials for Ford Escorts and Quasar television sets. Those commercials were noteworthy for the high quality of their production and the use of futuristic sets, emphasized by the presence of Leonard Nimoy, in a modified version of his Dr. Spock disguise from *Star Trek*. That "space opera" may be the most important cultural artifact in this dialogue with space because it domesticated space and created a whole new language to describe it.

When *Star Trek* was first beamed over the television screens in 1966, no one suspected that it would become a video classic. Years later, *Star Trek* is still going strong with reruns, "Trekkie" conventions, sales of memorabilia and, most significantly, with the persistence of the space jargon it pioneered. The male crew members dressed in pointed boots and pajamalike uniforms while the ladies wore space miniskirts, and they defended themselves with "phasers"; the ship itself warded off the attacks of Klingons and Romulans with "photon torpedoes." Telekinesis was achieved with an electronic "transporter," and the routine command, "Beam me up, Scotty" became a catch phrase for the devoted fans. The ship's computer, outfitted with a sultry feminine voice, contained "data banks" on every conceivable subject, while Dr. McCoy's "sick bay" sported a collection of weird electronic scalpels and diagnostic equipment capable of reviving even the moribund spacemen. But the focal point and nerve center of the mythical *U.S.S. Enterprise* was the bridge, under the command of Captain James T. Kirk, played by William Shatner.

Oh, the bridge of the *Enterprise!* What a stupendous assortment of widgets, screens, dials, switches, and lights! Sitting in his overstuffed chair, Captain Kirk becomes the ultimate pilot, the supreme space driver as he maneuvers his ship through black holes, asteroids, tractor beams, and enemy torpedoes. The bridge is dominated by a vast screen that magnifies the starry space surrounding the ship. Here, reality is what appears on the screen; there is nothing else to "see." The *Enterprise* redefines space at the same time that it redefines movement as Captain Kirk throws the big ship into "warp drive," until the ship, moving through "Warp Factor One, Two . . ." and so forth gradually approaches the speed of light, and, in fact, achieves it, thus slowing "time" in a way that Albert Einstein had so accurately forecast. Before the NASA Space Program had put men on the moon, before the *Columbia* space shuttle had lifted off the ground, and at a time when the Vietnam War was appearing in vivid colors on the nightly news, *Star Trek* invaded the living rooms of America and inculcated a new love for space, for speed, and for electronic technology that would open "the final frontier," as Captain Kirk solemnly called it at the opening of each week's episode.

Only two years later, in 1968, Stanley Kubrick, in collaboration with Arthur C. Clarke, would offer the definitive film on space, *2001: A Space Odyssey.* Visually and thematically, *2001* was infinitely more complex than the *Star Trek* series that preceded it. The special effects, alone, established a level that has not really been equaled in any subsequent film. If *Star Trek* provided the verbal language for space fantasies, then *2001* offered the visual text, a sublime coordination of models, filters, painted mattes and mirrors that, taken as a whole, enchanted and elevated the viewer (who was literally unprepared for what flashed across the screen). For our purposes, the most important sequence occurs after Dr. Heywood Floyd has left the giant orbiting wheel known as Space Station One and boarded the Aries-1B lunar carrier on his way to the Clavius Base on the surface of the moon. We ride inside the lunar carrier, which is suffused with an eerie green light. We are looking over the backs of the pilot and copilot and a marvelous computer console that monitors every aspect of the shuttle's flight, printing out instantaneous coordinates and providing gyroscopic guidelines for effecting a perfect landing. At a time, then, when Americans were plagued by snags and snafus of planned obsolescence, from toasters to televisions, here was a piece of perfect technology that was not only efficient—it was beautiful! Here was an object lesson in computer guidance, which had long been used in rockets and satellites, now applied to a small-scaled, manned vehicle. In ten short years after the making of that film, computers would be designing automobiles, while guiding the robots that weld, spray, and align them, later controlling internal components like carburetion and the metering of fuel. Consoles would feature clocks, radio dials, and even fuel gauges and speedometers that used LCD or LED components.

By the time *Star Wars* appeared in 1977, the language of space travel and computer guidance had become a virtual *lingua franca*, enabling us to participate in common fantasies like Spielberg's *Close Encounters of the Third Kind* or the sporadic but predictable outbreaks of UFO sightings. *Star Wars* did for the movie audience what *Star Trek* had done for the television viewers: it made space accessible and glamorous and, hence, all the more seductive. By the time *Star Wars* appeared on the cultural scene, the basic groundwork had been laid, a common language of fantasy had been introduced and articulated, and *Star Wars* was able to absorb the successes of its predecessors so well that it could afford to include a love story, a mythical story line ("A long time ago in a galaxy far, far away . . ."), and two anthropomorphic robots (See-Threepio and Artoo-Detoo). Han Solo's spaceship, the *Millennium Falcon*, is a rather familiar craft, even though it goes into "hyperspace" instead of "warp factors." And the "X-wing" fighters have cockpit instrumentation that was lifted right off the lunar shuttle in *2001*. *Star Wars* outdid its predecessors in one significant way, however: it elaborated the sense of *being inside* a space vehicle; it gave us an artistic approximation of a space ride, the pinnacle of joy riding, especially in the spectacular sequence where Luke Skywalker pilots his X-wing through the tunneled surface of Darth Vader's Death Star and manually shoots a "proton torpedo" into the exhaust port of the larger vessel. Luke's X-wing is guided by electronic gyroscopes and computer printouts first used in *2001*. The exhilaration in this sequence doesn't arise from the intricacy of the gizmos but from the pitching and yawing of the ride itself, that snug, dangerous feeling of being in a tight cockpit pursued

closely by enemy fighters where one is likely to crash against surrounding walls at any moment. It was interesting to see Clint East-
wood virtually duplicate this scene in his film *Firefox*, where we also
sense the internal space of the cockpit and its fingertip controls.

All these metaphors of high-speed travel in outer space are crucial
to our designing of internal space in contemporary automobiles. The
way they corner and steer, assisted by front-wheel drive and lower
centers of gravity, the way they absorb bumps and cling to the roadway, helped here by MacPherson Struts and air dams and spoilers, all
these engineering changes add up to a new dialogue with space and
distance. Cars, after all, are ways of addressing space, and the newest
ones rolling off the production lines are closer in feeling to the lunar
shuttle in *2001* or the X-wing fighters in *Star Wars* than to any other
artifacts in our culture. In their silent contact with the surrounding
environment and in their mathematically designed interiors with
warning lights, flashers, and light-emitting diodes, they are the clos-
est most of us will ever come to space travel. They have become the
spaceships of our fantasies and our films, and they are available on
forty-eight-month loans for a "mere" 12 percent interest.

As far as I can determine, no one has written a definitive history of
internal vehicular space, the particular feelings, "ride" characteristics,
and suspension qualities of automobiles. Although we may remember
the general shape of the cars we have loved and owned, or even little
details like the emblem or the lettering of the instruments, what stays
with us permanently, I believe, is a depth perception of the ride
itself, the actual *experience* of driving that vehicle in snow, rain, or
mud, up mountain grades and over flat prairies, on winter mornings
at twenty below, and on summer afternoons in the high nineties.

In 1949, when I was five years old, my grandfather took me for my
first ride in his 1929 Model A, a rigidly sprung black box that bounced
along the dirt roads while its little four-banger coughed hoarsely. I
remember the Spartan, no-nonsense ambiance of that little black car,
virtually stripped of upholstery or chrome, with a dashboard that truly
looked like a black board divided by a small ovoid plate on which the
rudimentary gauges were nestled. This Ford was a farmer's car, and it
was meant to work as hard as anything else on the place. My grandfather had been its only mechanic, body man, and driver for twenty
years, and the Model A seemed to understand its role in a rather rough
scheme of things. Its angularity and hardness (rectangular window
openings, pointed door handles, vertical windshield) stood as a kind of
defiance to a world of tropical heat, dust storms, hurricanes, and

yellow clay ruts that deepened in the spring rains and hardened into canyonlike troughs by summer. I can still hear that old car coughing, and in my bones I feel the bumpiness of those dusty roads that bounced me up and down on the seats until my head made the first of many contacts with the steel roof above. I think that is how I earned a permanent soft spot for automobiles.

Certainly, I had a weakness for my neighbor's 1939 Packard, which we all regarded as a museum piece that was somehow ours. Maroon in color and as long as a yacht, it had a high, vertical feeling and made me think I was in an old-fashioned railway car. That Packard had the armor plating of a Sherman tank and the constitution of a Caterpillar tractor. It accelerated at a glacial pace, but once it achieved highway speeds, it fairly hummed. I made many trips to the ocean in that old gunboat, deep-sea fishing gear streaming out of the rear windows, and the bustle-shaped trunk loaded with Coke bottles iced down in galvanized tubs. I nearly sobbed when the Packard disappeared and a 1957 Dodge took its coveted place. Of course, I was seduced by those crazy tailfins and the push-button drive, but the Dodge seemed hollow and insubstantial, a two-tone imitation in cheap sheet metal that would never compare with the solid steel of the old Packard.

Those old heavy sedans mashed out the undulations of the roughest roads by dint of their sheer weight, like my best friend's 1950 Buick Roadmaster, a slick beauty with massive chrome bumpers, portholes in the fenders, and a hearse-black finish built up from dozens of coats of hand-rubbed lacquer. The Buick had oversized balloon tires that made wonderful sibilant noises on pavements wet or dry. Its huge cavernous interior was taken up by sofalike seats with deep, pleated cushions. The straight-eight engine produced amazing bursts of acceleration in that black behemoth, and it rode like a railway car adhering to invisible grooves in the surface of the road. Underfoot, the old Dynaflow transmission hummed in gallons of oil, and gentle centrifugal pressures pushed the passenger into the back of the overstuffed seats as the Buick settled into cruising range. You didn't drive the Buick; you ran it like an engineer, you sounded the horn in fair warning, and you prayed that other vehicles stayed off your track. That strange combination of immense body weight and cushiony seats gave the driver a heady sense of luxury and power: the Roadmaster lived up to its proud name, indulging every whim of a driver intoxicated by the power to move such a massive thing with delicate precision.

The Model A, the Packard, and the Roadmaster were all cars of the past. My first encounter with the cars of the present occurred on a wintry day in 1975 at a huge foreign car dealership in suburban St. Louis. I had driven there in my rather quaint Volvo station wagon for the express purpose of eyeballing the new Triumph TR-7, heralded in newspaper and magazine advertisements as "the wedge," or "the shape of things to come." The salesman for this aerodynamic marvel looked as if he had just stepped out of a disco. In spite of near blizzard conditions, his shirt was unbuttoned to the waist, and various chains and medallions jangled around his throat. He didn't say anything at first, just smiled and lightly pirouetted around the car, as if he had finally found a suitable dance partner. His was the softest sell I've ever encountered. Bopping over in my direction, he casually slipped the keys in my hand as if they were jewelry and delivered himself of one solemn opinion. Sketching the shape of the car with his mobile hands, he asked rhetorically, "Doesn't it look like a jet? Even standing still, doesn't it look like a jet?" Was he trying to tell me that it could fly, or that I would *feel* as if I were flying? As I entered the compact interior, I could sense the dynamics of the little vehicle, its spear-point design that pushed the sharp nose down and raised the hind quarters proudly in the air. The wedge accelerated like a turbine, and the front-wheel drive gave that Triumph an uncanny rock-like stability as I nudged it up the icy ramps of the expressway or floored it on the boulevards. The seats seemed more like the ejection seats of military jets, and the cramped interior with console and overhead lamps seemed more like a cockpit. When I parked it in the dealer's hangar, that is, showroom, I felt a profound depression overtake me, and my Volvo, parked in a snowbank, looked dowdy and hopelessly middle class. It might have been a white mule harnessed to an ice wagon.

The Triumph TR-7 came to mind again when, armed with a press pass, I studied the delights of the 1979 Chicago Automobile Show, a kind of automotive smorgasbord held annually in the huge enclosure of McCormick Place. An experimental Japanese car was on display, a wedge to out-wedge all others. It sported a fiberglass body, plexiglass windows, and gull-wing doors that popped overhead like those of the old Mercedes Gull-Wing sports car. The seats sloped backward at such a rakish angle that one literally lay down in the cockpit, surrounded by speakers, ventilation ducts, diodes, flashers, and warning lights. This brilliant red wedge was equipped with various laser-activated sensing devices that "read" and interpreted the immediate and long-distance conditions of the road surface as well as the density of the traffic. The price tag read $50,000, which seemed steep even in the inflationary spiral of our era! What was this car, exactly? Was it a dream machine like the specially outfitted numbers that 007 drove across the screen in the James Bond sagas? Was it another version of Luke Skywalker's X-wing? Or was it still another tangible piece of evidence that the contemporary automobile is a fusion of fact and fantasy, part dream machine and part inheritor of various technologies that intersect and overlap in the design and production of the vehicle?

In the decade or so before World War I, rickety automobiles and flickering movies came into their own and might be called the dominant technologies of the Edwardian period—certainly they were the most visible. Since the films and Tin Lizzies appeared virtually at the same time, it is hardly surprising that many of the earliest films are unthinkable without automobiles, especially in Mack Sennett's Keystone Kops, whose zany car chases, wrecks, near misses, and gargantuan pileups are classic examples of automotive humor. It is clear that Mack Sennett saw the automobile as a funny and fascinating object that everyone would want to see, and all the great stars of the silent era used automobiles as integral components of complex comic situations. The other technology that appeared in this period was the liquefaction of gas, at first used for vacuum flasks on Edwardian picnics and later applied by the young American Robert Goddard in the manufacture of rockets. The story of rocketry reaches its first climax at Peenemünde on the Baltic, where German scientists like Wernher von Braun created the V-2 rocket. But rockets and space travel were on the screen long before they became part of newsreels or the six o'clock news on the family television screen. As early as 1902 Georges Méliès made his little classic, *A Trip to the Moon*, a film which was sixty-seven years ahead of its time! And three years later, in 1905, an English filmmaker named R. W. Paul made an animated film called *The Motorist* in which a motorist in duster, goggles, and driving cap steers his open touring car around the rings of Saturn. Since that little film was made over seventy-five years ago, it offers graphic proof of the interdependence and cross-fertilization of these three technologies. We saw it on the screen, we lived it in our fantasy lives, and then we tried to buy it from a local dealer. Cinema, automobiles, and space travel have been thrown together like siblings who can never outlive their family resemblances and influences.

Exactly eighty years separate *Tron* from Méliès's *Trip to the Moon*, but the dialogue with space and the future never ceased during those eighty years; more significantly, that dialogue continues today. During the late forties and early fifties, we watched as the beautiful classic jets were produced, models like the Starfighter and the F-85. At the same time the V-2 was evolving into ever-larger forms, always pencil-shaped and neatly finned. Perhaps it was inevitable, then, that those first vestigial fins, little teardrops on the rear fenders, began to appear on the postwar Cadillacs until they expanded into the soaring sheet metal of the late fifties and early sixties, like the manta-ray wings that formed the rear deck of the 1959 Chevrolet or the outrageous sharklike dorsal fins on the Chryslers and DeSotos of the same period. *Star Wars* style has been with us for over two decades, taking different forms, and like genes the style is recessive in some individuals and dominant in others. The fins died slowly, or perhaps they just went underground. Those "slab-sided" cars of the early seventies (e.g., the Ford LTDs) tucked the fins into folds and swellings of the fenders. Although the main influence in the new cars may occur in the feeling of internal space and the diode-studded consoles, I must observe that, seen in profile, all those wedge-shaped cars (like the new Chevrolet Celebrity) have sharp pointed snouts and flaring rear ends that surely remind *me* of fins.

Yet all those early "space cars," the fully finned sedans (like the 1957 Chevrolet) were rather vulgar in their symbolism, vulgar but not necessarily ugly. In their design they amounted to crude representations of the myth of outer space; those cars were loud and childlike in their enthusiasm for the starry worlds beyond. Today's vehicles, like the X-cars and K-cars, have a cool, professional air. Their interpretation of the space theme is more profound because the paradigms for vehicular travel in outer space have become a hundred or even a thousand times more complex. NASA, *Star Trek*, and *Star Wars* have allowed us to dream in technicolor and Dolby sound, as it were, after generations of silent black and white. We now have real astronauts (Glenn, Armstrong) and imaginary ones (Spock, Skywalker) to suggest the frigid beauty of space travel, its silence, its smoothness, its computer-driven swiftness and precision. And we want those values to carry over in the design of our automobiles. We demand a soundproofed, climate-controlled, hermetically sealed environment with all the appointments of the imaginary *U.S.S. Enterprise*. With catalytic converters, plastic undercoating, and P-metric radial tires, these cars are refined and obedient, down to their signal-seeking radios. Technologically, they belong to a new generation of cars that are wedge-shaped, front-wheel driven, and powered by transversely mounted engines, with computer chips monitoring and regulating the consumption of fuel. We have come a long way from the "muscle cars" and "gas hogs" of the late sixties and early seventies. Yet it is where we are *going* and *how* we get there which interest me the most.

In his book *Zen and the Art of Motorcycle Maintenance*, Robert Pirsig compares the experience of riding a motorcycle with that of driving a closed sedan. In the car we are insulated from the environment, whereas on the bike we are thrust head first into the winds, smells, and temperatures of the living environment. In space, there is no "environment" as such, so the ideal space vehicle is the one that most effectively insulates us from the vast, airless, space outside. And I believe that our cars are approximating this ideal with every succeeding year, not merely because our environment has become poisoned, not merely because our cities are more dangerous, but because on the level of our imaginations we crave the vastness and mystery of outer space. The interface where inner and outer space make contact is the windshield, a kind of television screen, not unlike the giant visual screen on the *Enterprise.*

Space is deeper and sexier than anything we can imagine: it has preoccupied the great minds of our civilization from Plato to Newton to Einstein. It is our privilege or curse to be the first generation living in a dual existence, one foot planted firmly on earth, the other on the threshold of space. In less than a century we have created the enabling technologies to make space travel possible. The *Columbia* shuttle has dramatically proven the feasibility of multipurpose vehicles that can cross the magic threshold—and return. The youngsters in the video arcades are already there, and when they buy cars, we should cater to their expectations. We had better offer them the vehicles they are *already* controlling on thousands of video terminals. When these youngsters become old men and women, laser light and star light may have become the highways and beacons of an entirely new age. Who knows how long these changes will take? Who can doubt that they are surely coming? We may, any day now, climb into the old family bus and take off for the stars.

VI. HISTORIOGRAPHY

ROBERT C. ACKERSON

SOME MILESTONES OF
AUTOMOTIVE LITERATURE

Literature examining and evaluating the impact of the automobile on American life has never been wanting; in fact, it appeared coeval with the car itself and evolved along the same lines as the product it described. Early views were almost always laudatory, although Lewis Mumford presciently warned in 1926 that trouble was on the way. But at a time when the American businessman was a national hero (think of Sinclair Lewis's Dodsworth), and the corporation regarded as a modern blessing, most commentaries remained favorable, if not fawning. The Great Depression swept away a lot of that optimism, and even more of it has disappeared in the last twenty years. The huge size and depersonalized nature of many automobile firms have made them easy targets of contemporary critics, and new priorities in the culture at large have provoked increasing criticism of the automobile itself. It may be useful to discuss some works from the 1970s which recapitulate the century-old arguments about the nature and function of the horseless carriage.

John B. Rae's *The Road and The Car in America* (The M. I. T. Press, 1971) not only traces the development of roads and highways in the U.S., his ostensible subject, but also challenges the chief complaints made by the car's detractors up to 1970. He has a large field to cover. There is Woodrow Wilson's famous lament that the automobile would stimulate Socialism by "inciting the poor to envy the possessions of the rich." "In this attitude," Rae comments, "Mr. Wilson was reflecting the frequent propensity of the intellectual to express his concerns for the common man by undertaking to determine what the common man should go without." Rae makes the essential point that the car, because it has been "an instrument of social revolution," has in fact benefited "ordinary people" more than it has increased the prosperity of the rich. Whether the result was Socialism, as some now claim, or an enhanced form of democracy, the social effects have been positive.

Rae also answers critics who blame the car for congested cities, a breakdown in moral values, and the destruction of rural landscapes and wilderness. He concedes that the car intensified urban congestion but tries to balance present-day traffic problems with evidence that before the car arrived there was substantial urban congestion in all large cities, even in ancient Rome. It is the city and not the car which is the culprit, for "congestion will remain as long as economic and other activities are concentrated in a limited central city area." As to whether the car stimulated moral degeneracy, Rae first notes the obvious: it is impossible to accurately determine if people really are less moral than in the distant past. Recent scholarship on the sexual habits of "the other Victorians," for example, suggests that hedonism was not invented at the turn of the century, nor did business practices in America during The Gilded Age remain untouched by the iniquities we associate with, say, General Motors (see below). If changes did take place, for example in church attendance, the car can hardly be isolated as the primary culprit when so many other social patterns were also experiencing revision. It must be remembered that the car could take people to church as well as away from it. (In fact, automobile advertising of the early period depicted both nuclear and extended families using a car to travel to church.)

Many historians have been comfortable with the view that the automobile, since it supports the American preference for mobility and individuality, accommodates and manifests some of our most basic social values. Rae accepts this position. "Freedom of movement," he notes, "provides greater opportunities for both work and play, as well as a wider choice of places to live. . . . [The motor car] offers individual, personal mobility, as nothing before it has ever done, and as nothing else now available can do." On this latter point he is supported by a report on transportation prepared by Cornell University, which concluded that "the automobile itself is so exasperatingly convenient that it drives the transportation inventors almost mad trying to devise competitive substitutes." The idea that unfettered mobility ought *not* to be a primary American cultural value does not occur to Rae; he would categorize it with Wilson's prescription for the lower classes as a form of snobbery. Nevertheless the idea will gain strength among automotive historians in the 1970s, as we shall see.

Finally, Rae disputes the view that cars are ravishers of open space and despoilers of natural beauty. He points out that such an assumption "ignores the elementary point that the situation is an unavoidable consequence of a massive growth in population." He maintains that most of our existing roads would have been built (obviously in different form) even if cars didn't exist. He cites a useful fact in this regard: in 1920 nearly ninety million acres or 5 percent of the total land area of the United States was given over to the growing of feed for mules and horses. Today the need for this commodity requires under eight million acres. As a result, "by replacing the horse, the automobile has released for other purposes almost four times as much land as is occupied by the entire highway system."

Like most social scientists, Rae recognizes that no other invention of the twentieth century has affected our manners, customs, and living habits as has the automobile. But "trying to evaluate the impact of the automobile on American life seems like an exercise in measuring the immeasurable." All revolutions have both pleasant and unpleasant features to them and those wrought by the motorcar, at this moment in history, may seem to lean heavily toward the unfortunate. Yet Rae stands firmly by four propositions that summarize the dominant view of the automobile, by historians and public alike, for most of this century: 1) "It goes without saying that any society is better off for having better roads." 2) "The growth of the highway system has been due to the fact that it has filled . . . needs better than anything else that has appeared so far." 3) "Freedom of movement provides greater opportunities for both work and play, as well as a wider choice of places to live." 4) "The Road and the Car together have an enormous capacity for promoting economic growth, raising standards of living, and creating a good society. The challenge before us is to implement this capacity."

If Rae's book represents the majority opinion till 1971, another book which appeared in that year suggested ominously that nay-saying would soon become the fashion. Kenneth R. Schneider's *Autokind vs. Mankind* (Norton, 1971), is "positive" only in the sense that it reads like an automobilized version of Marxism, complete with redemptive vision at the end. On the far side of the rainbow Schneider finds not the proverbial pot of gold but a de-automobilized utopia in the tradition of Edward Bellamy. In this brave new world the city dweller has no need of cars, for his food and material needs are conveyed to him by a network of underground delivery systems. Thanks to a restructured environment in which work, shopping, school, and public life are closely integrated, walking will become a viable mode of human mobility. The car will still exist but only for pleasure use, not for wasteful purposes like the assembling of provisions.

As Schneider sees it, for most of the twentieth century the "Iron Law of Automotive Expansion" swept all opposition out of its way. It became firmly entrenched as the city's "most prominent citizen" thanks to the virtues Rae enumerates. This honor enabled the automobile to determine the nature of its environment, just as distinguished people exert influence upon political, social, and economic affairs. But as Schneider observes, "rarely in history is there a tyrant who creates intolerable social problems and then presents himself as the Savior." The car achieved this feat by means of surrogate forces, e.g. a government that collected highway use taxes, and the activities of numerous pro-automobile organizations. In Schneider's scenario, however, the car proves its own worst enemy, simply by being "technically impossible for basic urban transportation." Its hunger for more highways, more parking spaces, and more accommodations at the expense of the (human) public prompts a coalition of urban interests to take legal and practical action against it, leading to the utopia already mentioned.

The following year the same publisher issued another text with many of the same arguments, John Jerome's *The Death of the Automobile* (Norton, 1972). Jerome was a former managing editor of

Car and Driver magazine, generally regarded as the first American automobile publication to seriously question the social consequences of policies followed by the Detroit manufacturers. Jerome condemns the car, more severely than Schneider and perhaps more knowledgeably, as "a bad machine," one that has murdered and injured thousands of Americans in highway accidents, wasted irreplaceable natural resources, exacerbated national problems like poverty and race, altered sexual customs, loosened family ties and held the economy hostage to its unreliable engineering. This is the litany of complaints Rae attempted to answer, with a major exception: Schneider argues that the cost, complexity and poor reliability of the automobile itself make its one putative virtue, mobility, of dubious value to the culture. Mobility, he claims, was the illusion surrounding the automobile, but the reality was an emphasis on styling and status symbology that vitiated the car's capacity to drive reliably from point A to point B. When "mobility" *was* summoned as a virtue, it was only to promote cynical ends: used-car dealers passed off worn-out cars as "transportation specials," or, more serious, roadbuilding lobbies promoted superhighways as a grandiose tribute to this magical god, "Mobility." Jerome comments, "We stopped building roads to places. We began building roads for automobiles."

As the automobile became less and less of a viable product (Jerome depicts the Chevrolet Impala of the early Seventies as the archetypal Detroit product, a "stagnant monstrosity"), the first waves of a consumer's revolt began. Its opening volley probably was the publication in 1965 of Ralph Nader's *Unsafe at Any Speed*, and by the early Seventies it was in full cry, manifested by a growing preference for foreign cars (which Jerome views as more "rational" vehicles), a turning away from arrogant styling, and a growing indignation about shoddy construction. Exactly how the automobile will die and what will replace it are questions left unanswered by Jerome. He writes that "the force that will finally finish off the automobile as the basis of our transportation system still lies unrevealed in the future." Many readers a decade later, of course, will jump to the conclusion that the mysterious force may be a shortage of oil, but another book touching on this subject disputes this now-widespread assumption. *Running on Empty: The Future of the Automobile in an Oil Short World* (Norton, 1979), by Lester R. Brown, Christopher Flavin, and Colin Norman, concludes that "the expected levelling off in world oil production does not necessarily mean the end of the automobile age. But it does suggest that things will never be the same again." This may not satisfy Jerome but Schneider will take heart from the abundant evidence for the decline of the Road and Car in influence.

Most of the evidence for Schneider's and Jerome's critiques derives from the 1950s and 1960s. One might ask, didn't the automobile companies learn the lesson from their failures? Why didn't they just build a perfect car? In 1970 General Motors did produce a vehicle to its entire satisfaction; it would be "everybody's car," according to advertisements. "Little but Big, Adventurous but Substantial, Womanlike but Manly, Old but Young," and so on down the cliché path. Furthermore, according to a major GM executive, from the very beginning of the project the company had "set out to produce an American car with size, economy and performance to serve the American people. . . . We set out to improve this country's balance of payments." Against this rhetorical backdrop of great expectations the Chevrolet Vega made its entry into the market. In many ways the Vega seemed certain to succeed. Its design was contemporary; it was produced in a highly automated plant in Lordstown, Ohio, trumpeted as the ultimate in efficient design; and GM directed its most creative energies into the marketing of this new brain-child.

The ensuing career of the Vega, to be charitable, fell somewhat short of the mark. Its early sales record was respectable enough but its reputation reeled and faltered under the unfavorable publicity surrounding a series of recalls. To compound GM's agony, the Lordstown plant underwent intense labor conflict culminating in a prolonged, well-publicized strike in 1972.

Emma Rothschild's *Paradise Lost: The Decline of the Auto-Industrial Age* (Random House, 1973), uses the Vega scenario as the starting point for a probing yet sympathetic look at the car industry's impact on the quality of life in America. Like many automotive historians she focuses on two individuals, Henry Ford and Alfred P. Sloan, Jr., but unlike their usual biographers she anatomizes them as forces who inflicted serious damage on a precariously humane social organization. Rothschild's approach is in a certain sense philosophical, as opposed to the nuts-and-bolts complaints of critics like Schneider and Jerome. Rothschild's work seems to derive from the tradition represented at its best by Mumford, and behind him John Ruskin and William Morris, who commented on the same range of industrial ills.

Ford's contribution to industrial management, labeled "Fordism"

by Rothschild, was his relentless obsession with reducing the manufacture of an automobile into ever-smaller units of human labor. His
refinement of the division of labor concept led to increased pay for
workers, and an ever-rising standard of living. On the other hand, it
led as well to a routine of unsatisfying labor that alienated workers
from their work and the products they assisted in constructing. In
1921 Samuel Marquis attributed his resignation as head of Ford's
Sociological Department to the departure of "the old group of executives, who at times set justice and humanity above profits and
production." In their place, he believed, came managers "whose
theory was that men are more profitable to an industry when driven
than led." At Lordstown some fifty years later Rothschild found the
same kind of managers behind the computers, and the same kind of
dehumanized workers on the assembly line. Her documentation of
"Fordism" in action is probably the strongest part of her study.

But there is also "Sloanism," which is less a manufacturing principle than a marketing strategy. Sloan lured buyers to cars by making
them symbols of upward mobility and eternal youth. Within the
market there were GM products at every rung of the economic
ladder. The Chevrolet owner could aspire to a Pontiac, the Pontiac
driver to an Oldsmobile, and so on up to the Cadillac. Since it was
not engineering but superficial grace that distinguished the car,
advertising became central to the triumph of "Sloanism." Ad copy
suffered from ever-increasing amounts of overstatement as the years
passed, until, in Rothschild's words, cars were sold "with the frivo-
lous extravagance of detergents or deodorants." Thus the Vega, was
"a normal car with normal troubles, but a car which, with its lavish
and advanced advertising campaign may perhaps have suggested
intimations of modernity that it proved unable to support." "Sloanism,"
in fact, was doomed the moment foreign competition or a slippage in
the standard of living compelled the public to abandon the blithe
fantasies on which this pseudo-philosophy was based. At this writing
it is as dead as Zoroastrianism.

Or is it? J. Patrick Wright's *On a Clear Day You Can See General
Motors* (Wright Enterprises, 1979) focuses on the seventeen-year
career of John Z. DeLorean at GM in order to portray a corporation
caught up in "technical hibernation," and "management dereliction"
of the worst sort. Though much of the book is a celebrity profile of
DeLorean's meteoric rise through the GM executive power struc-

ture, it also contains a critical evaluation of GM's "public relations" that suggests elements of "Sloanism." For example, DeLorean claims that "Never once did I hear substantial social concern raised about the impact of our business on America, its consumers or the economy." Short-run interests reigned supreme, providing temporary profits at the expense of long-range planning that would benefit company and society alike. GM's emphasis upon profits, in DeLorean's view, was so pervasive that it blatantly violated its own cardinal precept of free enterprise. His depiction of the relations between Chevrolet and its dealers reads like a modern rendition of the bad old mercantile trading systems, with the Chevrolet Division playing the role of Mother Country and the dealers relegated to colonial underlings forced to buy not only automobiles but all spare parts from the home company. Thus the retail dealer is "squeezed for every last nickel of corporate profit." "Sloanism," one remembers, emphasized the centralization of power as one of its most canonical laws.

Even GM's current move toward production of small cars is credited not to a sincere effort to offer a product demanded by the marketplace according to the script of supply and demand, but instead is "based on costs and government action, pure and simple. Nothing else." Wright's muckraking book is enjoyable reading, if only as a corrective to Sloan's own sunny accounts of GM in his two autobiographies.

There is more to be said about "Fordism" however. Perhaps one can never say too much about it. James J. Flink, in *The Car Culture* (The M.I.T. Press, 1975), remarks that Ford's major innovations—the movable-belt assembly line, the five dollar a day wage, the Model T and the Fordson tractor—influenced America in the twentieth century more than the Progressive Era and the New Deal combined. Ford, in Flink's view, "set the pace and direction of a new social order based on mass production and mass personal automobility until the early 1920s" when other industries followed suit. Ford's belief that the average worker wanted "a job in which he didn't have to think" allowed him the moral freedom to devise and refine the assembly line process. Flink notes that "mass production meant that neither physical strength nor the long apprenticeship required to become a competent craftsman was any longer a prerequisite for industrial employment." The cultural results of this change were many and profound. Respect for age and parental authority was undercut in blue-collar families as the son became a more valuable worker than the father whose skills had been rendered obsolete by

Ford's technology. And according to "Fordism" the assembly line worker could not partake of the myth of upward mobility; a new negative attitude toward work was forged in the proletarian consciousness, as Rothschild discovered at Lordstown.

Flink's book is "partisan and controversial," and contains a wealth of significant data. He himself can speak best for its intentions and its place in the evolution of automobile historiography.* I would like to return to the subject of Ford, and specifically to an obscure topic of prime importance as an element of labor history: Ford's attitude toward and treatment of his black workers. In *Black Detroit and the Rise of the UAW* (Oxford University Press, 1979), August Meier and Elliott Rudwick trace Ford's complex feelings about his black workers. He was a man who believed that the black "needs a sense of industrially 'belonging' and this ought to be the desire of our industrial engineers to supply." The authors observe that between the Great Depression and World War II "the Ford Motor Company [was] one of the largest and least discriminatory employers of black labor in America." Yet within the Ford empire it was only in Detroit that blacks held industrial jobs and then more often than not they were of the most grueling and disagreeable nature. Outside Detroit, virtually all blacks who worked for Ford were employed as janitors.

Ford developed a close liaison with what the authors label the black bourgeoisie in Detroit. Black ministers in particular played a major role in this relationship. But his paternalism gradually degenerated into covert and overt hostility, and his racism increased. Though blacks were treated worse at other automobile firms, such as Packard, Chrysler, and GM, they suffered at Ford Motor Company also. They were tempted by the UAW, but the racism displayed by white rank-and-file workers in the union made them fearful. Meier and Rudwick weave the union's story and the condition of black workers into a fascinating narrative. The research is thorough, the references possess integrity, and the text is buttressed both by annotated footnotes and a valuable bibliographical essay. Especially masterful is their treatment of intraunion conflicts, the coalition between the UAW and the NAACP, the hate strikes that accompanied the movement of black workers into jobs previously closed to them, the beginning of federal actions aimed at combating job dis-

*See the following essay by Flink.—Ed.

crimination, and above all the welding of a black worker-UAW alliance that survived for two decades. One sees in this book, in short, how the excesses of "Fordism," despite their generous origins, led to significant social action by the oppressed of all races.

As is obvious from this review, it is difficult to discuss the car without focusing on Detroit. But The Road is more important to most Americans than either the labor or management conflicts of one big city. Even when it wasn't much more than two ruts running along a dusty trail the lure of the open road captivated the early motorist. No sooner had the automobile achieved a modicum of reliability than drivers appeared in their four-wheeled wonders ready and willing to dash off to the countryside and the pleasures of "auto-camping." In actuality this idyllic escape from the daily grind promised more than it delivered to many of its early advocates. The lack of basic amenities and sanitation facilities soon cooled the ardor of early autocampers. Yet as Warren Belasco records in *Americans on the Road: From Autocamp to Motel, 1910-1945* (The M.I.T. Press, 1979), the advantages of the automobile as a recreational vehicle were substantial. Even with roads of uncertain quality, family vacationing by car was free from the restrictions of the railroad timetable, not to mention its limited route alternatives and unexciting facilities. And the idea of touring and camping with an automobile nicely expressed the American pioneering spirit. It was a democratic act; all men on the open road were brothers and the camaraderie induced by a campfire was worth the inconveniences of semi-primitive conditions.

But this neo-pioneer adventure didn't last long. The automobile improved, roads were upgraded and expanded, and before long manuals and travel guides appeared in abundance. Belasco traces the decline of the large summer hotel and the degeneration of autocamping from "fad to institution." Before long campgrounds became civilized, and the rise of the motel caused a virtual end to primitivism altogether. Belasco's study offers us another chapter in the history of Vanishing Americana, especially the wandering form of it associated with the automobile.

But one should not close this survey on a nostalgic note, for whether or not the autocamp survived to service the needs of vacationers, a robust machine continues to convey a mass of vagabonds back and forth across the continent. I refer to the truck, invented as a mechanical beast of burden and already hauling payloads over the road in the car's first heyday. Firms like Mack and Kenworth supplied quality trucks to businessmen, but not until the mid-Thirties did truck stops, cabs with sleepers and other creature comforts become part of the long-distance truck driver's world.

The truck was a product of the twentieth century but the man behind its wheel is the living embodiment of America's nineteenth-century heritage. He is, in the words of Jane Stern in *Trucker* (McGraw-Hill, 1975), the "last American cowboy." The rigors of long hours on the road and days and weeks away from home make the trucker's nomadic life-style legendary. In the beginning he wore Western hats and cowboy boots; his truck, whether an aging Mack Thermodyne diesel or the latest Freightliner, was as much a part of his life as the cowboy's horse. He still is a living symbol of a people on the move, in love with motors and the individualism of the frontier. In its graphic descriptions of the seamier side of the trucker's world, *Trucker* may be offensive to some, but it conveys the milieu of the "gear grinder" realistically and powerfully. Its approach is not ruminative, not even analytical, but the world of truck stops, jackknifed tractor-trailers and grueling hours behind the wheel defies cerebration. What we do find is a memorable profile of that hardcore of perhaps 100,000 independent owner-operators, with cast-iron stomachs and rugged constitutions, who sustain their loyalty to "wheels" when others are losing faith.

Trucks are as essential a part of the car culture as the Model T or the shopping mall. In fact, John Jerome, having ruminated on the death of the automobile, reported in a later text on the surprising possibilities of the truck as an instrument of salvation. In *Truck* (Houghton, Mifflin, 1977), he praises the heavy vehicle as a boon to the austere ecological life-style he chose to pursue in the New England countryside. *Truck* and *Trucker* remind us, as some of the weightier tomes described above do not, that down to the smallest bit of food we take in order to survive, the horseless carriage makes us what we are.

JAMES J. FLINK

THE CAR CULTURE REVISITED:
SOME COMMENTS ON THE RECENT
HISTORIOGRAPHY OF AUTOMOTIVE
HISTORY

At its eighty-sixth annual meeting in New York City on December 29, 1971, the American Historical Association gave formal recognition to a growing interest in automotive history by holding its first session on the social impact of the automobile. The session emanated from and reflected a shift in automotive historiography away from narrow, uncritical concentration on the automobile industry, and toward an emphasis upon automobility as a force influencing American life. Those of us who participated in the session[1] were keenly aware that these developments in scholarly interest and awareness in turn had been conditioned by the new, critical attitudes toward automobility that had emerged in the United States during the 1960s. My paper, "Three Stages of American Automobile Consciousness,"[2] presented a long overdue synthesis of the American automobile revolution, which greatly expanded and amplified became *The Car Culture* (Cambridge, Mass.: M.I.T. Press, 1975). Despite its controversial, critical view of the American automobile culture, *The Car Culture* was selected by the United States Information Agency in 1976 for inclusion in its bicentennial exhibit of the more important recent university press books on American history. The book has been extensively and, in general, favorably reviewed; the paperback edition has been widely adopted as a supplemental text in college American history courses; and a Japanese edition was scheduled for publication by Chikura Shobo, Tokyo, in late 1980. In his review for *The Journal of American History*, Ralph D. Gray observed that "The book, which also offers an interesting cultural-technological alterna-

---

[1]Glenn A. Niemeyer chaired the session. John B. Rae and I read papers. David L. Lewis and John Hancock commented.

[2]Published in revised form under the same title in *American Quarterly*, 24:451–473 (October 1972).

tive synthesis to recent American history, signals a new departure in automotive history scholarship."[3] In retrospect, my synthesis was in the mainstream of a growing body of scholarship that made the decade of the 1970s a watershed for automotive history, and which deserves critical reappraisal.

To appreciate the great advances made in our knowledge and conceptualization of automotive history over the past decade, one need only recall that as recently as 1965 the publisher of John B. Rae's brief synthesis, *The American Automobile*, could claim on its dust jacket that the book was "the first complete, authoritative treatment of the whole span of the automobile industry." As Rae pointed out in his pathbreaking *American Automobile Manufacturers: The First Forty Years*, although a voluminous literature on the history of the automobile industry existed, it was extremely varied in quality. Up to the 1970s automotive history was dominated by the ghostwritten reminiscences of auto industry pioneers and by unfootnoted, appreciative, popular accounts, invariably beginning with a statement about the author's long and passionate love affair with the car. Probably the best of the popular histories was Edward D. Kennedy's *The Automobile Industry: The Coming of Age of Capitalism's Favorite Child* (New York: Reynal and Hitchcock, 1941). And among the ghostwritten reminiscences two stand out as exceptional: Charles E. Sorensen, with Samuel T. Williamson, *My Forty Years With Ford* (New York: W.W. Norton, Inc., 1956); and Alfred P. Sloan, Jr., *My Years With General Motors* (Garden City, N.Y.: Doubleday, 1964). Another large portion of the literature focused on the mechanical development of the motorcar and automobile racing. This remains largely the province of the automobile buff, and by far the most useful reference on the topic is *The American Car Since 1775*, by the editors of *Automobile Quarterly* (New York: E.P. Dutton, 1971). Only a handful of scholars had given attention to the American automobile revolution, and well into the 1960s two revised doctoral dissertations published in 1928 remained important references: Ralph C. Epstein, *The Automobile Industry: Its Economic and Commercial Development* (Chicago and New York: A.W. Shaw Company, 1928); and Lawrence H. Seltzer, *A Financial History of the American Automobile Industry* (Boston and New York: Houghton Mifflin Company, 1928).

---

[3] Ralph D. Gray, Review of James J. Flink, *The Car Culture*, in *Journal of American History*, 62:1042-1043 (March 1976).

An impressive awakening of interest in the automobile industry among scholars became evident in the late 1950s and early 1960s with the publication of Rae's aforementioned *American Automobile Manufacturers* and with the ,monumental three-volume history of the Ford Motor Company undertaken by Allan Nevins in collaboration with Frank E. Hill. Other important books of this period—all incidentally published in Michigan—were William Greenleaf's *Monopoly on Wheels: Henry Ford and the Selden Automobile Patent* (Detroit: Wayne State University Press, 1961); Glenn A. Niemeyer's *The Automotive Career of Ransom E. Olds* (Lansing: Michigan State University Press, 1963); and Sidney Fine's *The Automobile Under the Blue Eagle* (Ann Arbor: University of Michigan Press, 1963). In addition, several articles of continuing significance had appeared, including Harold G. Vatter's "Closure of Entry in the American Automobile Industry," *Oxford Economic Papers*, New Series, 4:213-234 (October 1952); George V. Thompson's "Intercompany Technical Standardization in the Early Automobile Industry," *Journal of Economic History*, 14:1-20 (Winter 1954); and Charles C. McLaughlin's "The Stanley Steamer: A Study in Unsuccessful Innovation," *Explorations in Entrepreneurial History*, 7:37-47 (October 1954).

As their titles suggest, these studies focused rather narrowly on the development of the automobile industry, to the neglect of the social impact of the road and the car. A notable exception was Ashleigh E. Brilliant's "Social Effects of the Automobile in Southern California During the 1920s" (unpublished Ph.D. dissertation, University of California, Berkeley, 1964),[4] which merits more attention than it has thus far received. The deficiencies of the existing body of academic literature on the automobile were summarized well by Lynwood Bryant, the leading authority on the history of the internal combustion engine, in his *Technology and Culture* review of my *America Adopts the Automobile, 1895-1910* (Cambridge, Mass.: M.I.T. Press, 1970). "Why has not this book been written before?" Bryant asked.

> It cannot be because there is a lack of documentary evidence, for the literature on the automobile and what it has done to us is immense. Perhaps this literature is hard to manage because it is so voluminous and disorganized, or perhaps historians avoid the topic because it concerns such things as hardware and popular enthusiasms, which are not academi-

---

[4] See also Ashleigh E. Brilliant, "Some Aspects of Mass Motorization in Southern California, 1919-1929," *Southern California Quarterly*, 47:191-208 (October 1965).

cally respectable. . . . One part of the story has attracted sober academic writers: the history of the *business* of producing automobiles has been recorded at some length, and the life and work of the hero of that industry, Henry Ford, has been recorded at very good length. . . . But there has been no adequate study of the transformation of American life effected by individualized motorized transportation in this century. This book looks like the beginning of such a study.

In sharp contrast with previous studies, *America Adopts the Automobile, 1895-1910* moved away from preoccupation with the internal dynamics of the automobile industry and its prominent personalities to focus on the development of the industry within its socio-cultural and socio-economic context. The development of garage facilities, motor vehicle regulation, automobile clubs, roads, etc. as well as the cultural values and socio-economic conditions underlying mass adoption of the automobile in the United States formed the subject matter of the book. One of my major goals was to shift attention away from Henry Ford as an heroic figure and toward understanding the automobile revolution as a socio-cultural process, from the perspective of the anonymous mass of Americans. As Bryant observed, "The central message of the book, amply documented, is that America had a well-developed automobile culture before 1908, the year of the Model T. This is an important lesson for any general historian who still thinks that the automobile appeared in 1908 and began to transform our institutions in the 1920s."[5]

The trends exemplified in *America Adopts the Automobile, 1895-1910* were echoed in Reynold M. Wik's *Henry Ford and Grass-roots America* (Ann Arbor, Mich.: University of Michigan Press, 1972), which focused on the social impact of the Model T and the impact of Henry Ford as a folk hero, and they were mirrored in Blaine A. Brownell's pathbreaking "A Symbol of Modernity: Attitudes Toward the Automobile in Southern Cities in the 1920s," *American Quarterly,*24:20-44 (March 1972), a model of what needs to be done for other regions as well. But most important, these trends were first fully expressed in John B. Rae's *The Road and the Car in American Life* (Cambridge, Mass.: M.I.T. Press, 1971). "For the first time in automotive historiography, the road and the car are dealt with as an integral unit, integrating two distinct bodies of historical literature to the mutual benefit of both. For the first time too, primary emphasis

---

[5] Lynwood Bryant, Review of James J. Flink, *America Adopts the Automobile, 1895-1910,* in *Technology and Culture,* 12:661-664 (October 1971).

is given to the impact of automobility on American life, rather than to the internal dynamics of the automobile industry and its prominent personalities," I wrote in my review for *Business History Review*. "The topics covered include highway policies; economic and social effects; urban transportation systems; the suburban decentralization of business, industry, and residential patterns; and ecological issues and automotive safety. The author's objective seems to be to inform contemporary debate over the merits and faults of automobility from the perspective of history." *The Road and the Car in American Life* was written under a research grant from the Automobile Manufacturers Association, Inc. Although I found the book "incontrovertible in its main arguments" and agreed with Rae that "mass automobility has been on balance beneficial," I was nevertheless critical that "Far from being the 'balanced view' promised on its dust jacket, the book is written from the narrower perspective of traditional value-laden assumptions that increasingly have come to be questioned—e.g., virtuous materialism, unbounded faith in technological progress, the primacy of consumer need, and the existence of consumer democracy." I then went on to criticize the book in more specific terms, saying that "Critics of the road and the car are not usually identified, and their arguments are not presented at the level of sophistication warranted. Especially on automotive safety and ecological issues, Professor Rae's own arguments in favor of automobility too often seem insensitive and strained."[6] *The Car Culture* was an attempt to set the record straight on these issues from the value perspective of a younger generation of Americans.

As Ralph D. Gray observed, *America Adopts the Automobile, 1895-1910* was "a basically adulatory account" of the American automobile culture, and *The Car Culture* marked a definite change in my perspective. My maturing conception of the American automobile culture was especially influenced by Blaine A. Brownell, who demonstrated in his study of the automobile in southern cities in the 1920s that "Then, as now, ownership of automobiles did not necessarily reflect a complete and unquestioning acceptance of their consequences. The views expressed about the motor vehicle in the 'circulating media' in southern cities during the decade . . . suggest a much more complex pattern of response. Such views ran the gamut from complete acceptance of the automobile to rather deep suspi-

---

[6] James J. Flink, Review of John B. Rae, *The Road and the Car in American Life*, in *Business History Review*, 46:123 (Spring 1972).

cions concerning its impact on American life. Not surprisingly, most conceptions of this significant technological innovation were highly ambiguous."[7] Brownell's work, which my own research for *The Car Culture* bore out, convinced me that previous automotive historians, including myself, had overly simplified a very complex popular response to the road and the car and that we had erred by simplistically stressing consensus and uniformity where the evidence often revealed conflict, complexity, and diversity.

The critical thrust of *The Car Culture*, however, was directed in the main not at mass personal automobility, which I portrayed as having had both beneficial and deleterious consequences, but against the American automobile industry. Far from casting the industry pioneers in an heroic mold, as Arthur Frank Wertheim noted, the chapters on Henry Ford and William C. Durant were "dipped in acid." I was "highly critical of their business methods and of the giant corporations in general."[8] These two chapters were followed by two others (in a seven chapter book!) attacking the industry on a number of grounds—from creating the conditions that led to the Great Depression of the 1930s, through the consumer and environmental complaints of the 1950s and 1960s, to the abuses of monopoly power and technological stagnation alleged by critics in the 1970s. *The Car Culture* was thus, in my opinion, not anti-automobile, but highly critical of Detroit's Big Three, which I pictured as regressive and irresponsible. Conversely, American Motors and the Japanese automobile manufacturers were portrayed as progressive influences, an interpretation that seems more than vindicated by the events of the past five years. The continuing increase in the share of the domestic new car market captured by imports (currently 45 percent in California and approximately 25 percent nationwide), the relative health of American Motors at a time when sales of American-made cars are suffering their worst drop in five years and Chrysler is on the verge of bankruptcy, the fact that we have entered an automobile-industry-induced major recession, and the imminence of $2-a-gallon gas with further OPEC price increases—these are further confirmations of fundamental flaws in the structure and business strategy of the post-World War II American automobile industry. They also are

[7] Blaine A. Brownell, "A Symbol of Modernity: Attitudes Toward the Automobile in Southern Cities in the 1920s," *American Quarterly*, 24:23 (March 1972).

[8] Arthur Frank Wertheim, Review of James J. Flink, *The Car Culture*, in *The History Teacher*, 10:159 (November 1976).

evidence that, as *The Car Culture* argued, American society and the American economy are disastrously over-dependent on the road and the car and on the automobile industry.

In the concluding paragraph of his 1958 *American Automobile Manufacturers*, John B. Rae boldly stated that "The growth of motor vehicle manufacturing in the United States provides, in fact, as convincing a case for freedom of enterprise as can be found. . . . The most fitting summation seems to be to paraphrase Patrick Henry and say, "*If this be Capitalism, make the most of it.*"[9] This adulatory view of the American automobile industry was shattered irrevocably in the early 1970s by Lawrence J. White's *The Automobile Industry Since 1945* (Cambridge, Mass.: Harvard University Press, 1973); Emma Rothschild's *Paradise Lost: The Decline of the Auto-Industrial Age* (New York: Random House, 1973), which was based on her earlier series of articles in the *New York Review of Books*; and Detroit labor reporter William Serrin's *The Company and the Union* (New York: Knopf, 1973). Through careful quantitative analysis, White's coldly objective study demonstrated that in automobile manufacturing a tight joint-profit-maximizing oligopoly in the post-World War II period had made excessive profits while being unresponsive to changing consumer preferences and to public concerns about automotive safety and atmospheric pollution. He further demonstrated that the American automobile industry was a technologically stagnant industry both in product design and in manufacturing methods, especially when compared with its foreign competitors, and that the concentration of monopoly power within the industry was well beyond what was necessary or desirable for maximal efficiency in manufacturing through economies of scale. Emma Rothschild pointed out the inevitable limits to both the domestic and worldwide automobile markets and brilliantly conceptualized the dilemma of the American automobile industry as an unresolvable contradiction between "Fordist" production methods and "Sloanist" philosophies of design and marketing, which would inevitably shift the center of automobile manufacturing to Third World countries with large supplies of cheap labor.[10] From

[9] Rae, *American Automobile Manufacturers*, p. 206. Italics Rae's.

[10] On the automobile industry in Third World countries, see especially William Chandler Duncan, *U.S.-Japan Automobile Diplomacy: A Study in Economic Confrontation* (Cambridge, Mass.: Balinger Publishing Company, 1973); and Rhys Owen Jenkins, *Dependent Industrialization in Latin America: The Automotive Industry in Argentina, Chile, and Mexico* (New York: Praeger Publishers, 1977).

the insider's perspective of a Pulitzer Prize-winning reporter intimately familiar with both the company and the union, Serrin detailed the reactionary nature of General Motors, the United Automobile Workers, and the socially destructive partnership that formed between them in the post-World War II period, focusing on the 1970 GM strike.

These three books, published *after* Rae had completed *The Road and the Car in American Life*, in my opinion remain incontrovertible in their main contentions and immeasurably influenced the last chapter of *The Car Culture*, "The Disenchantment," which has proved to be the most controversial in the book. One can only conjecture whether and how Rae's 1971 synthesis (or indeed his 1965 synthesis *The American Automobile*) might have been different had these books by White, Rothschild, and Serrin been available to him as well. It therefore makes little sense to consider *The Car Culture*, as George S. May has done in his review for *The American Historical Review*, as "a useful counterbalance to the scholarly defense of this [post-World War II car] culture by John B. Rae, another automobile historian."[11] For ultimately the points of disagreement between Rae's synthesis of our automobile culture and mine (which have been too generally and facilely counterposed as alternative explanations) may reflect far less our differences in value perspectives than that we published at different points in a rapidly expanding and maturing field of inquiry. Most certainly, a revisionist synthesis of the car culture would have been unthinkable were it not for John B. Rae's pioneering books and articles, and much more of *The Car Culture* than a casual reader can be aware of simply follows the lines of Professor Rae's scholarship.

Hopefully, automotive history has reached the stage of maturity where we who practice it recognize both the interdependence of our work and that scholarship in any field of inquiry is a cumulative endeavor. Hopefully, we will also recognize that in our intellectual house there are many mansions. Since publication of *The Car Culture*, a number of significant books have advanced our knowledge of the American automobile revolution, and any future synthesis of American automobility will have to take account of them.

Among those reflecting a more traditional historiographic approach, George S. May, *A Most Unique Machine: The Michigan Origins of*

---

[11] George S. May, Review of James J. Flink, *The Car Culture*, in *American Historical Review*, 81:1276 (December 1976).

the American Automobile Industry (Grand Rapids, Mich.: William B. Eerdmans Publishing Company, 1975), is a copiously and carefully researched survey of the formative years of the Michigan automobile industry (1890-1909) which adds much new information and corrects many factual errors made in previous accounts. It must now be considered the standard source on the early automobile industry. May's *R.E. Olds: Auto Industry Pioneer* (Grand Rapids, Mich.: William B. Eerdmans Publishing Company, 1977) greatly expands our knowledge of one of the more important industry pioneers, as does Ralph D. Gray's excellent *Alloys and Automobiles: The Life of Elwood Haynes* (Indianapolis: Indiana Historical Society, 1979). An invaluable contribution to our understanding of public relations in the developing automobile industry as well as of its most prominent personality is David L. Lewis, *The Public Image of Henry Ford: An American Folk Hero and His Company* (Detroit: Wayne State University Press, 1976). Lewis's book is undoubtedly the best balanced, most carefully researched, and most judicious interpretation of this complex and controversial figure to yet appear, and demonstrates that important new things can still be said about Ford.

In my opinion, however, the most noteworthy and exciting development has been a growing interest in the impact of automobility on American life. The 1971 session of the American Historical Association noted at the outset of this essay proved to be a precursor of other sessions on the social impact of the automobile at annual meetings of the Organization of American Historians, the Southern Historical Society, the American Studies Association, and the Missouri Valley Historical Association. And in addition to the works already cited by John B. Rae, Reynold M. Wik, Blaine A. Brownell, and myself a number of first-rate books on various aspects of the social history of the automobile have been published. One of the first, which I regret came to my attention only after publication of *The Car Culture*, is Norman C. Moline's *Mobility and the Small Town, 1900-1930: Transportation Change in Oregon Illinois* (Chicago: The University of Chicago Department of Geography, Research paper no. 12, 1971). More recently, Howard L. Preston has employed the techniques of the new social history in his study of the impact of the automobile on Atlanta—*Automobile Age Atlanta: The Making of a Southern Metropolis, 1900-1935* (Athens, Ga.: The University of Georgia Press, 1979). Preston's study is particularly useful because he makes a notable attempt to compare Atlanta with other American cities. A broader perspective is taken in Michael Berger's *The Devil*

Wagon in God's Country: The Automobile and Social Change in Rural America, 1893–1929 (Hamden, Conn.: Archon Books, 1979). In a study intended to complement the work of Rae, Wik, and myself, Berger uses a wide variety of types of evidence to analyze and synthesize contemporary observations of the motorcar's impact. Warren James Belasco, *Americans on the Road: From Autocamp to Motel, 1910–1945* (Cambridge, Mass.: M.I.T. Press, 1979) is a superb class analysis of American tourism and the formation of the motel industry. And Mark H. Rose, *Interstate: Express Highway Politics, 1941–1956* (Lawrence, Kansas: The Regents Press of Kansas, 1979) offers a first-rate analysis of the origins of the Interstate System. Finally, an excellent analysis of the impact of the motorcar on urbanization processes in the 1920s is Mark S. Foster, "The Model T, the Hard Sell, and Los Angeles's Urban Growth: The Decentralization of Los Angeles During the 1920s," *Pacific Historical Review*, 4:459–484 (November 1975).

Individually and collectively these works have vastly expanded and deepened our understanding of the American automobile revolution. They add up to a respectable body of scholarly literature, making automotive history by 1980 a distinct specialization within American social history. Paradoxically, this has occurred concomitantly with the ending of a period of over two generations of American history that can aptly be called "The Age of the Automobile." Domestic and world markets for cars are saturated, and dwindling world oil reserves with no viable alternative to the internal combustion engine in sight make continuation of our automobile culture into the 21st century seem doubtful. More important, the automobile and the automobile industry are no longer significant forces for change. As I observed in *The Car Culture* (p. 4), "Just as the centrality of Turner's frontier could be perceived only after the frontier had closed, so the overwhelming impact of automobility had to wait for formal recognition by the historical profession until the automobile and the automobile industry no longer called the tune and set the tempo of American life." That formal recognition came in the 1970s, not with a whimper, but with a bang.

Postscript 1983: I am grateful for the opportunity to update my 1980 essay. The rapidity with which automotive history is developing as a field of inquiry is evidenced not only by the increasing amount and diversity of the literature, but by new directions that challenge the predominant paradigm of a distinctive and generally shared automobile culture.

In large part, our emphasis on uniformities to the neglect of differences in the American experience with the car has been a function of our over-reliance on "literary" (i.e., nonstatistical) evidence. The impressions of contemporary observers too often have been relied upon while the available quantitative data have been neglected. Indeed, we have attempted in the main to reconstruct a participant's view of the automobile culture, while explaining away the divergent views of the participants. The resulting overview of the car culture has been a biased one—an accurate portrayal of social reality at best from the perspective of native-born, Caucasian, middle-class males. We also have been historical in overly stressing continuities rather than change over time.

For these reasons, I am even more impressed now than I was in 1980 with Howard L. Preston's *Automobile Age Atlanta* (1979), which is comparative and utilizes the research strategy of the new social history. His case study of the impact of the automobile on Atlanta relies preponderantly on statistical data to construct an objective observer's interpretation. And among other fresh insights, he illustrates not only that Black Atlantans did not share in the benefits of mass automobility, but that up to at least 1935, the automobile revolution affected them adversely. Similarly, the techniques of the new social history have been employed to excellent advantage by Joel A. Tarr in his *Transportation Innovation and Changing Spatial Patterns in Pittsburgh, 1850–1934* (Chicago: Public Works Historical Society, 1978). Contrary to conventional wisdom, Tarr's data demonstrate great differences in automobile ownership and use among Pittsburgh's middle class and working class and between urban and suburban residents up to the Second World War. His data also demonstrate far less auto-dependence in 1930s Pittsburgh than generally has been assumed for medium-sized American cities. Such evidence makes increasingly untenable the overview of an all-pervasive car culture portrayed most notably in Robert S. Lynd and Helen M. Lynd's classic 1929 *Middletown* and 1937 *Middletown in Transition*.

Other recent work has begun to examine the triumph of the automobile from the broader perspective of urban transportation planning. The first general scholarly work attempting to interrelate mass adoption of the automobile with the decline of urban mass transit is Mark S. Foster, *From Streetcar to Superhighway: American City Planners and Urban Transportation, 1900–1940* (Philadelphia: Temple University Press, 1982). Of particular excellence among specialized works is the case study of Chicago in Paul Barrett's *The*

Automobile and Urban Transit: The Formation of Public Policy in Chicago, 1900–1930 (Philadelphia: Temple University Press, 1983), and his earlier article, "Public Policy and Private Choice: Mass Transit and the Automobile in Chicago Between the Wars," *Business History Review* 59 (Winter 1975):473–97. Contrary to the pervasive misconception that the automobile succeeded over mass transit because of its inherent technological superiority, Barrett concludes that "Chicagoans changed their mode of transportation for reasons which often had little to do with either transportation or technology." Still another corrective to prevalent notions about the inherent superiority of automotive transportation over mass transit alternatives is David James St. Clair, "Entrepreneurship and the American Automobile Industry" (Ph.D. dissertation, University of Utah, 1979).

Just as the uniformity of American experience with the car is coming to be questioned, so too is the prevalent assumption of the distinctiveness of the American automobile culture. Underlying the appearance of several important books dealing with the automobile revolution in worldwide and comparative perspective are the realities that levels of automobile ownership and use in European countries are now at the United States levels of the 1950s and 1960s, that Japan surpassed the United States to become the world leader in automobile production in 1980, and that national differences in automobile design and methods of manufacture have all but disappeared. Of particular importance is Jean-Pierre Bardou, Jean-Jacques Chanaron, Patrick Fridenson, and James M. Laux, *The Automobile Revolution: The Impact of an Industry* (Chapel Hill, N.C.: University of North Carolina Press, 1982). This first scholarly comparative study of the worldwide impact of automobility—multiauthored by two historians, a sociologist, and a labor economist—was first published in French in 1977. At the level of popular history, this approach is evident in Raymond Flower and Michael Wynn Jones, *100 Years on the Road: A Social History of the Car* (New York and London: McGraw Hill, 1981), in my opinion the best done and most useful popular history of the automobile to date. And in the field of transportation planning, James A. Dunn, Jr.'s *Miles to Go: European and American Transportation Policies* (Cambridge, Mass.: MIT Press, 1981) deserves mention as a comparative historical study of European and American transportation policies regarding railroads, urban mass transit, highways, and the automobile that is particularly useful to automotive historians. Dunn demonstrates that our overdependence on automotive transportation compared with Europe stems basically from historic differences between the European transportation policy paradigm of centralized, authoritative planning and the American paradigm of relying in the main on the invisible hand of the market.

Important work continues to be done, of course, using the traditional approaches of biography and company history. Bernard Weisberger, *The Dream Maker* (Boston: Little, Brown and Co., 1979), deserves special mention. This first comprehensive biography of William C. Durant is copiously researched, balanced in its interpretation, and well-written. It adds much new information on Durant and on the early automobile industry. John B. Rae's *Nissan Datsun: A History of Nissan Motor Corporation in U.S.A., 1960–1980* (New York: McGraw Hill, 1982) also deserves mention as an exceptionally fine company history that reveals much about the successful penetration of the American market by Japanese auto manufacturers.

Looking into the immediate future, I believe that we can expect present trends to accelerate toward comparative studies employing the research strategy of the new social history. The paradigm of a distinctive, uniform American car culture, primary reliance upon literary (as opposed to statistical) evidence, and assumptions about the inherent technological superiority of automotive transportation over mass transit alternatives are all coming to be challenged. And scholarly attention is broadening from a myopic focus on the American automobile culture to the worldwide implications of the automobile revolution. My own revaluation will appear in *The Automobile Age: A Study in Comparative History*, scheduled for publication by the MIT Press in 1985 to coincide with the centennial celebration of the first successful Benz car.

CONTRIBUTORS

SAM ABRAMS teaches writing and literature at the Rochester Institute of Technology, and "feels confident that Thoreau's essay *Walking* will have historical influence equal to that of his *Civil Disobedience*."

ROBERT ACKERSON is a teacher and automotive historian whose articles have appeared in *Old Cars, Cars and Parts, Special Interest Autos, Car Collector*, and elsewhere.

MICHAEL BARONE, who grew up in Detroit and Birmingham, Michigan, is a member of the Editorial Page staff of *The Washington Post*. He is a coauthor of *The Almanac of American Politics*, issued every two years since 1972.

WARREN BELASCO is Assistant Professor of American Studies at the University of Maryland Baltimore County, where he teaches courses on popular culture, television, and cars. He is the author of *Americans on the Road: From Autocamp to Motel, 1910–1945*, and currently is working on a book, *Retailing Revolt*, which examines the commercial exploitation of discontent.

MICHAEL BERES, a novelist and short story writer, lives in Tinley Park, Illinois, where he is an active member of the South Side Creative Writers.

MICHAEL L. BERGER is the author of a number of books and articles concerning technology and culture. Most recently, the Shoe String Press published his *The Devil Wagon in God's Country*, a study of the automobile and social change in rural America from 1893 to 1929. He teaches at St. Mary's College of Maryland.

DAVID E. COLE is Director of the Office for the Study of Automotive Transportation at the University of Michigan, where he is also Assistant Professor of Mechanical Engineering and Applied Mechanics.

STEVEN DIMEO has published fiction in *Playboy's Oui Magazine*, *Fireland Arts Review*, and *Pyramid*. A columnist for *Amazing Stories* and *Cinefantastique*, he presently edits the *New Oregon Review*.

WILLIAM S. DOXEY, a resident of Carrollton, Georgia, is presently at work on a collection of short stories.

JAMES J. FLINK is the distinguished author of two classic studies of automotive history: *America Adopts the Automobile, 1895–1910* and *The Car Culture*. He teaches in the School of Social Sciences of The University of California, Irvine.

MARK S. FOSTER, Associate Professor of History at the University of Colorado at Denver, is the author of *From Streetcar to Super-highway: American City Planners and Urban Transportation, 1900–1940*, from Temple University Press, and a history of the University of Colorado, as well as many journal articles concerning automotive history.

HELEN FRYE, of San Gabriel, California, became interested in auto fashions after she and her husband acquired several pre-1915 cars and began collecting early auto costumes and fashion literature. Fashion editor of the *Horseless Carriage Gazette*, Ms. Frye re-draws and does the color overlays for most of the artwork accompanying her writing.

PAUL W. GIKAS, M.D., is Professor of Pathology at the University of Michigan Medical School and a Staff Pathologist at the University Hospital. He has a special interest in the pathogenesis of highway trauma and has argued for crashworthy automobiles in scientific publications and before State Legislative and Congressional hearings.

WILLIAM E. GILES served twenty-five years with Dow Jones before accepting the post of Distinguished Editor in Residence at Baylor University. He taught journalism there until 1977, when he became Executive Editor of *The Detroit News*.

LAURENCE GOLDSTEIN, Associate Professor of English at the University of Michigan, is the author of a book of literary history, *Ruins and Empire*, and a book of poetry, *Altamira*. He is completing a study of the response of American poets to the achievements of aerial technology.

DANIEL L. GUILLORY, Associate Professor of English at Millikin University, is a regular reviewer for *Library Journal*. He has served as a Poet in the Schools in Illinois and recently held a fellowship at the National Humanities Institute at the University of Chicago.

LAWRENCE T. HARBECK is Director of Management Projects at the Office for the Study of Automotive Transportation at the University of Michigan.

KENNETH HEY is Associate Professor of Film Studies at Brooklyn College, CUNY, and has written extensively on modern cinema.

JOHN HILDEBIDLE is a teacher and administrator at Harvard University. His poetry has appeared in *Ploughshares, Poetry Northwest, Southern Poetry Review,* and elsewhere.

JOSEPH INTERRANTE received his B.A. from Brown University in 1974, and his M.A. from Harvard University in 1975. He is currently a doctoral candidate at Harvard University, where he is completing his dissertation, "A Movable Feast: The Automobile and the Spatial Transformation of American Culture, 1890–1940."

SIBYL JAMES operates a one-person consulting firm called Appropriate Translations which specializes in editing material for energy research firms. Her poetry has appeared in *Calyx, Tendril, Pig Iron, Poets On, Room of One's Own,* and the *Ocooch Mountain News.*

FOLKE T. KIHLSTEDT is Associate Professor of Art at Franklin and Marshall College. He has contributed essays to *The Prairie School Review, The Journal of the Society of Architectural Historians,* the *Winterthur Portfolio,* and *Alternative Futures.* He is presently working on a book about the interaction between the automobile and architecture and design in America between 1920 and 1940.

DAVID LAIRD is Professor of English and American Studies at California State University, Los Angeles. His articles have appeared in *Journal of English and Germanic Philology, Renaissance Quarterly, South Dakota Review,* and *Studies in Philology.* He recently held fellowships at the National Humanities Institute at the University of Chicago and at the Folger Shakespeare Library.

DAVID L. LEWIS, is Professor of Business History in the Graduate School of Business Administration at the University of Michigan. He is the author of the award-winning book, *The Public Image of Henry Ford,* as well as some 350 articles on the subject of automotive history. He is currently writing a biography of Edsel Ford, a romantic novel with a campus setting, and an illustrated book on the impact of the automobile on courtship and romance.

ROBERT M. LIENERT has been a newspaperman since 1946, with the *Nebraska State Journal,* the *Detroit Free Press,* and *Automotive News,* which he has edited since 1974.

CHARLES A. MADISON, a specialist in the field of Jewish writing and publishing, has recently completed his autobiography, from which the essay in this issue was excerpted.

CATHERINE MARSHALL is a carfree resident of Pittsburgh, where she is managing editor of the University of Pittsburgh Press.

EDWARD MORIN, who teaches at Wayne State University, has recently published a book of poems, *The Dust of Our City.*

JOYCE CAROL OATES' selected poems, *Invisible Woman*, has recently appeared, as well as a collection of her plays. She is currently teaching at Princeton.

JON T. POWELL, Professor of Communication Studies and of Instructional Technology, is Chairman of the Department of Communication Studies at Northern Illinois University. His articles have appeared in many journals of communication research.

JOHN B. RAE is Professor of the History of Technology, Emeritus, at Harvey Mudd College. A series of works on automotive history, culminating in *The Road and the Car in America* (1971), has made him one of the most eminent figures in this field.

JOHN R. REED's first volume of poetry, *A Gallery of Spiders*, has just appeared from the Ontario Review Press. He is Professor of English at Wayne State University.

CHARLES L. SANFORD, Laflin Professor of Technology and Culture at Rensselaer Polytechnic Institute, is the author of *The Quest for Paradise* (1961), and the editor of *Automobiles in American Life* (1977).

FRED SETTERBERG lives in Oakland, California, and has written for *The Nation, American Arts, The Cultural Post,* and other national and regional publications. He is a Contributing Editor for *Ampersand.*

GERALD SILK, Assistant Professor of Art History at Columbia University, is a frequent contributor to *Artsmagazine,* and is completing a book on the automobile in modern art.

Primarily a playwright, LYDIA SIMMONS has had five plays produced off-off-Broadway, and is currently the recipient of a National Endowment grant in creative writing. She holds a doctorate in English from New York University.

JULIAN SMITH is Associate Professor of Film Studies at the University of Florida. The author of *Looking Away: Hollywood and Vietnam,* he is now working on a study of Hollywood and Detroit.

KATHLEEN SPIVACK's books include *Flying Inland* (Doubleday, 1973), *The Jane Poems* (Doubleday, 1974), and *Swimmer in the Spreading Dawn* (forthcoming). She directs the Advanced Writing Workshop in Cambridge, Mass.

PETER STEINHART is a California writer who specializes in environmental affairs. Aside from a regular column in *Audubon* magazine, he has contributed to *Harper's*, *National Wildlife*, and *The Los Angeles Times.*

STEPHEN W. WHITE is a high-technology advocate who teaches philosophy in the serenity of the mountains in East Tennessee. His most recent book is *Population and Environmental Crisis*, and he is currently serving as Editor of *National Forum: Phi Kappa Phi Journal.*

REYNOLD M. WIK, formerly May Treat Morrison Professor of American History at Mills College, is the author of *Steam Power on the American Farm* and *Henry Ford and Grass-roots America*. He is an ex-president of the Agricultural History Society.

ROBLEY WILSON, JR., has recent poems in *Poetry, Quest/80*, and *Georgia Review*. His two collections of short stories are *The Pleasures of Manhood* (Illinois) and *Living Alone* (Fiction International). He edits *The North American Review.*